Bridging the River of Hatred

Great Lakes Books

*A complete listing of the books in this series
can be found at the back of this volume.*

Philip P. Mason, Editor
Department of History, Wayne State University

Dr. Charles K. Hyde, Associate Editor
Department of History, Wayne State University

Bridging the River of Hatred

The Pioneering Efforts of
Detroit Police Commissioner
George Edwards

MARY M. STOLBERG

   WAYNE STATE UNIVERSITY PRESS   DETROIT

Library of Congress Cataloging-in-Publication Data

Stolberg, Mary M.
    Bridging the river of hatred : the pioneering efforts of Detroit
Police Commissioner George Edwards / Mary M. Stolberg.
        p.   cm. — (Great Lakes books)
    Includes bibliographical references (p.   ) and index.
    ISBN 0-8143-2572-6 (alk. paper)
    1. Edwards, George C. (George Clifton), 1914– . 2. Police
chiefs—Michigan—Detroit—Biography. 3. Police administration—
Michigan—Detroit—History—20th century. I. Title. II. Series.
HV7911.E37S76   1998
363.2′092—dc21
[B]   97-15023

To Peg,
A loving helpmate to George Edwards, Jr.,
and an inspiration to the rest of us.

CONTENTS

7

INTRODUCTION

Twenty-two-year-old George Clifton Edwards, Jr., arrived in Detroit with two changes of clothes and a head full of dreams. Along with thousands of other migrants during the thirties, Edwards was drawn to the booming city and its auto plants which seemed to epitomize the best and worst of the nation's industrialism. To the workers who flocked to Detroit from around the nation and world—but especially to those who poured in from the economically moribund South—the city offered jobs, high wages, and a foothold in the American middle class. To union organizers, communists, and such socialists as Edwards, Detroit was a sweatshop writ large where exploited workers toiled heroically against the hardships of capitalism.

Before settling in Detroit in December 1936, Edwards spent two years as an itinerant socialist organizer. The young Harvard graduate hoped to glean enough experience of working life to write a novel chronicling society's evils. Failing that, he hoped to take his place among the pantheon of the nation's great labor organizers. After two years witnessing the underbelly of Depression-era America, Edwards chose Detroit as the backdrop for his dreams. He never found time to write his book, but he did take an active role in the rough-and-tumble world of labor organizing and city politics. For twenty-five years, Edwards played a key role in Detroit's history. Propitiously, Edwards arrived in the city just as the Reuther brothers helped lead the United Auto Workers Union (UAW) to power. Edwards joined the fray during the UAW's formative years. When the 1938 recession led to massive unemployment in Detroit, he became head of relief efforts for the UAW and spearheaded the expansion of the Works Progress Administration (WPA) rolls in the city. When Walter Reuther, not one to share power, stymied Edwards's ambitions within the union, he began looking for other fields of endeavor.

With the outbreak of World War II and the expansion of war industries, Detroit experienced massive housing shortages. In 1940, Edwards left the UAW to direct the Detroit Housing Commission. For the next two years, he pioneered the battle for integrated public housing in the face of bigotry in city and federal government. In 1941, he ran as a successful dark-horse candidate for city council, a job in which he was often the lone voice for progressive change. Edwards was favored to win the 1949 mayoral race, but lost largely because he took a courageous stand for racial equality. He then devoted his time to the law practice that he had set up in 1946 after years of night classes at the Detroit College of Law. In 1951, Edwards was appointed as a Wayne County probate judge. In that job, he overhauled the county's disorganized juvenile justice system and joined the vanguard of reform just as juvenile delinquency was becoming a national obsession. Later, Edwards served as a Wayne County Circuit judge and a justice of the Michigan Supreme Court. In 1962, he abandoned the serenity and security of the appellate court to take over the Detroit Police Department.

Edwards's two-year tenure as the city's police commissioner occurred in an era of fascinating political and social change. John F. Kennedy's election in 1960 was one of those rare political watersheds that promised to fulfil the expectations of idealists like George Edwards. For the first time since the heady days of the New Deal, liberalism seemed to be in the ascendancy. Hope that government could improve peoples' lives breathed vigor into national and local politics. Racial justice appeared to be within reach. Politicians and social scientists believed that they could devise programs to eradicate poverty. Cities, as they had been at the turn of the century, regained center stage as the engines of national possibility.

But there was a dark side to the decade of optimism and political upheaval. As in other periods of rapid and dramatic social change in American history, nay sayers voiced their uneasiness in terms of concern about crime and law and order. In the sixties when student protesters, civil rights advocates, and Black Power agitators took to the streets, it was not surprising that middle-class reformers focused their attention on juvenile delinquency and minority crime. Edwards and other civil libertarians, reluctant to join in an attack on groups they championed, found an even more sinister scapegoat for the nation's ills in organized crime.

All of these crosscurrents became especially pronounced in Detroit, which began the decade as the nation's model city and ended it as the nation's most tragic example of urban disintegration. In the early 1960s, the coalition between white liberals, working-class Catholics, and African-American voters that propelled Kennedy into the White House also swept a new generation of young, charismatic, activist mayors into office in cities across the country. In Detroit, the harbinger of change was Jerome P. Cavanagh, a thirty-three-year-old lawyer and political unknown.

As the most articulate and savvy of the maverick mayors, Cavanagh drew national attention to himself and to Detroit. Once hailed as the nation's "Motor City," respectful observers in the early sixties began calling Detroit the "Model City." Cavanagh helped set a local and national agenda for urban problems by addressing concerns that ranged from suburbanization, job loss, racial tension, equitable housing, color-blind policing, and inner-city poverty. Cavanagh, recognizing that state legislatures had traditionally shortchanged large cities, joined the successful fight to supplant meager aid from the states with federal assistance. One bureaucratic symbol of the degree to which city problems became Washington problems was the creation of the U.S. Department of Housing and Urban Development (HUD). Cavanagh played a crucial role in the commission that recommended establishing HUD during the summer of 1964, and President

11

Lyndon B. Johnson unsuccessfully tried to persuade him to become the agency's first secretary in 1965.

During Cavanagh's first year in office, contemporary admirers credited him with easing the city's racial tensions. Detroit tottered on the brink of riots in 1961 when Cavanagh was elected, and he moved quickly to address minority concerns. He appointed Alfred M. Pelham as the city's first African-American comptroller. Even more significantly, Cavanagh appointed George Edwards as police commissioner. Blacks and liberal whites hailed Cavanagh's choice of Edwards almost as much as conservatives and the rank and file of the police department reviled it. Some critics pointed out that Edwards, who had been arrested and jailed twice during his student and labor organizing days, was a poor role model to become the city's chief law enforcement officer. Others lambasted Edwards's fight for racial equality and his liberal opinions on the bench. But Cavanagh recognized that it would take someone of Edwards's stature with the African-American community to signal his administration's determination to break from past policing practices.

Looking backward from the standpoint of our own era's muddled efforts for racial equality, the early sixties provide a contradictory picture of horrors and hopes. Between 1940 and 1960, African Americans flocked north in record numbers and settled in the nation's twelve largest cities. In Detroit during the 1950s, the percentage of blacks increased from 16 percent to 29 percent. Despite their numbers, they were largely ignored by the city's powerful. Nothing pointed up their voicelessness more than a police crackdown during the fall of 1960. After two white women were murdered, police stopped, questioned, frisked, and jailed thousands of innocent African Americans. When NAACP leaders protested the blatant violations of constitutional rights, the city's leaders wrongly dismissed their complaints as the work of a few troublemakers rather than the outrage of an entire community.

Such a sweeping, racially biased crackdown would be inconceivable today. Ironically, the simplicity of the solution to racial problems advocated by Edwards, Cavanagh, and African-American leaders at the time seems equally incomprehensible now. They worked under the assumption that equal justice was

12

the key. Once blacks had a voice in politics, once they received equitable treatment from the police, once they had a right to equal housing and education, then racial problems would be resolved. Their vision was becoming outmoded even while Edwards was Detroit police commissioner. Two disparate African-American views of race problems emerged in Detroit and the nation during the early 1960s. Martin Luther King, Jr., whom Edwards and Cavanagh accompanied on a Freedom March in Detroit during June 1963, espoused a philosophy of racial harmony and peaceful civil disobedience. The more radical Malcolm X, who preached the need for black independence, also came to speak in Detroit during Edwards's tenure as police commissioner. Despite their differing messages, both leaders threatened to disrupt the city's equilibrium. It was largely because of Edwards's calm and restrained leadership that their visits proved uneventful.

Edwards's handling of racial problems stands in stark contrast to normal police policies and practices in the 1960s. Police actions precipitated most of the urban riots and civil disturbances during that tumultuous decade. Edwards also was on the cutting edge of a movement that would produce unprecedented police reform. During the 1960s, contempt for police reached new heights at the same time sanctions and tolerance for abuse by police reached new lows. The Civil Rights movement and television coverage that highlighted police excesses prompted calls for change. The U.S. Supreme Court under Chief Justice Earl Warren's leadership whittled away at excessive police force in a series of rulings. Yet, police across the nation stymied reform—especially when the safeguards applied to minority suspects. Although he came to recognize his men's frustration at court rulings that freed criminals, Edwards shared the Supreme Court's views. He repeatedly invoked U.S. Supreme Court Justice Benjamin Cardozo's vision of "ordered liberty," a belief that social order could exist only if government respected the rights of its citizens.

Edwards and other reform-minded police chiefs tried to bolster police respect for civil liberties by pioneering the concept of community policing. They argued that increasing police and community interaction could break down barriers of prejudice on both sides. When Edwards became commissioner in 1962, many members of Detroit's black community saw the mostly

13

white police force as a hostile, often brutal enemy. Policemen blamed African Americans for most of the city's crime. For two years, Edwards worked to undermine those stereotypes. He ordered members of his force to treat all citizens equally, he required them to hold community meetings, he hammered away at the code of silence by which police sanctioned each other's wrongdoing, and he encouraged members of the community to cooperate with police.

Edwards's successors as police commissioner were unable to consolidate his reforms. Detroit's 1967 riots became a symbol of urban desperation and a sign of liberal hopes gone awry. That Edwards's reforms were short-lived was more of a commentary on American policing than it was on Edwards. During the past three decades, many police departments have instituted his ideas. In the early 1990s, police chiefs resurrected his vision of community policing. Most police departments now have affirmative action programs to hire and promote minorities. Federal and state courts have continued to vindicate Edwards's belief that police should work within constitutional guidelines, despite some public and political pressure to weaken defendants' civil rights.

Unfortunately, too many of the battles that Edwards fought more than thirty years ago remain unsolved in Detroit and in cities across the nation. Many police, hardened by the crimes they witness each day, see constitutional safeguards as hindrances to be circumvented. A continuing police culture of cronyism works against reform from the top or from the outside community. Despite affirmative action hiring, it remains difficult to find enough minorities to make police departments demographically representative. In many inner cities, residents continue to view police as uncaring at best and menacing at worst.

Cavanagh and Edwards lived in an era when there was optimism that social problems could be solved. Their vision stands in stark contrast to our own era's pessimism about hard-core problems of crime, race, and urban renewal. Edwards's entire career, but especially his days as Detroit's police commissioner, stands as a testament to the energizing spirit of American liberalism. The common thread of his multifaceted public service was a concern for the downtrodden. Detroit's failure to achieve his ideals of unity and social justice became one of the city's greatest tragedies.

PART I

THE MAKING
OF A POLICE COMMISSIONER

1

A REFERENDUM FOR REFORM

In 1961 when 33-year-old attorney Jerome P. Cavanagh decided to run for mayor of Detroit, the city was noted for three things: automobiles, bad race relations and civic sloth.

—Journalist Ernest Dunbar[1]

On December 7, 1960, Marilyn Lou Donohue began what should have been an ordinary work day at the Robert C. Engel Company. The twenty-three-year-old stenographer arrived before the other employees to open the office at 19741 James Couzens. Her attacker lay in wait. As she opened the door, he grabbed her. They struggled, but the five-foot two-inch petite woman was no match for her assailant. He threw her to the floor and thrust a knife at her. She raised her left arm to ward off the attack; he slashed her forearm twice, then stabbed her four times in the chest. He rifled her purse and flung her empty wallet to the floor as he fled. She dragged herself to a nearby chair and sat, too weakened and stunned to summon help. Thirty minutes later another employee arrived and called police. When they arrived, the office showed signs of a "terrific struggle." Chairs were upended. Papers were amiss. Donohue's earrings and shoes were scattered around the floor. In the ambulance, Donohue described her attacker as a black man with a trim mustache wearing dark, shabby clothes. She had seen him several times before, when he applied for work at her firm and several others in the same block. Although she was fit and athletic, Donohue did not survive her wounds and died on the operating table at Mt. Carmel Mercy Hospital.[2]

Three weeks later, Betty James, a nurse's aide at Children's Hospital, was walking to work at 6:30 A.M. December 28, 1960, along Kirby East, when a disheveled ex-convict, Ernest Embry, Jr., jumped her and beat her senseless with a four-pound brass bar. The bloody thirteen-inch weapon, typical of the driving pins used in factories and garages, was found four blocks away where Embry dropped it as he fled the scene. Embry netted $53 from the robbery. James, 26, died five days later of skull fractures. Newspaper accounts detailed the sorrow of her husband and three young sons. Embry's identity was not yet known, but witnesses described him as a dark-skinned African American, about thirty-five years old, wearing a long brown overcoat. James's murder brought Detroit's total killings for the year to 157—the highest number since 1931.[3]

The two murders ripped open the festering wound of Detroit race relations and provided the improbable catalyst for a political transformation that would sweep Jerome Cavanagh into the mayor's office. But most of the city's leaders had neither the insight to recognize that the crimes called for a new kind of racially sensitive restraint, nor the foresight to realize that conducting business as usual would disrupt twelve years of Democratic machine politics. Detroit's establishment interpreted James's murder as the harbinger of a massive crime wave engulfing the city. Propelled by press and public outrage, Mayor Louis C. Miriani ordered an "old-fashioned" police crackdown. Chief Herbert W. Hart complied. Hart, a millionaire who had made his fortune as president of D. F. Smith Co., a grocery chain, served as Miriani's campaign treasurer and had been police commissioner since 1958. Known as a dapper dresser, Hart had a fondness for wearing ties printed with hearts.[4]

On December 28, Hart declared a state of emergency and ordered members of his force to work six-day weeks. He gave his officers wide powers to stop, frisk, and arrest. Hart said, "The police should be able to go into places where they believe there are suspicious persons and make searches on suspicion. Then let the courts decide whether they did right or not." Vincent Piersante, a member of the force, recalled that "the police department response to the mayoral order was to round up all known street thugs and to question everyone who was out and about at night in those areas where the crimes had been committed."[5]

The two-week dragnet yielded impressive numerical results. Arrests city-wide increased from a normal weekly average of 1,600 to 1,955. During the first week, police questioned more than 1,000 suspects in the Donohue and James murders, most as the result of tips from callers hoping to reap the $5,000 rewards for information about the killings offered by the *Detroit News*. A week into the crackdown, the *Free Press* reported that "Council Offers Hart Full Backing: More Funds, Men Available To Aid His Battle on Crime."[6]

On January 11, Hart announced an end to the "state of emergency" and the six-day work week, but his superintendent, Louis J. Berg, said police would continue to use "old-fashioned methods." By the end of the month, Hart declared the crackdown an "unbelievable" success. He said police had stopped, questioned, and searched more than 150,000 people, and as a result, the city's overall crime rate was 30 percent lower in January than it had been in December. Nevertheless, he ignored the facts that unusually cold weather that month kept perpetrators inside and 150,000 "street contacts" led to only four court cases. Donohue's death remained unsolved, and police found James's killer by following routine investigative techniques after the emergency ended.[7]

Although its impact on crime may have been in dispute, one aspect of the crackdown was clear: it laid bare the deep divide between Detroit's blacks and whites. African-American leaders viewed the police effort as an unconstitutional, unwarranted assault whereas white leaders deemed it a great success. Many rank-and-file members of Detroit's mostly white police force used the crackdown as a license to intimidate and harass African Americans. As Richard V. Marks, then director of the Detroit Commission on Community Relations, remembered, "The way the police department defined criminals was, literally anybody that was black that wasn't where they were supposed to be." For many patrolmen, "suspicious" behavior by African Americans became little more than being well-dressed, driving a good car, or walking down the street, according to Mackie C. Johnson, one of the few blacks then on the police force. As one journalist noted, "Negroes were indiscriminately picked up on the streets, frisked, searched, and subjected to humiliating questioning. O-verzealous policemen booked those deemed to be acting 'suspiciously' on flimsy charges and held them overnight at precinct stations."[8]

Prominent African Americans caught up in the dragnet included Arthur Johnson, then executive director of the Detroit Chapter of the NAACP. On the night of January 4, Johnson was sitting in his car, in front of his house, with the motor idling. A policeman searched Johnson for concealed weapons and asked to see his identification. Johnson filed a complaint about the incident with the local precinct. Charles J. Wartman, writing in the African-American *Michigan Chronicle,* called Johnson's harassment "one of those things that all right thinking citizens sincerely wish had not happened. It is all too hard to explain and such explanations as are given severely strain the credulity of the listeners."[9]

Wayne Circuit Judge Wade H. McCree, Jr., who later became a federal judge and solicitor general of the U.S., cited three other incidents to show police racism. When the wife of a Detroit Street Railways employee called police to report that she had been accosted by a white man as she walked home, police responded by arresting her on suspicion of prostitution. On another occasion, police arrested a prominent African-American businessman for no discernable reason. In the third episode, police seized another man and held him for four days without questioning or formally charging him. After McCree intervened, police released him immediately.[10]

The police actions prompted widespread dissatisfaction. William Patrick, then Detroit's only African-American city councilman, likened the crackdown "to old shotgun justice, where you shoot first and ask questions later." On January 13, George Edwards moderated a discussion of the city's law enforcement problems at a public forum sponsored by the Americans for Democratic Action (ADA). The meeting drew nearly five hundred people to a jammed room at the Veterans Memorial Building. Edwards set the tone for the evening by making several points about crime. First, he said, it was everybody's business because it cost the nation $22 billion and had taken 155 lives in Detroit during the previous year. Second, he urged his listeners to help fight the causes of crime, which he listed as poverty, inferior housing, and racism. Third, he said, "Crime has no religion, or country, or color. There is no sociological or criminological basis for suggesting crime has any racial, ethnic or religious origin." Finally, he concluded: "In our efforts to deal with a current crime wave, we should remember that no one has the right to suspend the Constitution of the United States."[11]

Other speakers included Arthur Johnson; Harold Norris, chair of Detroit's chapter of the American Civil Liberties Union; Frank Hartung, a professor from Wayne State University; Max Silveran, an assistant district attorney; Richard Marks, executive director of the Detroit Commission on Community Relations; and Thomas R. Cochill and Philip Van Antwerp, detective inspectors from the police department. Cochill defended the crackdown, telling the overflow crowd: "If your house is on fire, you don't send the Fire Department next door." He explained that even though the crackdown primarily affected blacks, it did not mean the police department was "prejudiced or discriminatory." Instead, he explained, it meant that black offenders outnumbered whites by nineteen to one in Detroit. Cochill's comments did little to appease the crowd. The ADA's board met later and passed a resolution suggesting that the police department abandon its unconstitutional methods, hire more police, provide them with better pay and better training, and establish an independent review board to evaluate citizen complaints. The resolution also called on the mayor to reshape the Detroit Commission on Community Relations "which at this time of crisis and need has been paralyzed by apparent subservience to other city agency heads who dominate its machinery." Three nights later between 1,500 and 2,000 people showed up for an NAACP–sponsored rally at Ford Auditorium "to get the facts about crime in Detroit, about the police crackdown and about . . . constitutional rights." Various speakers, including ministers, union leaders, lawyers, and judges, called for a reorganization of the police department and an investigation of police violations.[12]

Members of the city's establishment discounted the outrage in the black community. Hart denied that the crackdown was aimed at any particular group and lambasted both the NAACP and the African-American press for stirring up unwarranted complaints. Hart said "99% of the letters he received" supported the crackdown, and he added that they were from ordinary "citizens, not professional do-gooders." He denied that the increased enforcement created any community tensions, and he said what tensions did exist "were created by Arthur Johnson of the NAACP." Superintendent Berg expressed similar views. He said police had to interview blacks in the James and Donohue murders because the suspects were African Americans. He added that his officers could not fight crime effectively if they could not question people acting suspiciously. White homeowners' groups agreed. They lauded the crackdown, called for its extension, and opposed demands for investigations of police misconduct. Typical was an editorial in the *Northeast Detroiter,* the newspaper put out by the Northeast Council of Homeowners Associations, which said "further commissions or investigative committees would serve only to undermine the morale of law enforcement in our city."[13]

Mayor Miriani and the police union also defended the crackdown. Miriani insisted the police department was run by "sympathetic and humane leaders." Patrolman Robert C. Fassett, president of the Detroit Police Officers Association opined, "The results of the emergency program proved gratifying and demonstrated that the Detroit Police Officer can provide the best law enforcement in the land, if he is given effective means." In a veiled reference to the African-American community, Fassett added, "Remove the pressures being applied by certain groups and lift the restrictions that shackle the attempts to provide efficient law enforcement, and the Detroit Police Department will provide the assurance of safety that the people of our city have a right to expect." Fassett concluded by commending Miriani and the members of Common Council "for withstanding and resisting pressures being made upon them to take actions which would not be to the best interest of effective or good law enforcement."[14]

Some whites did recognize the legitimacy of African-American complaints. Vincent Piersante recalled how many police officers were outraged by the abuses, "but they were stuck with the success of the program and thus became defensive of it." The

Detroit Council of Churches urged that an impartial emergency public committee be created to evaluate charges of police abuse. On February 9, a group of clergy, labor, and business leaders met with Miriani to request an easing of tensions. In early February, five Wayne State University sociologists called for a conference to discuss crime. They argued that the crackdown occurred because inflammatory coverage in the city's two major newspapers created the false impression that a crime wave was gripping Detroit. They criticized city officials for failing to support civil liberties and demanded that police receive more adequate training in constitutional rights.[15]

Many members of Detroit's establishment were as unsympathetic to the white liberals as they had been to the African-American outrage. Hart dismissed the Council of Churches request for a public investigation saying, "I don't approve of any committee. The Detroit Police department and the government of the city of Detroit can handle its own problems." Jack Manning, a columnist for the *Free Press,* attacked the sociologists who asked for a conference, claiming that police statistics proved the existence of a crime wave and the success of the crackdown. He said the sociologists' report charging racial bias was "not only unfair but a disservice to the very people its authors sought to defend. They implied the police and newspapers held to a feeble-minded conception that crime is related to race—that's just drivel." He singled out two of the sociologists, Leonard Moss and Mel Ravitz, for being especially "querulous in their accusations. You gather from their attitude that they deem the police commissioner either a dolt or a spotlight speaker who loves to strut under an imposing title."[16]

As the controversy raged, the mayor and police chief held to their belief that the crackdown had been a success, that the police had acted in a proper, unbiased fashion, and that complaints were the result of a few troublemakers. The *Free Press* agreed in a March 6 editorial:

> Our observation indicates that there has been wide approval of stepped up policing measures. The results have been too impressive to overlook. Unfortunately the whole contention about police methods has been endowed with a racial aspect. Those who try to exploit this aspect are guilty of some oversights. There are high crime rate white areas just as their are

high crime rate colored areas. Policemen use identical methods in both, and for a single reason. The honest citizen who perforce must live or work in such neighborhoods is entitled to protection. Of these there are many, both colored and white.

The writer concluded that the *Free Press* had never received any complaints about the crackdown from citizens, of any race, living in high-crime neighborhoods.[17]

Mainstream leaders' reactions revealed their naive belief that they spoke for a community that they had never consulted. Their reactions mirrored the attitudes of whites in the South, who were responding in a similar fashion to the turmoil prompted by Martin Luther King, Jr.'s, crusade for racial justice. In Mississippi and Alabama, politicians claimed that "their" blacks were content until stirred by outside agitators. Whites in both the South and the North failed to see that the Civil Rights movement was inspiring blacks to air longstanding grievances and demand a political voice.

Had Detroit's political leaders paid attention, they might have seen some of the many signs that indicated African-American voters planned to show their displeasure at the polls. During the mid-January rally at Ford Auditorium, William R. Ming, Jr., an NAACP lawyer who had represented Martin Luther King, Jr., when he was arrested the previous year in Alabama, accused Miriani of "ineptitude" and urged members of the audience to vote against him. Two weeks later, columnist Bill Lane, writing in the *Michigan Chronicle,* said, "When mayor Miriani tosses off with smirks and shrugs the complaints of Negro leaders against the police department's storm trooper tactics, he is obviously not caring about what happens during election time. He might figure the 'other side' will support his attitude sufficiently to override angered Negroes' votes." In mid-February, when the police department finally called off its "crash program" of law enforcement, a *Chronicle* editorial decried the "basic sicknesses in our community," and predicted that without political changes "the kind of social mentality which would embark upon such a program last December would do it again if crime involving Negroes and whites, particularly white females, were to occur again."[18]

Miriani and most of Detroit's leaders discounted the possibility of an African-American political insurgency and conducted business as usual. They failed to recognize how much Detroit's changing racial composition during the previous decade had altered the city's political landscape. Between 1950 and 1960, Detroit's total population dropped from 1.85 million to 1.67 million. An estimated 575,000 whites moved to the suburbs, and the percentage of African Americans rose in the city from just over 16 percent in 1950 to just under 29 percent in 1960. In other words, much had changed since 1949, when Miriani's predecessor, Albert Cobo, defeated George Edwards with a strident, race-baiting mayoral campaign. Virtually all of Detroit's African-American community had voted for Edwards, but they lacked the numbers to ensure his victory.

The first sign of change came in 1954, when Charles C. Diggs, Jr., defeated fourteen-year incumbent George D. O'Brien in the primary, and then went on to defeat three other candidates in the general election to become Michigan's first African-American member of Congress. The following year, Remus Robinson, a fifty-year-old surgeon, won election to the Board of Education. His victory signalled that African Americans could win city-wide races. In 1957, thirteen black activists became concerned that the UAW was not moving quickly enough for racial change. The group, headed by Horace Sheffield, Nelson Jack Edwards, and Robert "Buddy" Battle, joined with other such unionists as Frank Holly, John C. Brown, Elizabeth Jackson, and Hubert Holley to form the Trade Union Leadership Council (TULC). The TULC, which represented Detroit's 75,000 African-American union members, became an important force in city politics. Soon after its founding the group persuaded Walter Reuther to back Harvard-educated William Patrick, who became the city's first black council member.[19]

The alliance between the TULC and Detroit's white liberal establishment fell apart in the 1961 mayoral race. Liberal leaders of the UAW and the Democratic Party did not want to alienate the party establishment or their more conservative rank-and-file members, so they supported Miriani for reelection. That move was unacceptable to members of the TULC, which along with the rest of African-American Detroit was still smarting from the recent effects of the police crackdown. The TULC joined hands with the NAACP and the Cotillion Club to defeat Miriani in what became nicknamed the "Phooie on Louie" campaign. The Cotillion Club, a middle-class professional group which never had previously endorsed a candidate, created a political action committee to mobilize against Miriani.[20]

African-American leaders and disaffected liberals found the vehicle for their plans in Cavanagh, a political unknown. As George Edwards aptly described him, Cavanagh was "very young, very blond, and very blue-eyed. He looked the epitome of the Irish politician in a younger and more idealistic version." Cavanagh was only thirty-three years old when he ran for mayor. A Detroit native, he was one of six children born to Irish immigrants. His father worked at the Ford Motor Company's River Rouge plant, and the family lived in Detroit's Grand River-Livernois neighborhood. Cavanagh attended parochial schools, then received his bachelor's degree in political science and his law degree from the University of Detroit. He practiced law from 1955 to 1962 with the firm of Sullivan, Romanoff, Cavanagh & Nelson. His previous government service included serving as a deputy sheriff, an administrative assistant for the Michigan State Fair Authority, and a member of the Metropolitan Airport Board of Zoning Appeals. As chair of the Wayne County Young Democrats, he had been a delegate to county, state, and national party conventions.[21]

Cavanagh filed for office on July 29 with little more than "nickels and novenas" and a firm belief that the nation's fifth largest city could do better. He blasted the sixty-four-year-old Miriani's propensity for pomp and ceremony at the expense of meaningful change, and he provided a laundry list of needed improvements. He decried the city's $15 million deficit which violated the charter's call for a balanced budget. He criticized $55-million Cobo Hall as a white elephant plagued by labor gouging and corruption and described it as "the worst place to hold a convention in the world." He called for revitalizing a city increasingly marred by vacant stores and absurdly low rents. And he ridiculed the inefficient city transportation system as "a joke."[22]

Although his initial announcement included no mention of the city's racial problems, Cavanagh came to appreciate the depth of the problem in meetings with African Americans. He heard constant complaints throughout the campaign about the police crackdown from its victims who recounted

their experiences with the Detroit stop and frisk. Not just young street toughs but the lawyers, doctors, businessmen, and teachers who comprised the epitome of Detroit's black leadership. The pattern was approximately the same. A police flasher and siren for no apparent reason—an abrupt order to the male driver to get out of the car and another to spread-eagle over the hood for search. If compliance was delayed or questioned, the commands were backed up with abrupt physical force. Those whose protests were most vehement had experienced the degradation of being physically manhandled in front of wives and children.[23]

Horrified at such stories, Cavanagh took up the cause of equal justice, although he downplayed that fact while campaigning in white neighborhoods. For example, he omitted the following from a draft of one speech: "A hot potato in Detroit, like in most northern urban areas, is the so-called race issue. It is either ducked by the vote peddlers or made into an emotional conflict having nothing to do with reality. I will not back away from this subject as too dangerous to discuss. It is a reality that many of the colored and white demagogues identified with this problem have, as their own motives, the feathering of their nests after they have come up with solutions which amount to buying and selling prejudice by the ton and cash intake." During his campaigning in the African-American community, Cavanagh never wavered. In a speech at Olivet Baptist Church, Cavanagh assured his listeners that "police arrest is a subject that all lawyers deal with early in their schooling and in their practice. Arrest based on any other basis than that provided for in the Constitution is wrongful, and the police who are my responsibility as Mayor, will not engage in it willfully." The candidate vowed that, if elected, "the treatment of any one group of our citizens will be the same as that of all of our citizens."[24]

To show his good will, Cavanagh endorsed a proposal by William Patrick to allow the city's Commission on Community Relations to investigate citizen complaints about the police. Although Miriani took no public position on the question, his appointees lobbied heavily against the so-called Patrick Amendment. The measure was defeated in a five-to-four vote by the Common Council and became a rallying cry for both camps in the mayoral race. Cavanagh argued that passage of the amendment would carry symbolic importance for civil rights. Critics claimed that Cavanagh's support for the measure indicated he was "the property of the colored people."[25] His positions in favor of police restraint and the Patrick Amendment solidified his support among African-American groups. They provided his only major backing; the rest of Detroit's establishment, including the UAW, endorsed Miriani. The election boiled down to whether enough blacks would go to the polls and whether enough white voters would swing over to Cavanagh.

He placed ahead of ten other candidates in the September 12 primary, but his 35,856 votes put him a distant second to Miriani who garnered 80,557. He launched a vigorous campaign to gain ground. In a whirlwind of eighteen-hour days, he campaigned on a theme of "aggressive new leadership" and promised to create a "new image for Detroit" based on improved city services, increased employment, and better fiscal management. By contrast, Miriani approached the campaign with "self-confidence, if not smugness. He was the unanimous choice of the entire power structure in Detroit: the UAW, the Teamsters, the AFL–CIO council, the Chamber of Commerce, the auto companies, the newspapers. . . . No one in the establishment took Jerome P. Cavanagh seriously." Miriani refused to debate, despite Cavanagh's taunts that "throughout his life the mayor has stood for nothing, except his tailor and the press photographers." On the eve of the election, Cavanagh told radio listeners that Miriani "has never admitted that any serious problems do exist in Detroit. His campaign and the techniques which he has employed are an insult to the intelligence of the voters." He made a last-ditch appeal to white voters by offering to raise other kinds of taxes to ease the property tax burden and pay off the city's $15 million debt.[26]

On November 7, Cavanagh's campaign strategy succeeded. He received 85 percent of the African-American vote and 55.8 percent of the total vote. The final returns were 200,413 to 158,778. Pundits scrambled to explain the biggest upset in recent Detroit political history. Herb Levitt and Earl B. Dowdy of the *News* attributed the victory to Cavanagh's aggressive, negative campaigning, his appeal to black voters, and the fact that he had no record to defend. They contrasted how "Cavanagh dwelt on the personal problems of the voters" while Miriani discussed "efficiency and Detroit's future expansion." The *Free Press* said "Cavanagh's victory caught even his own supporters off guard." Its lengthy editorial damned the mayor-elect with faint praise, predicting that he would have difficulty evolving from a mere vote getter into a "responsible administrator." Still, the editorial conceded, "Many a successful candidate has done it, and Mr. Cavanagh may manage it as well as anyone else." His ultimate achievement would depend on respecting the rights of all Detroiters, not just the groups that elected him. "That will call for going very easy on meeting demands that the police department give, not equal consideration to all groups, but special consideration to certain elements."[27]

Voters also elected five liberal councilmen who supported Cavanagh's agenda. As B. J. Widick of the TULC said, "Suddenly it appeared as if a new day had dawned for Detroit. Almost overnight the city gained a new image under the direction of the talented, articulate, and personable mayor. . . . It seemed that Detroit had also found racial peace." On election night, Cavanagh visited TULC headquarters, promised that key positions in his new administration would go to African Americans, and predicted that his administration would provide the nation with a model of racial cooperation. The highest ranking black in his administration was Alfred M. Pelham, who became city controller. Pelham was a former member of the Wayne State University Political Science Department who had served as Wayne County's budget director. Cavanagh also appointed Theodore Morgan, a UAW official, to become secretary of the Department of Public Works Commission, and Esther La Marr, a former juvenile court probation officer, to head the Mayor's Commission on Children and Youth.[28]

Cavanagh joined the ranks of other idealistic mayors who were trying to remake the face of America's urban landscape. As journalist Fred Powledge noted, "In the early 1960s, a number of mayors of the new style took office. Most of them were liberal Democrats; many of them had no previous experience in elective politics. Some bypassed the machinery and the machines that had dominated city politics, and they got elected anyway, and then reelected." Cavanagh stood out from the others because he was the most articulate and provided the most insightful "description of the urban crisis."[29]

Perhaps because he was from Detroit, Cavanagh waxed especially eloquent about the plague of racism in urban America. Immediately after his election, he said, "I wish for myself and my family exactly what I wish for other parents and children; new horizons and the dawn of a new era in our sorely beset city." In his inaugural speech, he added, "Justice demands and morality dictates equality of treatment and opportunity in all phases of municipal government. Harmonious community relations must and will be, under this administration, a positive factor in our city."[30]

Cavanagh recognized that the one real test of his campaign promise for racial equality would be his choice of police commissioner. He discussed the importance of the appointment with the Pioneers Club, whose members included such prominent African Americans as Dr. J. J. McClendon, Judge Wade McCree, the Rev. A. A. Banks, Jr., Roy Morton, Horace Sheffield, the Rev. James E. Wadsworth, and Dr. Ira Whitby. After the election, club members reminded Cavanagh of their meeting. "While all your selections will be important, the Pioneers were agreed that probably the most sensitive and significant will be that of Police Commissioner." A qualified candidate, they argued, should "1) have demonstrated through action his belief in racial fair play; 2) be an intelligent and knowledgeable civilian; 3) have stature in the nation or in the community, and 4) possess a high degree of personal integrity, moral courage and independent judgement." They concluded, "We need not tell you how much the naming of a person with these qualities will reestablish this important city department in the eyes of the total community." Pioneers Club members did not provide names, saying that would be "presumptuous," but they offered to provide a list if asked.[31]

A handful of the city's black leadership may have shared the desire of Raymond C. Jenkins, head of the Peoples' Community Civic League, Inc., who urged Cavanagh to appoint an African American to the commissioner's job. Jenkins recommended Jesse Stewart, a uniformed sergeant who had been on the force since the 1940s and was working towards his doctorate in sociology.[32]

More savvy observers recognized that Detroit was not ready to accept such a dramatic change. Instead, they were pleased when Cavanagh decided to appoint a white liberal with an unquestioned record in the black community and a proven knowledge of the criminal justice system.

Finding a candidate who filled both of those requirements limited the pool. Ray Girardin, one of Cavanagh's political advisors, suggested that no one could fit the bill better than George Edwards. The bold recommendation was typical of Girardin, who was one of the city's most colorful and charming characters. Born in Detroit's Corktown section, Girardin worked as a boxer and carnival barker before attending Notre Dame and the University of Michigan. In 1929, he landed a job as a reporter with the *Detroit Times*. Contemporaries likened him to a character from a Damon Runyon novel because, as one friend noted, he could "make an intrigue of the simplest thing." Another writer described him as "a slight man with a face that looked as if it had been created with a potato masher." Girardin met Edwards as a police reporter, and the two became friends. When the *Times* folded in 1960, Edwards recommended Girardin for a job as Wayne County's chief probation officer, noting: "Over these many years on many occasions, Ray and I have had the opportunity to talk crime, its causes, the means of prevention and cure. To say that he has far more insight into and knowledge of the problem than would be expected of an ordinary run-of-the-mill crime reporter is to understate the matter."[33]

It was not surprising, given their mutual admiration, that Girardin believed Edwards would make an ideal police commissioner. Edwards enjoyed an unparalleled reputation as a champion of equal opportunity for African Americans. He was a member of the Michigan Bar Association's Committee on Crime Prevention and was a nationally recognized expert on juvenile delinquency. Earlier in the year, he had begun speaking out against organized crime.[34]

Still, in other ways, Edwards seemed an unlikely candidate for the police job. He had lived in Lansing since 1956 when he joined the Michigan Supreme Court. Immersed in judicial work, he had kept abreast of events in Detroit with only distant and detached interest until the crackdown. Virtually every African-

American friend he had in Detroit had told him about the police abuses "in graphic detail," and he had been outraged at their tales of "being stopped and searched with no pretense of probable cause, and generally with a rudeness that doubly infuriated them." He followed Cavanagh's campaign at a distance, through enthusiastic friends. Although he continued to care about Detroit, he saw himself as a permanent outsider to the city's fortunes.[35]

After the election, Detroit's unfolding political rejuvenation was far from Edwards's mind as he worked on opinions in his chambers, which he described as a "quiet oasis" on the fourth floor of the Old Capitol in Lansing. He was surprised when Girardin called him one afternoon in mid-November to tell him about Cavanagh's desire to make him police commissioner. His immediate response was, "Ray, you must be joking, Supreme Court Justices don't resign to become Police Commissioners." Girardin asked Edwards to meet with Cavanagh anyway. Edwards agreed, but added, "Don't give him any idea I will take the job. I like the one I have." They set an appointment for a week later, when Edwards was going to be in Detroit.[36]

Edwards travelled to the meeting with a sense of anticipation. He was "curious about the somewhat brash young man Cavanagh who had scored an upset victory over a lackluster incumbent." Edwards was impressed when Cavanagh chose Pelham to become the city's controller. He considered Pelham to be "one of the most able public officials in Michigan—imaginative, gifted in handling both people and problems, impeccably honest." The appointment convinced Edwards that "however young and brash Cavanagh might be, he was certainly not stupid."[37]

Edwards met Cavanagh at Girardin's apartment. Edwards remembered that when they were alone together, the "mayor-elect launched into his police problems and why he wanted me to serve as police commissioner." Cavanagh believed Edwards's appointment would reassure Detroit's African-American voters that there would be no crackdowns while he was mayor. Edwards was particularly impressed when Cavanagh described "his convictions about equal rights and constitutional law enforcement. . . . I didn't need convincing, but I was surprised by his command of the legal arguments and the strength of the convictions he expressed." Edwards said later he was equally taken that Cavanagh had thoroughly researched his career as a politician and judge. The mayor-elect concluded his pitch by promising Edwards that he would have a free hand to run the department.[38]

During their conversation, Cavanagh had touched on two of Edwards's deepest concerns about race relations: avoiding a riot and promoting color-blind law enforcement. Largely because of his experiences in Detroit, Edwards was convinced "that race hatred and race conflict constituted in domestic affairs, the greatest threat of all to the American dream . . . and that the police-black community problem had to be solved if 'domestic tranquility' was to become a reality." Still, Edwards was not convinced he was the man for the job. He told Cavanagh "that challenging as his offer was, I very much doubted that I could justify leaving the Supreme Court, but that I would surely think about the matter and would give him a considered answer fairly soon."[39]

He drove back to Lansing in a quandary and spent the next two weeks weighing his options. Inevitably the matter became public. Radio station WWJ broke the story on December 6 and contacted Edwards, who was attending a judicial meeting in Minneapolis. He confirmed that he was considering the appointment. The following day, Detroit's newspapers scrambled to put their spin on the story. The *News* speculated that Edwards was having trouble making up his mind because he wanted to insure that Governor John Swainson would find a suitable replacement for him on the supreme court. *Free Press* Managing Editor Frank Angelo reported that "persons close to [Edwards] indicate that he has been getting restive in recent months and that he misses the feeling of being in the middle of things. The job of police commissioner, particularly at this junction of Detroit's history, guarantees that he would be pretty busy."[40]

Edwards remembered those weeks of indecision as among the worst of his life. "There were so many reasons to say 'No.' I loved the work on the Michigan Supreme Court. I felt that much good had been accomplished in the six years I had served. . . . I was two years into a six-year term. . . . Peg and I had many friends in Lansing and East Lansing. As compared to the very real world in which we had lived in Detroit, Peg and I referred to East Lansing as 'fairyland.' We had thought never to leave it."[41]

Edwards continued to weigh his future, now with the benefit of editorial advice. The *Free Press* opined: "If Supreme Court Justice George Edwards accepts the invitation to become Detroit's new police commissioner, Mayor-elect Cavanagh will have scored a political ten strike. Even more important, the appointment of Justice Edwards could turn out to be a very good thing for Detroit and for the police department." The editorial noted that "conservative elements of the community are undoubtedly having fits at the prospect of one with Mr. Edwards' known liberal tendencies being given responsibility for law enforcement." But, it added, those potential problems would be more than offset by Edwards's "ability to communicate with large sections of our population among which there unfortunately exists suspicion and feelings of frustration. Detroit's Negroes comprise nearly one-third of the city's population. Just as the city has its obligation to them, so do they have an obligation to the city. When that is fully understood and accepted, whatever intra-community tensions now exist will be well on their way to being eliminated."[42]

The *News* weighed in with an article headlined, "Bold is the Word." It praised Pelham's appointment and Edwards's selection, saying: "We'll hear some moaning from traditionalists certain that the first Negro in top departmental office and a crusading liberal in police department command portend troublesome days to come. The *News* disagrees. We feel that the mayor-elect has chosen boldly but well." Although its editors disagreed frequently with Edwards's liberal rulings on the supreme court, the newspaper admitted it was precisely those stands that made him the best candidate for tearing down the "anger curtain" that divided Detroit's black and white communities. The editorial stressed the unlikeliness of Edwards accepting the thankless job, saying: "Who would have idly speculated that Edwards would be tapped? Or that he would be willing to quit the prestige and security of the State's highest court for the dubious honor of putting his neck on the block of the city's roughest appointive office? Edwards knows the police job is a maze of political fishhooks, that no police commissioner since James Couzens has gone from Beaubien to high political office. Why then would a man in whom the love of political life still runs strong risk losing everything?"[43]

Hundreds of friends and associates added their advice. Many attorneys urged Edwards to remain on the court. Some lawyers, like Robert J. Baker of Adrian, worried that given Talbot Smith's acceptance of a federal judgeship, Edwards's departure "would be a great blow to judicial liberalism" in Michigan. Most of his African-American acquaintances urged Edwards to accept the job. Charles C. Diggs, Sr., a former state senator and father of Congressman Diggs wrote, "Your acceptance as police commissioner will be a god send to all people of Detroit and will reflect itself in large cities all over America. We need dedicated men to step forward even at a sacrifice to meet these trying and turbulent times."[44]

Ultimately, Edwards pushed aside considerations of comfort and political expediency; he found Cavanagh's offer irresistible. From an intellectual standpoint, the police job offered a unique perspective from which to further study criminal law. He first became interested "in the legal and human problems posed in criminal law" while serving as a Wayne County juvenile judge in the early 1950s. As a Wayne County circuit judge and a Michigan Supreme Court Justice, he became even more intrigued by the delicate balancing act of reconciling constitutional safeguards with the necessities of criminal law enforcement. Later, he recalled, it was "for these reasons, I welcomed the opportunity to look at the problem of crime at a closer and intensely practical level in the Detroit Police Department."[45]

Edwards recounted an even more compelling, moral reason for taking the job. "If Detroit did blow up . . . in another race riot like the one we had lived through in 1943, I knew I could not live with the knowledge that I had been offered a chance to stop it—and had refused to try." On Sunday, December 10, he called friends to ask their advice. He realized that without support from city leaders, he could not succeed and taking the police commissioner's "job would only be a gesture—a silly one at that." He contacted *Detroit News* editor Martin S. Hayden, Walter Reuther, NAACP Detroit Chapter president Ed Turner, and Willis Hall, director of the Detroit Board of Commerce. Each expressed surprise that Edwards was seriously considering the commissioner's post, but they all encouraged him. Edwards was especially moved by his conversations with Hall and Turner. "From very different points of view [they] expressed great concern about impending racial conflict in Detroit. Both urged me to take the job. I particularly remember Turner saying that just my taking the job would avert disaster. I didn't express the skepticism I felt about that comment."[46]

While Edwards worked the phones, his wife, Peg, went to services at All Saints Episcopal Church in East Lansing, where Edwards served on the vestry. She returned home excited. The lessons for that Sunday seemed to be an omen advising them to return to Detroit. She was especially struck by the apparent relevance of a passage from St. Paul's letter to the Romans, "If there be any other commandment, it is briefly comprehended in this saying, namely, Thou shalt love thy neighbor as thyself. . . . now it is high time to awake out of sleep: for now is our salvation nearer than when we believed. The night is far spent, the day is at hand: let us therefore cast off the works of darkness and let us put on the armour of light."[47]

Edwards called Cavanagh for reassurance that he would have a free hand to run the police department without political interference. He then agreed to take the job. As he wrote his oldest son George, who was serving in the Peace Corps in Africa, "I guess I couldn't resist trying to find out whether it is possible to make the Constitution a living document in one of our great cities. In any event, HOLD YOUR HATS!" On December 12, Edwards and Cavanagh held a press conference at the Pick-Fort Shelby Hotel. The mayor-elect praised Edwards for his unimpeachable honesty and integrity, administrative ability, knowledge of the law, and "understanding of the police department's relationship to the total community. . . . These are rare, even difficult qualities to capture in any individual. I know Mr. Edwards possesses them." For his part, Edwards described how the passage from Romans had influenced his decision, and he provided copies for the media. His comments did not impress the *Free Press* reporter, who described how "Edwards soft-pedalled his background of liberalism and avoided flat statements that the police department even has problems." A few days later, Ray Girardin wrote Edwards, perhaps too enthusiastically, "the reaction to your acceptance announcement has been overwhelmingly favorable—from the man in the street to the jet pilots."[48]

Although he realized that people in Michigan, for better or worse, would understand why he accepted the police commissionership, Edwards worried that many of his political backers in other parts of the nation might see his decision as inexplicable. He launched a letter writing campaign to put his acceptance in the best possible light. On December 15, 1961, he wrote Selig Harrison, an associate editor of *The New Republic,* sending him background articles from Detroit newspapers and asking him to "do whatever you can properly do by word of mouth or otherwise to convey some understanding to our mutual friends in Washington and elsewhere." Harrison reassured Edwards that taking the police job did not constitute political suicide, pointing out, it "is not inexplicable, it's admirable—and if it's admired by the people, it's brilliant politics in the long run." Edwards wrote labor journalist John Herling, who lived in Washington, D.C., and coyly said he did not expect Herling to put an article about the matter in his nationally distributed newsletter. He also persuaded Michigan Senator Philip A. Hart to explain his decision to Attorney General Robert F. Kennedy and Labor Secretary Arthur Goldberg. A month later, he followed up by writing his own letter to Goldberg, who had appointed him to an international labor tribunal during the previous summer. "Many of my friends are of course perturbed about the pitfalls of this new post. It may be that your success in walking so surefootedly through so many [controversies] helped give me some confidence."[49]

The announcement that a sitting supreme court justice, who still nursed Congressional ambitions, had given up his peaceful public tenure for a highly contentious, politically risky job, where the annual salary of $22,500 could never compensate for all of the headaches might have surprised some outside observers. Even some of Edwards's friends had doubted that he would give up the security of the Michigan Supreme Court for the thankless task of curbing bigotry within the police department. But those who knew him best were not taken aback; they recognized that the police commissioner's post was just the kind of challenge that had always galvanized him. Everything in his background assured that he would accept the job.

2
WHO WAS GEORGE EDWARDS?

I suppose that somehow in the course of a lifetime fate will knock corners off of most ambitions until maybe some way or another the whole bundle will fit together—how I do not know.
—George Edwards, Jr., November 3, 1936

George Edwards brought the unique perspective of a southern liberal to Detroit's complex racial problems. His radical family background and his childhood experiences in Texas dictated that he would devote his life to wrestling the social injustices of racism and poverty. A native of Dallas, he came to the Motor City in 1936 as part of one of the greatest internal migrations of the twentieth century. The diaspora of southern whites and blacks to Detroit and other northern cities began after World War I and continued for the next fifty years.[1] It remade the face, culture, politics, and economics of the nation's largest cities by, among other things, bringing some of the most intractable problems of the South to the North.

Edwards was born on August 6, 1914, to parents who shared a deep commitment to social justice and a quixotic determination to do good in the face of evil. His mother, Octavia, was one of the first women to graduate from the University of Texas. His father, George Clifton Edwards, Sr., was perhaps the most radical activist lawyer of his day in Texas. He began his life of public service as a teacher offering night classes to impoverished workers in Dallas's cotton mills. His success convinced reluctant public school officials to build a school in the city's poorest neighborhood. Edwards's radical politics eventually ran afoul of the school board's conservative leadership. After his dismissal, he read law and opened a practice dedicated to helping the downtrodden.

In *Pioneer-at-Law,* Edwards's biography of his father, he described his father as "the labor lawyer, the ACLU lawyer, the NAACP lawyer. Into the bargain, he was anti-Ku Klux Klan, pro-Prohibition, and politically a Socialist." Even more radical for the South, he espoused racial equality. His fight against racism as a lawyer began on March 3, 1910, when he watched a mob lynch his first criminal client, Allen Brooks, a mentally ill, elderly black man charged with molesting a three-year-old white child. If justice had prevailed, Brooks would have been judged innocent by reason of insanity. Instead, an angry mob broke into the courthouse just as Edwards was scheduled to meet Brooks for the first time. In horror, the lawyer watched as the crowd seized his client and threw him out of a second story window. Brooks fell to the ground head first, breaking his neck. The mob dragged his lifeless body six blocks, ripped his clothes off for souvenirs, and then hanged the corpse.[2]

Brooks's lynching took place before young Edwards was born. But while working as a clerk in his father's office during the summers, Edwards had ample opportunities to witness the injustices his father fought on daily basis. Two incidents would remain vivid for the rest of his life, helping to animate his zeal for reforming the Detroit Police Department. The first occurred when he accompanied his father to interview a client in the Dallas jail. As Edwards recalled years later, he saw police lead a prisoner to a nearby interrogation room. A few minutes later, he heard groans and screams. When the door opened, "The scene in the room was unforgettable. A man on each side of a heavy table had the prisoner's arms twisted so that he was bent forward over the table. His ankles were shackled to the table legs so that his legs were spread apart. A big man stood behind him with a length of rubber hose in his hand. The subject was stripped to the waist and long, red welts stood out on the white skin of his back." There was a break in the moaning, "Then came the most fearsome shriek of pain and terror I had ever heard. On one occasion the door was open when this occurred and I saw the big man who had been wielding the rubber hose reach down between the prisoners spread-out legs and grab and twist his testicles."[3]

Edwards remembered even more vividly the night in early March 1931 when his father was kidnapped by the Ku Klux Klan. The drama began when two young communists arrived in Dallas preaching trade unionism and racial equality. City police arrested both men for vagrancy, even though each had $20 in his pocket—more than enough for a week's room and board during the Depression. Under Texas law, that evidence provided a complete defense against vagrancy. As their lawyer, Edwards argued that the police knew the vagrancy charge was specious and were using it as a fig leaf to cover their real aim—depriving the two radicals of their constitutional rights to free speech. The judge countered that the U.S. Constitution did not extend to his Texas courtroom. In the ensuing wrangling, Edwards launched into an impassioned defense of the Bill of Rights and the judge fined him $100 for contempt of court. The quirky courtroom drama drew amused stories from the *Dallas Morning Herald* and prompted an embarrassed change of heart from the prosecutor. He called Edwards and offered to forget the case if the lawyer could get his clients to leave town quietly.[4]

Sixteen-year-old Edwards drove his father to the courthouse to pick up the pair and drive them to the train station. He waited and waited. Finally, he went in only to learn that his father and his two clients had "left" through another entrance. After several hours and repeated inquiries, the desk sergeant finally took pity on the worried teenager and told him: "Listen son, you go on home now. Your Daddy ain't gonna get hurt." Later that evening, Edwards Sr. arrived home and described his misadventure. As police escorted Edwards and his clients through a side door of the courthouse, they were seized by six or eight men with drawn guns. Two men shoved Edwards and the communists into one car while the other abductors followed in speeding cars. The Klansmen drove about ten miles, released Edwards at a gas station, then took his clients to the Trinity River bottom, tied them to trees, and beat them unconscious with doubled ropes. When they regained consciousness, the two staggered to a nearby farm where an African-American family nursed them for five days until they were strong enough to walk and hitchhike to Corsicana, Texas. From there, they called Kansas City for the railroad fare home. Meanwhile, in Dallas, newspapers reported the kidnapping, Edwards and his son testified before the grand jury, and the local bar association condemned the incident. None of the Klansmen were ever charged, and Edwards Sr. later learned that three of his kidnappers were on the city prosecutor's staff.[5]

When George turned fifteen, his father encouraged him to become a lawyer by persuading him to read Blackstone's *Commentaries on the Common Law*. Later, Edwards recounted that he read the legal classic "with all the comprehension I would have brought to Sanskrit." His tedious encounter with Blackstone combined with his harrowing observations of the inequities of Texas justice persuaded the young Edwards that he never wanted to become a lawyer. After graduating as salutatorian of his class at North Dallas High School, Edwards set off for Southern Methodist University (SMU) to study literature with hopes of some day writing the great American novel.[6]

Edwards's decision to attend the local university proved fortuitous. After graduating from the University of the South, his father had taken a master's degree in literature from Harvard in 1901, and he cherished the hope that his son could spend four years there. But even though the prestigious university accepted Edwards Jr. and offered him a scholarship to cover tuition, the family did not have enough money to pay for travel costs to Massachusetts or his room and board. Instead, Edwards accepted a tuition scholarship at SMU, so he could live at home and commute to school. Edwards thrived on the small, friendly campus. He became a popular student leader, joined the debating team, and wrote for the student newspaper. Inspiring professors nurtured his love of literature—especially writings by the social realists Upton Sinclair and Theodore Dreiser, who chronicled the nation's ills. Edwards graduated in three years as one of the top four students in his class. In addition to his English literary skills, he read French fluently, and had a working knowledge of German and Latin.[7]

Following in his father's footsteps, at age nineteen Edwards headed north to Harvard for a year's study of literature. He left Texas in September 1933 imbued with his father's socialist beliefs and the ambition to learn what he would need to become a

41

writer. He took only a Royal typewriter and a battered suitcase that contained as many books as clothes. The highlight of his trip was spending a few days in New York City. Years later he still remembered his first visit to the metropolis. "That weekend was full of fascinating experiences and impressions. I walked over the Brooklyn Bridge and took the Staten Island Ferry, but I also saw the garment district, the tenements on the Lower East Side, and heard a fierce street corner debate between a Trotskyite and a Lovestonite."[8]

The highlight of Edwards's weekend came when he attended a lecture by Norman Thomas. His father gave him a letter of introduction to Thomas, the nation's leading Socialist and the chair of the party's social reform agency, the League for Industrial Democracy (LID). Thomas introduced Edwards to Mary Fox, the LID's executive secretary, and its two student organizers, Monroe Sweetland and Joseph Lash.[9] Lash, who would remain a lifelong friend, later gained fame as a biographer of Franklin D. and Eleanor Roosevelt.

In later years, Detroit political critics made much of Edwards's Harvard background, implying that his Ivy League experience showed him to be a mere dilettante in the muddier affairs of life. In reality, Edwards never felt comfortable in Cambridge. He chafed at Harvard's stodgy atmosphere, which contrasted sharply with the friendly informality of SMU. He found his classes interesting, but uninspiring. His two most famous teachers left him cold. Philosopher Alfred North Whitehead "thought and talked about what interested him at the time—always at the edge of his knowledge and usually well beyond ours." Edwards also disdained George Lyman Kittredge, Harvard's legendary Shakespeare scholar. To Edwards, Kittredge came to symbolize the university's "strange mixture of excellence and arrogance." Edwards enjoyed the theatricality of Kittredge's classes, but believed he was "hearing much more Kittredge than Shakespeare."[10]

Edwards might have been happier at Harvard if his creative writing had met with more than a lukewarm reception. In that, too, he was disappointed. On the basis of a gory story about a beating at the Dallas jail, Edwards was admitted to one of Harvard's most legendary and selective courses—Advanced English

Composition. As Edwards recalled, "Famous men taught [the course]. And men who had taken it had gone on to fame. . . . The happy 15 who were chosen felt that we had a guarantee that we would find the writer's Valhalla of our predecessors." Robert Hillyer, a minor novelist, presided over the class. Each week students submitted short stories, poems, or essays, and Hillyer chose a few to analyze. The discussions quickly degenerated into arguments between the two camps of passionate would-be writers. Edwards and a few allies who had fallen under the spell of social realism spent the semester battling the formalists who believed in art for art's sake. Hillyer sided with the formalists. His critiques praised Edwards's heartfelt fictional efforts but lambasted their overly emotional style.[11]

Years later, Edwards could still muster passion about those ivory-tower debates:

> The country was in the depths of the depression; unemployment was at the peak; the news was full of bankruptcies, suicides, starvation and riots. Hitler was in full power in Germany; his American admirers were making shrill imitations of him here. In such a world some of us thought Joyce, Proust, T. S. Eliot were effete. When some of our classmates attempted imitations of them, we who classified ourselves as realists descended upon them with vigor, and when a piece which we felt dealt with the issues of the times was read, it received the scornful ridicule of the art for arts sake group.

The unofficial leader of the art-for-art's-sake camp was *New York Times* heir C. L. Sulzberger. Years later, Edwards met Sulzberger covering a General Motors strike. He remembered that they "elected to pick up the conversation from there—without a reference to past history."[12]

The high point of Edwards's year at Harvard did not come in the classroom. He joined Harvard's Liberal Club soon after arriving in Cambridge. The club had enjoyed an interlude of activism in the years around World War I but by 1933 had degenerated into little more than a discussion group. Edwards and a handful of his friends revitalized the club by securing its affiliation with Norman Thomas's LID. The highlight of their efforts came on April 13, 1934, when the club sponsored an antiwar rally at Harvard that was part of a nationwide 25,000-student protest. As one of the speakers, Edwards experienced his first heckling. The *Harvard Journal* reported that more than 3,000 people milled about the library steps to hear speakers interrupted with shouts of "We want war," "We want Hitler," "We want Moscow," and "Down with Peace." When LID organizers were unable to bring order, they took to the nearby streets, tying up traffic on Massachusetts Avenue for more than half an hour.[13] The chaos provided good preparation for Edwards's life after Harvard.

By June 1934, Edwards was so eager to embark on his activist life that he did not stay for graduation. His year had been "pleasant" and "stimulating," but he had "come to think of Harvard as the epitome of the ivory tower." With a $10-a-week job as a college recruiter for the LID beckoning, Edwards had much grander goals in mind. Forty years later he could still list those "small" ambitions: "I wanted to help (1) end war; (2) end poverty; (3) end race injustice. In my spare time I thought I might try writing the great American novel."[14]

Later, in Detroit, political opponents resurrected Edwards's work as an LID organizer to portray him as an unpatriotic left-wing radical. During the 1930s, however, many Americans, horrified at the Depression's social ravages, joined the socialist cause, convinced that it provided the only means of salvaging the national economy. Most of Edwards's work as an LID organizer consisted of touring the nation, lecturing to students, meeting social activists, and participating tangentially in union organizing. He later estimated that he saw "at least a hundred thousand miles of the United States hitchhiking" during those two years.[15]

Edwards's first personal taste of brutal law enforcement came in February 1935, when police in Fort Smith, Arkansas, arrested him for helping to lead a strike of relief workers. During the nineteenth century, Fort Smith enjoyed a wild reputation as a gateway to the West and later to Indian Territory. In the Gilded Age, the town gained national opprobrium as the court seat of "Hanging" Judge Isaac C. Parker, who earned his dubious place in history by sentencing a record seventy-seven men to the gallows. By 1935, Parker was long dead and Fort Smith was a sleepy town on the Oklahoma border. Still, the town's police maintained a tough law-and-order outlook, especially when it came to rabble-rousing outsiders preaching racial and economic equality.

Trouble began early in the month when 2,000 unemployed coal miners, who had been hired as relief workers under the WPA, went on strike to protest a cut in their wages from thirty to twenty cents per hour for ditch digging and other manual labor. Edwards was dispatched to Fort Smith to help six local organizers led by Rev. Claude Williams. At a rally on February 18, Edwards told a crowd that farmers in Oklahoma paid $9 a month to feed their mules—more than the state of Arkansas paid to feed its relief workers. City employee Bob Williamson testified that he was offended by Edwards's metaphor because it made it appear that "they thought more of jack-asses in Oklahoma than they though of humans in Arkansas." Edwards further infuriated the authorities by leading a chorus of the national anthem. Police arrested Edwards and his six allies and charged them with barratry. Under common law tradition, barratry is an offense limited to lawyers who prosecute frivolous lawsuits. But Arkansas had broadened its barratry statute to include virtually any activity that the authorities found repugnant. The state's law defined a barrator as "one who excites or maintains suits and quarrels, either in courts or elsewhere in the country; a disturber of the peace who spreads false rumors and calumnies, whereby discord and disquiet may grow among neighbors."[16]

Fort Smith police did not permit Edwards to make any phone calls, so he persuaded a fellow inmate's wife to contact the LID. She sent a telegram to New York saying: "Am in jail. Wire instructions. Signed, George Edwards." Mary Fox telegraphed Edwards's father who handled many LID cases in the South, and he arrived in Fort Smith on February 21. Edwards Sr., arguing the spurious nature of the barratry charges, said they were "about equivalent to the New Testament charge against Jesus of stirring up the people." He wrote his wife that their son "was about as guilty as I was but those petty rural mine-dominated officials were as little open to reason, justice, or law as the Massachusetts officers were in the Sacco-Vanzetti case." The case took a curious twist during one hearing when the prosecutor called Edwards Sr. to the stand and tried to portray him as a socialist troublemaker. The defense attorney, however, successfully parried his attackers and continued his efforts on behalf of his clients. He posted bond for his son, who left Arkansas to consult with Roger Baldwin, head of the ACLU. Meanwhile, Edwards Sr. continued representing the others—especially Rev. Williams, who drew special wrath from Fort Smith's police chief by telling strikers that if they followed God, their cause would be vindicated. Finally, in June, prosecutors dropped the case.[17]

Edwards had another harrowing experience a few days later in eastern Arkansas, where the Southern Tenant Farmers Union was organizing. He attended a meeting of five hundred sharecroppers in Marked Tree while lookouts kept tabs on a planters' lynch mob massing down the road. The first two dispatches said "nothing, really to worry about—they're just starting to drink." Then came a third message, "Not much to worry about, there's just about a hundred of them and they're gettin' warmed up." Then came the alarm, a note telling the sharecroppers to disband because the planters were "pretty liquored up and they're getting in their cars and it's time to go." Edwards and the other organizers sat, terrified, as their driver sped for the Tennessee state line, their car nestled between a dozen cars in front and a dozen behind.[18]

After the Arkansas incidents, Edwards Sr. urged his son to leave the LID. On March 2, 1935, he wrote: "I hope you will send us a card every day, for I am bound to be anxious as long as you are working in our glorious, free, native and democratic South. Try to be as discreet as possible. Remember your style is greatly cramped in jail. The powers of violence are all on the other side and knowing that we have got to learn to evade their thrusts, not to take them breast on. We are not ready to be martyrs yet." The following month, he advised his son to consider law school because as a lawyer he could accomplish much more than he could as an organizer. "I have an abounding dislike for mere talking, such as preachers and itinerant lecturers are tempted to do."[19]

It would take another year for Edwards to tire of his life on the road. In the meantime, he enjoyed his vagabond existence and revelled in his meetings with national leaders. On November 17, 1935, Edwards, along with other student activists and such leading socialists as Norman Thomas, Earl Browder, Upton Sinclair, Heywood Broun, and Max Lerner, met with Franklin D. Roosevelt. Edwards described his youthful and cynical impressions of the president in a letter to his parents. He found Roosevelt's "famous smile" and behavior "quite studied," adding: "his face in relaxation impressed me even more than his acting did. It was lined and worn. He not only appeared haggard, but unless I was indulging in some self deception, his face was crossed with lines that come not simply from overwork but from knowledge and fear of the hypocrisy of one's own acts." It was, Edwards speculated, probably the same kind of look that Woodrow Wilson wore at Versailles. Edwards predicted that "when the time comes he will lead this nation into war again with all the too obvious sincerity and idealism which was Woodrow Wilson's in 1918. That is if we don't see to it otherwise." Ironically, by the time World War II began, Edwards had become an ardent supporter of both Roosevelt and the war effort.[20]

That time, in the late 1930s, when most socialists, including Edwards and his father, abandoned their idealism for the more pragmatic New Deal programs of the Democratic party, was still several years away. During the mid-1930s, American socialists and communists were enjoying a brief heyday. Their new-found sense of power became manifest in bickering. On December 2, 1935, Edwards wrote to his parents from the Socialist party convention; he was worried about a split within the ranks. Later that month, during a three-day convention in Columbus, Ohio, the socialist-leaning student LID merged with the communist-leaning National Student League to form the American Student Union (ASU). The delegates voted overwhelmingly to support the Oxford Pledge, refusing to support the U.S. in any war. They also elected Edwards as the new party's national chairman.[21]

Throughout his political career, critics seized on Edwards's ASU activities as a sign of his willingness to work with communists. In reality, Edwards, along with Norman Thomas and his socialist followers, had disdain for communism; the student group merger was more a matter of expediency than common philosophy. Even so, by the time he assumed the presidency of the ASU, Edwards's interests had begun to shift from student to labor organizing. In early December 1935, Edwards wrote his parents that he was ready to leave the student movement, although he planned to stay in it until at least April while he figured out how to get a foothold in a labor union. Three months later, he wrote that his impending speech at Oberlin College would seem anticlimatic compared to his experiences in Akron, where he had helped with the strike of 14,000 workers at the Goodyear Rubber Company. He now saw a labor organizing job as the "sina qua non" of his aspirations. Edwards stayed with the LID through the fall campaign in which Norman Thomas ran as the Socialist candidate for president. By October, he was clearly disillusioned, writing his parents that the radical movement based in New York City had become too isolated from the rest of the nation, despite the fact that it was "comparatively large in numbers and vociferous."[22]

The following month, Edwards hitchhiked to Detroit with $50 in his pocket and one suitcase containing two suits, two sweaters, a sweatshirt, rubber boots, a winter coat, and a pair of resoled shoes. Several myths grew up surrounding Edwards's reasons for moving to Detroit. Later critics claimed that he was sent by unnamed socialists and communists to infiltrate and help radicalize the autoworkers union. Opponents within the labor movement claimed that John L. Lewis, who founded the Committee of Industrial Organization (CIO) in 1935, sent Edwards to Detroit to entice the auto workers union to change its allegiance from the rival American Federation of Labor (AFL). Edwards perpetuated the most romantic story of all when he claimed he came to Detroit to write the great American novel. He told the tale so many times that he came to believe it himself. At the time, however, Edwards informed his father that he had done little writing lately and was unlikely to pursue a career as a novelist. If factory work did not pan out in Detroit, he promised to return to Texas, read law, and join his father's practice. It was probably best that his literary dreams went unrealized, judging by one piece that was rejected for publication by *The Story*—a New York magazine devoted to short fiction. In the tale, entitled "Texas Communist," Edwards used purple prose to describe the travails of a writer chronicling the life of an inspiring socialist speaker murdered by the police.[23]

In reality, Edwards's reasons for moving to Detroit were far more prosaic. He wrote his father that he was tired of his hectic life on the road and yearned for the "sane, well-rounded existence [needed] to maintain life in the radical movement." Detroit seemed a good place to settle. Along with thousands of others, he was attracted by its teeming factories and its burgeoning labor movement peopled by such socialists as Roy, Victor, and Walter Reuther. Edwards knew the Reuther brothers through their LID activities. Roy had taught at Brookwood Labor College in Katonah, New York. Brookwood was founded after World War I as a school for workers, but by the mid-1930s its mission had shifted to provide training for radical labor leaders. Frank Winn, a close friend of Edwards from his SMU days, spent most of 1935 studying there. By 1936, Winn had landed a job editing the UAW newsletter, and he invited Edwards to live with him. On November 15, Edwards left New York and began hitchhiking to Michigan. For the next six months he shared an apartment with Winn at 234 Alfred Street, just a few blocks from UAW headquarters.[24]

As would be true throughout his career, Edwards showed an uncanny knack for being in the right place at the right time. He arrived in Detroit just as the UAW was poised for greatness. Worker dissatisfaction in the auto plants arose from industry practices that today seem almost unimaginable. As one government report explained, unrest stemmed "from insecurity, low annual earnings, inequitable hiring and rehiring methods, espionage, speed-up, and the displacement of workers at an extremely early age." Although conditions were ripe for unionization, the AFL was sharply divided over how to handle conditions in Detroit. The AFL traditionally drew its support from skilled craft unions, and its leadership eschewed the great pool of unskilled workers who made up the bulk of autoworkers. Congress's passage of the National Industrial Recovery Act in 1933 spurred a flurry of unionization—some of it independent of the AFL. To regain some semblance of control, in August 1935 the AFL chartered the United Automobile Workers of America as a new union but refused to make it self-governing. AFL President William Green appointed Francis J. Dillon, whom contemporary labor writer Benjamin Stolberg described as "an archaic . . . organizer, flat-footed from a long life as a walking delegate." Stolberg said "the workers protested bitterly against Dillon. They wanted to elect their own leaders. But they were told that it was Dillon or nothing, and for the time being they took Dillon. Green and Dillon immediately began sabotaging the growth of the new national organization. After one year of Dillonism, 52 of these industrial union locals died from sheer neglect, and membership figures dropped precipitously. But underneath this official sabotage the rank and file, under its own leadership, was organizing feverishly all along." Walter Reuther was one of those feverish organizers and began laying the groundwork for his power in the West Side of Detroit, where he persuaded six locals to amalgamate into one and elect him president.[25]

In April 1935, workers struck a Chevrolet plant in Toledo; their resulting victory revitalized other auto locals. The following year, in April 1936, 30,000 workers sent delegates to the first independent UAW convention in South Bend, Indiana. They threw out Dillon and replaced him with Homer Martin, a former Baptist preacher who was one of the most inspiring speakers in American unionism. Under its new leadership, the UAW affiliated with the CIO which welcomed unskilled workers into its ranks. CIO members also prided themselves on being more militant. One sign of their militancy was the use of sit-down strikes in which workers took control of their work stations to stop production. Because most factories consisted of many interdependent departments, this meant that a small number of workers could close an entire plant. As historian Sidney Fine points out, sit-downs worked especially well for the UAW, which by late 1936 had only a handful of workers in any one factory.[26]

Edwards arrived in Detroit in November, just in time for the great wave of sit-down strikes that would revolutionize the UAW. Two thousand strikers paralyzed the Midland Steel Corporation factory that made body frames for Chrysler, Dodge, and Plymouth on November 27. UAW leaders called it the most significant strike in Detroit history. Initially, at least, the Midland strike complicated Edwards's job hunting because without the essential frames, Chrysler, Dodge, and Plymouth laid off their workers, who then flooded the job market. Edwards's most vivid memory of job hunting came at the Ford Motor Company's River Rouge Plant. As he recalled years later, workers began lining up at 10 P.M. hoping they would be among the first hired when the employment office opened at six o'clock the next morning. "It was a bitter cold night. . . . [W]hen I got there there were already thousands of people queued up ahead of me but before the night

advanced too far, there were more thousands by far queued behind me. . . . I'm reasonably sure that this selection process did
have a tendency to weed out the unfit. Occasionally there was a
splash up and down the line—it was one of the most macabre
nights I remember spending." The workers stood in stony silence
all night, shuffling their feet and waving their arms to stay warm.
The next morning would-be applicants were asked only one
question: "What do you do?" If they could not guess what jobs
Ford was hiring for that day, their efforts came to naught.[27]

Even before the Midland Steel strike was settled on December 4, UAW leaders began looking for their next target. They
chose the Kelsey-Hayes Wheel Company which made brakes for
Ford and General Motors. In his memoirs, Victor Reuther described how his brother, Walter, decided that Kelsey-Hayes
would provide the opening salvo in his war to enlarge Local 174
on Detroit's West Side. Reuther found it difficult to recruit
enough men to create a strong union presence in each plant, so
he decided to focus on just one site where he could place a handful of his own men. Reuther chose Kelsey-Hayes because it was
small enough to be manageable. At the same time, it was large
enough to disrupt Ford because it provided half of the giant auto-
maker's wheel and brake drums. Its $9-a-day wages were exces-
sively low; Ford, which had been forced to cut wages during the
Depression, still paid $19.80.[28]

Reuther learned that Kelsey-Hayes was hiring workers, and
he recruited applicants, including Edwards, who had still not
found a job and was keeping busy by volunteering for the kitchen
crew that fed the Midland Steel strikers. Kelsey-Hayes hired Edwards, Victor Reuther, and future UAW education director Mer-
lin Bishop to work at its McGraw Avenue plant. Edwards began
work on December 2. He earned 37.5 cents per hour as a proba-
tionary employee in Department 49, where he dipped brake
plates and shoes into vats of black enamel. In a letter home he
wrote: "My job very much resembles Charlie Chaplin's only it
is messier and faster." Although the work was not dangerous,
Edwards said, the "speed and constant weight of lifting and turning the plates make it difficult." When he was hired at Kelsey-
Hayes, Edwards qualified for membership in the UAW and he
signed up as a member of Local 174. Along with Victor Reuther

and Bishop, he began recruiting co-workers to the union. They held small meetings in their homes to limit repercussions in case there were informants among the new members. They met stiff resistance from workers fearful of losing their jobs. For example, the man on the assembly line next to Edwards refused to speak to him. The forty-five-year-old worker, approaching the age that usually signalled dismissal in the car industry, feared drawing any attention to himself. He worried that a pink slip would mean that he would never find another job to support his wife and six children.[29]

By early December, only 200 of Kelsey-Hayes's 4,500 workers were members. Nevertheless, within a week after Edwards's hiring, the union called a strike to protest a production speed up. Kelsey-Hayes required the increased production from its workers when Ford Motor Company experienced a parts shortage and ordered more brake and wheel parts. On December 9, Edwards and Victor Reuther led a sit-down strike in Department 49 which closed the entire plant. The protest ended several hours later when Kelsey-Hayes managers met with Walter Reuther and reached an oral agreement for a wage increase, overtime pay, a forty-hour work week, and an end to the speed up. When company officials reneged on the agreement, workers staged brief sit-downs on December 11 and 12. A fourth sit-down began on December 14 and closed the plant. As Christmas neared, the strikers became restless. To entertain them, Bishop set up discussion groups while Edwards organized "hillbilly bands" and barbershop quartets.[30]

Edwards gleefully wrote to his parents, "For once we seem to have Ford Motor Company in a squeeze. . . . I've got to go. Everything is swell—we're set to win." His prediction was right. Ford pressured Kelsey-Hayes to settle so it would not have to shut down its own production. On December 23, the wheel manufacturer raised experienced workers' salaries from 60 to 75 cents, probationers from 37.5 to 50 cents per hour, and provided a guarantee that foremen could not fire workers for arbitrary reasons.[31]

There would be other sit-downs in Detroit that month, but Kelsey-Hayes ranked second in importance to Midland Steel. The Kelsey-Hayes strike brought another firm, closely allied with major automakers, into the union. It gave the Reuthers, Bishop, and Edwards their first prominence within the UAW. It encouraged the rapid growth of West Side Local 174. The strike also provided valuable experience as a trial run for the famous General Motors strike in Flint that began December 30.[32]

After the Kelsey-Hayes strike ended, Edwards flew to Chicago to attend an ASU meeting. The convention marked the end of his career in student organizing. He wrote his parents that the four hours of sleep he enjoyed that night in Chicago was the longest stretch of rest he had gotten since the Kelsey-Hayes troubles had begun three weeks earlier. Nevertheless, he looked forward to returning to his factory job, telling his parents: "The crew of my department has in it some of the most natural, unaffected, warm hearted and courageous people whom I have ever known. If the whole of the working class resembles the workers at Kelsey-Hayes—then it is certainly worth spending a life time fighting for."[33]

Edwards's assembly line experience was cut short by the General Motors strike, which forced Kelsey-Hayes to lay off 40 percent of its work force. Edwards, Reuther, and Bishop who had the least seniority were among the first let go. Walter Reuther put Edwards to work part-time for the West Side Local, hoping he would build on the momentum generated by the success at Kelsey-Hayes. Because he was in Detroit, Edwards played only a tangential role in the great General Motors strike taking place in Flint. The West Side Local had three General Motors plants—Cadillac, Fleetwood, and Ternstedt Manufacturing Company—none of which had UAW members. By early January, the UAW had recruited enough people at Cadillac for a strike. When that settled in mid-January, it added pressure for General Motors to reach an agreement in Flint.[34]

While the General Motors strike raged, UAW president Homer Martin hired Edwards as a full-time organizer. The UAW was growing like topsy. On February 11, the Flint strike ended when General Motors granted several concessions, including agreeing to rehire the strikers. By bringing the world's largest corporation to the table, the UAW had scored a stunning victory and paved the way for other union action. Eight days later, Edwards wrote an exuberant letter to his parents. "As you can gather from the papers we are riding the crest of the greatest labor upsurge I have ever dreamed about in this country. Today in Detroit there are no less than a dozen sit-down strikes in three auto plants, three in cigar factories, two in bakeries, two in meat packing houses—and all of these want to join the UAW. That, of course, they can't, but we are free to help organize them. It is work—but it is certainly thrilling work for we are winning on every hand."[35]

Many Detroiters did not share Edwards's enthusiasm for the labor unrest. One newspaper reporter caustically noted that strikes had become so common in Detroit that "sitting down has replaced baseball as a national pastime, and sitter-downers clutter up the landscape in every direction." Company officials turned to the courts for redress. One such crackdown led to Edwards's most notorious experience as a UAW organizer.[36]

In March 1937, Edwards helped to organize strikes in eight West Side Local plants, including Yale and Towne, which made locks for Chrysler. Most of the workers at the company were young women. They shared the same complaints as their male counterparts in other factories but suffered from even lower pay and the added pressures of sexual harassment. Foremen and managers felt free to invite the women out on dates, then link job security with "friendliness." When the UAW strike at Chrysler forced cutbacks at Yale and Towne, the company responded by laying off women sympathetic to unionization. Yale and Towne's would-be organizers contacted Walter Reuther, and he dispatched Edwards who led a sit-down. The month-long Chrysler strike overshadowed troubles at Yale and Towne. But even after Chrysler settled, the Yale and Towne strike continued. Local company officials wanted to negotiate with the union, but executives in the firm's headquarters at Stamford, Connecticut, refused. Instead, they appealed to Wayne County Circuit Judge Arthur Webster for an order requiring the strikers to vacate the factory. He complied, rejecting UAW lawyer Maurice Sugar's claim that the strikers were within their rights because the company would not discuss their complaints. Webster said the argument was as nonsensical as excusing "kidnappers who claim their crime is justified because the kidnapped child's parents refused to enter into preliminary negotiations."[37]

As historian Christopher H. Johnson points out, the Yale and Towne strike "emerged in an atmosphere of growing intolerance of the sit-down concept by public authorities, the media, and, finally, public opinion." On April 15, after Yale and Towne workers ignored Webster's order to end their sit-down, two hundred policemen and sheriff's deputies arrived, firing dozens of rounds of tear gas. The fleeing strikers were arrested. Their attempt to disrupt their arraignment hearing by singing "Solidarity Forever" only hardened Webster's resolve; he found their leaders guilty of contempt of court. The judge spoke for Detroit's establishment when he said: "This has ceased to be a labor controversy: It is not even a question of legality of a sit-down strike; it has passed beyond this stage, and it has now become a question of whether we have a government of law and order or not. The order of this court was not appealed from. It represents law and public authority. If these respondents may defy the lawful order of this court, then any person has the same right to defy any and all ordinances and laws."[38]

Webster fined and sentenced Edwards and three of his UAW compatriots. Edwards and Peter Sedler, a shop steward at Kelsey-Hayes, received the stiffest penalties; Webster gave each thirty days in jail and fined them $250. Two others, Bruce Wilson, Yale and Towne strike chair, and George Cicich, a shop steward for Cadillac, received ten-day sentences. As Edwards explained in a letter to his parents, the four were voluntary prisoners. They refused Webster's offer to release them if they apologized, and the union decided against appealing, reasoning that the injustice of their jail sentence would inspire other strikers. Besides, Edwards wrote, he needed a rest and his cell in Wayne County was "palatial" compared to the jail in Fort Smith. The sheriff, who did not want to alienate potential voters by mistreating his star prisoners, gave the union leaders special quarters in a section of the jail normally set aside for witnesses. They ate special meals, stayed in private rooms with washstands and toilets, had their own shower and bathroom, and enjoyed use of a large reception room. Edwards found the sheriff's hospitality amusing. "It's a funny situation. A flock of the sheriff's deputies are trade unionists and the sheriff has always made a strong play for labor. They weren't willing to be on labor's side to the extent of taking a rap from the court; but they're damned apologetic about the whole show—and consequently we are being treated more like guests than prisoners. The Sheriff had us in this afternoon—cursed the judge in order to salve his conscience and declared we were 'civil not criminal prisoners' and that we would get the best of the house."[39]

Edwards's jail stay took on comic tones when the *Detroit News* described his efforts to unionize jail workers and inmates. In its tongue-and-cheek story on May 3, the newspaper reported how Edwards had recruited thirty new members to his local and vowed to sign up the other 320 prisoners before his jail term ended. His membership included seven deputies who had worked in auto factories, a traffic violator from the Murray Corporation, five short-term violators from Chrysler, and an ex-Packard turnkey. The story continued: "And then what? Well, Edwards admits he isn't sure. He is seriously considering demanding a forty-hour week and vacations with pay." None of this organizing was surprising, the article noted, because "Edwards has been an organizer for nearly a year and giving him 30 days of leisure time in a field hitherto unorganized and figuring he wouldn't do anything about it was like putting woolen underwear on a man with the hives and expecting him to refrain from itching." If Judge Webster did not free Edwards soon, the article predicted, "the first thing he knows he may be bargaining across a table with John L. Lewis or one of his aids on terms such as the outright discharge of all inmates who have been around over 30 days and 50 percent reduction in the sentences of the remainder."[40]

Young Edwards may have found his jail term a lark, but his father was less sanguine. For the second time in two years, he worked to free his son from jail. Edwards Sr. arrived in Detroit on May 1, contacted UAW lawyer Maurice Sugar, and attended a local meeting chaired by Walter Reuther. Two days later, he arranged a meeting with Judge Webster, whom he described afterwards as "a tyrant, rigid, formal, dull, and self-righteous." He made little headway with the hard-nosed jurist, which was not surprising considering his view that Webster's sentence was "ten times as severe as there was any justification for *even given his point of view.* The other 9/10 were sheer stupid, unfeeling cruelty." In a letter home, he assured his wife that most people he met in Detroit respected their son. "All know that he has acted with intelligence and courage and they know him and look up to him. It is certainly an insane social system that tries to shame such as he and gives honor and high pay to judges and slave drivers and gamblers." Edwards even met with Governor Frank Murphy, who had won plaudits for his role in settling the General Motors strike. But Murphy refused to intervene, saying clemency could only be granted in criminal cases and Edwards's jail term was for civil contempt. Despite his lack of success, Edwards and his son enjoyed their visits—which included at least one dinner at a local restaurant thanks to the sheriff's largesse.[41]

His arrest and thirty-day jail stint for leading a sit-down against Yale and Towne Lock Company was relatively insignificant in the annals of UAW history. But it would dog Edwards's later political career and provide fodder for critics who would oppose his appointment as police commissioner. After he became a judge, Edwards looked back on his jail stint sheepishly, telling one interviewer, "It wasn't the piece de resistance of my life, but I suppose it has to be mentioned." In hindsight, he admitted that if he had been in Judge Webster's shoes, he would have meted out the same kind of sentence. He also took a more judicious and historical perspective of sit-down strikes. As he explained, Congress opened a new era of labor unrest when it passed the National Labor Relations Act of 1935. The act recognized workers' rights to organize and required employers to bargain with unions. Business leaders, represented by the Liberty League, argued that the NLRA was unconstitutional and refused to abide by its terms. Unions affiliated with the CIO responded by staging sit-down strikes. Employers argued that sit-downs constituted illegal takeovers of property; labor leaders argued they were justified because employers had broken the law first. Sit-downs raged until 1939, when the U.S. Supreme Court ruled them illegal. Ironically, there was never a major court test of sit-downs in Michigan because Governor Murphy repeatedly talked strikers into leaving plants by securing company commitments to negotiate.[42]

Edwards's release from jail on May 27 came the day after the Battle of the Overpass, one of the most famous episodes in Detroit labor history. With General Motors and Chrysler organized, the UAW had turned its attention to Ford, which had the most sweeping antiunion program of any of the major automakers. On May 26, Ford henchmen attacked a group of UAW organizers that included Walter Reuther and Richard Frankensteen as they handed out pamphlets to workers crossing the bridge to the River Rouge plant. Photographers caught the brutality on film, and the vicious attacks stirred the consciences of many Detroiters, even those previously skeptical of unionism. As Edwards wrote his parents: "No one in Detroit who saw the pictures of the fracas—and every Detroiter did—has any doubt of the fact that Walter and Frankensteen were carefully trapped and brutally beaten by Ford hired thugs called 'service men.' " Along with many other union workers, Edwards was energized by the attack and added: "Be sure that I am neither discouraged nor downhearted nor in any way embittered. The past is past—God keep it for it needs a guardian. But to live and work in the present and for the future—that's life worth living. I am much rested and eager for the battle."[43]

After regaining his freedom, Edwards headed to Stanford, Connecticut, where Yale and Towne Lock was headquartered. Because of its union troubles, the company had threatened to close its Detroit plants and move all of its operations east. But once the UAW began pressuring its home turf, Yale and Towne relented and signed a nationwide agreement organizing all of its factories. It was another sign that the UAW was on a roll. The General Motors strike, the seventeen-day Chrysler strike, and other successful settlements prompted a huge increase in membership. By the summer of 1937, the union had more than 350,000 dues-paying members. Ironically, the UAW's success also fomented chaotic divisiveness. In its early days, union leaders had been so busy fighting for recognition and recruiting new members that they had little time to fight among themselves. But success bred discontent. The impetus for organizing had come from the locals, which continued to call for more and more sitdowns—170 between mid-March and mid-June. Martin and other international leaders could not rein in their renegade members and began to fear that the labor unrest would undermine the UAW's credibility.[44]

Martin tried to reassert control and reorganize the UAW

into a more structured hierarchy in which the international set policy for the locals. He also believed that the union should consolidate its efforts before taking on Ford. Edwards and Reuther opposed Martin's agenda and formed the Unity Caucus, which represented more radical elements within the UAW, including socialists and communists. The Unity Caucus hoped to begin a campaign against Ford immediately and believed in more flexibility, arguing that decentralization had and would continue to pave the way for the union's rapid growth. The disagreement boiled over during the UAW's August 1937 convention in Milwaukee. Martin and Richard Frankensteen created "The Progressive Caucus" to oppose the Unity Caucus. Finally, Reuther offered a compromise proposal to keep the union's decentralized structure while putting members of both factions on a slate with Martin as president. Martin refused the olive branch and retaliated. Among other things, his goons threatened to throw Edwards out of a twelfth-story hotel room. Later, Martin and Frankensteen attempted to fire organizers associated with Reuther, including both Edwards and his friend Frank Winn. Edwards went to work often not sure whether he still had a job.[45]

Edwards found the factionalism disheartening. As he wrote to his parents:

> There has never been a more confused period in my young existence. Here is a young and militant union—the best beyond question in the U.S.—able and ready to organize its own industry completely . . . and what does our gallant president do? He fires about a dozen men who organized and will be essential to maintenance of union success at Ford; caves in to General Motors, dismisses organizers in the midst of a campaign. Either they are the most criminally irresponsible acts which any leader has ever been guilty of, or they amount to what the rank-and-file are openly charging—a sellout.[46]

Edwards's popularity allowed him to keep his job despite Martin's machinations. On April 9, 1938, he witnessed one of the most publicized events in Walter Reuther's career. Reuther was suffering from a cold and decided to stay home for his wife's birthday party. He invited friends, including Edwards, to their apartment on La Salle Boulevard for the celebration. Reuther ordered Chinese food, and expecting the deliveryman, instead opened the door for two gangsters. They flashed their revolvers and asked which of the partiers was Reuther. When no one answered, one of the thugs said: "It's the red-headed guy. Get him." The other put his revolver away and pulled out a blackjack. He headed toward Reuther, who ducked, grabbed the knife, then tossed it to Edwards saying, "Here George." The other gangster responded by shoving his gun in Edwards's stomach and saying, "Drop it." Edwards answered: "You'll never get out of here alive. You may kill me, you may kill two or three of us, but you won't get out of here either." Victor and Roy Reuther chimed in with similar statements. Years later, Edwards said, "There was no doubt in my mind that they intended to kidnap him. They would have beaten him to the point where he would no longer be effective, and maybe they would have killed him too." While the events in the living room unfolded, another guest, Al King, jumped out of the second story window and yelled for the police. Meanwhile, Victor Reuther's wife, Sophie, hurled a pickle jar at one of the assailants. As a commotion began outside, the pair fled. Local 174 paid an informer who identified the two men as Willard "Bud" Holt, a former Ford Service department employee, and Eddie Percelli, a former bootlegger. Evidence indicated that Ford had hired the gangsters to intimidate Reuther. Nevertheless, at their trial in September, a jury acquitted the pair, apparently swayed by the defense's false claim that Reuther had hired them to stage the attack in order to cultivate sympathy within the union for his ongoing battle with Homer Martin.[47]

The infighting continued and provided a constant backdrop to Edwards's final efforts for the UAW. In 1937, the union created a welfare department, which it modelled after the CIO's pioneering program to organize unemployed workers in federal and state relief job programs. Union leaders hoped that massive recruiting efforts among the unemployed would pay off in the short term by denying employers a ready-pool of strikebreakers and in the long term by increasing union membership when the economy improved and workers returned to their regular jobs. In Michigan, where the auto industry was sensitive to economic fluctuations, the program was particularly successful. The state had been hard hit by the long depression that lasted from 1929 to 1935. A brief recovery that attracted more workers to Detroit between 1935 and 1937 spelled even greater misery when the recession of 1937–1938 came. The UAW played a key role in lobbying the WPA to channel more money and jobs to Detroit. By March 1938, 80 percent of WPA workers in Wayne County were members of the new UAW auxiliary. By the end of May 1938, 60 percent of Michigan's WPA projects had been organized and well over 50 percent of all WPA workers had joined the UAW, which set up a grievance procedure, a steward system, and discussions that resulted in improved sanitation, less discriminatory hiring, and reduced intimidation of workers.[48]

In late 1937, Reuther assigned Edwards to organize the unemployed into a West Side Local Auxiliary. The following year, Edwards's efforts became ensnared in the larger web of the union's factional struggles. In May, fighting broke out over finding a replacement for Richard Leonard, who was resigning as head of the UAW relief efforts to become secretary-treasurer of the Michigan Industrial Union Council. Initially, Martin filled the welfare post vacancy with a close ally, William B. Taylor, who opposed Reuther, Edwards, and other Unity Caucus members. Taylor's tenure was brief, and Reuther fought for Edwards to replace him. In June, Edwards received the promotion, and wrote his father that the job was daunting, but "it looks like I have to take it and do what I can. If I do my job it should be important work."[49]

Edwards managed to hold his position despite the widening split between Reuther and Martin and their respective followers. Martin sought strength by trying to take the UAW into the AFL. Reuther allied with the CIO. The NLRB oversaw elections in 1939, and the rank and file overwhelmingly sided with the CIO. After his ouster, Martin began his own efforts to organize unemployed workers. Still, most of the impetus for helping laid off autoworkers fell to the UAW and Edwards. In March 1939, Edwards fought off one attempt to cut WPA funding in Wayne County. His efforts, however, were doomed in Washington, where Congressional conservatives, prompted by fiscal concerns and worried by increased radicalism among WPA workers, began curtailing the relief program. Edwards testified before Congress along with UAW Secretary-Treasurer George Addes and CIO unemployment director Ralph Hetzel, Jr. The WPA received its budget, but Congress passed the Work Relief Act of 1939 which slashed the number of jobs, imposed new wage cuts, and included crippling employment restrictions. Edwards lobbied hard to soften the blow. Due in large measure to his efforts, in October 1939 the WPA agreed to let 5,000 Michigan workers return to their relief jobs and in June 1940 granted a six-month extension in Michigan because of the state's high unemployment rate.[50]

As World War II pulled the nation and Detroit out of its economic slump, Edwards asked for reassignment back to the West Side Local as an organizer. There he found his path to union greatness blocked by Walter Reuther. As historian Nelson Lichtenstein argues, Reuther increasingly saw Edwards as a threat to his own ambitions. One sign of this rivalry came in March 1938, during Local 174's first meaningful election when Reuther took Edwards out of the loop of command and put him in charge of welfare efforts. Although Edwards would have been the logical choice to run as vice president, Reuther instead opted for Michael Manning, whose conservatism and "bumbling and maladroit" speaking style contrasted sharply with Edwards's vision and charisma. Reuther correctly calculated that Edwards was too loyal and had too little stomach for infighting to complain. Edwards began looking for an opportunity to leave the UAW. He expressed his feelings in a letter to his parents, "Frankly I am sorry to be getting out of active trade union work—for I like it and I feel that the UAW has been a very good base and experience for me. But it appears that from here on if I desire to serve in any other than my present capacity as an organizer, I would have to wait long and patiently—or organize to battle my friends as well as my enemies."[51] In characteristic fashion, Edwards did not waste time plotting revenge or mulling over his dashed aspirations. Instead, he began climbing the dual ladders of politics and law that would eventually lead to his appointment as Detroit's police commissioner.

3

THE CRUCIBLE OF POLITICS

Public service is the highest calling to which any citizen in our nation can aspire with the exception of the ministry and possibly some branches of education. The fact that there are . . . selfish persons, and just plain reprobates holding public office in my view no more serves to decrease the importance of the calling than the fact that similar fallible representatives are to be found in the ministry or in other walks of life.

—George Edwards, Jr., 1954

E dwards began his life-long career of public service in 1940 when he became director of the Detroit Housing Commission. The decision to take the post signalled his resolve to stay in Michigan and raise his family. The job also established his reputation as a champion of racial justice who relished the challenge of tackling intractable social problems, and it provided the first stepping stone in his political career. In 1941, Edwards became the youngest city councilman in Detroit's modern history. While he was away during World War II, Detroiters elected him council president by giving him the largest number of votes among the candidates. National newspapers and liberal groups hailed him as a shining star in the nation's political firmament. Then, abruptly, his political fortunes crashed into the harsh realities of Detroit racism when he lost the mayoral race in 1949. His political hopes temporarily dashed, Edwards sought refuge in the law.

When he first travelled to Detroit, Edwards planned on staying only long enough to secure a foothold in the labor movement. But, as he recalled years later, "I fell in love with that city and I fell in love with a girl who lived in that city and between the two facts, it accounted for my remaining in Detroit and in Michigan."[1] The girl was Margaret (Peg) Medill McConnell, the daughter of a successful Detroit stockbroker, Rollin Medill Mc-Connell. Her sister Florence's marriage the previous year to Semon Knudsen, the only son of William S. Knudsen, the president of General Motors, had been the highlight of Detroit's social season. The McConnells reacted less enthusiastically when their other child began dating a UAW organizer.

Peg and George Edwards were married on April 10, 1939. As Edwards wrote years later, "It rained, snowed, and sleeted. The weather outside was a good backdrop for the mood of most who gathered at the McConnell home for the wedding. In Peg McConnell's world her marriage to me was seen not merely as a social disaster. In the midst of the labor management conflict that had torn Michigan apart, it was received as something akin to treason." But the mutual friends who had introduced them recognized that Peg and George Edwards were made for each other. She had a degree in government from Connecticut College for Women, where she had joined the ASU, been elected president of the student government, and led a group of classmates on an Electric Boat Company picket line. Their relationship began as and would remain a love match for the next fifty-six years. The week before their wedding, Edwards attended a UAW meeting in Cleveland while Peg stayed in Detroit. He wrote his parents: "I never thought it would be true but in the middle of a convention I am lonely. I suppose that's what the poet calls love." The following month, he wrote his father again: "I am deeply in love with my wife and the business of marriage is wonderful." The next month, he said, "I do not believe I would have survived in the trade union movement this year without loss of hope and disillusionment and defeatism without the complete personal satisfaction that my courtship and marriage have meant."[2]

In addition to their lifelong devotion to each other, the Edwards shared a passionate commitment to liberal politics and social justice. Both supported Mayor Edward J. Jeffries, Jr., in Detroit's 1939 mayoral race. The son of a liberal politician and Recorder's Court judge, Jeffries gained useful connections as a member of the Common Council from 1932 to 1939, and as a lawyer for Maccabees, a well-known insurance company in Detroit. Historian Dominic Capeci describes him as "fun-loving, competent, and extremely well-connected, though politically nonpartisan. . . . As 'Mayor of all the people,' Jeffries challenged those who expressed class, ethnic, or racial intolerance." He provided an attractive alternative to incumbent Mayor Richard W. Reading, whose tenure had been marked by a bribery scandal. In the general election, Jeffries handily beat Reading by a margin of 226,185 to 108,973.[3]

Edwards first came to Jeffries's attention during his work for the campaign, and the mayor-elect considered rewarding him with appointment to either the housing or public lighting commission. On February 6, Edwards wrote his parents that he preferred the housing post as a logical outgrowth from his UAW work because "labor in Detroit is tremendously concerned with the housing program and it appears to be a somewhat less traditional job than the other." Nevertheless, he added, "Both of them are big jobs and important ones with many political implications. Either, if a good piece of work resulted, would promise much for the future. Both pay $5,000 a year or more which seems a scandalous and somewhat embarrassing salary."[4]

Jeffries's appointment of Edwards proved controversial. The *Detroit News* implied its displeasure in a story headlined "Dallas Intellectual to Guide Detroit's Housing Program." The article identified Edwards as being only twenty-six years old and the "son of a labor and Socialist lawyer in Dallas." The story contrasted Edwards's relative inexperience with the huge scope of his new job. The housing program in Detroit had a $10 million budget and long-range plans to build $60 to $80 million in new housing. The AFL, which disliked Edwards's affiliation with the CIO, also opposed his appointment. Frank X. Martel, president of the Detroit and Wayne County Federation of Labor, issued a statement saying, "Edwards' connections and background are inimical to the interest of the American Federation of Labor Unions, many of whose members are now employed by the Housing Commission. . . . Edwards' selection for this position jeopardizes the interests of those established unions in the building industry." Jeffries waved off the criticism, especially when the chorus included Edward Thal, an AFL member who served on the housing commission. On March 15, the mayor told reporters, "Up until now I did not realize that Mr. Thal thought the Housing Commission to be a playground for the AFL. Now that I realize he feels this to be the case, I will keep my eye on him to make sure that he doesn't make it one."[5]

Public housing was one of a handful of New Deal programs that survived the onset of World War II. Federal housing programs dated back to 1933 when the Public Works Administration announced that it would provide $3.2 million to local governments for slum clearance. That offer was welcomed in Detroit, where the huge in-migration of autoworkers had created serious overcrowding and chronic shortages. In response to the federal announcement, city officials promptly created the Detroit Housing Commission. By the time Edwards took charge, Detroit boasted the second-largest housing commission in the nation after New York City. On May 6, 1940, he wrote his parents that "our program at present is hitting on all fours and going ahead rather rapidly." The commission had signed a construction contract for a 350-unit addition to Parkside and was letting out $13.5 million bids for additions to complexes at Brewster Place and Charles Street. On May 15, the commission planned to advertise bidding for the $12 million construction of 2,150 units for 9,000 residents at James Herman Gardens.[6]

The first great controversy during Edwards's tenure came in early 1941 when a grand jury investigation revealed that several city council members accepted bribes for their votes on Herman Gardens. Edwards was never linked to the scandal and watched with disgust as the details surfaced. The probe began when an unsuccessful bidder admitted paying a city councilman $25,000 to vote for steel rather than concrete construction. By March, city councilmen John F. Hamilton and Robert G. Wald were indicted for accepting bribes of $15,000 and $5,000, respectively. Later, councilman Harry I. Dingeman confessed to taking $5,000 in cash, which he hid in the rafters of his home. All three councilmen resigned in the spring of 1941 and received prison sentences of three-to-ten years. In the wake of the scandal, Edwards wrote his parents: "I personally feel considerably relieved to know that there will be a definite end to the cloud of suspicion that has hung over this job from the very beginning even though that end results in the convictions of a number of city officials. These indictments are definite enough to establish guilt beyond much need for a trial and I feel that the whole conspiracy, on both sides, will be exposed before the matter is finished." Even though his own reputation was not tarnished, Edwards added that "unfortunately bribery charges are reflections on everyone who is connected with government."[7]

Perhaps because their attention was riveted on the housing scandal, Detroit's leaders were slow to appreciate the impact that the war boom would have on the city's already serious housing crunch. Edwards expressed his frustration in a letter home: "By next fall, we really anticipate a very serious housing shortage due to defense programs. I have tried to get the city officials excited about that shortage before it actually happens—but so far I have got no results." In late April, Edwards wrote his parents that "life in Detroit is busier and more hectic now than ever. The defense work is about to begin in dead earnest and for the next few months this place is due to have some aspects of a boom town or a mining camp. And the director of the Housing Commission is due to have a lot of headaches. However, life is never lacking in interest." Statistics bore out Edwards's impressions; between April 1940 and July 1941 the vacancy rate for city housing decreased from 3.5 to 0.9 percent.[8]

Edwards's greatest problems stemmed from the question of African-American occupancy at the Sojourner Truth project. Although all of Detroit was experiencing a housing shortage, the problem was particularly acute in black neighborhoods. During the 1930s, the city's African-American population rose slightly, and slum clearance exacerbated already crowded conditions. In 1937, the city responded by constructing the Brewster project for blacks, but it proved inadequate to ease the problem. Most of the city's poor African Americans were massed into a ghetto just east of Woodward Avenue that stretched from the Detroit River north to Highland Park and east to Hamtramck. They began moving into other neighborhoods, provoking racial tensions and creating a political and logistical conundrum for Edwards and other city officials.[9]

As one historian notes, "Defense production rather than racial antagonisms . . . goaded official action." The federal government, through the Federal Works Agency (FWA), attempted to coordinate defense production and housing. In May 1941, FWA officials proposed construction of one thousand government-financed housing units, two hundred of which would be set aside for African Americans. Immediately, a conflict arose about where to locate the black housing. As would be true throughout the war years, the conflict was complicated by competing federal and local interests. Federal officials rejected the commission's first choice—an undeveloped site at the northwest corner of Dequindre Road and Modern Avenue—and instead opted for the commission's second choice—a twenty-acre tract bordered by Nevada, Fenelon, Stockton, and Eureka near Conant Gardens, a middle class black neighborhood.[10]

Blacks from Conant Gardens and residents of a nearby Polish neighborhood joined hands to protest the development because they feared the subsidized housing would decrease property values. The Detroit Housing Commission and Edwards soon found themselves caught in the middle, trying to carry out a controversial federal decision that they had not made. In September 1941, the commission signalled that the housing would be set aside for African Americans by naming the projects after Sojourner Truth, an ex-slave, abolitionist, and feminist. Once middle-class blacks realized the racist overtones of the white protest, they switched sides and supported construction. Sojourner Truth became a racial lightning rod. Local and federal politicians vacillated in their support. Edwards worked behind the scenes in Detroit and in Washington to keep Sojourner Truth for blacks.[11]

Edwards's greatest ally during the Sojourner Truth controversy was the only African-American member of the housing commission—Rev. Horace A. White. White, the articulate and charismatic leader of Plymouth Congregational Church, supported a variety of liberal causes, including UAW unionization efforts at Ford and Jeffries's candidacy for mayor. During Jeffries's first term, White became the mayor's highest ranking African-American appointee. Peg Edwards described him as "a very brilliant well-informed man," and said that he helped George because, together, they constituted "a minority of two instead of one." White's first official action had been to support Edwards's appointment, and they continued to work together for fair housing even after Edwards left the commission to join city council.[12]

In the summer of 1941, Edwards took the first step in what

he hoped would become a long political career. That April, Mayor Jeffries and union allies urged him to run for Detroit's Common Council. The resignation of the three incumbents who had pleaded guilty for accepting bribes from Herman Gardens contractors created an unusually open race. Jeffries, who supported Edwards's candidacy, said Edwards could keep the housing job while he ran. Still, Edwards worried. He believed political opponents would criticize him for leaving the housing commission "midstream." In addition, while the CIO offered funding if he could get past the primary into the general election, in the interim he had no money to finance a campaign. Finally, it appeared unlikely that he would receive any newspaper endorsements.[13]

Nevertheless, in many ways, Edwards was an appealing candidate. His efforts for Sojourner Truth cemented his credibility with Detroit's African-American voters. As director of Detroit housing, he demonstrated an impressive ability to manage the authority amid corruption and in the face of shifting federal demands. Less visibly, in January 1941, he eschewed his Socialist party affiliation and became a Democrat. Along with his father, Walter Reuther, and many other prominent Socialists who had thrown their support behind the New Deal, Edwards had come to believe that the Socialists were too marginal, a fact that was "preventing their voices from being heard in a terribly critical period." Democratic party affiliation carried no concrete benefits in Detroit's nonpartisan elections, but Edwards undoubtedly helped his own political aspirations by dropping the socialist label which many voters rejected as too radical.[14]

Even with his proven track record, Edwards was a long shot. Apart from his association with radical politics, there was his age; at twenty-seven he would be the youngest councilman since Detroit's nonpartisan charter became effective in 1918. In addition, he was not the only aspiring politician who hoped to take advantage of the open race. A record 122 candidates ran in the October 7 primary; of those, the eighteen highest vote getters could run in the general election for the nine council seats. Perhaps his most formidable challenge was gaining name recognition in a large field with meager funding. One way of accomplishing that was by naming his wife as campaign manager. The novelty of the young, idealistic couple taking on entrenched politics charmed reporters. The *Detroit News* noted that Edwards's "attractive wife, Margaret McConnell Edwards, 26, . . . could pass any day as a college girl." Peg did all of the office work, filled orders for leaflets, planned his schedule, wrote his thank-you letters, and critiqued his speeches. She told skeptics who wondered why Edwards would give up his $7,000-a-year housing post for a $5,000-a-year council seat, "It's because we believe in certain governmental ideals, but if you say that people think you are crazy."[15]

Edwards's campaign became entwined with the effort of state Senator Charles C. Diggs, Sr., to become Detroit's first African-American city councilman. The Ku Klux Klan actively campaigned against Diggs while Edwards rallied to his aid. Diggs's candidacy drew national attention, according to the *Michigan Chronicle,* which encouraged its readers to vote. "We must show Detroit and the world that we are worthy of our franchise and that we are capable of fighting for ourselves within the framework of our democracy. The social forces that are opposed to our group progress have already shown their cloven hoof in attacking our Negro candidate and the slate which we must carry to victory." That slate included Edwards, whom the article described as a "champion of our cause."[16] Although Diggs lost the election, his candidacy prompted a heavy African-American turnout that helped Edwards.

Edwards also ran sixteenth in the primary because of Peg's management skills, an exhausting speaking schedule, and the work of committed supporters. UAW heavyweights lent their endorsements and help. Richard T. Leonard chaired Edwards's campaign committee, and President R. J. Thomas was honorary chair. West Side Local 174 President Michael J. Manning served as treasurer. Other UAW noteworthies who endorsed Edwards included George F. Addes, Melvin Bishop, Jack Ellstein, Clifford Fay, Richard Frankensteen, Harry McMillan, William Marshall, Stanley Nowak, Pat Quinn, and Walter Reuther. CIO officials August Scholle and Roy Scoggins weighed in with their public approval. In mid-October, Edwards wrote to his parents, apologizing for the fact that he had been too busy working all day and campaigning all night to write during the previous month. "Thus far the campaign has been fun and I feel that I have gained a great deal from it in knowledge and friends and experience that will be permanently useful. I believe in addition that I will definitely climb a few places in the vote standing—and that I may be elected." He garnered endorsements from the *Detroit News,* Labor's Nonpartisan League, the Detroit Citizens League, and Town Talk, but did not have enough money to buy space on billboards to list his supporters.[17]

The weather was so beautiful on November 4 that Peg said there was no reason for anyone not to vote. She remained skeptical that her husband would crack into the top nine and take a city council seat and said she would be "satisfied with tenth or eleventh." To her pleasant surprise, Edwards placed seventh. He assured his parents that he had incurred no financial or political debts that would compromise his ability to serve honestly. A month later he still was surprised at the speed with which his political career had been launched. "The win has been quite a shock to me in spite of all forewarning. The only thing to do now is apparently to see it thru."[18]

During the rest of November and December, Edwards worked overtime trying to ensure a smooth transition for his replacement at the housing commission. In a December 19 letter to his parents, he complained that his days were so hectic that he had no time for Christmas spirit. Still, he took pride in having accomplished most of his goals. Defense housing was under construction. Most of the projects that began under his tenure were built and their management was in place. The commission had gained land title and solicited architectural plans for other new projects, including Brightmore, Jeffries, and Douglass. The only source of worry was Edwards's successor, Charles F. Edgecomb. Although Edgecomb also came out of the UAW, he did not share Edwards's commitment to civil rights. Instead, he "held white 'do-gooders' in contempt and distrusted assertive black leaders." As Dominic Capeci writes, "Edgecomb lacked Edwards's self-confidence, avoided major issues and manipulated behind the scenes. He was capable of understanding other 'wheeler-dealers' like Rev. White and of personal relations with deferential black housing managers. Nevertheless, 'Choo Choo Charlie'—so called because of his desire to place the black homes at the alternative site, near a railroad track—dismissed all claims by black spokesmen and their liberal supporters."[19]

Edgecomb's failings became quickly apparent in the continuing controversy about the Sojourner Truth homes. The protests, vitriol, and violence that plagued the housing project laid bare the ugly truth about simmering racial problems in Detroit. On January 6, the day that Edwards left the housing commission to take his seat on the city council, federal officials reversed their decision to allow black tenants at Sojourner Truth. The timing, according to some observers, was no accident. Federal officials miscalculated, however, if they believed Edwards would forget his obligations to African Americans once he left the housing commission. As a politician, he became an even more vocal advocate for their rights. Although bungling federal bureaucrats had aggravated the Sojourner Truth situation with their indecision, inflamed passions came to rest on local officials—especially Edwards, who continued to support black occupancy, and Jeffries, who publicly concurred in late January.

Sojourner Truth became a rallying point for African Americans in Detroit and across the nation. Rev. White, Senator Diggs, and other prominent Detroiters organized the Sojourner Truth Citizens committee to protest racism in federal housing policy. In response, white neighborhood groups became even more combative. Edwards continued to support the African-American position unequivocally. Showing characteristic idealism, he wrote his father:

> This Sojourner Truth Houses matter has been as difficult a problem as I have ever known anything about, and it isn't over yet. As I am writing this the council chamber is crowded with protestants and protestees—white and black—each waiting to threaten the dire consequences of failing to act as it wishes.
>
> There is no answer to the problem. The Negroes have all logic, decency, civilization and ethics on their side. The whites have a simple argument "We don't want Niggers living near us" and probably a majority of Detroit citizens on theirs.
>
> Although the Mayor and 4 members of the council are on my side of this battle—the Mayor and I are catching most of the heat. And I greatly fear ending up in another minority of one.
>
> I have never had any difficulty in finding compromises on issues that I have faced—provided that such compromises offered us some possibility of gain. But where the issues were drawn so vividly—as they are

here—I have always had trouble keeping quiet—and it isn't in my nature to give up. Something tells me that my head will show a few more years when this is over. . . . The Negroes haven't lost yet, but I think they will.

I don't know how the Sojourner Truth issue will turn out but I intend to stand my ground. And I will try to keep my temper—that's the toughest part.[20]

In retrospect, it is not hard to see why Edwards had trouble keeping his composure. During one council meeting, when he charged white neighborhood leaders "with inflaming racial hatred for selfish real estate interests, he was jeered by members of the audience who loudly asked: 'What color are you?' " Civil rights activist Geraldine Bledsoe, who attended the meeting, compared Edwards's courage to the other council members' cowardice. She recalled how police had to escort Edwards, who "looked so young" that he could have passed for a "college sophomore," from the council chambers "to keep him from being really attacked by the mob."[21]

In the face of well-organized African-American protests and Jeffries's support for their cause, federal bureaucrats reversed their position. When blacks tried to move into the project on February 28, however, KKK members provoked a violent confrontation. Finally, the protests were quelled, and in April occupancy resumed. Bolstered by its success, the NAACP demanded that more public housing be set aside for African-American defense workers. On April 29, 1943, Jeffries tried to avert another divisive debate by persuading the Common Council to adopt a policy against using public housing to upset the racial balance of existing neighborhoods. Edwards cast a lone, dissenting vote.[22]

The public housing controversy was just the most visible aspect of the city's worsening race relations. Concerned observers, both black and white, predicted a major riot, and few were surprised when trouble broke out on June 20, 1943, an especially hot, humid Sunday afternoon. An estimated 100,000 people had jammed on to Belle Isle seeking relief from the heat when rumors about a racial attack spread through the crowd. African Americans later recalled hearing rumors that a white mob tossed a black mother and her baby from the bridge connecting the island to the city. Whites recalled hearing that a crowd of blacks had either raped, murdered, or thrown a white woman off of the

73

bridge. Whites and blacks began fighting. The violence escalated and spread; black mobs looted and burned stores in the Paradise Valley ghetto while white mobs massed on Woodward Avenue to begin an attack. After two days in which thirty-four people died and hundreds more were injured, federal troops brought peace to the city. Decades later, Edwards remembered the riots as "the worst 48 hours I have ever spent as a human being, and I made a deep resolve that if ever I had an opportunity to do what I could to avoid a similar situation recurring in the city which I loved, I would do it." Edwards's vow became the major reason he accepted the police commissioner's job. He believed that police malfeasance had fueled the 1943 riots, and twenty years later he hoped to stop a similar conflagration by providing calm, unbiased leadership to the department.[23]

In 1943, African-American leaders and white liberals like Edwards, who believed the violence stemmed from deep-seated injustices aggravated by police wrongdoing, were in the minority. In the aftermath of the riots, Edwards asked city council to demand a grand jury investigation, to request an FBI study and report, to seek future military support in case of further trouble, and to appoint two hundred more African-American police officers. He also urged Common Council to create a committee that could analyze the need for additional housing, recreation, and other public facilities in the city's minority neighborhoods. Edwards cast the lone vote in support of his measures, and his stand for racial justice drew national attention. James A. Wechsler, the editor of New York's *PM* newspaper, said: "Risking his political future in this explosive, race-conscious city, a youthful member of Detroit's City Council today challenged county and local officials who have resisted a grand jury probe of Detroit's race riot." Edwards also won plaudits from the NAACP which reported: "There is overwhelming evidence that the riot could have been stopped at its inception Sunday night had police wanted to stop it. So inefficient is the police force, so many of its members are from the deep south, with all their anti-Negro prejudices and Klan sympathies, that trouble may break out again as soon as the troops leave."[24]

Most white leaders sought explanations that cleared the city and its police of wrongdoing while shifting the blame to black "troublemakers." Mayor Jeffries traced the violence back to the Sojourner Truth riots. In reality, there was little connection between the two episodes except for the racial disharmony they revealed; Sojourner Truth remained relatively peaceful during the 1943 riot. Police Commissioner John H. Witherspoon appeared before the Common Council a week after the violence to lambast African Americans and to defend his men for showing "rare courage and efficiency." He admitted the existence of white mobs but dismissed their role as "retaliatory action." Jeffries and Governor Harry F. Kelly appointed committees to investigate the riots, and both issued reports that minimized white violence and police malfeasance.[25]

The riot became a national disgrace, a subject of Congressional investigation, and fodder for the 1943 mayoral campaign. The CIO, civil liberties groups, and African-American voters, angered by Jeffries's pro-segregation housing stance and his handling of the riots, switched their support to his opponent, liberal court commissioner Frank Fitzgerald. The two-man race put Edwards in an ideological and a pragmatic quandary. As he wrote to his father before the primary, "Jeff in my eyes, has made a good many mistakes—but he has also done a great deal for good. I think the race riots were far from being his creation although in my eyes he could have done something toward preventing them and should have commanded the police more effectively during them." Edwards was fond of Jeffries and privately believed him to be a more appealing candidate than Fitzgerald, whom he described as "a nice, weak liberal whose fundamental leanings are Democratic tempered by Catholicism, or vice versa." Publicly, however, Edwards did not want to alienate his CIO backers, so he remained neutral in the race.[26]

The idea of a labor-loving mayor and a former socialist turned council member pushing for African-American rights proved too much for white extremists. Publisher Floyd McGriff led the charge. McGriff attacked Edwards with the same passion he had mustered as a foreign correspondent in London covering World War I. He arrived in Detroit during 1926, ostensibly to retire. But he missed the fray and eventually bought the eight small papers that made his Detroit Suburban Newspapers the largest chain of weeklies in Michigan. In the *Home Gazette* of Strathmore, McGriff wrote:

> The future of Detroit, of this neighborhood, of property values in this immediate area, hinge upon the outcome of the election Nov. 2. Whether this community will remain a white neighborhood, or whether it will be infiltrated with NEGROES. Whether the city hall is turned over to become a General Headquarters for the CIO, now dominated . . . by Communists, and all city workers made slaves of a Communist-directed, city political machine. . . . Whether a great and powerful sized Negro police contingent is to be inaugurated immediately upon Fitzgerald taking office.

In another article, he singled out Edwards. "Observance of the customary rules of decency will not permit publication in this newspaper of the complete story of the organizational propaganda of the American Student Union of which George C. Edwards was the first national chairman. Mothers and Fathers would object." McGriff claimed Edwards had "cut his eye-teeth on Karl Marx" and advocated overthrowing the nation's social order, sabotaging munitions factories, creating bi-racial housing, and disseminating graphic sexual information.[27]

Edwards wisely ignored the *Home Gazette*'s hysterical attacks and ran a positive, issue-oriented campaign, stressing the accomplishments of his first term. In a radio talk the day before the October 5 primary, he described how he had supported anti-inflation measures, helped pass a forty-eight-hour work week for city employees (to meet President Roosevelt's call for more work from public servants), and fought for improved municipal services. Edwards's progressive agenda drew favorable reviews; New York's *PM* newspaper called him one of the most "fearless" liberals in the nation. The *Michigan Chronicle* called him "the lone incumbent who has won the respect and admiration of the Negro people." Edwards was confident. On the eve of the election, he wrote his parents: "I think I am doing all right in spite of the mayor's race. I have been viciously attacked by small groups and several neighborhood newspapers, but I do not think they can profoundly influence a city-wide vote."[28]

Edwards placed fourth out of the forty-six candidates in the primary and fifth in the general election. But it was the mayor's race that attracted most political observers' attention. Fitzgerald ran ahead in the primary, netting 97,548 votes to Jeffries's

59,545. Jeffries pulled out all stops to win the general election by running a racist, antiunion campaign. The mayor won reelection by a close margin, but his tactics disgusted Edwards who decried them as "reactionary."[29]

Edwards had only three weeks to rest on his political laurels. On November 24, he received his reclassification card for the draft and decided not to appeal even though Peg was expecting their second son in April.[30] Along with many Americans, Edwards had spent the 1930s focussing on problems closer to home and came late to appreciate the crises unfolding in Europe and Asia. The harsh realities of World War II prompted him to renounce the pacifism of his student activist days. He first took note of events in Europe on May 13, 1940, while still with the housing commission. He chronicled his horror in a letter to his parents: "This is the first day for some reason, that the full impact of the recent developments has reached me emotionally. . . . Hitler has trampled too many of my dreams under foot for me to see the issues coldly." He wondered what personal impact the war would have:

> My wife is a constant and never ending joy. My work is a source of satisfaction and contentment. My family has always been my reliance and inspiration . . . and yet those beliefs for which I work and the dreams for which we live have been torn and bloodied and trampled in a thousand ways.
>
> You know and probably feel the story more sharply than I— Germany, Austria, Spain, Denmark and Norway etc. And to top the incongruity of it all while the world is going to hell in a handcart I am at a Housing Conference. While thousands of men are dying, Peg and I are producing another human being. While dozens of cities are being actually blown to bits I am trying to get a few thousand houses built.
>
> Perhaps that's the way the world goes, anyhow—from life to death, from peace to war, from construction to destruction with always a few hopeful souls that shelter and guard the light that they hope will sometime shine even more brightly than ever in the peace that must always come again.

He concluded by thanking his parents, again, "for extending in my soul a faith . . . that makes me perfectly content to continue to try to build White Cities from a Bellamy Utopia when only too many of the actual cities of the world are being leveled to the ground."[31]

With his impending draft, Edwards's days became even

more hectic. He arose early to take classes at the Detroit College of Law, where he had been a part-time student since 1938. In an effort to earn money for Peg while he would be away, the previous April he began working forty hours each week at Timken-Detroit Axle Co., which supplied parts for Jeeps and truck axles for Chrysler, Ford, and General Motors. He worked the afternoon shift from 2:30 to 10:30 and took off Tuesdays so that he could attend morning and Tuesday night council meetings. His only day of relative freedom came on Sunday. Finally, Edwards received his military summons and was inducted into the U.S. Army as a private on January 10, 1944, at Fort Sheridan, Illinois.[32]

Edwards's departure for military duty prompted even his critics to set aside partisan politics. He received a send-off worthy of a war hero. On January 9, the *Detroit News* said that as soon as Edwards entered public service as director of the Detroit Housing Commission, he "removed all doubt that he intended to hew to the principles of liberalism and individual human rights which had made him a union power. Two years later, upon his promotion to the Council, it was made equally clear that direct participation in politics had cost him none of his militant personal integrity. Union leaders who assumed they would receive special favors because of Edwards's labor affiliations were doomed to disappointment." In an editorial four days later, the newspaper opined: "It is a loss to the council, and a loss to Detroit that George Edwards should have to go into the army. But he has been fighting in this war ever since it started, whether in the City Hall or on his factory job. He has merely moved as a soldier from one activity to another, as his orders demanded. He is the sort of citizen and patriot of whom this community can be proud; the unselfish man, who does his duty as he sees it, and does it to the full."[33]

Edwards kept up with events in Detroit. He wrote occasional letters to the newspapers commenting on unfolding events, especially the city's omnipresent racial problems. In March 1944, for example, he praised Mayor Jeffries's appointment of a permanent race relations commission in a letter to the *Detroit News*. For the next two years, however, most of his attention would be focused on the military. After his processing at Fort Sheridan, the army sent Edwards to Camp Wheeler, Georgia, an infantry training replacement center. If Edwards had graduated with his class, he would have been shipped off to Europe. Instead, in his seventh week at Camp Wheeler, he broke his wrist playing touch football. While his injury healed, the army assigned Edwards to "gofer" duty as a file clerk and instructor. Edwards spent nearly eleven months at Camp Wheeler, gaining a promotion to corporal in October and drawing the attention of superiors who recommended him for officer candidate school.[34]

He attended officer's school at Fort Benning, Georgia, from November 1944 to March 1945, and graduated as a second lieutenant on March 19, 1945. From there, Edwards went to Camp Maxey, Texas, to receive advanced infantry training for the invasion of Japan scheduled for that November. Edwards was at Fort Maxey from April to August 1945. During part of his time there, Peg and their two sons moved in with his parents in Dallas, so they could be close. In early August, when the war was cut short by the U.S. dropping of atomic bombs on Hiroshima and Nagasaki, Edwards's mission changed. The army sent him to the Philippines to investigate Japanese war crimes. His brief stint with the War Crimes Division provided Edwards's only experience as a prosecutor. Judging by what little information he left behind, he felt little affinity for what must have been a relatively minor role in the proceedings.[35]

With the war won, Detroit officials pressured the War Department to release Edwards. In October, the *Free Press* noted that since Edwards's departure, council had been conducting business with only eight members instead of the nine required by the city charter. The newspaper editorialized: "Detroit is in a period of turbulence. . . . Clear-headed and courageous, he would, if back in the City Hall now, be a powerful influence for bringing sanity back into the labor situation with which no one at the moment appears able to cope. As a balance wheel, George Edwards is needed in Detroit." In December, the city council agreed and passed a resolution asking the War Department to send Edwards home early.[36]

Edwards did not object; he was eager to return to Peg and his more active life in Detroit. He left the military in December 1945 and arrived home in January 1946. Edwards's council career added political weight to the adage that distance makes the heart grow fonder. He had taken a leave of absence from the city council to join the army. In 1945, while he was still away, Peg ran his absentee campaign, and he won by a huge margin. As the top vote getter, he became president of the city council. Once Edwards returned, however, he again became a thorn to the city's more conservative elements.

Especially noteworthy was his ongoing battle with his familiar nemesis Floyd McGriff, who geared up to defeat him in the 1947 election. This time the reactionary publisher joined forces with Councilman Charles G. Oakman, a Detroit native who worked in the insurance and real-estate businesses before entering city government as Jeffries's secretary in 1940. In 1941, Jeffries appointed him to become the city's comptroller. In the 1945 council race, the forty-one-year-old candidate surprised political observers by placing sixth in the general election after coming in only thirteenth in the primary, a parallel to Edwards's startling council victory four years earlier. Aside from their upset election bids and youth, the two councilmen had little in common. During the 1947 campaign, the UAW charged that Oakman, "with the support of the most hysterically reactionary, antilabor forces in the community has launched a smear campaign . . . in an effort to defeat Edwards as Council President." Meanwhile, McGriff created and published a composite picture of a youthful Edwards as a "Communist-sympathizer" peering through jail bars after his arrest in the Yale and Towne strike. McGriff also complained that Edwards "is spearheading a movement to require bowling alleys to open up their alleys to Negro athletes. He wants mixed bowling, just as he wants mixed housing in northwest Detroit and other areas."[37]

McGriff's dirty tricks alienated many liberals and good government advocates, such as James Hare, head of the Detroit chapter of the Americans for Democratic Action; Edward Swan, secretary of the NAACP; Adelia Starrett, president of the Detroit Welfare Commission; Joseph McCusker, director of the UAW-CIO, and Rev. William B. Sperry, pastor of Christ Episcopal Church in Grosse Pointe. They pressured Wayne County District Attorney James N. McNally to launch an investigation. McNally charged McGriff with illegally taking $3,750 from Oakman to editorially oppose a political candidate and not identify a special edition of his *Home Gazette* as a paid political advertisement. The district attorney charged Oakman with failing to file an adequate account of expenses in his campaign. The councilman denied knowing that the money went to McGriff and tried to draw attention from his own troubles by falsely accusing Edwards of failing to report $34,500 spent on his election campaign.[38]

Edwards watched the unfolding mess with bemusement. After winning the election with the largest plurality, he wrote his parents: "The echoes of the last campaign are still rumbling. Oakman at this stage is a bit unhappy that he ever got into this business and I hope to keep him unhappy. There will, of course, be repercussions coming my way but maybe it will teach a long range lesson to the next guy that tries a smear campaign." The following month, Edwards characterized Oakman's charges against him as "fantastic" and opined that the councilman and McGriff "represent a group of political racketeers; their enmity is an honor."[39]

Unlike his most strident opponents, Edwards took the political high road—informing voters about his own accomplishments and criticizing the opposition in relatively generic terms. He turned his youthfulness into an asset by arguing that he was on the cutting edge of progressive change, fighting against entrenched, old-fashioned politics. In a pamphlet he issued for the 1947 election titled "A Councilman Reports to the People," he warned voters that "topsy-turvy, fast growing Detroit has been mired for years for lack of planning, lack of money and lack of civic enthusiasm. . . . Many of the problems of Detroit remain unsolved, many half-answered and for some the solution seems unattainable." In contrast, Edwards said, he supported revamping the city's rundown waterfront, building twenty new schools to ease overcrowding, creating one hundred new parks and play fields, constructing the Lodge and Edsel Ford expressways, improving public transportation, and trying to find ways of solving the city's perpetual housing shortage.[40]

He also addressed some controversial questions always lurking behind the city's more concrete problems: "If we are not to have our town a constant battleground for labor-management or racial conflicts, then, there must be a public opinion powerful enough to say to both sides that the public interest is paramount to any group greed or prejudice." He advocated creation of a Labor-Management-Citizens Committee that would finance and work on steps to reach industrial peace in Detroit. Edwards praised efforts by Detroit's Interracial Committee and the police department to improve treatment of minorities. He urged revamping city government, which he claimed was too remote from voters. Edwards blamed that distance on the city's nonpartisan politics but said, "I am not yet willing to call it quits on our nonpartisan Charter, but I do think we must start in on a deliberate effort to bring the City Hall closer to the people and the people closer to the City Hall."[41]

Edwards did not limit his political horizons to Detroit. He nursed ambitions to one day join the U.S. Senate—a goal that would entail gaining statewide support and national recognition. During his last term on city council, Edwards began laying the groundwork for his wider aims by working to liberalize the Democratic party. In January 1947, he joined Eleanor Roosevelt and Walter Reuther to found the Americans for Democratic Action (ADA), an anticommunist organization that promoted government action to address social problems. It evolved into the major progressive force within the Democratic party during the late 1940s and 1950s. He and Peg also played a significant role in the effort to revamp the flagging fortunes of Michigan's Democratic party. In 1948, they worked to elect G. Mennen Williams as governor. The progressive, charismatic World War II veteran signalled his activist agenda in a letter to fellow Democrats in August. Williams exhorted: "Let us take to the people of Michigan our answers to the problems of the high cost of living, housing, social security and all those 'hot potatoes' untouched by Republican hands." His program included, among other things, subsidies for housing, increased unemployment compensation, higher teachers' salaries, larger welfare payments to the poor and elderly, creation of a state Civil Rights agency, and an end to overcrowding in state prisons and mental hospitals. He also promised to end the corruption and cronyism that marked state politics. Williams handily defeated the Republican incumbent Kim Sigler, and his election set the stage for changes unrivalled since Frank Murphy had been governor a decade earlier. His many accomplishments would include promoting Edwards's career.[42]

That wunderkind political career, which seemed so promising, crashed into the brick wall of Detroit racism in 1949. As long as Edwards was merely one of nine council members, many mainstream voters were willing to overlook his "radical" racial views so they could reap the benefits of his energy on other issues. They were less willing to elect him mayor. Still, his campaign began with all of the optimism, promise, and excitement that had marked his city council races. He enjoyed his usual support from the African-American community, liberals, and labor leaders. He faced his usual opposition from conservative groups, but he had triumphed over their smear tactics in the past, which made it easier to dismiss their vow that he would "never grace the mayor's chair."[43]

Edwards declared his intention to run for mayor on April 5, 1949, at an informal gathering in the City Hall press room. His announcement came as no surprise; Detroit's newspapers had been speculating about it for more than a year. He had served four terms on Common Council and was ready for new challenges. In the last two council races, he racked up huge margins as the front runner. Political pundits had little doubt he could ride that same wave of support into City Hall. Incumbent Mayor Eugene I. Van Antwerp seemed a desultory opponent. Many believed he had won the previous election only because voters had tired of Jeffries, who had sought a fifth term. Van Antwerp, an engineer, World War I veteran, and sixteen-year member of Common Council, capitalized on Cold War hysteria to criticize Jeffries for his alleged "lamentable disregard for the seriousness of the Communist in-road into the social, civic, and economic life of Detroit." During his two years as mayor, Van Antwerp's obsession with radicalism did little to endear him to voters concerned with more concrete issues. By contrast, Edwards offered an activist alternative. He promised to sponsor a host of improvements, including construction of freeways, development of the waterfront, construction of a municipal auditorium, extended recreational facilities, improved garbage collection, and better management of public transportation. By the time Edwards formally filed on June 22, many believed he had a clear path to the mayor's chair. Few could have predicted the strange and ugly turns the campaign would take.[44]

Detroit's 1949 mayoral's race provided an uncanny preview of the 1961 election that would sweep Jerry Cavanagh into office. Both elections became pivotal in deciding the course of the city's future, especially its racial future. Many political watersheds are recognized only with historic hindsight, but the 1949 and 1961 elections were unique because contemporary voters and candidates recognized the high stakes. As a result, the two elections were hard fought and vitriolic. The candidates shared many similarities. Edwards, like Cavanagh, was in his mid-thirties, and his youth, idealism, and activism appealed to many voters who believed the city needed new direction. Like Cavanagh, he recognized the danger to the city represented by suburbanization and shifting tax revenues. Edwards, like Cavanagh, realized that racial disharmony, especially the racially biased actions of the Detroit Police Department, threatened to undermine all other civic improvements. By contrast, their opponents enjoyed establishment support, stood proudly on platforms of maintaining the status quo, and opposed extending power to the city's African Americans. Perhaps the only major difference between the elections was that Edwards, unlike Cavanagh, started out as the clear favorite.[45]

Perhaps no other issue came to symbolize the difference between Edwards and Van Antwerp more deeply than the latter's management of the Detroit Police Department. Van Antwerp had appointed a suburban lawyer and criminal justice hardliner, Harry S. Toy, as his police commissioner. Toy's harsh leadership and his pride in running the department on a "semi-military" basis undid his predecessors' efforts to improve relations between police and African Americans. The police problem burst back into public debate with the shooting death of a black teenager, Leon Mosely, in June 1948. Some facts of the case were undisputed. Mosely stole a car and was joy riding when Patrolman Louis Melasi spotted his haphazard driving and gave chase. Mosely sped to get away, then crashed into a light pole. Versions of what happened next differed. Melasi said Mosely got out of the car in a menacing fashion, then tried to flee. African-American witnesses said Mosely stepped out of the car too dazed to walk; Melasi beat him, and then shot him when he tried to defend himself. A coroner's jury, sifting through the evidence a month after the incident, concluded that the killing was "unnecessary, unwise, and unjustifiable."[46]

Although he followed the routine practice of suspending Melasi until the matter could be resolved, Toy refused to condemn the patrolman's actions. Melasi fought to keep his job, and in December Wayne County Circuit Judge Arthur E. Gordon ruled in his favor. Gordon ignored the autopsy report of wounds and bruises on Mosely's head and attributed the boy's fractured skull to his fall on the pavement after being shot. He commended Melasi as "an alert police officer," awarded him $2,021 in back pay, and added, "it is worthy of notice that those witnesses who made the wildest accusations. . . . were of the group produced by the National Association for the Advancement of Colored People and set to . . . be interviewed by the pink devotees of agitation. . . . If the handful of Communist agitators who are trying to ruin the creditable work of the NAACP cared to do a good deed for once in their pink lives, they would raise money to replace the automobile stolen by Mosely." The *Detroit News* reported that after Gordon's ruling, Melasi said he "never had any doubt" about the outcome, and "high police officials" escorted him from the courtroom to Toy, who "immediately restored him to duty." Four days later, the Young Progressives of Michigan asked Toy to answer troubling questions about the Mosely shooting. The police commissioner responded in predictable fashion: "The rate of crime committed by members of the colored race is extremely high; and you and your young progressives could help clear it up, rather than coming to the aid of those who violated our laws." He then attacked the progressives saying they were "just another one of the many front outfits inspired by Communists in the United States."[47]

Debate about the incident continued into January. Early in the month, Rev. Robert L. Bradby, Jr., newly elected president of Detroit's NAACP chapter, called Toy "the worst police commissioner in many years." Citing the growing distrust between African Americans and the police, Bradby asked Van Antwerp to fire Toy: "Resentment against police brutality is greater now than at any time since 1943. Brutality is on the increase throughout the city and particularly in the Woodward precinct." The mayor rushed to defend Toy, telling reporters: "The commissioner has been running the department in the best interests of the city and is very capable."[48]

With Van Antwerp's continued approval, Toy launched ever more bizarre law enforcement campaigns. In late January, he infuriated Detroit's three newspapers by requiring that all reporters covering the police department sign non-Communist affidavits before they could receive their 1949 press cards. Amid outcries about freedom of the press, Toy rescinded his decision the following month. During the summer, Toy cut back the department's nationally recognized women's bureau and reorganized the Detective Bureau. His efforts demoralized members of the department and drew negative reviews from outsiders. In July, the *Free Press* ran a scathing editorial about Toy's mistreatment of Jack Harville, the twenty-nine-year police veteran who ran the detective bureau: "Most of what Harry Toy does in his role of police commissioner can be laughed off as municipal comedy relief. But that is not true of his latest grab for headlines." The newspaper predicted that Van Antwerp would get more votes if he could "jettison" Toy before the election. The commissioner launched his weirdest crusade in August, when he declared that campaign stickers in car windows posed traffic hazards. The target of his antisticker program was Edwards, who was among Toy's harshest critics and whose campaign committee had printed window decals. Theodore Bohn, Edwards's campaign manager, decided to test Toy's pronouncement. He placed stickers in the front and back of his car, then drove to Detroit's Public Safety Building where he promptly received a ticket. A month later, Traffic Judge John D. Watts sat in Bohn's car, decided the stickers did not block the driver's vision, and dismissed the case.[49]

Although the sticker incident provoked journalistic guffaws, the larger questions associated with Toy's ham-handed leadership did not. In late August, the Michigan Bar Association criticized Detroit's police for making 20,169 arrests without warrants during 1948. Toy shrugged off the report, saying: "Ninety percent of criminals guilty of serious crimes would go free if we weren't permitted to arrest these men without warrantless searches." He added: "If the Constitution were construed as attorneys would like it, crime would run rampant in the city."[50]

Edwards found Toy's racial views and his disregard for constitutional principles repugnant. On August 25, he delivered a fifteen-minute speech in which he lambasted "Headline Harry" Toy and gave a preview of the philosophy that would guide his own tenure as commissioner twelve years later. "I do not believe in selective law enforcement. I believe that all citizens of Detroit deserve impartial protection all of the time, not only in their person and in their property but in their civil rights as well." Edwards accused Toy of alienating many law-abiding citizens of both races by acting "as though he is the commanding general of an army of occupation who views the citizens of Detroit as subjects of the police department."[51]

Toy defended his record in a letter to the editor on September 9: "We have had no race riots in Detroit in this administration like former administrations and like many other cities today. . . . Every policy of this department is calculated to provide friendly and courteous relations between the police and our law abiding citizens regardless of creed, position, or race. We recognize only two minority groups in our law enforcement: Criminals and Communists. We admit we are prejudiced against these." Toy concluded by impugning the city council president: "Mr. Edwards is going to fire me, he says. This is an old dodge borrowed from Communists in Detroit who produced a booklet which they circulated among the Negro residents, entitled 'Toy Must Go,' and which contained practically every charge now made by Mr. Edwards against me in my operation of this department."[52]

Unfortunately, Toy was closer to the mood of Detroit's voters than Edwards. He recognized that many whites feared African Americans, saw their aspirations as radical, and had a vested interest in maintaining the city's status quo of racial injustice. When it became apparent that Edwards could defeat Van Antwerp, Detroit's leaders began looking for another candidate. They tapped city Treasurer Albert E. Cobo, who entered the race in July. Cobo was not the only splinter candidate. Richard Frankensteen, a former UAW member and long-time foe of Walter Reuther, and Luke Tiller, a forty-eight-year-old African-American real estate agent, also entered the primary. But it was Cobo who posed the real threat. He had been mentioned as a possible mayoral candidate in every election since the mid-1930s. A former salesman for Burroughs Adding Machine Company, Cobo first entered government as an assistant city treasurer in 1933. He was elected treasurer in 1935 and had been reelected ever since.[53]

Cobo ran on a platform of fiscal conservatism, criticizing Edwards as an advocate of big government spending. Their differing philosophies became apparent in their views of public housing. Both candidates supported slum clearance projects. Edwards advocated clearing slums and replacing them with public housing projects. Cobo argued for limited public housing; he maintained that the city should sell most of the cleared land to private developers and use the profits to increase middle-class services and cut taxes. As he explained, "there is no reason why some Detroiters have to 'carry' others who are well able to pay their own way. The helter-skelter construction of public housing units could result in one home owner, getting an identical salary, subsidizing another Detroiter who lived in a housing project." Cobo draped his opinions with a racially neutral patina, which did little to obscure the underlying racist message. His opposition to public housing was directed mostly at the city's African-American residents, and he was vocally against integrated housing.[54]

As the campaign evolved, various factions came to recognize that the election marked a crucial point in the city's history. Edwards termed his campaign a "civic crusade" to modernize city government, extend services to the poor, and offer racial justice. Cobo offered a different vision of Detroit as a place where private enterprise was paramount, taxes would remain low, the poor would fend for themselves, and African Americans would accept their second-class status. White neighborhood groups were especially fearful of Edwards's candidacy. For example, John Laub, head of the Northwest Civic Federation, endorsed Cobo, saying: "This election is one of the most important, if not the most important, in our municipal history." Perhaps because the candidates and the voters perceived that so much was at stake, the campaign took on an increasingly bitter tone. Political observer Helen Berthelot recalled how "from the start there were no holds barred. Mock-up pictures of George Edwards behind bars were

tacked up on street corners. Vicious cartoons were everywhere
. . . cartoons distributed in black neighborhoods showed him in
cowboy hat and boots, swinging a lariat that took the form of a
noose. In the heavily white . . . neighborhoods of Detroit, pictures
were distributed showing George meeting with black ministers—a blatant attempt to stir up racial hatred and make enemies
for him among white voters as well." Edwards had always attracted vitriolic criticism from the margins, but Cobo moved negative, personal campaigning to the mainstream. In a typical
speech, he declared that the only reason he had entered the race
was "because that man George Edwards must never be mayor of
Detroit."[55]

Edwards's campaign was further complicated in August
when he contracted a mild case of polio. Peg, who, as usual, was
working yeoman hours for her husband's election, said the illness
added more stress to an already tense situation. Edwards recov-
ered quickly, but Peg still worried. As she wrote to Eleanor Roosevelt: "I am sure you can appreciate the combination of polio,
campaign, and all the newspapers against us, as few others
can."[56]

The former first lady was one of the many outside political
observers following Detroit's municipal election. Roosevelt and
Edwards knew each other through their work in the ADA, which
had recently formed a political action committee with the CIO.
The *New York Times* called Edwards's candidacy a referendum
on the power of the ADA–CIO alliance. Meanwhile, the *Pittsburgh Courier,* the nation's most prestigious African-American
newspaper, viewed Edwards's candidacy as a ray of hope in the
nation's otherwise bleak political landscape. "We support Edwards for Mayor on the basis of his platform for a clean and
efficient government, and particularly on the basis of his promise
to get rid, not only of Police Commissioner Toy, but also the Toy
psychology of fear and oppression in the Police Department."
Not all of the outside attention was positive. Columnist Drew
Pearson, who hosted a fifteen-minute Sunday radio program, predicted that Detroiters would never elect a former jailbird as
mayor. Edwards's friends protested Pearson's attack as unfair.
During his broadcast the following week, the columnist conceded
that Edwards's jail sentence in the Yale and Towne strike had

been for a youthful offense, but he still predicted a Cobo victory.[57]

Time drew national attention to Detroit when Edwards lost the September 13 primary. The magazine reported that his loss came as a surprise because "almost every preelection poll had shown the thirty-five-year-old George Edwards, a Harvard-educated member of the United Auto Workers out in front in Detroit's mayoral race." Cobo won a "landslide of unprecedented proportions," netting 169,566 votes to Edwards's 114,173. Van Antwerp came in a distant third with 52,690, and Frankensteen logged only 16,659. Returns showed that Cobo had swept every part of the city except African-American neighborhoods, where Edwards won overwhelmingly. The record turnout of 373,143 topped the previous record of 335,000 set in 1937. Journalists in Detroit and elsewhere scrambled to explain the heavy turnout and unexpected result. The *Free Press* attributed Edwards's loss partly to a split in the union vote. The UAW and CIO backed Edwards, while the AFL endorsed Cobo. August Scholle, president of the Michigan CIO, was quoted as saying "too many members thought the election was in the bag and didn't bother to vote." The newspaper was closer to the truth when it noted how "poisonous propaganda fanning racial prejudices had brought out the conservatives."[58]

After his primary loss, Edwards took a drastic step to revive his candidacy by breaking with Detroit's fifty-one-year tradition of nonpartisan municipal elections. Edwards decided to run openly as a Democrat. He argued that was the only way to break the powerful political hold of the city's elite. He maintained that Cobo was the handpicked choice of Detroit's wealthiest citizens. "They—the Board of Commerce, the Republican newspapers, and the Republican Party head, the Downtown property association, and the big real estate lobbies have opposed every candidate who has ever offered a constructive program of accomplishment to the people of Detroit. . . . Their negative policy of obstructions has meant years of do-nothingness—a snail-paced government guided by the selfish motivations of private interest and big pressure groups." Edwards's partisanship reaped immediate rewards. With urging from Governor Williams and his law partner, Democratic state chair Hicks G. Griffith, the party provided financing, took over management of Edwards's campaign, and opened five headquarters in Detroit to back his candidacy.[59]

Edwards's action drew predictable criticism from his opponents. The *Detroit News* reported that many Democrats had distanced themselves from Edwards. The *Free Press* editorialized that Edwards's arguments for running with a party label reflected "desperation . . . trickery and subterfuge." Ultimately, the newspaper argued, it showed his unfitness for office. Harking back to the Yale and Towne Strike, the editorial stated, "Edwards demonstrated then that he considered his own purposes and ambitions as above the law. . . . He is doing so again. And in so doing, in flouting the spirit of the Detroit Charter and the nonpartisan tradition, he is proving that he lacks the first qualification for becoming mayor—the qualification that the chief executive of this City represents not a group or party, but All the people." Even some long-time Edwards's supporters believed he had compromised his integrity. The Detroit Citizen League, a twenty-five-year-old civic organization, withdrew its longtime support of Edwards, calling his decision an "arrogant and defiant attack on a basic non-partisan principle."[60]

The 1949 election broke all previous records. An unprecedented 529,360 voters—nearly 62 percent of those registered—showed up at the polls. Cobo took 309,067 of those votes—beating Edwards by more than 105,000. Cobo's victory easily overshadowed the previous high of 275,159 set by Jeffries in the 1945 election. Cobo swept all of the city's white wards; Edwards did not win one precinct west of Woodward Avenue. Edwards did carry seven African-American wards in the eastern part of the city, but blacks did not yet have enough numerical strength to push him to victory as they would Cavanagh twelve years later. Cobo's win was a clear indication that Detroit's establishment intended to continue ignoring minority demands. In his victory speech, Cobo downplayed the racial underpinnings of the election, declaring simply that his triumph represented a success for the taxpayers of Detroit who would not have to fund costly civic improvements. Louis Miriani, Detroit's future mayor and Cavanagh's future opponent, replaced Edwards as city council president.[61]

In retrospect, the 1949 election was a referendum on race

relations. Edwards's decision to run as a Democrat may have cost him a few votes. It may also have provided many of his opponents with an opportunity to cloak their racial attacks in the loftier rhetoric of clean government. In its analysis, the *Michigan Chronicle* noted:

> Cobo's victory over Edwards is generally conceded to be a victory of conservative stand-pat forces against the liberal and progressive elements of the city. . . . Although concentrated in all-white neighborhoods and rather closely guarded in secrecy, it is known that the most vicious types of anti-Negro, anti-labor literature was distributed and a very damaging whispering campaign was waged. Edwards was unable to beat such a combination in a city which is noted for its race prejudice and anti-liberal sentiment.

Years later, Robert J. Greene, who worked on Edwards's campaign, recalled how questions of race permeated the election. Edwards's opponents "were skilled in the use of code words even back then. Welfare was code for unworthy persons, largely Negro; public housing soon came to be a cipher for black, often for nigger."[62]

The 1949 campaign was also noteworthy because it revealed the growing conservatism of labor's rank and file. Many CIO and UAW members did not approve of their leaders' endorsement of Edwards. They disliked the candidate's support for African Americans and rejected his "radicalism" as a relic of labor's early days. As one CIO member wrote Edwards after his defeat, "We don't want you or any part of your stuff. . . . I suggest you go to Washington they take care of lame ducks there. Or better yet, go back to the Heart of Texas. . . . We may belong to the CIO in the shops but when we vote we vote American."[63]

Edwards took his loss hard. He faced the massive disappointment of someone who had always succeeded, was set in the sureness of his own cause, and then with great shock found his belief in his own invincibility shattered. Now he faced the awesome triple tasks of dealing with his loss, recasting his life's ambitions, and keeping hold of his ideals. On Christmas night 1949, he wrote a long, thoughtful letter to his father recounting the events of the ending decade and pondering his political future:

> I leave it with much the same strange sense of frustration that I experienced in relation to the army. All the time I was in the army I was preparing for combat; my reason and emotions both tell me Thank God I never

had either to participate in battle or suffer its horrors. And yet I doubt that I will ever think much about the army without a feeling of frustration at never having done that which I spent two years of my life learning how to do.

My common sense and many of my feelings too now tell me— Edwards sit down and thank the Lord that you are not having to drive yourself crazy trying to make this big overgrown industrialized village act like a modern city with a soul. Under favorable circumstances with a reasonably united electorate and a not unfriendly press, both of which I had dared to hope for after election when I made up my mind to run a year ago, the job is a man killer for anyone with a conscience and a program. With a bitterly divided electorate and an utterly hostile press, the job—if I had won—would have been almost impossible. But reasoning that in fact I am probably very lucky cures none of the sense of frustration at not doing what I spent a good many years learning and preparing to do.

The years ahead are hardly likely to be dull ones or fruitless—but I find considerable disease in my inability to figure out which way they will lead.

Edwards rejected the declaration of Detroit's newspapers that his political career was over, noting, after all, that 205,000 people did vote for him for mayor. Nevertheless, he conceded that his immediate prospects looked dim. As he wrote his father: "I am not just interested in a living or a pension which quite a few political jobs represent." His most likely political avenue would have been challenging Congressman George O'Brien, whom Edwards characterized as "a thoroughly undistinguished Irishman who drinks too much, does nothing on floor or committee, but manages to remember to vote right." But Edwards feared his candidacy would split the party, and "waiting for the gent to pass on is not a particularly intriguing idea either." For the time being, Edwards said he would take refuge in his blessings: his family, his recent recovery from polio, and a law practice based on his union contacts.[64]

4

THE CRUCIBLE OF LAW

I hope I shall always remember that the people look to the courts to
defend their fundamental freedoms and that I have no right to sacrifice one iota of those rights for the least significant person because of
the ranting of demagogues or the pressures of press or politics.
—A Judge's Meditation, George Edwards, Jr.

George Edwards's unique qualifications to serve as Detroit's
police commissioner included the fact that he had melded
two distinct but complementary careers in law and politics. His
experience in politics provided him with an intimate knowledge
of the workings of Detroit's government along with insights into
the city's diversity. Ultimately, however, it was Edwards's judicial
experience that set him apart from his immediate predecessors.
His six years as a judge on Wayne County's juvenile and circuit
courts tempered his idealism with judicial restraint. His six-year
tenure on the Michigan Supreme Court overlapped with the constitutional rights revolution wrought by the U.S. Supreme Court
under Chief Justice Earl Warren. As a result, when Edwards became police commissioner, he already had wrestled with the implications of the court rulings that were transforming American
policing.

Nevertheless, in 1949, Edwards did not foresee the distinguished judicial career that awaited him. Instead, he struggled to
make meaning of the election defeat that had turned his career
from politics to law. He feared settling down to the drudgery of
a full-time law practice with a caseload that would consist largely
of workmen's compensation, damage actions, and picket-line vi-

olations. Edwards had studied law only after much nagging from his father. Edwards Sr. predicted, correctly, that his son did not have the ruthless temperament necessary to become a successful labor leader. In late 1937 and 1938, he urged him to leave union work and bombarded him with information about law schools. His campaign began in May 1938 when he wrote that UAW work "looks to me to be almost a dead end." He advised his son:

> You are 23. Consider the men in the labor movement who are old in it. Do you see in their work the sort of life you want to live and work at? Interminable petty squabbles and personal conflicts. . . . You never get time to read a book or to write a letter or to have a room to yourself. . . . I know you got involved in this work because of the way I have lived and I have no words of criticism for you: I only want you to make the best of your life and not to fritter it away, as I have frittered so much of mine, in the senseless squabbles of the kites and the crows.[1]

Edwards considered applying to Yale and the University of Michigan law schools, but he did not want to give up his union and political work. He decided to study law part-time at the Detroit College of Law, enrolling in September 1938. For the next six years, he fit his course work into an already numbing work schedule. During his first semester, he studied between 6:00 and 8:30 in the morning, attended one class, worked at the UAW office until 5:30, took two more classes, studied two hours, then went to union meetings.[2] Even though he eventually cut down on the hours of classes, his schedule became even more hectic as he tried to balance marriage and his work at the housing commission and city council. His perseverance paid off. During World War II, the Michigan State Bar instituted special exemptions allowing military inductees who were close to completing their law courses to receive a "certificate of completion" for purposes of taking the Michigan Bar. The certificate allowed Edwards to become a lawyer in 1944, although he would not complete the three courses needed for his degree until 1949. When he returned from the military, Edwards began practicing part-time with Theodore H. Bohn. In 1950, the firm of Edwards & Bohn became Rothe, Marston, Edwards & Bohn. It eventually evolved into Detroit's largest labor firm.

From 1946 to 1948, Edwards devoted most of his time to politics, using his law firm as a sideline from which he earned about $8,000 a year to supplement his salary as a city council-man. When he became a full-time attorney, his income jumped to about $20,000 a year.[3] Amid the exhausting routine of a busy law practice, Edwards managed to make occasional headlines. Perhaps the most famous episode of these years came in his first publicized brush with organized crime. It began when Edwards pressured reluctant authorities to investigate the attempted assassinations of three friends who were UAW officials, including Walter and Victor Reuther. Edwards believed the attacks stemmed from the union's ongoing struggles with a gangster on the East Side of Detroit, Santo Perrone, a Sicilian native known by his nicknames "The Shark" and "The Enforcer." Perrone earned his early fortunes bootlegging but branched out into strikebreaking in 1934. In exchange for his help against unionizing efforts that spring, John A. Fry, president of the Michigan Stove Works on East Jefferson Avenue, gave Perrone a lucrative scrap metal contract with which to start his own business. Edwards and the Reuthers believed that Perrone used his company as a cover for other illegal activities, including labor racketeering. Their suspicions gained ground when union workers began receiving threats at the Briggs Manufacturing Company soon after the firm gave Perrone's son-in-law, Carl Renda, its business.[4]

The wave of violence took an ugly turn on May 31, 1946, seven weeks after Briggs hired Renda. Attackers brutally beat Ken Morris, secretary of Briggs Local 212, in the parking lot outside his apartment at the Parkside Housing Project. He nearly died from thirty-seven fractures to his skull, arm, and right leg. On the day after the attack, Edwards visited Morris in the hospital. Later, he recalled how Morris "was conscious but very weak. When I returned to the car, I told my wife that I didn't think that Ken would make it. [But] Morris's relative youth and conditioning from his military service stood him in good stead." No charges were ever filed in the case, even though Morris's wife had identified Dick Lambert, a Perrone associate, as the man who had visited her apartment the day before the attack looking for her husband.[5]

Perrone and his henchmen grew bolder. On April 20, 1948, Walter Reuther returned home from a union meeting and was preparing a late-night snack in his kitchen. A shotgun blast

96

ripped through the window, nearly tearing off his right arm. As historian John Barnard notes, "Only a quick turn at the moment the shot was fired, which allowed his right arm instead of his chest to take the brunt of the blast, saved his life. . . . The arm's nerves were in shreds, and doctors feared that he would never recover its use." Reuther was eventually able to regain some function in his arm through exercise and surgery. His brother, Victor, was not so lucky. On May 24, 1949, a gunman shot Victor through a living room window. The gunshot ripped into his face, tearing off part of his jaw bone and blinding his right eye. His wife, Sophie, told neighbors to call Edwards, who rushed to Redford Receiving Hospital. As he recalled, "I waited beside the motionless body of my wounded friend, feeling that my presence might forestall any attempt of the would-be assassins to finish the job. Vic's eyes were bandaged. I thought him unconscious and never spoke to him. I stood silent guard for what seemed like hours—probably one-half of one—until a police guard had been assembled and put in place. I left after attempting to assure Sophie that Vic would live." His assurances proved correct; Reuther did survive.[6]

Edwards was upset at the lackadaisical manner in which police investigated the attacks. When he began practicing law full-time in 1950, he prodded the authorities by filing a lawsuit on Morris's behalf against Briggs Manufacturing. Edwards charged that the firm had engaged in a criminal conspiracy by hiring Perrone to intimidate union officials. As evidence, Edwards cited the nearly fatal beating of his client two years earlier. Although Briggs's contract technically was with Perrone's son-in-law, Carl Renda, Edwards said that was a fiction because Renda had just graduated from college and had no business experience. Edwards's investigation led him to Wayne County Circuit Judge George B. Murphy, who admitted that he had been ready to indict Perrone, but instead fled to Florida for a vacation after being threatened.[7]

Edwards's visit with Murphy coincided with Congressional hearings into organized crime. Led by Tennessee's Democratic Senator Estes Kefauver, the 1950–51 investigation constituted a major effort to peel back the secrecy of organized crime. Edwards recognized that Kefauver's efforts could help his lawsuit, and he conducted some behind-the-scenes maneuvering to insure that the Congressional investigators subpoenaed Judge Murphy's records. When Senate staffers wrapped up their business and left for Washington, Detroit reporters and Edwards convinced them to leave a copy of Murphy's report behind. Years later, Edwards recalled how "we worked until the small hours of the following morning and then the three reporters from competitive newspapers debated what to do with the massive record, a debate which resulted in my agreeing to keep it and make it available at my law office to each of the three."[8]

Kefauver's hearings and the ensuing publicity shed light on many of Perrone's activities. In 1953, he and three others were convicted of bribing Michigan Stove Works employees to resist unionization; they were fined $1,000 and put on probation for a year. That year the NLRB successfully sued to void Perrone's $100,000 scrap metal contract with Briggs Manufacturing. Nothing, however, ever came of the more serious charges accusing Perrone of masterminding the attacks on Morris and the Reuther brothers. A Wayne County Circuit judge dismissed Edwards's civil suit because the statute of limitations had run out on Morris's beating. Meanwhile the police investigation into the Reuther shootings dragged along, then ran aground. Private investigators hired by the UAW located an informant, Donald Joseph Ritchie, a convicted felon from Canada. After his arrest, Ritchie told authorities that he heard Perrone say, "We'll have to get this guy [Walter Reuther] out of the way." Ritchie said he witnessed the shootings carried out by his uncle, Clarence Jacobs, a Perrone henchman. Relying on Ritchie's testimony, Wayne County District Attorney Gerald K. O'Brien charged Renda, Perrone, Jacobs, and another Perrone associate, Peter Lombardo, with conspiring to attack the Reuthers. Detroit police detectives, who were guarding Ritchie at the Statler Hotel, allowed him to escape on January 8, 1954. He fled across the border into Canada, and the case never came to trial. The botched investigation made a deep impression on Edwards, who said: "I learned that Santo Perrone operated in mysterious ways and with astonishing invulnerability." Edwards believed Perrone's power stemmed from his protection by the city's anti-union business leaders, politicians, and police. Years later, when he became police commissioner Edwards vowed to smash those ties. In the early 1950s, however, he turned his attention to other matters.[9]

Edwards continued to nurse political ambitions. Along with other progressive Democrats, he recognized that continued reform in Michigan meant keeping G. Mennen Williams as governor. Williams's activist, good-government agenda, however, offended many of the party's old guard. Assuring his re-election in 1950 meant revamping the party at the local level. To further the cause in Detroit, Edwards became a legal advisor to the Wayne County Democratic party. In that capacity, he represented Helen Berthelot and other reformers who sued to invalidate illegal signatures gathered by Democratic leaders in the 17th District. Edwards also played an instrumental role in uncovering Republican vote fraud in Macomb County that would have denied Williams's re-election in 1950.[10]

In 1950, Edwards won election as a precinct delegate and a congressional district chairman. Peg optimistically predicted that the latter would "probably be the first step towards his running for Congress two years from now. The present Congressman supported George's opposition and is a very weak specimen." Although neither he nor Peg recognized it in the early 1950s, Edwards's idealism and temperament were much better suited to the intellectual nuances of the law than to the hurly-burly compromises of politics. This became readily apparent in September 1951, when Governor Williams appointed Edwards to fill a vacancy on Wayne County's Probate Court left by the death of Judge D. J. Healy. As a signal of his commitment to impartial justice, Edwards arranged for Wayne County Circuit Judge Arthur Webster to hold his robes for his swearing in ceremony. Webster was the judge who had sentenced Edwards to jail on contempt charges fourteen years earlier.[11]

Edwards became the only judge in charge of Wayne County's juvenile court. He accepted the appointment, telling Williams that he would fill the job until he could run for Congress. Edwards earned $17,500 a year—$2,500 a year less than he made from his law practice, but he was excited about the new challenge. He wrote to his mother: "The job seems to go fairly well. I am working hard to get the dockets in hand and to learn the job. There is a lot of heartache in this job as Dad knows. There are a number of legal and a number of policy questions which bother me—but all in all I believe I will end up glad I took it."[12]

His appointment to probate court coincided with one of the nation's recurring, periodic obsessions with juvenile justice. In the early 1950s, in many jurisdictions, children enjoyed few of the same constitutional rights guaranteed to adults. For example, the U.S. Supreme Court dictated that adult defendants were entitled to a hearing within seventy-two hours of their arrest; yet, in Wayne County, juveniles sometimes waited one hundred days for a judge to hear their cases. The early 1950s also saw renewed interest in reforming delinquents and housing them separately from neglected children. During his tenure, Edwards implemented many of these reforms, and, in the process, remade Wayne County's Probate Court into a national model.

He began on January 3, 1952, by overhauling the court's scandalous procedures. He took greatest pride in his introduction of preliminary hearings, in which "every child apprehended by the police will be seen by the court within 24 hours. It may have seemed impossible but previously they were just held on police complaint until hearing—which takes thirty days or more— unless someone came down and put up a scrap to get them out." Edwards also cut the period between the complaint and hearing from sixty to thirty days. As a result of both reforms, he reduced the number of children held in the Detention House from two hundred to one hundred. He noted proudly that "I don't think we have turned loose any children who constitute menaces to the community."[13]

Edwards played a key role in persuading county officials to build a separate shelter home for abused children and a new juvenile detention home for youthful offenders. Along with most other 1950s juvenile justice reformers, he believed that delinquency stemmed largely from family and social breakdown or what he called "disordered life." In one speech to the Detroit Rotary Club, "What Can Be Done About Juvenile Delinquency," Edwards argued that "it is vitally important to this community to realize that criminals are not born, and juvenile delinquency is not a built-in factor of a child." Institutions, he said, could not stop delinquency; at-risk children's problems had to be solved by schools and social agencies before they ran afoul of the criminal justice system.[14]

Many voters, police officials, and newspaper writers who had criticized Edwards's mayoral campaign applauded his efforts at juvenile court. In a lengthy story, the *Detroit Times* noted that Police Commissioner George F. Boos and his chief aides favored the overdue reforms. Another newspaper praised Edwards for vowing to require parents to assume part or all of the costs of their children who ran afoul of the law—a move he estimated would save taxpayers $30,000 to $100,000 annually.[15]

Public support, newspaper endorsements, and UAW backing rolled in when Edwards announced his decision to run for reelection in May 1952. He had no trouble gathering the 13,500 signatures needed to get his name on the ballot for the August primary. He came in first with 300,000 votes—40,000 more than the nearest candidate. Before the general election, the Michigan and Detroit Bar Associations gave him their highest rankings, and he handily defeated his opponent, Joseph Maher.[16]

Edwards's win was noteworthy because it came amid a scandal that fueled an anti-incumbent backlash from voters. The uproar began in the spring when the *Detroit News* published stories detailing favoritism and corruption in Wayne County's Probate Court. The court had six judges; five sat downtown, handling estates, while the sixth sat by himself at the juvenile court facility located on the near East Side. In one story, the newspaper published pictures of judges Thomas C. Murphy, William J. Cody, Patrick H. O'Brien, James A. Sexton, and Joseph A. Murphy. The caption identified them as "the five Wayne County probate judges who pay off political obligations by appointing friends, relatives and election workers as appraisers for estate work. The practice costs tens of thousands of dollars annually to heirs." In late April, Judge Joseph A. Murphy responded with a plan to rotate the judges. But his plan to transfer Cody to juvenile court and Edwards downtown failed, after both Edwards and the Michigan Supreme Court objected.[17]

The scandal did not touch Edwards, but Peg worried anyway. In a letter to her in-laws on May 30, 1952, she wrote: "Yesterday Justice Budget of the Michigan Supreme Court and one of the two justices making the investigation of Probate Court called

George and told him that they had absolutely no criticism of the present handling of the juvenile court and would point this out in their report. This report also will appear after the bar poll is taken." She added that "it seems as though we have a positive genius for being present when things are the most difficult. For years no one has paid any attention to Probate Court and now although George is not one they are after, it reflects on all the judges."[18]

Edwards's ability to rise above the scandal and his obvious skill at revamping the court added lustre to his judicial career. His reputation as a juvenile justice reformer brought him national prominence. He joined such legal luminaries as Harvard Law School Dean Roscoe Pound on the advisory council of judges for the National Probation and Parole Association (NPPA) and struck up friendships with such politicians as Senator Kefauver.[19]

Edwards found his job fascinating. As he wrote to his parents in March 1952,

> It has thrown me head over heels into these endeavors: 1) A general study of human behavior and misbehavior. . . . Rather a large and inconclusive study—but a thoroughly interesting one. 2) Learning the law and procedure of Juvenile Court. . . . 3) Investigating and starting to lay plans for completely replacing the Juvenile Jail which I also administer. 4) Getting to know all of the institutions to which the court makes commitments and trying to figure out what can be done to get something done to build those which don't exist—like a treatment hospital for children with serious mental disturbances.

He added, "Even the newspapers haven't given me much trouble since the appointment." He guessed that he probably received more favorable press than any judge in Wayne County, but, "this is not saying too much."[20]

Edwards's NPPA activities attracted the wrath of FBI Director J. Edgar Hoover, who became a lifelong enemy. Hoover's attacks began after Edwards, along with other members of the NPPA's advisory council of judges, opposed a model penal code that had been drafted by the American Law Institute and enjoyed Hoover's support. Edwards and the NPPA criticized the new code, especially its treatment of youthful offenders, as a draconian throwback to the days before enlightened criminology. In a February 1957 editorial in the FBI *Law Enforcement Bulletin*,

Hoover asked, "Are we to stand idly by while fierce young hoodlums—too often and too long harbored under the glossy misnomer of juvenile delinquents—roam our streets and desecrate our communities?" Citing a growing number of teenaged gangs, Hoover predicted "a resurgence of the brutal criminality and mobsterism of a past era" if juvenile justice groups continued to promote "the illusion that soft-hearted mollycoddling is the answer to the problem." Edwards and other NPPA members responded by publicly condemning the FBI director's position. The judges also suggested that police chiefs should be more independent of Hoover in their approach to crime problems. Hoover was so outraged by Edwards's action that he began a smear campaign, using U.S. District Judge Edward A. Tamm as a conduit. Tamm had served as Hoover's assistant in the FBI for eighteen years before President Harry Truman appointed him to the federal bench in Washington, D.C. Hoover sent Tamm six copies of a blind memorandum, prepared by the FBI, outlining Edwards's activities as a socialist and condemning his father as "a Socialist nominee for the Governor of Texas." As author Alexander Charns writes, the memo "had no markings revealing its sources, so Tamm could pass it to other judges or to the press."[21]

Edwards retained an interest in juvenile justice long after leaving probate court. Three governors appointed him to the Michigan Youth Commission from 1955 to 1963, and he continued to speak to national groups and testify before Congress about juvenile problems. Edwards retained his belief that most criminal behavior resulted from social dislocation rather than innate character defects. Thus, the ultimate solution to much crime rested with helping children at risk. In a letter to a University of Michigan graduate student who sought his advice for a zoology project, Edwards wrote: "I completely reject the notion that there is such a thing as a criminal type definable either by heredity or physical characteristics."[22]

In August 1958, Edwards came up with his so-called "recipe" for creating a criminal in a speech at the American Bar Association convention in Los Angeles. It became the most telling exposition of his views of juvenile delinquency and the causes of crime, and he recycled it for the next several years. After he became Detroit's police commissioner, several journals and newspapers across the country reprinted it. Edwards's recipe began with one normal baby, two drunken or drug-addicted brawling parents who frequently separate, and a half dozen other children living in squalid slum housing. He added that the child should have little adult supervision. "Because he is unkempt and unruly, the teacher will pay no attention to him because she sees him as a troublemaker. By the seventh grade, he will be three years behind in reading but much bigger than the other kids in the class." Edwards added that it was important that the community offer no organized sports or other after-school activities for the child. To guarantee continued "progress," he said, it was important to make sure that the school counselor, social workers, and juvenile probation officers were all overworked so they could not intervene to help the child. "Even at this late stage good probation efforts might wreck progress. It's better if public indignation and a juvenile court judge who wants to 'make an example of him' sends him without any intermediate attempt at rehabilitation to the state training school." At the crowded juvenile detention center, Edwards said, the child would experience peer pressure to behave badly. By his release at age seventeen, he would be free to get a gun, commit a robbery or violent crime, and end up in the penitentiary. Edwards concluded that no child "is born predestined to be a criminal." He optimistically predicted, "As medicine has defeated dread diseases of the past, one after the other, so we can, if we will, learn to cure the socially ill."[23] In 1962, the only members of the Detroit Police Department who welcomed his appointment as commissioner worked in the juvenile division.

Edwards took time out from his busy judicial schedule for civic events. He was active in the American Cancer Society's annual drives, served on the boards of an outpatient psychiatric clinic for indigents at Harper Hospital, the Boy Scouts of America, and a Christian council for social action. He was a popular speaker to Parent Teacher Associations, religious and women's groups, business clubs, university panels, and bar and probation associations. His success in persuading these groups to back his juvenile reforms helps explain why he implemented community meetings when he took over as police commissioner.[24]

Edwards's volunteer work reflected his belief that democratic government functioned best with citizen input. In 1954, he wrote a long letter expounding those views to his minister at the Mayflower Congregational Church. Upset at a series of sermons in which Rev. Phillip W. Sarles spoke disparagingly of politicians, Edwards took up his pen and launched his most eloquent defense of public service.

> As a long time public official I am proud of my calling. I take much more pride in public service than in my profession of law. . . . I would even be inclined to the assertion that public service is the highest calling to which any citizen in our nation can aspire with the exception of the ministry and possibly some branches of education.
>
> The fact that there are . . . selfish persons, and just plain reprobates holding public office in my view no more serves to decrease the importance of the calling than the fact that similar fallible representatives are to be found in the ministry or in other walks of life.
>
> In my mind one does the general cause of democracy little good by holding the field of public service in contempt by reference to elected officials generally only as politicians etc. The fact that this is the commonest of popular attitudes these days, of course, is of no justification for it; and the fact that it pleases most of your parishioners isn't either. . . .
>
> The same popularly held attitudes keep "good" people . . . from soiling their skirts with the "dirt" of political life. And many times these attitudes keep people who could perhaps make a real contribution from any participation in political party activity. . . . [I]n fact, I would hazard a guess, that 30% of the members of your church were not registered for voting. And yet all of these good citizens, if asked would assert . . . fervent loyalty to the democratic way of life. . . . If the people who consider themselves Christian in motivation hold themselves aloof from the essential processes of government, God help democracy. . . .
>
> Too few people these days seem to realize that the great ideas of democratic government—the equality of men before the law and God, the concern of all of us for the least of us, the brotherhood of all mankind—are ideas drawn directly from the ethics of Christianity. Their realization in government can hardly be safely entrusted exclusively to those who make no pretense of Christian belief.[25]

In May 1954, Governor Williams appointed Edwards to fill an opening on the very busy 3rd Judicial Circuit, Wayne County's court of general jurisdiction. In an average year, he handled 150 cases and various miscellaneous matters. He compiled a remarkable record for a busy trial judge. Only one of his decisions was modified and none were reversed on appeal.[26]

Within weeks of his appointment, Edwards geared up for re-election. With Pat Taylor as the secretary of his campaign committee and Norval "Doc" Mueller as his campaign treasurer, he had no trouble gathering roughly 25,000 names to get on the ballot. As usual, Edwards won wide support in the African-American community. Edwards won the November election handily, and he was pleased when two friends joined him in the race. The first was Theodore Bohn, his former law partner, and Wade H. McCree, Jr., a thirty-four-year-old lawyer who became the first African American elected to the Wayne County bench. After his election, Edwards won more praise in the *Michigan Chronicle* by appointing an African-American law student, Jesse Eggleston, as his clerk. Eggleston, a native of Winston-Salem, North Carolina, had served with Edwards in the infantry and was attending night classes at Wayne State University.[27]

During his tenure on the circuit court, Edwards continued to be a champion for the downtrodden, even when it entailed exhaustive research and creatively reading new interpretations into old statutes and rejecting precedent. This was true in the negligence case brought by Theodora Dahlstrom against the Mohawk Lumber & Supply Co., and one of its employees, Playford Jackson. On August 13, 1954, an official at Mohawk asked Jackson to drive him to the airport in the company Cadillac then go back to work. Instead, Jackson stopped at his cousin's house, and the two of them went for a joy ride. Jackson ran a stop sign, speeding at sixty to seventy miles per hour, and struck Charles Dahlstrom's car. Dahlstrom died in the wreck, and his widow sued. On June 15, 1955, the jury ruled that Mohawk and Jackson had both been negligent and awarded her $12,000 in damages. Mohawk's attorney asked Edwards to set aside the verdict because Jackson was not acting within the scope of his employment at the time of the accident. After extensive research, Edwards decided to follow his own "conscience" and throw out the legal precedents that supported the company's position. He wrote, "It must be obvious, and should perhaps be confessed, that such a lengthy opinion bespeaks a troubled Judge. But it appears to this court that on these facts the widow of an utterly innocent victim should have the benefit of the language of the statute itself in determining the liability of the owner who turned a car over to a driver whose recklessness occasioned the death of her husband."[28]

During this time, Edwards's natural sympathies for the underdog were becoming tempered by his experience on the bench, and he was developing the judicial philosophy that would mark the rest of his career. As he would tell an interviewer in later years, "You have opinions, of course, but you don't make up your mind as a judge until you approach the matter in the context of the case. You don't decide your personal view, you decide what is or should be the law, and that is a very different decision." Edwards's emerging philosophy became apparent in his 1955 ruling in the case of May E. Fisher against the City of Detroit. Fisher's husband worked for the city's Department of Public Works from June 1921 until his death on June 20, 1951. On May 28, 1951, Fisher filed an application for retirement which would have provided a pension for his wife. But he died before the thirty-day requirement was met, and the city paid his widow only $2,200. Edwards sided with the city against Fisher. He noted that even though her situation was regrettable the statute was clear and he concluded: "The cure of this situation lies, however, not by the Court's seeking beyond its authority to rewrite Charter provisions, but by remedial amendment."[29]

As a circuit court judge, Edwards developed a lifelong fascination with criminal law, which was one reason for his willingness to become Detroit's police commissioner. In April 1955, he spoke to the Chicago City Club in his capacity as chair of the law school curriculum committee of the NPPA. Soon after, he began planning a book on criminal law that the NPPA would publish for law schools. His proposal revealed the same philosophy of criminal justice that marked his tenure as police commissioner. He believed that law courses and the courts placed too much emphasis on the narrow aspects of the criminal law and did not pay enough attention to larger questions of social justice, prevention, and reformation. In a letter to his parents, he said the book would differ from most law school texts that "teach the problem as essentially a who-dun-it and the lawyer's role as being exclusively that of the defender of the innocent person charged with crime (or the guilty one who has a chance to create a reasonable doubt)." Instead, he would focus on "the possibility of correction of criminal misbehavior at least with the younger offenders and first offenders." Such an approach made more sense, he claimed, because "90–95% of all criminal cases are handled on guilty pleas without trial—and currently law schools limit their preparation of lawyers to the 5 to 10% of the cases which are tried."[30]

Edwards continued to nurse political ambitions throughout the 1950s. In October 1955, he considered running for a seat in a neighboring district, which opened when Congressman John Dingell died. As he wrote to his parents,

> Some would like me to run and there is some real temptation to do it. I could probably be elected because the [illegible] are so bad and the Democratic majority is so large. . . . But it would be quite a tour de force. There is no great popular demand for Edwards—I do not live in the District—I am recently elected judge and would have to resign from the job and a whole host of involvements in the space of the next week. We would have to move the family right in midstream. All in all I guess that Congress will have to wait—though it actually is my ultimate goal.[31]

In June 1956, Governor Williams appointed Edwards to the Michigan Supreme Court to fill a vacancy left by the death of Justice Neil E. Reid. At age forty-one, Edwards became the court's youngest member. By accepting the job, he took a pay cut from $25,000 to $18,500. He accepted the lower salary for the opportunity to serve on the more prestigious court, which, he believed, needed a more liberal direction. Several months before his appointment, Edwards complained that the high court was "far from sensitive to social questions." He commiserated about the court's philosophy with Talbot Smith, a liberal Democrat whom Williams appointed to the supreme court on January 11, 1955. Smith developed an independent streak growing up in the western mining and cattle towns where his father served as an Episcopal missionary. He and Edwards shared a deep philosophical commitment to what they believed should be the liberalizing effects of the law. Smith regularly dissented from the court's other, more conservative justices, especially in workmen's compensation cases. After one such ruling in December 1954, Smith wrote Edwards: "Quite a beating again today. I am sorry I cannot persuade my brethren. I must become more eloquent, or something."[32]

Edwards accepted an invitation to give a speech honoring Smith to a civil bar group on May 18, 1956. When Williams announced his nomination, Edwards worried about the propriety of keeping the engagement and speaking publicly about a future colleague. He decided that Smith's efforts deserved a defense from critics, mostly Republican and conservative, who said the justice's many dissents had undermined the court. Edwards, whose own judicial career would be marked by conscientious dissent, said Smith's disagreements with his colleagues were not "born of stubbornness or petulance or whim." Instead, they provided "evidence of a sincere and determined spirit, significant because it may well help to shape our law." Edwards outlined his colleague's championing of civil liberties and rights of common people. He concluded by citing a recent speech that Smith had given criticizing judges who believed in maintaining the status quo: "Let those who will, counsel caution and silence and the need for certainty and stability. There can be no silence while wrongs done our people cry for relief. And as for stability, the only real stability is that of the grave."[33]

In his speech, Edwards touched on the growing divide between judicial "activists" and "conservatives" about the nature of American law. Conservatives argued for the principle of judicial restraint—the idea that judges should be bound by precedent. They generally criticized Supreme Court rulings for school desegregation, consumer rights, and protections for criminal defendants as usurpations of legislative authority. Activists such as Edwards and Smith believed that courts had a fundamental duty to protect individual rights against the powerful interests of corporate America and government. Governor Williams eloquently referred to this divide at Edwards's swearing-in ceremony on June 5, 1956, "On this high court it is of the greatest importance that we have men of integrity, men learned in the law, and men who have had experience with the trials and tribulations, the hopes and aspirations of the men, the women and the children of this state." Others spoke at Edwards's swearing-in, including Ira W. Jayne, one of five Wayne County Circuit judges who attended the ceremony. But Edwards's most vivid memory came when his father was asked to say a few words. He said simply, "Mrs. Edwards and I are very grateful to all of you that the famous State of Michigan has given our son this opportunity for service to the people. We hope and pray that in his work on this court, he will do justly and will have mercy, and will walk humbly with the spirit of goodness and love, who is our God." As Edwards remembered years later, "Everything that came after seemed irrelevant."[34]

During the 1950s, Michigan's Supreme Court heard an average of 300–360 cases per year. Edwards wrote opinions in about sixty of those cases annually. His presence was felt immediately. Along with Talbot Smith, he worked to belie the court's reputation as a bastion for corporate America and a bulwark for the status quo. Many court observers believed that the changes Edwards wrought were epitomized in his 1957 ruling in the case of *Bishop v. New York Central Railroad*. It was a personal injury suit brought by a motorist who had been injured when a train hit his car at a railroad crossing on January 30, 1954. Lawyers for the New York Central argued that the driver contributed to the accident by failing to look both ways before proceeding across the tracks. Evidence showed that he had waited ten minutes for one train to pass. Then, when the gates went up, he began to cross the intersection and another train hit him in the side. The jury agreed with the driver, who claimed he could not have been expected to see the second train coming.[35]

Under previous rulings, the court would have set aside the jury verdict because the burden of proving the accident would have rested with the driver instead of the railroad. Edwards, however, changed that, and in the process issued a ringing endorsement of the democratic strengths inherent in the jury system. He wrote: "The jury is drawn from the community. It lives, and thinks, and decides, with the standards of conduct of the ordinarily prudent persons in that community. . . . It is part of the genius of our system of law that a jury trial inevitably brings into each case thus decided the color of life in the country or city concerned, the habits of the people who dwell there, and the ordinary standards of their conduct in their relation to the problems of their day and time."[36]

Edwards's most famous decision during his five years on the high court, *Comstock v. General Motors,* struck a major victory for consumers across the nation. Ironically, the product liability case grew out of problems in brakes made for Buick by Edwards's first Detroit employer, Kelsey-Hayes Wheel Company. Evidence showed that sealers in 1953 Buick power brakes sometimes leaked fluid, causing brake failure. General Motors learned about the problem and notified its dealers, but argued that it had no further obligation to inform car buyers. A lower court judge agreed that the responsibility for warning customers rested with dealers, and he dismissed General Motors from the case before it went to the jury. Edwards reversed that decision, arguing that General Motors's liability was a fact that the jury should have decided. His ruling set a precedent for recalls in the auto industry.[37]

The Comstock case became important as a symbol of the dramatic change that Edwards and his liberal colleagues wrought on Michigan's Supreme Court. Before Smith joined the court, lawyers cynically joked that the state's highest court "opens and closes on motion of General Motors." By the time Edwards left in 1962, critics accused the court of bowing to the whim of the CIO. Both claims were simplistic but indicated the dramatic changes in the court. Williams appointed three other Democratic justices during the late 1950s—Eugene F. Black, John D. Voelker, and Thomas M. Kavanagh. Edwards became the unofficial spokesman for the group, who in his words, "made the 20th Century welcome in Michigan courtrooms." Together they "telescoped twenty years of progress into three years," according to Dean Charles H. King of the Detroit College of Law. According to James Robinson, writing for the *Detroit Free Press,* "Some lawyers called them radical. Others said they were brilliant. All, however, agree that never before in the history of Michigan—or perhaps any other state—have so many court reforms been accomplished and so many legal concepts altered in such a short space of time." Robinson said that reporters eagerly waited to see what "bold action [would be taken] to wipe out concepts of the past." The court's liberalization of the law favored working men, the unemployed, accident victims, and criminal defendants. Above all, reliance on precedence had been replaced by what Edwards had called "common sense applied to the problems of today."[38]

Such changes came at a cost to collegiality, and during Edwards's tenure the court became more fractious. The rift took on national overtones in August 1958, when the five Democrats chastised the court's chief justice, Republican John R. Dethmers.

Dethmers, while attending a conference in California, joined chief justices from southern states in a resolution criticizing the U.S. Supreme Court for its "hasty, impatient" rulings in such cases as *Brown v. the Board of Education.* The conservative jurists accused the nation's highest court of using its rulings to make public policy decisions better left to legislators. Edwards, Smith, Voelker, Black, and Kavanagh responded with a statement praising the U.S. Supreme Court as "courageous and competent." The *Los Angeles Times* contacted Edwards, who opined that "the desegregation decision will be regarded as a great historic contribution to the future of this nation."[39]

Although the most visible divide on Michigan's Supreme Court was between its Democratic and Republican members, there was also growing discontent among the Democrats. Some of this stemmed from what his colleagues believed to be Edwards's grandstanding. The Dethmers resolution was one example. Thomas M. Kavanagh came up with the idea of condemning the chief justice's action, but his role was dwarfed when Edwards won national attention by giving an interview to the *Los Angeles Times.* Tellingly, Edwards referred to this discrepancy in a letter to Governor Williams, but he never mentioned it when he sent a copy of the resolution to Earl Warren. The U.S. Supreme Court chief justice said he already had read about the Michigan jurists' resolution "because it was publicized widely throughout the country." Eventually, even Smith became jealous of Edwards's growing reputation, and their friendship cooled. Edwards, who left the labor movement in part because of its infighting, tried to downplay divisions among his colleagues. While attending the Michigan Judicial Conference in Dearborn in 1957, he told reporters that even though "the Supreme Court is composed of eight strong-minded and thoroughly independent men" attacks "on the integrity of the court" were unfounded. Black was less tactful. In 1960, he told the Midwest Convention of Attorneys General meeting in Mackinac Island that the court "is bogged down by politics; shot with conditions that prevent satisfactory work."[40]

Although his high public profile grated on his colleagues, Edwards welcomed the increased visibility that came with being a member of Michigan's Supreme Court. He continued to be known as a leading authority on juvenile justice and delinquency. Detroit Police Commissioner Edward S. Piggins valued his willingness to address civic groups about prevention of youth crimes. He helped lobby for construction of a new Boys Vocational School north of Ann Arbor to replace the state's overcrowded, century-old facility for youthful offenders in Lansing. The St. Peter's Home for boys gave him its annual award for outstanding achievement. In 1961, at the behest of Governor Swainson, he testified before the U.S. Senate for creation of a Youth Conservation Corps to provide jobs to unemployed young adults between the ages of 16 and 22. He was a tireless speaker on the need to temper increased antidelinquency efforts with enlightened treatment. His views impressed Attorney General Robert Kennedy, who appointed him to the President's Commission on Juvenile Delinquency and Youth Crime in April 1962. His many speaking engagements around the country included the American Bar Association's annual meeting in 1958, the U.S. Conference of Mayors in 1958, and White House Conferences on Children and Youth in 1960 and 1961. After a conference of the Missouri Association for Social Welfare, an attendee wrote: "If he ever runs for president, he has my vote and I don't care what ticket he runs on. . . . I rate Judge Edwards's talk as one of the few really good ones that I have heard in my lifetime."[41]

Edwards also remained vocal on civil-liberties and racial-justice issues. During the 1957 Michigan Judicial Conference in Dearborn, Edwards made headlines by unsuccessfully introducing a resolution asking the judges to send a telegram to President Dwight D. Eisenhower praising his stand on racial integration. As the *Detroit News* reported, Edwards called protests in Little Rock, Arkansas, over the integration of Central High School "the worst threat to national unity since the Civil War." Three years later, Edwards drew more attention when he delivered a speech declaring that constitutional guarantees to all Americans of life, liberty, and the pursuit of happiness were still a distant dream. He pointed out that the Fourteenth Amendment to the Constitution, which attempted to give full citizenship to former slaves, had been ratified ninety-two years earlier and "it was high time we honor it." He added: "I am glad that both the Supreme court and the youth of our land are making clear that the days of segre-

113

gation and second-class citizenship for Negroes are numbered." In another speech that year, Edwards predicted that the nation would either have to honor the democratic ideal by desegregating society or watch as "America moved toward the backwash of history."[42]

Edwards's reputation as a champion for the working man gained him international attention in August 1961, when Department of Labor Secretary Arthur Goldberg appointed him to be deputy judge of the Administrative Tribunal of the International Labor Organization (ILO). He was the only American jurist on the panel which met in Geneva and heard cases concerning private contracts, employee contracts, and pension disputes of the ILO and six other agencies of the United Nations. In order to free time in his busy schedule for the tribunal's work, Edwards resigned as a trustee of the Amalgamated Clothing Workers of American Insurance Fund Board, a post he had held since 1957.[43]

Given his political ambitions and his bent towards social activism, Edwards, more than most judges, continually wrestled with the question of how to strike a balance between public outspokenness and judicial circumspection. The line was thin. Edwards kept up membership in such political and civil rights organizations as the ADA, the ACLU, and the NAACP. He continued pushing for a model penal code through his work for the NPPA, and he remained active for juvenile justice reform efforts as a member of the Child Welfare League, Inc., an advocacy association based in New York City. He spoke at the 88th Annual Congress of Corrections, decried the prison cell as "a bird cage for humans," and proclaimed "there is not sufficient continuing contact between society and the prisoner to help him become a better man." Nevertheless, in 1956, he refused to join the legal advisory board of the social action committee of the American Jewish Congress (AJC). The board was well known for civil rights work, and its members had included Harry Schulman, a former dean of Yale Law School; Thurman Arnold, a former assistant U.S. attorney general; Frank P. Graham, a former U.S. senator from North Carolina; and future Supreme Court Justice Thurgood Marshall. Edwards was flattered but concluded that his membership in the AJC would hurt, rather than help, the cause if he were forced to recuse himself from deciding cases in which he had taken a strong public position. "After viewing the activities of the Commission I am inclined to feel that my best service in the field of civil rights can be offered through opinion writing from the bench rather than in any other way." He used the same reasoning three years later to refuse an offer to join the ACLU's advisory board.[44]

Edwards's high profile drew mixed public reactions. Predictably, liberals praised it while conservatives decried it as inappropriate. For example, Arthur Johnson of the NAACP said he was "heartened" by Edwards's praise of the *Brown* decision. The civil rights leader added that because of judges like Edwards "I have never had any real doubts about the outcome of this struggle or even despaired of the inevitable stress and strain involved in it." By contrast, George M. Zimmerman, a Detroit insurance agency owner, wrote Edwards an angry letter after one speech. "May I respectfully comment that pious double talk about 'Civil Rights' comes with poor grace from our organizer of the righteous sit down strikes and over the mikes of the UAW–CIO. Among the worst violators of Civil Rights are labor monopolies, some of which 1) confine membership to the white race, and 2) closed union shops which levy a private tax upon an otherwise free American as a condition of employment."[45]

Despite his strong liberal leanings, Edwards never considered himself to be a judicial activist. His tenure on the supreme court strengthened his belief that judges should follow the law set by legislatures and precedent rather than their own predilections. He said if judges had to "write bad law to do justice in a single case, that's too high a price to pay for the result." He told one interviewer,

> I agree with Cardozo that we don't have a "roving commission" to do justice, and I'm not sure I'd like it if I had. It might be one way to live, but it's not judging. I'm certainly a liberal in political and social policy, but in law I identify with values—I'm hesitating over which one to say first—of "ordered liberty." I identify with the Bill of Rights of the Constitution strongly, and recognize that any government must be the guarantor of the people's welfare, including the opportunity to live in peace."[46]

Edwards's professionalism won plaudits from bar association groups and voters. As former Detroit Police Commissioner Frank D. Eaman wrote when he sent Edwards a campaign contribution for the 1956 supreme court election, "You deserve to be elected, and I was pleased to see that members of the Detroit Bar Association gave you their endorsement in spite of their party labels." In the April 6, 1959, primary he easily won against Circuit Judge John Simpson. In the general election, he defeated his nearest Republican opponent, William Baldwin, by the largest majority ever received by a candidate for state office in the history of Michigan.[47]

Criminal cases posed an ongoing source of potential conflict between Edwards's personal passion for civil liberties and existing law. His tenure on Michigan's Supreme Court came just before the U.S. Supreme Court, under Earl Warren's leadership, was about to embark on its revolutionary efforts to expand the reach of the Bill of Rights in criminal cases. For much of the nation's history, the U.S. Supreme Court had stopped short of saying that the safeguards set out in the Bill of Rights applied to the states. That began to change in the 1920s, when the Court ruled that some rights—such as free speech—were so fundamental that states could not violate them. Still, the high court gave states latitude to deviate from specific federal provisions as long as their laws were consistent with constitutional principles of justice. This hands-off policy was particularly evident in criminal law, which traditionally had been recognized as primarily a state concern. As a practical matter, it meant that states could adopt their own rules about such issues as search and seizure, jury composition, and right to counsel. Still, the Court's rulings created problems as states struggled to apply vague principles to concrete situations.

In some cases, there was no problem; the wrongdoing was so blatant that there was little question of constitutional violation. Edwards found that in the Kafka-esque case of Embre Maddox, an African American, who had been arrested by Detroit police as a "criminal sexual psychopathic person" after he married a white woman. The examining doctor decided Maddox must have committed some sexual offense to have been arrested. He further reasoned that Maddox's refusal to confess wrongdoing provided proof of criminal intent. Maddox was committed to the Ionia State Hospital for the insane on May 11, 1952. When it became clear six months later that he was not insane, hospital

authorities transferred him to the Southern Michigan Penitentiary at Jackson. Embre filed a habeas corpus petition, arguing
that his imprisonment violated his Sixth Amendment rights to a
fair trial. In an opinion ordering his release, Edwards agreed: "In
short, the defendant on this record is shown to be confined in
a penitentiary largely because certain police officers and certain
doctors believe that he was guilty of criminal offenses to which
he has never admitted, and as to which he has been denied a jury
trial. In the event that defendant was actually innocent of the
offenses charged, his right to proper medical treatment would
have been as badly violated by his imprisonment as his constitutional rights."[48]

The U.S. Supreme Court's failure to enunciate clear standards became apparent when Edwards twice wrestled with the
case of Louis Stolz Gonzales. The facts were relatively simple. On
October 18, 1955, state troopers in Flint stopped a car which had
a defective light; they asked the driver and his two passengers,
including Gonzales, to step out of the car. Police found a revolver
and arrested Gonzales for carrying a concealed weapon. Before
his trial, the judge suppressed evidence of the gun, ruling that a
Michigan statute allowing police to search for guns when they
believed they had probable cause violated the Fourth Amendment. In his 1957 opinion, Edwards agreed that the judge's interpretation flew in the face of Supreme Court rulings that held the
Fourth Amendment had only "limited applicability to the states."
He sent the case back for trial. Two years later, after Gonzales
had been convicted, the case came up again on the same argument. In his second opinion, Edwards pointed out the division
that then existed on the U.S. Supreme Court between the majority of justices, who believed in limited applicability of the Bill of
Rights to the states, and the minority, led by William O. Douglas
who believed that U.S. Constitutional protections should be uni-
versally applied. "As interesting as it may be," Edwards said the
minority view "offers no reason for failing to give effect to the
interpretation adopted by the majority of the U.S. Supreme Court
until and unless it is changed."[49]

Although he felt bound by the Supreme Court's majority
rulings, Edwards was far more sympathetic to the minority, as he
indicated in letters to justices Douglas and William J. Brennan.

In June 1959, he praised Douglas's dissent in a search and seizure case, *Frank v. Maryland*. The majority held that Fourth Amendment provisions did not apply to housing or health inspections. Douglas argued that authorities should be required to have warrants in civil as well as criminal cases. In April 1960, while preparing to speak on a television program, Edwards reviewed recent U.S. Supreme Court decisions in criminal cases. That prompted him to reread several Michigan Supreme Court decisions, including Gonzales. He wrote Brennan, "I think that our majority is much closer to your opinion and that of the minority than we are to Mr. Justice Frankfurter and the majority of your Court." He suggested Brennan might like to look at the Michigan cases, adding, "May I close by expressing my admiration for your courage and clarity of thinking in Abel." In the Abel case, Brennan wrote that immigration officers did not have the right to seize forged birth certificates without a warrant.[50]

Edwards publicly endorsed the expansion of civil rights. Early in his tenure on the supreme court, he prodded his colleagues to require the state to pay the costs of transcribing trials for indigent defendants. He suggested that the court invite the American Civil Liberties Committee of the state bar association to join the state attorney general in arguing the matter. In 1960, he wrote an article for *This Week,* a Sunday supplement that appeared in about fifty newspapers across the country, explaining appellate court work. In a letter to Brennan, Edwards explained that he had originally wanted to write a more pointed piece defending U.S. Supreme Court decisions that extended rights to criminal defendants. But, he said, "I quickly found that this I could not get printed. The stated objection was that readers refused to identify themselves with criminals to the extent of accepting the argument that when the Court guaranteed the Constitutional rights of a criminal, it likewise did the same for the average citizen. I am not completely convinced on this score—but then, I don't edit a magazine."[51]

In a 1961 law review article, Edwards vigorously defended constitutional notions of liberty, which he said were based on two assumptions: "first, that every individual should be free because he is a child of God—and second, that a free society should be maintained because it is the most creative system." He added that both beliefs are "denied, despised and challenged by our modern tyrannies, either communist or fascist. Indeed, we cannot rest content with our theory. We must either prove it—or perish." Edwards admitted that "freedom" was sometimes difficult to define, especially when it collided with the concept of "order." Sometimes, he explained, "order became the prerequisite of the maximum of liberty for all" while at other times order was "in direct conflict with individual freedom." Edwards welcomed recent court rulings that leaned more heavily toward liberty than toward order, observing that "it seems clear that the constitution and the Supreme Court of the United States have clearly ruled out of our system such old-fashioned police measures as third-degree procurement of confessions, dragnet arrests without probable cause, and star-chamber evidence without the right of confrontation and cross-examination."[52]

Edwards praised a number of court decisions that angered police. The first and most contentious group of cases centered around the principle that police had no right to search or arrest a defendant without probable cause. Edwards wrote: "Reading some current civil rights debate one could assume that the requirement of probable cause was a recent invention of some liberal-minded court." In reality, he said, "probable cause" was a principle enshrined in the Fourth Amendment to the U.S. Constitution. He cited the 1957 decision of *Mallory v. U.S.,* in which the Supreme Court overturned a rape conviction because police failed to arraign the defendant before a magistrate, instead holding him—without informing him of his rights—until he confessed. The court ruled that such "unwarranted detention led to tempting utilization of intensive interrogation, easily gliding into the evils of the 'third degree.' " Edwards supported other rulings that upheld the Fifth Amendment principle that suspects cannot be compelled to incriminate themselves. One such case was *Spano v. the People of the State of New York* (1959), in which the court ruled that even though "law enforcement officers [have] become more responsible, and the methods used to extract confessions more sophisticated, our duty to enforce Federal constitutional projections does not cease. It only becomes more difficult because of the more delicate judgments to be made." Finally, Edwards addressed a case that would become a pillar of modern criminal trials, *Jencks v. United States.* In 1957, the U.S. Supreme Court reversed the perjury conviction of Clinton Jencks, a New Mexico labor leader, because he had not been allowed to see all of the interviews that FBI agents had conducted with the witnesses who testified against him. The case established the right of defendants to review prosecution documents, thus bolstering the principle that defendants should be fully able to confront their accusers. As Curt Gentry noted, "Nothing frightened the FBI more than the Jencks decision. It did not mean . . . that anyone could go fishing in the FBI's files. But it did mean—and this was equally frightening to Hoover—that possible inconsistent earlier statements . . . would have to be made available if the defense requested them." Although he never publicly denounced the Supreme Court ruling, behind the scenes Hoover successfully lobbied Congress to pass a bill granting the FBI special exemptions to Jencks. It remained in effect for other cases. Edwards conceded that some aspects of the FBI's work warranted special consideration, but he reaffirmed his view that "the Jencks case accurately mirrored the spirit of the Sixth Amendment and the case law of the United States."[53]

Edwards offered advice for police wrestling with the changing law. He suggested that departments should put more emphasis on investigation before rather than after arrests, conduct more thorough investigations to avoid having to rely on confessions, provide more detailed explanations for a search or an arrest than a mere "hunch," increase use of the judiciary to issue warrants, and arrange prompt arraignment of defendants. Such changes would fit in well with U.S. Supreme Court Justice Benjamin Cardozo's concept of "ordered liberty," which Edwards believed to be the best way of balancing the individual's rights with those of society. As Edwards explained, "Because this concept includes order, it can never mean complete individual freedom. Because it includes liberty for the individual, it can never mean perfect order. We pay a price for freedom." He recognized that the result of this balancing act could often be difficult to accept, especially when the guilty were set free. Nevertheless, he added, "It must be remembered that the constitutional tests of the Bill of Rights are almost always made by people charged with or found guilty of crime. It was never written in the constitution that these rights be guaranteed to all except those upon whose conduct we look with dismay. And we must remember, too, that these rights which all of us value will weaken and wither when denied to the weak, the friendless, or the guilty."[54]

Edwards concluded his article by repeating an impassioned defense of liberty that he had first delivered in a February 1961 speech to recruits at the Michigan State Police Training School in East Lansing. In a series of rhetorical questions, he asked:

> What is liberty? It is the right to go to sleep quietly at night; the right to know that there will be no midnight knock when armed men invade your home without authority based on judicial warrants and due process of law.
>
> What is liberty? It is the right to walk the streets or drive our highways knowing that no man's whim can interfere with your freedom of movement and that only a breach of published law cause arrest and incarceration.
>
> What is freedom? It is the right to participate in voting for those who will make our laws. It is the privilege of obeying them, once made, and knowing that they will be equally enforced, and obeyed, by all others.
>
> What then is liberty? It is the right to dream of better things for our children and to know that there is no legal or class barrier to their abilities and their ambitions.
>
> What is freedom? It is the right to look on a police officer, not as an instrument of the state, but as a protector of ourselves, our families and our homes.
>
> What is liberty? It is the privilege of being able to teach our children that the police officer is our friend.[55]

In 1961, the U.S. Supreme Court began resolving the ambiguity of its previous positions by moving towards a much broader application of the Bill of Rights. The change finally came in *Mapp v. Ohio*, a landmark Fourth Amendment case that mandated that federal rules excluding illegally seized evidence be extended to all of the states. The following year, two conservative justices—Felix Frankfurter and Charles Evans Whittaker— retired. Their replacements, Arthur Goldberg and Byron White, sided with other justices who favored nationalizing the Bill of Rights.[56] The resulting changes came too late to affect Edwards's tenure on the Michigan Supreme Court, but they had a profound impact on his role as police commissioner. Police and judges had always played differing roles in the criminal justice system, but the split between them was especially marked during the 1960s. The growing disparity between judicial standards and police practices made the police rank and file especially suspicious and hostile to a judge with Edwards's strong record on civil liberties.

Edwards's support for defendants' rights made him a lightning rod during his early days in office. In large measure, Edwards's reputation as a civil libertarian first drew Cavanagh's attention and ensured his support. Both men believed that effective law enforcement and respect for civil rights were complementary, not mutually exclusive, goals. But, it was exactly those views that alienated many Detroit police officers, who believed they needed special license to deal with criminals. Race further complicated debates about civil liberties in Detroit and other parts of the nation. Theoretically, at least, questions about police powers were racially neutral and centered on the battle between police and criminals. In reality, however, many mostly white police departments during the early 1960s felt they had a mandate to abuse minority defendants. Police shared the belief of many white citizens who saw law enforcement as the last bastion of defense against rising African-American expectations. Their fears of equal justice reflected a view of race relations as a zero sum game in which any advance for African Americans meant a loss for whites. Given Detroit's racially charged atmosphere and the changing complex of civil liberties law, Edwards could not have chosen a more challenging era in which to become police commissioner.

PART II

REFORMING THE FORCE

5

PUTTING ON THE ARMOR OF LIGHT

The night is far spent, the day is at hand: let us therefore cast off the works of darkness and let us put on the armour of light.

—Romans 13:8–12

When Edwards took the helm of the police department on a cloudy January 3, the battle lines of his future command were clearly drawn. On one side, he enjoyed support from the new mayor, civic do-gooders, and the city's African-American leaders. On the other side, he faced staunch opposition from many whites who mistrusted his liberal record on race relations and civil liberties. His greatest opposition came from his own rank and file, many of whom viewed Edwards, at best, as a neophyte and, at worst, as a threat to Detroit law enforcement. From the outset, the department's top command officers tried to undermine his efforts, seizing every opportunity to discredit him. But their early, clumsy attempts at sabotage, which made the job more difficult, only stiffened his resolve. Edwards recognized that his early days in office would be crucial, and he reckoned that if he could survive the first six months, he could last out the rest of his two-year term. He jokingly rated his chances of success at 30 percent.[1]

Edwards looked for inspiration and guidance to a predecessor, Frank D. Eaman, another Democratic lawyer-turned-commissioner who had managed to reform the police department despite entrenched opposition. Eaman, like Edwards, brought

varied political and legal experience to the job. Although he had
served as a prosecutor and president of the Wayne County Bar
Association, Eaman also worked for civil liberties. He helped
found Detroit's Legal Aid Society, served on the state prison committee, and drafted the statutes that created a psychiatric and
probation department at Recorder's Court.[2]

Eaman was a successful corporate attorney in 1939, when a
grand jury indicted hundreds of Detroit and Wayne County officials for taking bribes to protect a $10-million-a-year numbers
racket. The list of wrongdoers eventually included Mayor Richard Reading, Wayne County District Attorney Duncan McCrea,
Detroit Police Superintendent Fred W. Frahm, and eighty police
officers. The scandal led to a prison term for Reading and the
election of Mayor Jeffries. Jeffries appointed Eaman, who fired
Frahm and abolished the jobs of ten ranking officers. He replaced
Frahm with Louis J. Berg, Sr., the only man in the top echelon of
the department untouched by scandal. Eaman explained his efforts in words that Edwards would echo twenty years later in his
fight against organized crime, "I'm not a moralist; I know that
people have gambled, and always will. But I know too that widespread gambling can only go hand-in-hand with police corruption. That is going to be stopped in Detroit. I'm going to drive
the gamblers into the alleys where they can't make enough to buy
policemen." From his own perch within Jeffries's administration
as housing director, Edwards watched with admiration while
Eaman reformed the police department. In 1962, four months
into his own term as commissioner, Edwards told a civic group
that Eaman "was and is one of my personal heroes."[3]

Edwards drew several lessons from Eaman's experience.
First, he learned that an outsider faced an uphill battle in bringing
about change. Second, he recognized that because reform would
face staunch opposition from within the ranks, the key to success
would depend on identifying and removing uncooperative officers from positions of power. Third, he followed Eaman's example by taking the job for only two years. Edwards gave two
reasons for his self-imposed term limit: "I wanted to stay in the
mainstream of the law. I knew I did not have either the experience or training for a lifetime career in police work. . . . Most
persuasive perhaps was the knowledge that what I intended to do

in Detroit for equal law enforcement would prove so controversial that if I attempted to stay longer, the next mayoralty campaign would be fought over my administration of the police department in a political battle which would be very hard to win."[4]

Edwards's varied experiences shaped his agenda. His work as a juvenile judge gave him a strong belief in crime prevention. In December 1961, he told the *Free Press* that "the problem of crime is not merely enforcement." Instead, he argued that racial discrimination, poverty, and inferior housing all fostered crime. Admittedly, police could not address those underlying social problems, but he believed the department could do a better job of cooperating with social agencies and the community to help troubled youths before they became problems for the criminal justice system. His tenure on the Wayne County circuit and state supreme courts also confirmed his view that more thorough investigation and improved community cooperation could ease police work while eliminating many civil liberties violations. Edwards drew on his impressions of a trip he had taken to England two years earlier as a delegate to the United Nations Congress on Crime and Delinquency. "I had been greatly impressed with the politeness of the English bobbies and the almost universal respect and support they were accorded by the English people. There was a marked contrast between what I perceived to be the situation in England and that in the United States, particularly between the black population of Detroit and its police department." Edwards hoped that by encouraging politeness, increasing pay scales, and improving training, he could bring about greater professionalism. That, in turn, would "leave the Detroit Police Department with an increased possibility of avoidance of civil strife and some increase in real citizen support, including in the black community."[5]

While Cavanagh publicly praised his new commissioner and Edwards mapped his strategy, the department's officers worried about their futures. Cavanagh's choice of Edwards "hit the Detroit Police Department like the news of the first atomic bomb," according to Vincent Piersante, then inspector in charge of the Criminal Information Bureau. The *Free Press* confirmed that Edwards's appointment "has aroused more emotion in Detroit Police Headquarters than the total reaction caused by the selection of the department's three previous commissioners." Although some members of the force took a wait-and-see attitude, others, especially veterans who remembered Edwards's arrest in the Yale and Towne strike, opposed him. His liberal decisions on the Michigan Supreme Court also offended many police officers who believed that appointing Edwards was "like putting the fox in charge of the chicken coop." Many predicted that "the day of enforcing the law in Detroit was over and that the days of semi-independence from political control were at an end." One detective told reporters, "I can't understand why he wants the job unless he hopes to shoot at us from close range. He has been sniping away at the department for years."[6]

In the days leading up to Edwards's takeover, panic increased. According to Piersante, John O'Neill, a lieutenant with the vice squad who actively supported Cavanagh during the campaign, "surfaced as the voice of the mayor-elect within the police department. Everybody tried to catch his ear, especially the executives." O'Neill took advantage of the situation. He told Piersante that his support of Miriani would be forgiven if he would write a confidential evaluation of the command and executive staff of the detective division. Piersante feared that such an evaluation would mean career suicide, so he drafted a "careful, conservative evaluation" that contained "hints" of problems if the mayor-elect wanted to follow up with more thorough questions. Rumors were rife. One claimed that Piersante would be demoted from inspector in charge of criminal investigations to a noncommand post at the detective bureau desk. Another speculation was that Walter Wyrod, the chief of detectives, would become the new superintendent, replacing Louis J. Berg and his brother, James, who were going to be forced to retire. As Piersante recalled, "On and on it went to the point it seemed that everyone at the command or executive level was to be affected."[7]

Of all the top executives in the department, James and Louis Berg had the most to fear. When Edwards took over, Louis was superintendent and James was his deputy. As the city's most visible police commanders, they epitomized the department's actions. A contemporary reporter wrote, "Both are six-footers and resemble each other closely in both mannerisms and looks. The two have been marked for promotion ever since they joined the force. Some say because they are able; others say because of their father." Frank Eaman had promoted their father, Louis Sr., to the become superintendent of police in the wake of the Mayor Reading scandal. The two sons had caught the police bug as children hanging around the old Hunt Street Station, when their father was an inspector. Louis Jr. joined the department in 1934, after playing halfback at the University of Detroit and studying law for a year at Northwestern University. Eleven years later, when he was only thirty-four, he became the youngest inspector on the force. James also attended Northwestern University, where he planned to study dentistry. After sustaining a football injury, he dropped out of school and returned to Detroit and took a job as a salesman for Ford Motor Company. In 1943, he, too, joined the force. "The boys," as they became known in the department, rose rapidly through the ranks of the traffic division.[8]

Edwards felt the Bergs' hostility as soon as he reported to police headquarters for work on January 3. The massive, ornate building at 1300 Beaubien had been hailed as the most modern municipal police station in the world when it was built in 1922. It was still intimidating nearly forty years later when Edwards climbed the steps to begin his new job. He arrived at 8:30 A.M. and surprised employees by riding a public elevator to his office rather than taking the private one used by his predecessors. As Edwards recalled years later, his swearing in was "a brief, brusque ceremony, which seemed notable for its chilly atmosphere. Superintendent Berg made the usual presentation to me of the gold badge which went to every Police Commissioner." Edwards then signed the payroll papers to receive his $20,000 annual salary and shook hands with his top assistants. The *Free Press* reported that Edwards "displayed a mixture of sternness and jollity as he greeted his men in an office completely bare of pictures." He agreed to make a brief public statement, but that was delayed while technicians struggled to fix a broken television camera. While the crowd waited, he joked, "This is the time of time saving devices, and here we are waiting." In his brief comments to the media, Edwards said he hoped to study two means of improving Detroit policing—putting more officers on the

129

street and encouraging better cooperation from the public. He concluded by saying he would not make any personnel changes until he had spent "sufficient" time on the job.[9]

The whole enterprise took only forty-five minutes, and by 9:15 Edwards was ready to begin work. After the media left, he issued an address that was carried by loud speakers to the department's thirteen precinct stations and twelve command centers. "I am exceedingly proud to assume this post for this great city which we all love. I know the Detroit Police Department as a fine organization. From ten years in city government and eleven years in the judiciary, I know of its work and its recognition for efficiency and for honesty." Edwards acknowledged his firm commitment to constitutional law enforcement and his appreciation of the difficulties of police work. "To the degree that I can influence the matter you can look forward to more law enforcement and to more vigorous law enforcement. . . . I look forward to our mutual endeavors toward making Detroit the safest big city in the country and toward securing for its Police Department the greatest possible support from all of its people." Acknowledging the rumors that had accompanied his appointment, he advised his officers to ignore all predictions of a shakeup. After his speech, Edwards recalled, "I quickly became engrossed with the enormous paperwork of the department. . . . The mail that flooded in to my desk was quite a bit warmer than had been the swearing-in ceremony." It included many congratulations and invitations to speak.[10]

Probably no other police commissioner in Detroit's history received such accolades from the city's African-American leaders. Arthur Johnson, the executive secretary of the NAACP, who later went on to become a vice chancellor at Wayne State University, remembered "that Edwards's appointment was the equivalent for Detroit's blacks of President Lyndon B. Johnson's later appointment of Thurgood Marshall to the United States Supreme Court." African-American leaders flooded Cavanagh with complimentary letters about Edwards's selection. Robert Battle, president of the Trade Union Leadership Council, telegrammed: "We wish to offer our support and complete confidence in your choice for police commissioner. Justice Edwards is regarded by many people in all walks of life as an outstanding dedicated courageous citizen." The Cotillion Club voted its unanimous approval and pledged "full cooperation for improved community relations." L. M. Quinn, publisher of the *Michigan Chronicle,* promised to write an editorial saying that Cavanagh had made Detroit a better place because of the "stature" of Edwards's appointment. Perhaps the most moving tribute came from Broadus N. Butler, a former Tuskegee airman and assistant to the dean at Wayne State University, who wrote that Edwards had been his role model ever since he began his career working in juvenile court. "I was deeply impressed by your selection. . . . Justice Edwards' personal knowledge, wisdom, and dedication to the basic precepts of our evolving democracy as embodied in the concept of the equal worth and dignity of man has already contributed immeasurably to the amplification of legal democracy in the City of Detroit and the State of Michigan."[11]

Predictably, reaction among whites was more divided. Many civic leaders and business groups welcomed Edwards's appointment. Rev. Robert F. Allen, director of the Catholic Archdiocese's Department of Social Action, told Cavanagh that Edwards will "greatly assist you in the serious problem of Police-Community relations particularly with the Negro citizens of our city." John S. Humphrey of the Detroit Real Estate Brokers Association said: "I have lived in the city of Detroit for 23 years and know something of the record of George Edwards. I believe that no finer selection could have been made." There were also critics, whose views were typified by a letter to the *Detroit News,* from a self-proclaimed Cavanagh supporter now claiming to be a "befuddled voter." He wrote: "Mr. Edwards ran for mayor in our city and was rejected. As soon as he lost that election, he was appointed by Soapy Williams to be a judge. Now our mayor-elect picks him again for a public job, even though the people of Detroit turned him down. . . . Why can't new people be picked for these jobs?"[12]

As Edwards took command of the department, it became increasingly obvious that public support would not translate into a welcome from his officers. So, during his first weeks in office, he moved quickly to win their cooperation. In an attempt to appease his men, Edwards refused to reopen complaints of police abuse that had been filed during Hart's commissionership. In one especially well-publicized episode, Patrolman Abraham Assam shot and wounded William Green on September 18, 1961. Green, paralyzed from the waist down by the shooting, was still a patient at the Veteran's Hospital in Dearborn when Edwards took over the department. The Detroit Chapter of the National Lawyers Guild (NLG), an interracial association of lawyers, decried the police department's and district attorney's failure to discipline Assam as "a distorted approach to law and justice." As soon as Edwards became commissioner, the NLG asked him to investigate the incident. He declined to reopen Green's case and five other claims of brutality that occurred during Hart's administration. As he explained, "I will take responsibility only for those matters occurring since January 3, when I took office."[13]

Edwards embarked on a hectic schedule to meet and talk with as many officers as he could. Herbert M. Boldt, a reporter for the *Detroit News,* likened Edwards to a union organizer scrambling to learn more about the working conditions and concerns of the rank and file. "The new police commissioner has prowled basements of precinct stations, sat hours with police dispatchers, ridden scout cars in many areas and presided over countless meetings in an attempt to learn his job from the bottom up. Whatever he does and wherever he goes Edwards always brings questions. He has an insatiable appetite for knowing the why and the where." Edwards explained, "I don't intend to make any major policy statements, change orders or make personnel changes until I am satisfied I know something about the various jobs in the police department." Boldt recounted a typical day in the life of the new commissioner. It began at 7:30 when Edwards's driver, Patrolman Jack E. Jenson, picked him up at home. They drove to the nearby Palmer Park station, where Edwards shook hands with the men. By 10 A.M., Edwards was sitting at his desk downtown, reading mail and conferring with his executive officers. At noon he attended a Wayne County supervisors meeting; then, he gave a speech to the Detroit Kiwanis. After another meeting at his office, he went to the Vernor station, where he questioned patrolmen about their jobs, conferred with the inspector, and hurried home for a two-hour visit with his wife. That night he attended a PTA meeting at James N. Pepper School in Oak Park and then drove in a scout car for a few hours. He

132

returned home at 11:30 P.M. It was unclear how patrolmen responded to Edwards; Boldt reported only that some were "startled" by the commissioner's impromptu visits and curiosity.[14]

Edwards also took time during his first year to visit other police departments, including those in Washington, D.C., and Philadelphia. He came home impressed with the merits of his force, more determined than ever to build on its strengths, among which he numbered its ambulance squad, delinquency division, and gang-control unit. He believed many of the department's weaknesses could be resolved by improving community-police cooperation, and he began laying the groundwork immediately. The concept of soliciting citizen help to combat crime had become a popular idea by the early 1960s. Edwards had heard his predecessor, Herbert Hart, discuss the subject two years earlier when both men spoke at the Sixth Annual National Institute on Police-Community Relations at Michigan State University. Hart's speech was illustrative of how top members of the Detroit force viewed community relations. Although his speech followed serious discussions of civil rights and policing by Edwards and future Supreme Court Justice Thurgood Marshall, Hart ignored all questions of race in his speech. He blamed misunderstandings on the fact that citizens born in rural areas did not understand big city life. He added, "Those familiar with the situation know, of course, that there are elements who make a policy of discrediting the police. They sometimes make outrageously false accusations—and unfortunately citizens who should know better have been known to give the detractors a helping hand." Even though such misunderstandings were unfounded, Hart argued, they should not exist. His department addressed the problem by sponsoring community meetings, which, he said, produced "rewards greater than anything we had anticipated."[15]

Unlike his predecessor, Edwards believed that race was the primary factor in improving community relations, and his first efforts at reform came in the department's highly visible traffic division. As he recalled, his campaign for politeness was "hardly dramatic." Ever since his days as a city councilman, Edwards received numerous complaints that despite its "enviable record for traffic safety improvement," the division had "a bad reputation in the black community for a demeaning attitude toward blacks." He learned that such problems were still common from an old friend, Dores McCree, whose husband, Wade, served with Edwards on the Wayne County Circuit Court. Dores McCree wrote a letter to Edwards complaining about her treatment from a policeman who gave her a ticket for double parking in front of her daughter's school. McCree was not angered at receiving a ticket, but she became irate when the police officer repeatedly called her by her first name. As Edwards dryly noted, "Mrs. Mc-Cree considered this inappropriate, since the traffic ticket had hardly engendered a personal friendship and the officer was considerably younger than she."[16]

Edwards called in William H. Polkinghorn, a deputy commissioner and director of the traffic division. Edwards assured Polkinghorn that he would not exert political influence on tickets, but he "emphasized that . . . courtesy should apply to everyone and particularly in relation to the disaffected black portion of Detroit's citizenry." Polkinghorn listened and promised that he would tell his men to improve their manners. Edwards was skeptical at first, but within a few weeks he began receiving letters and congratulations from African-American citizens. George W. Crockett, Jr., a lawyer and president of the Cotillion Club, wrote after receiving a ticket for making an illegal left turn. "This is the first letter of appreciation I've ever written concerning a policeman. . . . Patrolman Harry E. Lee performed his duty courteously. My appreciation is extended to him and also to you for this change in attitude which appears to characterize our Police Department under your administration." Edwards remembered another incident: "One enthusiastic black caller, whom I knew, said that he had almost enjoyed the fine which he had to pay, because it was the first time in his life that any police officer had spoken to him with politeness. As the months went by, the Traffic Division became my favorite unit. Their many contacts on the street with black people served to demonstrate that something new had happened at the Detroit Police Department, other than a new commissioner."[17]

Edwards's early success with the traffic division contrasted sharply with the recalcitrance of other sections of the department. Edwards was forced to abandon the management practices he had honed in previous jobs. In other positions, he set broad principles and then let his subordinates figure out how to implement them. He quickly learned that this practice would not work with the police. For example, precinct inspectors dragged their heels when Edwards suggested that they meet with high school principals after "gang fights had resulted in mutual and public recriminations between the high school principals and the precinct inspectors." Two weeks later, when he learned that none of the policemen had followed through, he ordered them to make the visits and provide him with written reports within ten days. "We never had another school complaint about failure of police cooperation or vice versa."[18]

Subtle attempts at sabotage took place behind the scenes. On February 16, the department's leaders launched their first attempt to discredit Edwards publicly in the monthly crime report. Statistics for January seemed to indicate a dramatic growth in crime during Edwards's first month on the job. As he recalled, "Reading them I knew that my welcome to the department was complete. They showed a total 25% increase in crime . . . over January of the preceding year. There had been no unusual weather or public commotion. The department personnel offered no explanation at all. The faces which I searched were professionally impassive. But I felt there had been grins just below the surface." Edwards suspected the figures were false, but he had to accept them until he could discover the truth. Months later he learned that the increase "was accomplished simply by delaying the counting of crimes committed in the last two weeks of December, 1961, and counting them in January 1962."[19]

At the time, however, he was faced with a public relations disaster. His entire program was based on his declaration that racially unbiased policing would not undermine effective crime fighting. To skeptics the statistics proved that his two goals were mutually exclusive. Edwards moved quickly to allay their fears. At his press conference to announce the statistics, he made his first policy announcement: More police would begin working night shifts because more crimes occurred at night. In analyzing statistics for 1961, Edwards discovered that 52.8 percent of the city's most serious crimes had occurred on the four-to-midnight shift, and a disproportionate number of those occurred on Friday and Saturday evenings. Yet, only about a third of the department's patrol officers worked the afternoon and night shifts, and only a small number of those worked weekends. Nevertheless, the sensible reallocation of manpower was drowned out by hysteria over the city's alleged crime wave.[20]

As Edwards was soon to learn, his troubles had just begun. That night, as he addressed an African-American civic organization stressing his new program of equal and constitutional law enforcement, officials within the department planted a story in the *Free Press*. When Edwards picked up a copy of the newspaper on the way home, he was greeted with a banner headline proclaiming: "Police War on Street Crime. Edwards Orders Crackdown." He weighed his options. He initially thought of not responding but then rejected the idea. "I knew exactly what that word 'crackdown' meant to the Detroit Police and to the Detroit Negro community. To let that headline stand without immediate and effective contradiction would be abandonment of my mission in coming back to Detroit before six weeks had passed."[21]

Edwards called Louis Berg and arranged a meeting at 7 A.M. the next day with his top command officers. He also ordered all inspectors to be on duty at 7:30 A.M. with their day shifts. The next morning he issued an address over the loudspeaker system: "Not one extra policeman has been added to the force; not one policeman has been ordered to work special overtime; not one policeman has been detached from duties normal to his precinct or bureau. And most important no one in this department has ordered any crackdown." He emphasized there was nothing in the new crime statistics to "require alarm or to suggest emergency measures. There is certainly nothing to suggest dragnet arrests or arrests without probable cause which are historically associated with the term, 'crackdown.' " For added measure, Edwards sent copies of his address to Mayor Cavanagh, Detroit's nine city council members, seven radio and television stations, and twenty-two civic leaders, including Horace Sheffield, Al Pelham, and Dr. J. J. McClendon.[22]

Edwards suspected that the Berg brothers had manufactured the alarming crime statistics and leaked word of a crackdown. He had no proof, however, and was frustrated by his inability to learn what was going on within his own department. As a civilian appointee, he was isolated from the department's normal channels of communication. Traditionally, all information to the commissioner was funnelled through the superintendent and his chief deputy. So, in the beginning, Edwards was forced to depend heavily on the Bergs. As a result, he "never felt comfortable relying on any report which concerned a matter of real importance." After the "crackdown" controversy, Edwards continued trying to develop his own sources within the department by riding in squad cars and looking for command officers who would support his program. His efforts would take months.[23]

In the meantime, Edwards tried to work with the Bergs. Superficially, at least, their relations were civil.

> In the first couple of months, both Bergs were meticulous in treating their new commissioner with all formal courtesy. It was as if they were willing for me to be the typical commissioner—the figurehead of command—appearing at the multitudinous functions and public occasions involving the police. However, they did so, I felt, with an unstated proviso—so long as you let us run the department as it has always been run. The trouble was I had taken the job for the sole purpose of making major changes in both policy and performance. That was the rub.[24]

Edwards took the altered crime statistics and crackdown story as a warning. He acted quickly to show he would not be intimidated. On February 19, he gave a speech at the People's Community Church. He told the African-American congregation: "I come to you just one day after warning my own men against dragnet arrests or arrests without probable cause." He criticized those who "think it is impossible to be a police commissioner and hold the belief in brotherhood and the Constitution." On the contrary, he said, "This can be done. It is simple, desirable and necessary." Edwards provided a brief summary of landmark civil rights rulings and described the "joy" he had always felt while working to end the "fatal contradiction" that existed between constitutional guarantees and the realities of segregation. He read from his favorite Biblical passage, Romans 13:8–12: "Owe no man anything, but to love one another: for he that loveth another hath fulfilled the law. . . . it is high time to awake out of sleep: for now is our salvation nearer than we believed. The night is far spent, the day is at hand: let us therefore cast off the works of darkness, and let us put on the armour of light." He concluded by exhorting his audience: "Let us make this a shining city."[25]

Although African Americans responded to Edwards's program enthusiastically, many of the city's white citizens reacted quickly and negatively to reports of increased crime. Typical was a letter from one correspondent who expressed fear and outrage at the city's "100% increase in crime." She wrote Cavanagh: "When Police Commissioner Edwards took office you boasted that he was a 'liberal' and would be very 'nice' to the Negro population." By contrast, she said, former Commissioner Hart "knew from bitter experience that he had to be firm, indeed, with Detroit's colored population. You just can't afford to be too nice to them, for the minute you are, they take advantage of your friendship and consequently the crime rate shoots up again." As soon as Cavanagh appointed Edwards, she said, a lot of citizens became alarmed. "For we knew his past record. We remembered he was for labor, the underdog and all minority groups. It doesn't pay to be friendly with that type, for they are the very ones causing all the crime today."[26]

Although Edwards and his top command officers were on a collision course, they found common ground in the need for more police and larger salaries. To the Bergs, pay raises were the axiomatic rewards for a job well done. To Edwards, better pay was the first step towards increasing professionalism. The salary scale for Detroit's police lagged behind those in other major U.S. cities, and Edwards argued that an increase would help boost morale. Thus, during his first days in office the new commissioner devoted most of his time to drafting budget requests. When Edwards took over, the department employed 4,302 officers, 431 civilian employees, 134 school crossing guards, and had a total budget of $30.7 million. Along with pay increases, Edwards sought the hiring of 260 more police, and extra money to pay police who worked night and weekend shifts. In an address over the department's loudspeaker on January 26, Edwards said, "I consider this program both desirable and essential to the department and ultimately to the well-being and public safety of the people of the city of Detroit." Detective Donald Livernois, president of the Detroit Police Officers Association, praised Edwards for going "farther than any other commissioner on our behalf."

But, he complained that even with the proposed pay increases, Detroit would still lag behind other cities.[27]

Edwards campaigned hard for his budget requests in speeches to women's groups, churches, civic groups, and African-American associations. He proved persuasive. Many groups endorsed his demands. Al Barbour, president of the Wayne County AFL–CIO, wrote Cavanagh, urging him to approve Edwards's requests. The Cotillion Club and the NAACP also supported Edwards. It was the first time that either African-American organization endorsed a police department budget. In a letter to Cavanagh, NAACP President Edward M. Turner explained that the NAACP's vote was "a gesture of its confidence in the distinguished and respected citizens who now have the awesome responsibility of leading the Police Department and of rebuilding community confidence and support of its essential work. . . . Please note that you have the continued good wishes of our Association in your good efforts to make Detroit a better place to live for all our citizens."[28]

Edwards's budget fit in with Cavanagh's agenda to improve city services despite dramatic revenue losses. Cavanagh had inherited a $34.5 million deficit, which he attributed to growing suburbanization. To raise more money, Cavanagh won passage of a 1 percent income tax on all those who worked in the city. The proposal drew immediate ire from suburban politicians, including Mayor George W. Kuhn of Berkeley, who said: "I believe there is one thing we can all agree upon, Mr. Cavanagh, and that is—it is very easy to spend the other person's money—and to me, there is no end to this kind of business." Kuhn suggested that instead of taxing suburbanites who worked in the city, Detroit should limit fiscal spending. For example, he said, there was no reason to hire two hundred more police when the city's population was decreasing.[29]

Although Edwards did not get all he sought, the Common Council was more generous than many skeptics predicted. The department received funding for 160 new officers and money to provide premium pay for afternoon and night shifts. Edwards eased the way for council to approve his requests by offering to spend money more efficiently than his predecessors. He told one civic group what he had told the council, "I don't want to suggest to you, who have great interests as citizens and taxpayers in this community, that the only answer to crime is to spend money. This I do not think is true at all. . . . One of the things we need to do in the Police Department is to make sure that we are making the best use of our available manpower at every hour of the night and day, 24 hours a day, 7 days a week, and I doubt that we have succeeded in doing that, up to and including this present moment."[30]

Edwards explained how he reassigned more officers to work during peak crime periods. He said part of the department's budget increases would go to provide premium pay to those officers now working the less desirable shifts. The commissioner also promised to hire civilians to do mundane work so that he could transfer trained officers to more important jobs. For example, the council approved funding for one hundred police cadets to take over the parking-ticket detail. Lastly, Edwards argued that improving community relations would ultimately bear fiscal benefits. If more citizens came forward to help police, investigative costs would decrease.[31]

Although they worked together for the budget, Edwards and his executive staff parted company when it came to more serious changes. One simmering controversy stemmed from the department's failure to recruit and hire minority police officers. African Americans applied to the force in roughly the same proportion as their numbers in the city's population or about 28 percent. Yet, out of the department's approximately 4,300 officers, only 3 percent, or 136, were black. African Americans who were hired faced even greater obstacles to promotion. At the time of Edwards's appointment, no black had ever achieved the rank of inspector. No part of Detroit city government had an admirable record on minority hiring, but the police department's record was more dismal than most. Its exemption from normal civil service procedures exacerbated the problem. In most city agencies, promotion was 70 percent based on such concrete measures as written tests and seniority, while only 30 percent was based on subjective scoring of service ratings and oral interviews. By contrast, the police department used subjective ratings for 50 percent of a candidate's ranking, which made it easier to inject prejudice into the process.[32]

140

The department's discriminatory personnel policies were a festering sore for Detroit's African-American community. Three studies conducted in the three years before Edwards took office detailed the existence of problems. Detroit's Urban League and the Citizens Advisory Committee on Police Procedures had conducted the first two investigations. When nothing came of their suggested reforms, the Baptist Ministers Alliance complained to the Common Council on May 26, 1960. After a preliminary investigation by councilmen Ed Carey, William T. Patrick, Jr., and William G. Rogell, on November 30, 1960, the Common Council ordered the city's Commission on Community Relations to conduct an in-depth study. Using statistics for 1959, the last year for which complete numbers were available at the time of the study, the commission found widespread discrimination. Although 434 blacks had applied, only two were hired. The study found that at each stage of the hiring process, the preliminary interview, the written tests, the physical examinations, and the oral interviews, "the percentage of white applicants increased and the percentage of blacks decreased."[33]

Commission Director Richard Marks concluded that physical and medical standards were more rigorously applied to blacks. Written tests, which on their face were racially neutral, also discriminated against blacks. The few African Americans who passed through to the oral interviews often found themselves declared unfit for the vaguest of reasons. Some included the candidates' alleged immaturity, insincerity, and backgrounds. Marks said it was clear that the examination board's definition of "immaturity" varied greatly among the candidates.[34]

Marks suggested a variety of remedies. He advised the police commissioner to set specific eligibility standards and then require that they be applied equally. He urged increased recruiting of African Americans by, among other things, implementing an education program to show positive aspects of police careers. If the department continued to use oral interviews, Marks urged that all the reasons for disqualification be specified and consistently applied. He said that "nothing is more destructive to an objective personnel selection system than the inconsistent application of criteria during the oral interview, or disqualifications based on ambiguous, overlapping, and general appraisals." Fi-

141

nally, Marks offered the services of the Commission on Community Relations to monitor hiring and promotion within the department.[35]

Robert A. Lothian, the department's personnel examiner, angrily condemned Marks's conclusions. "In analyzing this report it has been difficult to refrain from expressing extreme resentment of the author's unsubstantiated derogatory criticisms of our recruiting system." In his telling apologia, Lothian revealed much about the department's ingrained discrimination. For example, he acknowledged that 51 percent of whites passed the written exams compared to only 19 percent of blacks. He maintained the discrepancy was not a matter of discrimination. Instead, he argued, it showed "that the better class of young Negroes are not applying for police service." He rejected Marks's recommendations, claiming the department already followed some and the rest were vague. Lothian concluded that Marks's report and its two predecessors "have probably done immeasurable harm by creating in the minds of qualified young Negroes the image that 'the cards are stacked against them' before they ever make application." He said the department sincerely wanted to hire more minorities, but its efforts had been stymied by African-American leaders who did not work hard enough to encourage qualified young people to pursue police careers.[36]

Edwards forwarded Marks's report and Lothian's response to Cavanagh. The mayor's assistant, Joseph B. Sullivan, summed up the controversy: "The essence of the problem would seem to be that the caliber of Negro applicants is exceedingly low. According to many persons, the reason for this, as you know, is the absence of promotional opportunity." He added that two black officers had told him that the police force needed more African Americans. "Why not then quietly promote applications from desirable men to the force through Negro leaders." To Edwards, Sullivan wrote that a black should be appointed to the police academy to screen black applicants and that more African Americans should be promoted. Edwards received the report two weeks after becoming commissioner, but he delayed publicly releasing it in order to give the Commission on Community Relations and police staffers time to reach a consensus.[37]

On February 19, Mayor Cavanagh appointed six new members to the community relations commission and asked that it hold its next meeting as quickly as possible so that it could analyze and discuss Marks's report. When the commission met a week later, Edwards sent a letter saying he had reviewed Marks's recommendations and Lothian's rebuttal. Edwards again tried to find a middle ground by not criticizing his men publicly. "For myself and for the present administration of the Police Department I am much more interested in the present and in the future than in analyzing the practices of the past with which this report deals."[38]

When it became apparent that Marks and the police department personnel had not been able to reach any agreement, Edwards released the commission's report. The *Detroit News* said Edwards agreed with all of Marks's recommendations except one. He did not favor the Commission on Community Relations serving as monitor for improved personnel policies. "These matters are a . . . responsibility of the Police Commissioner and unless I determine that I need some help on this I cannot confer that responsibility on the Commission." Edwards told both the commission and the newspaper that "the most important single statistic in this study . . . reveals that we have 136 Negro police officers out of a department of approximately 4,300." He said he would cooperate fully with the commission to improve that number.[39]

Discriminatory employment practices were not limited to the police department; they were endemic within city government. On February 22, Cavanagh addressed the overall problem in his first executive order, which said: "City employees shall be recruited, appointed, trained, assigned and promoted without regard to race, color, religion, national origin of ancestry. . . . All municipal departments and commissioners shall follow a clear, definitive policy of nondiscrimination in employment, personnel practices and procedures, and correct any which may contribute to the possibility of discrimination." To ensure that city bureaucrats followed the directive, Cavanagh required that their annual reports include descriptions of their efforts to improve personnel procedures.[40]

That same day, Cavanagh publicly explained the reasons for his order in a speech to the Coordinating Council on Human

Relations. Government, he explained, "has an affirmative duty . . . to promote the human conditions that will make equality possible. . . . We must work together as individuals, as members of groups or in our business and governmental actions to make the dream of Detroit—equality in its broadest sense—a living reality. The revolution of rising expectations starts at home, at business, in our every day contacts and finally with our children who will inherit happier community relations than you and I have witnessed during our lives."[41]

Edwards shared Cavanagh's belief in fair hiring practices, and he ordered the police department's personnel office to find better ways of recruiting and testing African-American applicants. In late March, Edwards appeared before the commission and vowed to increase recruitment of blacks. His promise won immediate praise from the *Michigan Chronicle,* which noted that Detroit lagged behind Chicago and New York in African-American police recruiting and promotion. In the past, the paper said, African Americans had to have far better credentials than whites to advance within the department. Although its numbers were off, the editorial's point was clear: "We used to speculate that the number of college degrees among the 100 or so Negro officers probably exceeded in ratio, if not also in number, the college degree held by the 3,000 white officers."[42]

Dr. Broadus Butler cited one example—the case of a black detective who was repeatedly passed over for promotion despite the fact that he had twenty-four merit citations and received scores as high as 96 percent on three written exams. Butler recalled how "it became an open secret among his fellow white officers that if anyone wanted to be promoted he had to score higher than this officer because the cut-off point was just above his name." Finally, the man made lieutenant, and friendly white officers kidded him that they were glad he had finally been promoted because it would now be easier for them. Even with higher rank, however, the man's job never changed. He "kept the same partner and the same job; he was never given a new job commensurate with his rank; he was put under the command of lieutenants with less seniority." Butler predicted that with Edwards on the scene there was real hope for change.[43]

By early April, some reforms were in place. Lothian reported that the personnel office had implemented a new program which included, among other things, the setting of a minimum rather than a fluctuating passing score for written tests. He said his office had developed a standard form for other kinds of examinations that would help promote uniformity. In addition, Lothian's office printed and sent out four thousand recruiting posters to precinct commanders for public distribution. Edwards would continue to advocate fair hiring practices during the rest of his tenure, but change came slowly.[44]

In mid-May, Edwards announced the largest number of promotions since he had taken office. He signalled his intention to institute nondiscriminatory personnel procedures by promoting George W. Harge to lieutenant and transferring him from the vice squad to the department's Community Relations Bureau. As the *Detroit News* noted, "for the first time in a number of years, Detroit has a Negro police lieutenant." Only two other African Americans had ever achieved a lieutenant's rank, but both had retired.[45]

Harge's career in the department illustrated the difficulties and complexities that would mark future debates about affirmative action. Discriminatory and subjective evaluations made it appear that Harge was less qualified than his white counterparts. As the *Detroit News* noted, he had ranked only sixty-fourth out of eighty-seven uniform sergeants eligible for promotion. In reality, Harge, like most African-American police officers of that era, was far better qualified than most white officers. In the wake of the 1943 riots, Detroit's Urban League issued a call for African Americans to apply to the police department. Harge accepted the challenge, but the examiner rejected him for a medical problem that did not exist. Two weeks later he enlisted in the Army Air Corps and, at the end of his three-year stint, achieved a lieutenant's rank. Even so, when he replied for a police job, the department again rejected his application for medical reasons. Under pressure from African-American leaders and Police Commissioner John Ballenger, the department reexamined Harge. This time he passed the test and on January 2, 1946, became one of only 35 blacks on the 2,400-man force. He began attending night classes at Wayne State University. Seven years into his career, he scored fifteenth out of 850 men competing for sergeant's rank.

After Edwards elevated him to lieutenant, Harge's career soared. In 1969, he became the first African American ever to reach the top command level of the department. When he retired in January 1972 as director of the Inspectional Services Bureau, which oversaw internal and organized crime investigations, he was the fifth ranking member of the department. Four years later, he took over security for the Detroit Public Schools.[46]

Edwards's goal for the first year was to maintain vigorous law enforcement while implementing reforms geared towards racial justice. During his first six weeks in office, he pondered how best to promote his agenda in a way that would signal real change to African Americans without alarming Detroit's white citizens. On February 13, at a meeting of the department's top officers, Edwards presented his "3-Point Police Program," which called for more vigorous law enforcement, fair policing, and greater public cooperation. Edwards believed his proposals would be uncontroversial, but he still wanted input before making them public. He miscalculated. Many command officers perceived Edwards's program as a threat, and the Bergs vehemently objected when Edwards ordered that a proclamation, summarizing the three points, be posted in every precinct. The statement read:

> The police Department of the City of Detroit seeks more law enforcement and more vigorous law enforcement.
>
> Secondly, it seeks equal protection of the law for all law-abiding citizens and equal enforcement of the law against all violators.
>
> And third it seeks the cooperation of all law abiding citizens in the city, in our efforts on behalf of law enforcement.

The Berg brothers argued that the proclamation should not be displayed where it was visible to the public. Edwards, however, stood his ground. As he recalled later, "After some discussion, I just ordered it done."[47]

In early March, he publicly unveiled his plan in a speech to more than two hundred businessmen, teachers, parents, and clergymen in the largely black 10th Precinct. Edwards promised to visit the city's other twelve precincts during the month to discuss his agenda and garner public comment. Edwards tried to downplay the racial aspects of his plan by arguing that it was little more than a return to the concept of community policing.

As he told the federal bar association in late March, he envisioned a return, in spirit at least, to the days before cars, when police were closer to the neighborhoods and citizens they patrolled.[48] Two days later, the department's high command launched its boldest move yet to undermine Edwards's program of racial justice. It came, not surprisingly, in a police brutality case. The Bergs and other officials assumed they could push through a cover-up. Edwards's bold refusal to go along set the stage for the showdown that would present the first crisis of his administration.

6

BRIDGING A RIVER OF HATRED

I feel that there is a river of hate running through a city which I love.
I feel that I have been asked to come down to that city to seek to
build some bridges over that river. . . . I'm going to try to build those
bridges.

—George Edwards, Jr., December 1961

E dwards's major objective for the police department during
his first year in office was "to end dangerous racial tension
while maintaining effective law enforcement." He harbored no
illusions about how difficult it would be to overcome decades of
hostilities. Historically, many whites, including members of the
police department, viewed the city's African Americans as violent, crime-prone menaces to be controlled at any cost. The racial
divide became apparent in discussions of Detroit's crime statistics. Although blacks made up only 29 percent of the city's population, they totalled 65 percent of all criminal defendants.[1] To
African-American leaders and white liberals the disparity indicated that police disproportionately targeted blacks. To many
whites the statistics proved their assumption that blacks committed most of the city's crimes.

During the 1920s and 1930s, when large numbers of blacks
began migrating to the city, Detroit police officials recruited
southern whites for the department. They reasoned that South-
erners would have a better understanding of the "problem" than
Northerners. Many of the white recruits were members of the Ku
Klux Klan. During the 1943 riots, some of those same southern-
born police officers stood by as white mobs randomly attacked

African Americans. In the riot's aftermath, police unjustly blamed blacks for all of the trouble. As the *Michigan Chronicle* noted, official reports of the riots ignored "the existence of the Ku Klux Klan, the National Workers League and a score of other fascist and Nazi organizations which are known to have operated extensively in this area . . . in the daily dissemination of the vilest of anti-Negro propaganda." Blaming blacks for the riots was, according to the newspaper, equivalent to Hitler's claims that the Jews had brought on their own abuse.[2]

Mayor Jeffries established a permanent race relations commission in January 1944 to succeed a temporary interracial peace committee of twelve people that he had appointed several days after the riot. The commission's report, which showed widespread disaffection with the police, prompted the Common Council to require inclusion of information about race relations during police cadet training. That early, feeble attempt to instill racial sensitivity was ineffective, and tensions continued to increase. In 1952, Arthur Kornhauser, a professor at Wayne State University, conducted a study that documented the ongoing problem. His survey verified that many of the city's African Americans brought a deep suspicion of law enforcement with them from the South. Their experiences in Detroit did little to alleviate their mistrust.[3]

Eight years later, on December 15, 1960, the NAACP highlighted continuing police brutality in Detroit when its executive secretary, Arthur L. Johnson, described the problem in a statement for the U.S. Commission on Civil Rights. In a city that provided "an impressive case study of the hard core existence of the racial discrimination problem in the North," Johnson said police brutality "by its very nature is perhaps the most openly oppressive form of racial injustice [that] Negroes suffer here." In the previous four years, African Americans had filed 149 formal complaints against the police with the NAACP. In one especially egregious 1957 case, a woman driving on East Jefferson was stopped for no reason by three police officers. One asked to see her license, then asked if she owned the car, and then struck her in the face while the other two officers restrained her. They drove her to the station, where the desk sergeant told them to take her to the hospital. After receiving stitches and a shot of painkiller, police dragged the woman to jail. The bogus charges of drinking and reckless driving were suspended the following day, and she was released.[4]

In another incident, a black couple leaving a bar were accosted by four white men who yelled at the woman: "Hey baby do you want some business?" Her date asked the men why they were bothering his girlfriend. "What do you mean?" they responded. "That nigger bitch going along there." Then they attacked him. When he fought back, one said: "You don't know who you're messing with—we're police officers." Another handcuffed him and shoved him into the back of an unmarked car between the two other policemen, who called him a "nigger" and a "monkey" as they beat him. After they arrived at the jail, they continued to strike him, and one said: "We'll give you something to tell the NAACP." The man was charged with soliciting but was later found not guilty.[5]

Two other groups had studied police practices in Detroit during the late 1950s. On August 12, 1958, Mayor Miriani appointed a Citizens' Advisory Committee on Police Procedures to investigate charges of brutality levelled by the NAACP. Johnson said the committee's report, issued on March 22, 1960, "whitewashed the wrong-doing of police officers. . . . In its evasive and indirect approach, however, the Committee did recognize that 'one of the major problem areas yet remaining in police-community relations involves complaints of police mistreatment.' " The report suggested that if the police department could not process charges more effectively, then the mayor should establish an independent citizen review board.[6]

In 1958, the Detroit Bar Association conducted its own study of police practices. The most alarming statistic in its report showed that out of 67,301 arrests in 1956, 26,696 were made without warrants. Investigators looked at 103 charges of police brutality between January 1956 and July 1957. In most complaints, the victims said police assaulted them, insulted them with racial epithets, and indiscriminately searched their wallets and pockets. When citizens questioned the violations of their civil liberties, police responded by beating and arresting them. Police insisted that the illegal arrests were necessary to control crime. Given the department's lack of money and manpower, police had no choice but to arrest suspects first, then find the evidence against them later. "The follow-up of clues, the shadowing of suspects, etc., are methods appropriate to television drama, but the entire police force would be quickly bogged down if these methods were pursued in every case brought to police attention." Finally, the police claimed that arrests formed a legitimate means of harassing illegal enterprises in cases where it would be impossible or time-consuming to prosecute. The bar association's report rejected such logic, pointing out that unreasonable searches were unconstitutional, engendered disrespect for the law, and bred mistrust—especially among African Americans. As Johnson noted, "While the Bar condemned these practices with unrestrained vigor, it expressed the view that a determination to correct the problem did not exist in the Police Department."[7]

In March 1960, the Presbytery of Detroit endorsed the NAACP's request for a permanent citizens' review board. It was the only white civic or religious group to take a stand against police brutality. Even Detroit's three daily newspapers denied there was a problem. Still, Johnson insisted, there could be no meaningful improvement in Detroit's charged racial climate unless police brutality was stopped. "For only in this way can healthier attitudes ensue, and fulfillment of the democratic ideal be more nearly realized in practice. The challenge here is one for the whole community."[8]

In addition to the citizen board, Johnson urged changes in police personnel procedures to ensure that more blacks were hired and promoted. He also suggested that the department provide white officers with better training, including more extensive instruction in human relations. Finally, he said, "The major leadership of the community from the mayor on down should speak more often, forcibly, and clearer in support of democratic practice and the great need to eliminate the problem of police brutality and all other forms of police mistreatment of Negro citizens."[9]

The *Free Press* spoke for many white citizens when it dismissed Johnson and the NAACP as unrepresentative trouble makers. The newspaper contended there was no evidence of a problem that merited permanent citizen oversight of the police. Its editors wrote: "Considering that a representative citizen committee appointed by the Mayor concluded about a year ago that

Detroit's Police Department is one of the finest in the country, the conclusion at this time, must be that those persons doing the talking for a few organizations either do not choose to follow established methods in the lodging of complaints or have no real evidence upon which to base their actions."[10]

Reaction from the police department was also swift and negative. Commissioner Hart complained, "I think it unfair for the NAACP to make allegations completely unfounded and to by-pass this department on charges against our policemen." Superintendent Berg gave a more extended criticism of the NAACP report in *TUEBOR,* the police officers' newsletter. He said creation of a police review board would "restrain the Police Officer in his effort to provide the law enforcement that the community must have."[11]

On May 17, 1961, Mayor Miriani announced a compromise that did not appease either side. He created a community relations bureau within the department rather than an external citizen review committee. Commissioner Hart explained that while the new bureau would review cases, it would have no investigative powers. The NAACP, and later Edwards, criticized the bureau as mere window-dressing.[12]

Although Detroit's politicians and newspapers dismissed Johnson's critique, his remarks impressed the U.S. Civil Rights Commission. In November 1961, the commission issued a report on the administration of justice that was based on evidence it had gathered from Johnson and other African-American leaders across the nation. The report stated: "Police brutality by some state and local officers presents a serious and continuing problem in many parts of the United States. . . . Negroes are the victims of such brutality far more, proportionately, than any other group." The report attributed the problem of police brutality to the poor caliber of local police and the inadequate training they received. It urged the federal government to help local authorities recruit and train better candidates. The commission also proposed more sweeping changes that, among other things, would have made local officials legally liable for police misconduct. In March 1962, Attorney General Robert F. Kennedy asked Congress to toughen federal statutes against police brutality by adding a section to existing civil rights laws that would prohibit beatings or attempted beatings to extort a confession or deliver "summary punishment."[13]

The commission's report sparked immediate criticism from veteran police chiefs across the nation. Along with the old-guard members of Detroit's Police Department, they saw African-American complaints as unfounded and viewed court-imposed restrictions as a hindrance to effective policing. One of the most vocal proponents of this view was Los Angeles Police Chief William H. Parker, who would later become a target of Edwards's derision. In a city known for racial turmoil, Parker denied the existence of any racial problems beyond what he believed was the unfounded "resentment of some minority groups." He criticized the commission's report, which he claimed was based on two "factors that militate against the public understanding of the police." The first stemmed from minority efforts to distract attention from the high incidence of crime in their communities by unfairly criticizing law enforcement. The second lay with media stories "magnifying police failures and . . . minimizing their successes and accomplishments." He disparaged recent Supreme Court rulings, saying "that in the guise of restricting the authority of the police such decisions actually amount to a lifting of moral restraints." Eventually, Congress ignored the criticisms of Parker and others by incorporating the commission's recommendations into the Civil Rights Act of 1964, but that did little to help Edwards in the interim.[14]

Edwards shared Johnson's views about the necessity of eliminating police brutality in Detroit. He got his chance to rein in the department's excesses during his first few months on the job. The situation arose, innocuously enough, from a dispute over a $20 debt. The trouble began on January 28, 1962, a quiet Sunday morning, when Permetta Jones called police to report that Willie Daniels had threatened her with a gun. She owed Daniels $20, and he had gone to her apartment at 1440 Webb to collect. Daniels denied having a gun, but he admitted going to see Jones. He said the two fought, and he left after she hit him over the head with a lamp. He returned to his house on Leicester Street and was putting up panelling in the basement when the police arrived. Mrs. Daniels told the four policemen that her hus-

153

band was not at home, but they insisted on searching anyway. They found Daniels hiding in the basement coal bin.

Officer John M. Organ came downstairs with his gun drawn, located Daniels, and handcuffed him. The three other officers came to the basement and began searching for a gun. When they failed to find a weapon, Daniels said, the policemen grabbed him, knocked him to the floor, and kicked him. They arrested him and took him to the Woodward Precinct Station. He was released the next day when Jones refused to press charges. She claimed that she had only called police so they would keep Daniels away from her; she never sought his arrest. After he regained his freedom, Daniels visited Dr. Elias L. Dickson, who treated his legs for bruises and abrasions. Dr. Dickson also noticed that Daniels's wrists and stomach were swollen.[15]

Edwards learned of the incident two days after it happened from an African-American acquaintance, who said five policemen brutally beat Daniels in his basement, and a doctor would verify the extent of the injuries. Daniels hired an attorney to sue the City of Detroit, the Police Department, and the five patrolmen who participated in the attack. Edwards assured his friend that the department would conduct a prompt and careful investigation. Reasoning that he should stay impartial in case the matter came to a trial board, Edwards asked James Berg to conduct the department's internal investigation.[16]

After Berg found that there were grounds for a trial board, Edwards convened one. Trial boards constituted the department's strongest tool for dealing with police misconduct. All cases began with an internal investigation. These were normally conducted at the precinct level, and reports were then forwarded to the higher levels of the department for final disposition. The accused police officers could be mildly disciplined, exonerated, or, in the most serious cases, cited before the department's trial board. The trial board operated as a civil court, with the city corporation counsel acting as prosecutor. The board consisted of the commissioner and two other high-ranking department officials. The accused police officer could hire his own attorney and had the right to subpoena and cross-examine witnesses. The media could attend the hearing, but the judges deliberated in private before making their decision public.[17]

Although the machinery for handling brutality complaints against police existed when Edwards took over, his predecessors had not convened a trial board since 1957. This had been an ongoing source of tension with Detroit's African-American community. The NAACP filed numerous brutality complaints in the previous six years, yet the department had not adequately processed any of them. This stemmed from a loophole in the city's charter. Although both the charter and the police department set guidelines for processing citizen grievances, the commissioner enjoyed broad powers to establish rules and regulations. Edwards's immediate predecessors never gave any impetus to the departmental guidelines. His decision to hold a trial board in the Daniels case won immediate plaudits from the black community and triggered apprehension within the department.[18]

The trial board met on March 15. It consisted of Edwards, Louis Berg, and Chief of Detectives Walter Wyrod. Edward Welch, a senior attorney in the city corporate counsel's office, served as prosecutor. Daniels's complaint originally named four officers—Organ, 25; William L. Weis, 32; Robert J. Anderson, 39; and Rudy Y. Roodbeen, 22. Before the hearing, charges against Roodbeen were dropped for lack of evidence. The first witness was Daniels's physician, Dr. Dickson. In a restrained, professional manner, Dickson described Daniels's wounds, which consisted of a cut to his lip and severe bruises on his wrists and abdomen. As Edwards recalled, "Such cross-examination as there was did nothing to shake his testimony. The net effect of it . . . was to establish that sometime, somewhere, something untoward had happened to Willie Daniels."[19]

Daniels appeared next and recounted his mistreatment. After police tightly handcuffed his hands behind his back, the senior policeman at the scene, Anderson, demanded to know where the gun was. When Daniels said there was no gun, Anderson punched him in the stomach. Anderson repeated the question ten more times. Each time Daniels gave the same answer; each time Anderson hit him again. Another policeman then picked up a saw, held it to Daniels's neck, and said, "Now Willie, where's the gun?" When Daniels again insisted that he had no gun, the policeman dropped the saw and picked up a baseball bat which he pushed between Daniels's handcuffed wrists and back.

The policeman rocked Daniels back and forth so that the handcuffs dug into his wrists. The rocking motion propelled Daniels to the floor, where he cut his lip. The police then took him to a waiting scout car. As they drove to the 2nd Precinct Station, another scout car drove up alongside, and a policeman yelled to the officer seated next to Daniels, "Willie looks sleepy, why don't you wake him up with your slap jack?" When the officer said he did not have a slapjack, the driver of the scout car threw him one. The police officer next to Daniels never used it. Mrs. Daniels substantiated her husband's story. After police went into the basement, she heard noises and her husband's cries. When she tried to go to his aid, police posted on the first floor prevented her from going downstairs.[20]

At the trial board, four officers, including Weis and Organ, testified that no beating took place. Patrolman Anderson invoked his Fifth Amendment right against self-incrimination. His decision not to testify created a minor controversy within the department. As Edwards later noted, the U.S. Supreme Court had not yet decided whether the Fifth Amendment applied to such quasi-judicial proceedings as police trial boards. That meant Edwards could have ordered Anderson to testify or face losing his job. It was not surprising that Edwards, the civil libertarian, refused to issue such an order.[21]

There was a numbing redundancy to the stories told by the four police who did appear. Edwards recalled, "It was detailed and definite as to everything which happened up to the point when Daniels was dragged out of his hiding place and handcuffed." Each officer confirmed that Daniels repeatedly denied having a gun, but none seemed able to recollect what else happened. They were all asked if they had beaten Daniels or had seen anyone else hit him in the stomach or threaten him with a saw or baseball bat. As Edwards noted, "Each of the four officers denied emphatically that they struck or injured Daniels in any way. But, significantly, every time the question was asked as to whether they saw anyone strike Daniels, the answer was always phrased in terms of failure to see or failure to recall."[22]

Edwards was appalled by the city attorney's performance. As he recalled years later, "A trial as most lawyers and judges understand it is a forum for finding truth, and the tool is cross-examination." Welch, who nominally was supposed to serve as prosecutor, asked few questions despite glaring inconsistencies in the policemen's testimony. For example, Welch failed to explore Daniels's motive for hiding in his basement. After all, as Edwards sarcastically noted, "The officers testified they had found him in a coal bin, hardly the place that most householders choose as a Sunday morning resting place." Admittedly, Daniels's motive for hiding was not directly relevant to the brutality charges, but it did provide further proof that blacks routinely feared police abuse in Detroit. In any case, by the time Welch finished his questioning, Edwards had "developed considerable professional contempt" for his performance.[23]

When Edwards first learned of the Daniels case, he decided to let the police department machinery "proceed according to its normal form and pace." But after seeing police officers lie and witnessing Welch's lackluster questioning, Edwards realized he had been wrong. He began to cross-examine the witnesses. As he recalled, "Any lawyer knows that shaking your finger at a witness and asking the critical question which he has already answered is going to produce nothing except a stronger reaffirmation of the former answer, all television detective stories to the contrary notwithstanding." So, Edwards took a different tack by asking one of the policemen for more details about the "flying slapjack." When the officer said he could not remember if the driver had thrown him the slapjack, Edwards honed in: "Officer, isn't it true that the answer to that question might be yes or it might be no, but it couldn't possibly be that you don't remember?" The officer conceded, "Well, if you put the matter that way, then the answer has got to be 'No.'" Edwards had made his point, and the hearing ended.[24]

As Berg, Wyrod, and Edwards left the room, Wyrod jokingly commented, "Liars' Club, hey, Boss?" Edwards had planned to return to his office to contemplate his decision, but Berg suggested that the three men go to the Detroit Yacht Club for lunch. Edwards was taken aback by Berg's invitation because it was the first friendly overture the superintendent had made since he became commissioner. After they finished lunch in the club dining room, Berg began talking about the trial board. The ensuing conversation revealed much about the department leaders' prevailing attitude in brutality cases.[25]

As Edwards remembered, Berg "reviewed the evidence we had heard about the complaint, pointed out that the four officers who had testified denied that they had seen or heard any violence, [and] pointed out that Daniels's testimony was suspect in part because of his obvious attempt to evade arrest." Berg concluded that where any conflict of evidence existed, police officers' testimony should prevail. Wyrod agreed with Berg. Edwards countered by contrasting the doctor's undisputed testimony with the police officers' evasive statements. He pointed out that the police had an obvious motive to protect each other, and he lambasted Welch's ineffective cross-examination. Edwards then concluded that his own questioning proved that the policemen had been evading the truth. Edwards reminded Berg and Wyrod that they shared his responsibility as fact finders, and there was no question that Daniels's beating violated department regulations, Michigan law, and the U.S. Constitution. He said it was clear that the three officers who participated in the beating should be found guilty. Wyrod objected: "Boss, we can't do that. Why, if I voted these men guilty, my own men would never work for me again."[26]

Edwards found Berg's argument more subtle and, in some ways, more alarming. "He reviewed some of the events which had occurred since I became police commissioner, said that he knew things had not gone too smoothly, said that if I went along on this Trial Board decision, everything would work out in the Department. He added that the crime statistics about which the *Detroit Free Press* had given me a great deal of editorial criticism would straighten out." Edwards listened and weighed each word. As he noted later, however, "There was one trouble with all of this. I had heard a lot of testimony in my lifetime and I had never been more convinced that four witnesses had not been telling the truth. . . . Also I knew that I was not going to join in exonerating the beating of a police prisoner to extract a confession."[27]

Edwards repeated his determination to hand down a finding of guilt; Berg and Wyrod pleaded with him. They insisted that the trial board's rulings were always unanimous, and they could not destroy department morale by voting against their own men.

Edwards offered a compromise. He said if they joined in finding the men guilty, then he would agree to a light punishment. He said that would be only fair, "particularly in view of the newness of this sort of approach to this problem in the Detroit Police Department." Berg and Wyrod refused to compromise, and the three men drove back to headquarters in stony silence. Edwards was beginning to realize that "police morale was a code name for a police officer's obligation to support another police officer, regardless of regulation or law unless he was so far out of bounds that saving him was impossible."[28]

When the trial board reconvened that afternoon and announced the verdict, most members of the audience applauded. When Edwards said it was not a unanimous verdict, the room grew silent. In his resonant baritone, the commissioner announced, "I find, after weighing all of the testimony, a deep conviction that Willie Daniels, after being handcuffed, was struck and that each officer struck him at least once." Neither Wyrod nor Berg offered any public explanation for their decisions. As Edwards recalled, "The three of us walked out of the board between grim faces."[29]

He got the first inkling of rank-and-file reaction later that day when he was leaving headquarters. His driver, Patrolman Jenson, waited until they were alone and asked about the verdict. When Edwards told him the officers were acquitted, Jenson sighed with relief and said, "Boy am I glad we have got you as commissioner." Apparently Jenson believed that Edwards's reputation as a civil libertarian would help mute criticism of the verdict in the African-American community. When Edwards said he dissented, Jenson looked at him with amazement and said, "You did?" As Edwards dryly noted, it was one of the few times his garrulous driver was left speechless.[30]

Edwards had little doubt that most of the 4,500 members of his department shared Jenson's view of the decision. He also believed that most of them probably knew more about what happened in Daniels's basement than he did, and therefore, knew that he had been right about the beating. But many members of the public were less sure. In its story about the trial board, the *Free Press* by-passed questions of brutality and focussed on the African Americans involved in the original skirmish. The newspaper suggested that Edwards turn his attention away from errant police and instead question the original complaint brought by Jones. Either Daniels had a gun or he did not. If he did not and Jones lied to police, the editorial said, she should be arrested and charged with making a false complaint.[31]

Edwards rejected the newspaper's suggestion as he contemplated how to handle the aftermath of the Daniels decision. As he noted later, "I knew that I could not stay aloof from the matter after my dissent unless I was prepared shortly to resign." Because Detroit's City Charter was drafted to curtail political patronage, he had no power to hire or fire police officers. Still, as commissioner he did exercise control over promotions, demotions, and assignments. He reasoned that no officer eligible for promotion would lie to him directly, so he decided to question the inspector in charge of the 2nd Precinct, Glenn C. Chittick. As Edwards remembered, Chittick "was a stocky, taciturn officer with a reputation for 'doing it by the book,' which meant in police parlance that he was unwilling to bend police regulations to suit the circumstances." Chittick said one of his men confirmed Daniels's story, and he passed that information on to James Berg, along with the officer's avowed refusal to repeat the story before the trial board. Chittick agreed to order the reluctant officer to visit Edwards the next day.[32]

The next morning the young policeman arrived in Edwards's office "paler and more nervous" than the commissioner remembered him from the trial board. The patrolman verified Daniels's version of the beating. As Chittick predicted, he also refused to repeat publicly what had happened. He told Edwards if he broke the code of silence, then he would no longer be able to work in the department. Edwards realized that there had been a conspiracy to protect the errant policemen in the Daniels case. When James Berg's investigation corroborated Daniels's story, the Bergs decided to keep the truth from him. As Edwards said later, "I hadn't yet heard the slogan with which I was to become very familiar, 'A police officer can do no wrong,' but I began to suspect that some such tradition was involved."[33]

Edwards faced a dilemma. The charter did not provide him with the power to set aside a trial board decision. Further action would have to be taken by the district attorney and the Wayne

George Clifton Edwards, Jr., late 1930s.
(Archives of Labor and Urban Affairs, Wayne State University)

Graduation photograph of Edwards's wife,
Margaret (Peg) McConnell Edwards, 1937.
(Archives of Labor and Urban Affairs, Wayne State University)

George Clifton Edwards, Sr., Edwards's father.
(Archives of Labor and Urban Affairs, Wayne State University)

Edwards with his family after returning from World War II,
January 14, 1946.
(Detroit New Archives)

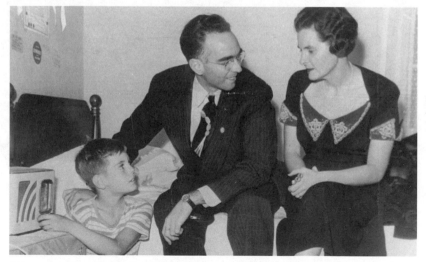

Edwards with wife Peg and son James.
(Archives of Labor and Urban Affairs, Wayne State University)

*Edwards speaking at a meeting on the evening of
the 1949 mayoral primary in Detroit.
(Archives of Labor and Urban Affairs, Wayne State University)*

*Edwards (center) campaigning at Michigan Steel Casting
during the 1949 Detroit mayoral race.
(Archives of Labor and Urban Affairs, Wayne State University)*

*Left to right: Franklin D. Roosevelt, Jr., Walter Reuther,
and Edwards at the 1949 UAW convention.
(Archives of Labor and Urban Affairs, Wayne State University)*

*Edwards (right) being sworn in as judge
at Wayne County Probate Court, 1951.
(Detroit News Archives)*

Left to right: Guy Nunn of the UAW,
Michigan Supreme Court Justice Talbot Smith, and Edwards
during an unidentified television program in the 1950s.
(Archives of Labor and Urban Affairs, Wayne State University)

Wayne County Circuit Court Judges,
Left to right: Ted Bohn, Wade McCree, George B. Murphy,
Damon Keith, George Edwards, Jr., Nate Kaufman, and Hazen Kunz.
(Archives of Labor and Urban Affairs, Wayne State University)

Santo Perrone testifying before the Kefauver hearings, February 1952.
(Burton Collection, Detroit Public Library)

Former Detroit Police Commissioner Frank Eaman, 1939.
(Burton Collection, Detroit Public Library)

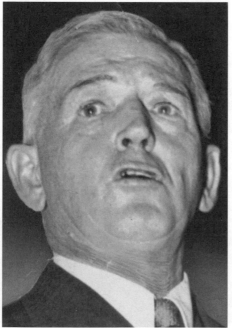

*Edwards (right) with Mayor-elect Jerome Cavanagh, December 12, 1961.
(Burton Collection, Detroit Public Library)*

Edwards (left) being sworn in as Detroit police commissioner,
January 3, 1962.
(Detroit News Archives)

Edwards entering a police squad car, February 11, 1962.
(Detroit News Archives)

*Edwards (left) arranging a ministers meeting, June 21, 1962.
(Detroit New Archives)*

*Vincent Piersante, head of the Detroit Police Department's
Criminal Information Bureau (CIB).
(Detroit News Archives)*

Edwards (right) with U.S. Supreme Court Justice William Douglas,
June 28, 1962.
(Detroit News Archives)

Bridging the Gap of Hatred
(Courtesy of Margaret Edwards)

Edwards (right) at the Detroit police Field Day exercises at Tiger Stadium, August 13, 1962. (Courtesy of James Edwards)

Ray Girardin, Edwards's successor as police commissioner, in front of Detroit police headquarters, December 1963. (Burton Collection, Detroit Public Library)

Edwards and Peg (center) receiving Amity Award, March 29, 1963.
(Detroit News Archives)

County courts, both of which had a history of favoring police in disputes brought by citizens. Even if he persuaded the district attorney's office to charge the police officers in the Daniels case with perjury, the only compelling evidence would have been against the officer who told him the truth. Edwards did not relish punishing the youngest and least culpable of the policemen involved in the incident. Finally, if the case ever did come to trial, it would come too late in his commissionership to eradicate police brutality. Edwards decided his only option was to deal with the problem internally by staging a showdown with his top officers.[34]

During the department's next bimonthly command meeting, Edwards put the Daniels case at the top of the agenda. He outlined what he had learned about the cover-up and vowed that future cases would be handled differently. Edwards said he would not pursue criminal charges against the four officers who lied or brutality charges against the three officers involved in the beating. Instead, he announced that he had asked Mayor Cavanagh to remove Welch from representing the police department in the future, and he vowed to ensure that trial boards would become vehicles for ascertaining the truth, not sham proceedings to protect department wrongdoing. Edwards ended the meeting by repeating that he would not tolerate unwarranted police violence against citizens.[35]

Edwards then called the corporation counsel, told him what he knew about the department's culpability, and urged him to settle Daniels's civil suit. Edwards believed that one reason for police misconduct was inadequate supervision on the street. On April 2, to minimize the risk of other incidents, Edwards issued an order requiring duty sergeants in each precinct to go to every situation involving a gun. Each morning Edwards read every detective report on events from the previous day and followed up by asking for explanations about "questionable" cases. When reports hinted at racial problems, he routinely asked the department's Community Relations Bureau to investigate.[36]

Edwards's actions won predictable plaudits from African-American leaders, who voiced their support for the commissioner and urged a complete shake-up of the old guard. Dr. D. T. Burton, medical director of Burton Mercy Hospital, said he was glad the dispute had become public because it showed the need to get rid of the department's senior command officers. "How long can the city afford such outrageous and open defiance of the commissioner's efforts to restore public confidence in our police department? How long must we retain these same men whose defiance of public concern for decent conduct . . . has hamstrung the good efforts of past commissioners and, now, threatens to continue in the same vein." Burton urged Cavanagh to fire the Berg brothers and Wyrod, because Edwards could not do his job "if he is not given the staff personnel at the top echelon to supplement his policies." The mayor responded by assuring Burton that he supported Edwards and his right to make any personnel changes "that the best interests of the community and the department dictate."[37]

On March 24, the *Michigan Chronicle* weighed in with a lengthy editorial titled "Standard Operating Procedure." The newspaper noted that while Edwards had explained his ruling, "Berg and Wyrod, who represent the hard-boiled rank-and-file of the department, had no comment to make regarding the basis of their judgment." The *Chronicle* said the two men's silence "opens a lot of doors to speculation . . . that there is no logical basis or objective basis for their whitewashing of the case . . . that this was the first opportunity of the police reactionaries to openly refute the liberal thinking of their boss . . . that Berg and Wyrod had their minds made up before the hearing." Although it predicted that Edwards would gain control in the long run, the editorial said, in the short term, the trial board incident would make it difficult for Edwards to garner community support for the police. "The recalcitrant members of the police department, regardless of the size of their breeches, will have to fall in line with modern concepts of police-community relations if progress is to be made in this area."[38]

Although African Americans supported Edwards, some doubted that he could change ingrained racism within the department. John E. Beckley, for one, asked: "How can our police commissioner expect a citizen to cooperate with the police officers of our city when his memory bears the scars of abuse and public embarrassment at the hands of these same officers. In the case of the Detroit Police Department, it is not one bad apple but several that are spoiling the entire bunch."[39] Concern within Detroit's

162

black community was mirrored by a different kind of anxiety among the city's white residents. Many feared that Edwards's "mollycoddling" attitude toward African Americans would foster a crime wave.

The *Times, Free Press,* and *News* ran stories detailing low police morale. Edwards was inundated with letters and phone calls from friends and enemies. As he recalled, "They all said the same thing: The word is out on the street; the police aren't working." Citizens took their cue from the newspaper reports and began writing to Edwards detailing how they were witnessing increased crime in their neighborhoods. Usually, they blamed black perpetrators. For example, Edmund J. Papineau, Sr., of 77 Custer Avenue, described how his ailing wife had been "attacked by a colored purse snatcher who pummelled her and after grabbing her purse, threw her to the ground." He said his wife's victimization was just one incident of many in his neighborhood and added, "Please understand that this is not meant to cast any reflection on the police force, but rather on the executive and administrative divisions of the police department."[40]

The department's forty top executive officers inflamed the situation even more by calling a meeting on April 16, 1962, at Tina's Pizzeria at 17322 Harper. The restaurant was closed to the public for the evening, so the police commanders could freely discuss their problems with Edwards. They invited Herbert Boldt of the *News* to publicize their grievances. Senior Inspector William Icenhower began the meeting by urging his colleagues to unite against Edwards. He was seconded by James Berg who said that if they banded together they could "wreck the administration of the commissioner." Piersante and a handful of others tried to provide voices of reason. They pointed out that under the city charter Edwards did not have the power to remove police officers. Therefore, he posed no threat as long as they did their jobs in a professional manner. The Berg brothers and Wyrod disagreed. According to Piersante, Wyrod vowed, "We'll get rid of that little son of a bitch in six months."[41]

Lower-ranking officers took their cues from their commanders and complained to citizens that they felt helpless to do their jobs with Edwards in charge. In one case, Dr. Walter Silver wrote the mayor about the increased gang activity near his clinic located at Evergreen and West Chicago. Silver said when he reported his problems to Inspector Fred Kirby and other officers of the 16th Precinct, they "convinced him that they feel their hands are tied, that they cannot make a legitimate arrest without subjecting themselves to physical injury or a lawsuit and that their morale is shot."[42]

Edwards reasoned that the best way to counter dissension within his own ranks was by bolstering his public support. Fortuitously, he received the opportunity to do just that when Allen B. Crow, president of the Economic Club of Detroit, asked him to speak to the association. Edwards believed that many of the club's members, who included most of the city's successful white businessmen, opposed his agenda. He welcomed the opportunity to persuade skeptics that his reforms could work.[43]

Edwards's speech drew a packed crowd to the meeting at the Veteran's Memorial Building. He tried to put Detroit's problems in a larger context by citing an article from *Fortune* magazine about the plight of urban America:

> The city is in trouble today because it isn't dealing successfully with its newcomers. They are still pouring in—not from County Cork or Bavaria or Sicily or Galicia, but from Jackson, Mississippi, and Memphis, Tennessee, and a host of towns and hamlets with names like Sunflower, Rolling Fork, and Dyersburg. The new immigrants are distinguished from the older residents not by religion or national origin but by color. Between 1950 and 1960 the twelve largest United States cities lost over two million white residents; they gained nearly two million Negro residents.[44]

Edwards said he did not share the belief that crime is a racial problem, but added, "the existence of suspicion and distrust between law enforcement officials and the Negro community certainly is." Granted, "some of that suspicion, some of the distrust . . . cannot be labelled 'Made in Detroit.' " Instead, much of it stemmed from two hundred years of history marked first by slavery and then by segregation. Edwards argued that white Detroiters had to ensure that "the law in this city is the law for everybody . . . regardless of who they might be." The most overlooked fact in debates about the city's policing was that "there is not one single neighborhood in the city of Detroit where the overwhelming majority of residents are not themselves law-abiding citizens." Edwards conceded that there were neighborhoods

164

"where the law-abiding citizens are not in the ascendancy," but he said the answer in those areas was to "forge a link between the law-abiding citizens . . . and the majesty of the law representing the people through the police department." He then recounted the small steps toward progress that had already occurred during his first months in office, including unprecedented NAACP support for the department's budget requests, his three-point plan, and more positive interaction between community groups and precinct commanders.[45]

He received polite applause and left the Economic Club "with the feeling that an important section of the community was favorably impressed. I knew that it would take much more than speeches to impress the 4,300 police officers whom, at least technically, I commanded." Still, the business leaders' "willingness to greet the program I had outlined with something between acceptance and support may well have been decisive in meeting the challenge of the Pizza Parlor Putsch." Later that month, Edwards received another vote of confidence from Detroit's establishment, when *Detroit News* editor Martin Hayden nominated him for the Jerome N. Frank Award. Although Hayden and Edwards liked each other personally, they often disagreed about legal and political issues. Nevertheless, Hayden had come to believe that Edwards's efforts to reconcile civil rights and policing could set a model for the nation. He argued that Edwards would be a fitting recipient for an award that honored Frank, one of the nation's most influential, progressive legal thinkers. Hayden admitted that Edwards's ambitious program might not succeed, but he said, "even in failure" it would constitute a noble effort "in a very difficult and controversial field."[46]

With a feeling of confidence, Edwards tackled the prickly question of how to permanently improve the department's methods of handling brutality complaints. The Daniels case renewed African-American demands for a citizen review panel. After the trial board, Edward M. Turner, president of the Detroit Chapter of the NAACP, told the *Detroit News:* "One of the things evident here is the problem of permitting the Police Department to sit in judgment on itself. Even with a commissioner of the caliber of Edwards, the inequity of the situation is built in. As a result, it makes his job more difficult." Rolland O'Hare, chair of the Detroit ACLU, agreed that the case pointed up the need for public review. His comments provoked a vitriolic response from *Free Press* columnist Jack Manning, who said "periodic pressure by volunteer reformers to create a 'public review board' . . . [was] as stubbornly repetitive as those damn birds to Capistrano." He warned that if the ACLU people had their way, eventually there would be "a public review board of Army court martials and even Supreme Court decisions."[47]

Although a handful of other cities like Philadelphia had instituted civilian oversight panels, Edwards believed that creating one in Detroit would demoralize the rank and file. Besides, he reasoned, it would be unnecessary if the department's top command made it clear that the use of excessive force would not be tolerated. He publicly rejected the idea of a civilian review panel and asked supporters to give him time to solve the problem. At least one group, the Detroit Chapter of the Anti-Defamation League of B'Nai B'rith (ADL), acceded. As its chair, Victor J. Baum, said, the ADL had not "abandoned its belief that a public Review Board is desirable. Temporarily, however, and with every hope that you will be able to correct that which needs correction, ADL will forego insistence upon the immediate creation of such a Review Board."[48]

Nevertheless, Edwards did set about revamping the system for handling citizen complaints within the department. Under the system in place when he took over, accusations of brutality were sent back to the precinct in which they occurred for further investigation. As Edwards noted, the investigating officer "was bound to be conscious of the fact that at some time in his working career, and perhaps on many occasions, he might have this same officer as a partner. On some one of those occasions, his own life might depend on whether or not the officer he was now investigating would loyally and eagerly come to his aid if he were in great danger. Such a system guaranteed that the investigating officer would try to find exonerating facts and not dig deeply for inculpatory ones."[49]

Edwards decided to eliminate such conflicts of interest by giving responsibility for brutality complaints to the Community Relations Bureau that had been established by his predecessor. When Edwards assumed command, Inspector Philip J. Van Antwerp ran the bureau whose members, according to Edwards, did little more than make speeches "about community relations rather than doing any of the hard nitty-gritty work to improve them." Van Antwerp was a cousin of Detroit's former mayor, Eugene I. Van Antwerp, and he also nursed political ambitions. In July, when Van Antwerp resigned to run for sheriff, Edwards took advantage of the vacancy to appoint a more committed leader. He chose Blake S. Wallace, "a no-nonsense officer [whose] honesty in reporting on street episodes had greatly impressed me." With Wallace in place, Edwards shifted all responsibility for investigating incidents with racial overtones to the bureau, which conducted less biased, more professional investigations.[50]

Edwards's program received another boost on May 21 when *U.S. News & World Report* ran an article about policing in Detroit. In mid-April, the magazine's reporter showed up in Edwards's office without an appointment. He spent the next several hours asking tough questions, and Edwards worried that the story would be negative. His fears proved unfounded. The author wrote, "At a time when major crime is rising alarmingly in U.S. cities, a new approach to the problem is being tried in Detroit." The story recounted that Detroit residents held differing views of changes in the city's police policy. It detailed how police and many white residents were still skeptical about Edwards's reform agenda while black leaders welcomed it. Some original critics, it added, including business leaders, were slowly coming around. A quote from William C. Matney, Jr., summed up Edwards's approach. Matney, a former managing editor of the *Michigan Chronicle,* explained: "The Commissioner didn't attempt to appease the Negroes. There have been no promotions of Negro officers since he took over. But he has been able to get across the feeling that he is impartial, that he will not tolerate racial discrimination by the police." The article concluded, somewhat optimistically, that the "cold war between Detroit's police and the city's Negro population may be coming to an end." Edwards was pleased. As he noted, "Without saying so explicitly, it gave the reader the impression that *U.S. News and World Report* thought the program might just work. I couldn't ask for more."[51]

Two weeks later, U.S. Supreme Court Justice William O. Douglas came to Detroit and gave Edwards's program more national exposure. Douglas, who delivered a speech at Cobo Hall to the Detroit Friends of Yeshiva University, wanted to forego a cocktail party and reception in order to tour the police department with Edwards. The two visited headquarters, rode in a police scout car, and talked to a surveillance team staking out the Lesod Gambling Club, which Edwards would later drive out of Detroit. When asked about his tour, Douglas told reporters, "This is quite an experience for a boy who grew up in Yakima [Washington] where there was a chief and two or three other officers." After returning to Washington, D.C., Douglas wrote a gushing thank you note: "It's a great job you are doing along the banks of the River of Hate—the most important one in America at this particular time. I was thrilled at your achievements. . . . Let me know if there are occasions when some people of prominence in Washington, D.C., can come out to help on a project." Edwards took personal satisfaction from Douglas's trip, writing the justice: "Your visit was tremendously important. This was partly true because it made me feel that others than myself realize the importance of this job: and, secondly, it was a great boost for the morale of the Police Department of the City of Detroit in giving them recognition for the importance of the service which they are performing."[52]

Douglas's visit came on the eve of a major test of Edwards's policy of police restraint. On June 10, the Nation of Islam (NOI) staged a national protest rally in Detroit at the Olympia Arena located in a predominantly African-American neighborhood on the lower west side. Malcolm X convened the meeting to protest an April 27 shootout in which Los Angeles police killed two NOI members. When Edwards first learned of the shootings in Los Angeles, his reaction was "thank heavens, it wasn't Detroit." He was less sanguine when the NOI chose his city as the place to vent its anger. As Edwards recalled, "my reaction to this . . . was in highly personal terms. How could a new Detroit police commissioner be so fortunate as to have Detroit, which was already a tinderbox, selected for such an event?"[53]

Edwards had good reason to be fearful. Although the NOI had been founded in Detroit more than thirty years earlier, the religious group received little attention until the years immediately preceding Edwards's commissionership. W. D. Fard, a yard goods peddlar who claimed to have been born to the same Arab tribe that included the prophet, Muhammad, began preaching in Detroit's slums in 1931. Taking advantage of the Depression's unsettling effects, Fard converted followers by arguing that American blacks were a lost tribe of Islam who could find redemption by returning to their true religion. In Detroit, he founded the University of Islam, a school to train children in his religious tenets. After Fard died mysteriously in 1934, his chief convert, Elijah Poole, took over leadership of the Nation. Poole changed his name to Elijah Muhammad and moved his headquarters to a nineteen-room mansion in Chicago. His converts included Malcolm X, who grew up in Michigan and went by the street nickname "Detroit Red" before he converted to Islam while serving a prison sentence in Massachusetts.[54]

In the years immediately preceding Edwards's takeover as commissioner, the NOI and Malcolm X received widespread negative publicity. In 1959, the "Mike Wallace Show" featured the NOI in a segment sensationally titled, "The Hate that Hate Produced." As Malcolm X noted in his autobiography, the program "was edited tightly into a kaleidoscope of 'shocker' images" that provoked a "public reaction [that] was like what happened back in the 1930s when Orson Welles frightened America with a radio program describing, as though it was actually happening, an invasion by 'men from Mars.' "[55]

Malcolm X and his mentor, Elijah Muhammad, preached a complex philosophy that combined principles of black separatism and religious self-discipline with strands of the Islamic faith. Mainstream journalists in the early 1960s, however, dismissed the NOI as a religious cult that advocated black supremacy, demonizing of whites, anti-Semitism, and violence. Their portrayal was an alarmist caricature. Admittedly, Malcolm X and Elijah Muhammad rejected Christian tenets of forgiveness and argued that victims of oppression had the right to fight their oppressors. They did not, however, encourage chaotic rioting in the streets. Such fine points were lost to most observers who blamed the April shootout with police in Los Angeles entirely on NOI members. For their part, NOI members were equally outraged when a Los Angeles County coroner's jury ruled that the police killings of two "cult" members constituted justifiable homicide.[56]

The NOI had many loyal followers in Detroit, and Edwards took comfort in the fact that "there had been no law enforcement problems specifically involving the Black Muslims in the immediate past." He met with the commanders of the traffic division and the two precincts most directly involved to devise a strategy to avoid conflict. As he recalled, "I said that we were going to treat this conclave as we would a national convention of the Junior Chamber of Commerce meeting. I wanted every single service which we would normally tender to such an organization to be tendered to the Black Muslims." He stressed that NOI members had "a right to meet in our city and a right to air their protests. So long as they did not pose any threat to Detroiters' lives and property, our job was to treat them with courtesy and respect."[57]

The commanders vehemently disagreed. As Edwards recounted, most "had heard some of the Black Muslim anti-white tirades and proceeded to detail their doubts that any approach except the application of maximum force would produce a solution which was consistent with law enforcement." Edwards pointed out that Los Angeles police had taken that approach with tragic results. He vowed that Detroit would be different. He told his officers to report back to him about their discussions with NOI members, and he also warned them not to try to undermine his orders by throwing up bureaucratic roadblocks for the issuance of meeting and traffic permits. During the next several days, the officers reported to Edwards that they met with NOI members who were surprised by the department's cooperation.[58]

A week before the rally, Malcolm X wrote a letter thanking the department for its help and inviting Edwards to attend the rally and sit on the speaker's dais. Edwards was disturbed by the request.

> My presence on the platform could easily be considered as some sort of endorsement of what was being said at the meeting. I felt exactly the same way about Malcolm X's hate white doctrine as I did about the Ku Klux Klan's hate black doctrine. Nonetheless, I knew that my mere presence at the meeting would guarantee the peaceful intentions of the Police Department on that Sunday better than any message, words or orders. In the highly explosive situation of those months, Detroit needed to give that guarantee.[59]

Edwards decided to attend the meeting, but he chose to sit in the audience instead of on stage with Malcolm X. When he

170

announced his plan to attend the rally, Louis Berg protested, saying the department could not protect Edwards because NOI members did not allow anyone, including police, to carry guns into their meetings. Edwards stood firm and showed up without a police escort. In case of trouble, Edwards ordered nine hundred men to wait in a nearby garage. He wanted them off of the streets to avoid sending a message that the department anticipated violence. When Edwards arrived at the rally, the NOI's security men searched him "somewhat roughly," then escorted him to his seat fifteen rows from the front. As he scanned the faces in the crowd, he recognized several black police officers. The meeting itself was anticlimactic. Only 3,500 people showed up instead of the 15,000 that the Nation predicted. Malcolm X introduced Edwards, welcomed him to the meeting, and praised him for trying to bring equal law enforcement to Detroit. At that point, the commissioner relaxed because he "knew that the 900 armed police officers on standby would spend a boring Sunday afternoon." Edwards remained in the hall listening to a two-hour speech from Elijah Muhammad on the need for separation of the races and the importance of Allah.[60]

In early June, Edwards took another step to show how better use of manpower, rather than force, could improve law enforcement when he assigned two veteran officers to revamp enforcement efforts in the crime-ridden 10th Precinct. Located in the northwest part of the city, the so-called Petoskey Precinct comprised a 6.5 square-mile area bordered by Highland Park and the Lodge Expressway on the east, Grand Boulevard on the south, Grand River on the west, and the Detroit Terminal Railroad tracks on the north. The 10th reported a 43.6 percent increase in crimes over the previous year, including car thefts, burglaries, petty thefts, gambling, and prostitution. Urban renewal projects, which displaced 175,000 people into the area, exacerbated the problems. Edwards transferred two veteran police to the troubled precinct—Lieutenant Robert Potts, an expert on community relations, and Thomas Turkaly, a twenty-two year veteran of the force who had served as an inspector in the 14th Precinct.[61]

In early July, the *Detroit Free Press* ran a series of five articles analyzing Edwards's police commissionership. Given the fact that the newspaper was consistently one of his harshest critics, the series provided one yardstick by which to measure whether Edwards had convinced his skeptics. The newspaper argued that an inherent contradiction plagued Edwards's efforts. He assumed that increased citizen cooperation would improve law enforcement and decrease crime. In fact, the newspaper argued, just the opposite had happened. The number of citizen calls to police had grown, especially in the African-American community, yet crime continued to increase. Each article in the *Free Press* series looked at this "contradiction" from various perspectives.

The series asserted that Edwards's agenda constituted "a radical, new approach to law enforcement in Detroit." Among other things, reporter John Millhone said, "He has abandoned traditional police methods under which, on a dark night, on a tough street, with officers facing a hardened criminal, the Constitutional niceties of search and seizure are occasionally forgotten." As a result of this new policy, statistics showed a dramatic decrease in the number of arrests. In analyzing the statistics, Millhone found that much of the decline came from a drop in the number of "investigative arrests" in which police booked a suspect, then tried to gather the evidence against him to make the charge stick. Suspects caught in these types of dragnets often languished in jail for several days before police presented their cases to a magistrate. Both the Michigan and Detroit Bar Associations had criticized investigative arrests as unconstitutional, but Edwards's predecessors defended them as a necessary part of police work. Millhone also found that even though arrests were down, the number of prosecutions remained constant. This statistic seemed to support Edwards's contentions. Millhone had much more trouble sorting through the statistics involving incident reports, which constituted the figures most often cited in newspaper accounts. These numbers showed a constant increase, and it was hard to discern whether they represented the fact that more people, especially African Americans, were reporting crimes or whether more crimes were occurring. Whites claimed there was a real increase; blacks claimed it was all a matter of reporting. This question would constantly dog Edwards's tenure.[62]

In his next article, Millhone turned his attention to Detroit's African-American community. His evidence supported Edwards's contention that crime was not a racial problem. One of the city's quietest areas was Conant Gardens, a middle-class black neighborhood bounded by Seven Mile, Ryan, and Nevada. Still, it was inevitable that most Detroiters associated crime with African Americans. Although they comprised only 29 percent of the city's population, 65 percent of all criminal defendants were black. The city's highest crime rates, not surprisingly, were found in the ghettos of the 10th Precinct, where social problems were legion. The precinct's 39 percent unemployment rate among adult men was the highest in the nation. Unemployment rates were even higher among teenagers, demographically the most crime prone segment of the population. Seventy percent of black men between the ages of 16 and 21 were out of school and held no job.[63]

Millhone argued that the 10th Precinct would provide the ultimate testing grounds for Edwards's program. During his tenure, police joined hands with approximately two hundred neighborhood block clubs in a pitched battle "against prostitutes, numbers peddlers, juvenile delinquents, and professional criminals." Together they were fighting against the opening of bars and lobbying for better lighting and more playgrounds. There had been a dramatic increase in citizen reports of illegal activity—especially after Edwards transferred Turkaly and Potts to the precinct. Police were also enforcing a curfew against teenagers. Yet, despite all of those efforts, statistics showed an alarming increase in crime between the first half of 1961 and 1962. Car thefts rose from 152 to 454. Burglaries and petty thefts increased from 1,573 to 2,115.[64]

Millhone also provided a portrait of Edwards, whom he described as "the child prodigy of Michigan public life." This was not necessarily a compliment. Millhone, along with many of Edwards's critics, portrayed him as a publicity hound "drawn to the public spotlight." At the same time, it was hard for any reporter not to recognize the idealism that infused Edwards's political ambitions. Millhone reported how Edwards still "bristled" when he recalled reading a Dallas newspaper article that noted "ten Negroes were killed on the Central Track last night" and then provided no names or personal details of the victims, who, because of their race, were deemed unnewsworthy. Edwards told Millhone that his ongoing concern for racial justice in Detroit prompted him to accept the commissionership, which he described as "the most challenging thing I've ever tried to do." Edwards dismissed critics who believed that rising crime statistics constituted a more serious problem than Detroit's ongoing racial tensions. Crime was rising across the nation; it was a trend that no one person could solve in six months. By contrast, Edwards believed racial tensions could be defused more quickly. If they weren't, he predicted, "the situation could become explosive." Millhone was surprised that Edwards, who was "as sensitive to publicity as a first-term councilman," ignored public criticism to implement his program. "Edwards has moved so fast that a major problem facing him is from those within his department who feel he has hamstrung them until they no longer can enforce the law adequately."[65]

Millhone concluded the series by reporting how members of the police department viewed Edwards and his agenda. For many, he wrote, the real test came in Edwards's handling of the Willie Daniels case. When Edwards voted to find the police guilty of brutality, Millhone said, "It showed the new commissioner intended to be boss. As the commissioner's action became clear, the reaction rippled through the department." A sergeant, speaking off the record, predicted that law enforcement in Detroit would collapse and Edwards would be out of his job in six months. A top officer offered a similar, if more restrained view. "To operate effectively, we can't be hamstrung within such narrow boundaries of the law. We should never use gestapo methods, but we should never be fettered as we are now getting to be." Other officers were more sanguine. Inspector Glenn Chittick of the 13th Precinct noted that "a lot of officers were skeptical at first that Edwards might soft pedal arrests. But he says he wants more vigorous law enforcement and you can't argue with that." Chittick said he had noticed much better citizen cooperation in his precinct, where 75 percent of the residents were African American. Inspector Thomas Nolan of the 2nd Precinct said, "Morale's good. Not high . . . not low. But good. I think this is an exaggerated issue. You don't have an avalanche of people retiring, do you?" Millhone concluded that "some crusty officers will never accept the new commissioner. But the majority will try his public relations and velvet-hammer approach."[66]

Throughout the summer, Edwards tried to garner support in a seemingly endless round of speeches to community groups. In a typical address on July 25, 1962, Edwards told the Detroit Rotary Club that "crime is not a racial problem." He reiterated his belief that fair, unbiased law enforcement was one of the best cures for the city's racial problems. In an interview with the *Detroit News,* Edwards said,

> While some of the animosities in this area have centuries of background and certainly are not going to be eradicated in a few months, we have made progress which has been astonishing to me. . . . I may be deluding myself but I think this program has been accepted by every important segment of the community, from the Economic Club to the NAACP, through the neighborhood improvement associations of Northeast and Northwest Detroit to the block clubs in Precinct 10. No doubt implementing this program is more difficult than stating it or getting it accepted, but I think we can report progress.[67]

Edwards's optimism was not unfounded. By early August, Detroit's Commission on Community Relations found significant improvement. Its report said: "Negroes are getting over their traditional fear of calling upon the police in times of difficulty." Another indicator of success came with a reduction in the number of complaints to the department's Community Relations Bureau. During its first seven months of operation after its creation by Mayor Miriani in 1961, the bureau received sixty-four complaints. By contrast, during the first seven months of Edwards's tenure the bureau received only twenty-one complaints, some of which dated back to the previous administration. By August 1962, the department reported it received no complaints of police brutality during the previous six months. Edwards's program would continue to confront hostility among police and many of Detroit's white residents. In October, for example, he told precinct inspectors to discourage patrol officers from using such "trigger words" as "Nigger, Dago, Wop, and Polak." He warned that the use of those epithets could turn a street fight into a riot, and he added that it was "not professional" for police to return insults even when their feelings were offended. All in all, by fall Edwards felt he had met his early goal of easing a potentially explosive racial situation. With the crisis past, he turned his attention to deeper reforms.[68]

7

Traffic, Trash, and Long-Term Change

The problem of crime is not merely enforcement. There is also great
need for action on crime prevention.
—George Edwards, Jr., December 1961

E ven though he attempted to learn about the day-to-day lives
of his officers, Edwards was necessarily removed from the
department's routine policing activities. This did not bother him.
Unlike some of his predecessors, Edwards never became enrap-
tured with the cops-and-robbers excitement and romance of police work. By temperament and intellect, he was much more
suited to the role of a policymaker, who was interested in setting
broad guidelines for the professionals. During his first few
months in office, Edwards set a tone for racially unbiased policing, and he made it clear that he would not tolerate brutality
against citizens. With those immediate concerns out of the way,
he was free to work for the long-range programs that could make
a serious dent in crime. Even so, he was not entirely freed from
the more mundane aspects of a police commissioner's job.

One of those ordinary concerns was traffic control, which
was perhaps the most visible aspect of the Police Department's
efforts. Like all of his predecessors, Edwards recognized the need
for constant improvement in monitoring traffic safety on Detroit's busy web of highways and streets. One of Edwards's first
victories in the cause of racial justice came when he ordered officers in the traffic division to issue tickets more politely. Traffic

control and safety were a recurring theme in Edwards's monthly meetings with his precinct inspectors. In April, for example, they discussed a campaign to encourage drivers to check their brakes regularly and a school education program to discourage children from crossing streets in the middle of blocks.[1]

On May 7, 1962, Detroit became the first city in the nation to use closed circuit televisions and electronic, illuminated signs to control freeway traffic. The pilot program relied on fourteen cameras placed along a 3.2-mile stretch of the John C. Lodge Expressway between Davison and the Ford Expressway. In the short term, engineers used information about traffic conditions gathered from the cameras and sensing devices to adjust speed limits. The television screens also helped police react more quickly to accidents and car breakdowns. Engineers planned to use the information gathered to design more effective highways.[2]

Another matter that came to Edwards's attention during his early days in office was corruption in the Department of Public Works (DPW). In February, Cavanagh received a tip that trucking companies, in order to avoid paying garbage handling fees, were bribing DPW employees working at the city's incinerators. The mayor's informant was unwilling to testify, which meant that police had to make their case from scratch. Cavanagh contacted Edwards, who asked Chief of Detectives Walter Wyrod to launch an investigation. On March 12, Wyrod handed the case over to Vincent Piersante and his Criminal Information Bureau (CIB).[3]

When Edwards took over the department, the CIB was "a small, highly specialized unit of the Detective Bureau which worked on organized crime problems. It had a considerable reputation for undercover capability and for incorruptibility." Edwards was especially impressed with Piersante, who would become his closest ally within the department. A native of Western Pennsylvania, Piersante came to Detroit to work for Ford. He attended Wayne State University and joined the department in 1941. Edwards respected Piersante's calm professionalism, his honesty, and his realistic assessment of problems and their solutions. To Edwards, Piersante represented "the epitome of what a police officer should be."[4]

Piersante's division did not have enough men to provide

177

twenty-four-hour surveillance, so he assigned them to conduct random checks of DPW incinerators at West Davison and Turner, 24th and West Jefferson, Wilkins and Orleans, and St. Jean and Harper. The city charged garbage haulers thirty cents per hundred pounds of food, and ten cents per hundred pounds of paper and wood rubbish. The police noticed that some trucks passed over the scales without being weighed at all; other full trucks were grossly underweighed.[5]

The four-month investigation revealed that the city lost more than $1.25 million in fees from five trucking companies. The thirty employees involved in the scheme received a total of $500,000 in payoffs in the form of money, cigarettes, and beer.

One foreman netted $17,000, while most raked in from $300 to $9,000. That constituted quite a bonus considering incinerator workers earned between $2.24 and $2.82 per hour. The scheme was so well organized that workers were paid in checks made out to "cash" by the trucking companies.[6]

Mayor Cavanagh took credit for the successful investigation, which he said signalled that he would not tolerate the graft and corruption that plagued previous administrations. He took advantage of the occasion to issue an antigraft directive ordering all city departments to tighten their operations. At the DPW that meant raising rates to pay for actual disposal costs, installing automatic, tamper-proof scales, and requiring frequent spot checks by city auditors rather than incinerator personnel. Cavanagh stopped short of a total house cleaning at the DPW. Because the probe did not turn up any corruption above the foreman level, Cavanagh allowed DPW Commissioner Glenn C. Richards, who was near retirement, to keep his job.[7]

Although he recognized the beneficial publicity that stemmed from the garbage investigation, Edwards was generally more interested in making long-term reforms than in fighting specific cases. Broadly speaking, there have been two major, sometimes conflicting approaches to crime and criminals throughout American history. The punishment model, normally adopted by police and other members of the criminal justice system, emphasized detecting crime, and catching and punishing criminals. The sociological approach, usually taken by social-welfare advocates and legal reformers, focused on prevention and rehabilitation.

These two strains of criminological thought have always coexisted, but in any given era one usually predominates. During the early 1960s, the teeter-totter effect gave the upper hand to Edwards and other reformers who favored the sociological approach. To them, the only way to prevent crime was to root out its causes by launching programs against poverty, substandard housing, juvenile delinquency, and other social ills that provided breeding grounds for would-be offenders. Edwards argued that the study of criminology was "as important as fighting cancer or getting to the moon. We must develop this science if we are to survive." His view that crime was a social, as well as a criminal justice issue, put him at odds with standard police thinking in Detroit and across the nation. Many career officers believed his "do-gooder" views were another indication of his unfitness to lead the department. They argued that they were trained as police officers, not social workers, and they insisted that the best way to approach crime was through harsh, swift justice, not nebulous social programs.[8]

There was no inherently racial cast to Edwards's views that poverty and despair fomented crime. Nevertheless, as a practical matter, Detroit's poor were disproportionally African Americans. Paramount among their problems was the city's unequal, inadequate housing conditions. Overcrowding in Detroit's ghettos stemmed in large part from hostility to ethnically and racially mixed housing. Unlike states in the South, Michigan and its northern counterparts did not mandate segregation in public accommodations or housing. Nevertheless, Edwards noted that Michigan's "customs and practices had . . . not been far removed from those in southern states." That harsh reality first drew national attention to Detroit in 1925, when Dr. Ossian H. Sweet paid $18,500 for a two-story house in an all-white neighborhood on the city's East Side. On the evening of September 9, a day after Sweet moved into his home, a mob milled around, intermittently throwing rocks and chanting "Let's get the Niggers." Shots rang out as gunmen began firing at the house. Sweet and his friends, who armed themselves against just such an attack, fired back. One of their bullets hit and killed Leon Breiner, a bystander who was visiting neighbors across the street.[9]

Sweet, his wife, two of his brothers, and seven friends, were charged with first-degree murder. The ensuing trial became a cause celebre. The trial judge was Frank Murphy, who later became Michigan's governor and ended his career as a U.S. Supreme Court justice. The NAACP persuaded the legendary Clarence Darrow to handle the defense. He was joined by Arthur Garfield Hays, a noted civil liberties lawyer, and a handful of African-American attorneys who worked behind the scenes. The first prosecution ended in a mistrial. In the second trial, Sweet's younger brother was the only defendant because he was the only one who admitted firing a gun. Even though a jury acquitted him, the Sweet case left a lasting scar on Detroit's historical consciousness. As author B. J. Widick noted, the Sweet "ordeal became a test for Detroit, and a preview of American society's dilemmas and agonies for the next four decades."[10]

Edwards had first confronted the conundrum of segregated housing when he had taken over Detroit's Housing Commission more than twenty years earlier. In the intervening years, African Americans continued to face violence as they moved into white neighborhoods. It was a national problem. During the 1950s, white attacks on black homeowners received national attention in Chicago, Birmingham, and New York City. In Detroit, the situation was exacerbated by a chronic shortage of public housing, the city's growing black population, and urban renewal projects that displaced a large number of people into already overcrowded neighborhoods. For example, when the ghetto of Paradise Valley was uprooted, most of its residents moved into the crowded 12th Precinct. There were few other places for them to go. According to Guy Nunn, the UAW's television and radio commentator, African Americans made up more than 20 percent of the city's population in 1957, yet they received less than 1 percent of its new housing. Many suburbs also adopted restricted deed covenants and other exclusionary racist tactics. A study released by Albert J. Mayer and Thomas Ford Hoult of Wayne State University in September 1962 verified that housing in Detroit was more segregated than it had been thirty years earlier.[11]

Detroit's housing problems did not normally come within the purview of the police, and Edwards's predecessors largely ignored the problem. But, because of his own experiences trying to obtain more public housing for blacks and his sociological approach to crime, Edwards was more willing to see the plight of black homeowners as a law enforcement issue. Technically, he noted, the Civil Rights Act of 1866 gave "all citizens of the United States . . . the same right . . . to inherit, purchase, lease, sell and convey real and personal property." After Reconstruction, however, courts refused to enforce the act—an omission that was not corrected until the Supreme Court's ruling in *Jones v. Alfred H. Mayer Company* in 1968. Although the Court's ruling would not come for another six years, Edwards had no doubt that Michigan's own law "calling for protection of privately-owned property . . . was unequivocal."[12]

In the years before Edwards took over as commissioner, there had been an increasing number of violent incidents as African Americans moved into white neighborhoods. William Patrick decided to run for the Common Council in 1957 after white thugs terrorized one of his clients, Ethel Waters, when she bought a house in Northwest Detroit. Patrick said he was appalled by the fact that no city officials cared about Waters's plight. In late 1961, two mobs in the same area showed their displeasure when real estate agents showed houses to potential black buyers. On September 2, the *Michigan Chronicle* criticized police failure to take action. The newspaper said it was time for the police department to formulate a policy rather than leaving it up to men on the scene to decide how to handle each incident. If the department failed, the newspaper predicted that "Detroit is going to be the focal point of national and international publicity."[13]

Edwards got his chance to make his mark on the problem soon after taking office. In early November 1961, Culley Griffin, a Korean War veteran, and his wife, Mary, signed a contract to buy a house at 19139 Riverview in a predominantly white neighborhood on Detroit's West Side. As Edwards wryly noted, the area in the 16th Precinct was nicknamed "Copper Valley" because so many police officers and firefighters lived there. The Griffins' next door neighbor was a policeman, and other officers lived on their block. But their presence did little to deter trouble. At 1:30 A.M. on December 29, the day the Griffins were scheduled to move in, a fire caused $9,000 worth of damage to the house. Investigators found that someone had removed the furnace blower, which caused the furnace to overheat and start the

181

fire. On February 20, before Griffin, his wife, and their two small children could move in, arsonists cut through the porch screen, poured gasoline on the floorboards, and set another blaze.[14]

Edwards learned of the second fire from a member of the Detroit Commission on Community Relations. He summoned Inspector Frederick G. Kirby of the 16th Precinct, who arrived late, sullen, and defensive. As Edwards remembered, "When asked for the report, he replied that he had been told by the duty officer that the damage had been minimal and the fire probably resulted from defective wiring." He denied knowing anything about the torn porch screen or the gasoline can found at the scene. When Edwards ordered him to post a patrol car round-the-clock at the Griffin home, he balked and complained about manpower shortages. Even with guards, the trouble persisted. While police watched the front of the house, vandals hurled paint bombs and rocks at the back door and windows.[15]

In April, the family finally settled into the house. Edwards visited several times and remembered, "The loneliness of the Griffins and their hazardous living in such a beleaguered home with two small children bothered me." On one occasion, Edwards saw two white youngsters playing on the sidewalk in front of the house. One threw a ball deliberately onto the yard. When the other went to retrieve it, he shouted, "Don't go on the nigger's lawn." As Edwards noted, "The voice was obviously intended for everybody within earshot, particularly me, to hear." Although he offered the family assurances that the police would help them, his words rang hollow. "Even though I increased the patrol and surveillance . . . the harassment and undetected assaults on the Griffin property continued." On April 17, vandals uprooted a hose which was part of an underground sprinkling system. That same night, pellet guns blasted out a front and side storm window.

On May 7, a neighbor began teasing the Griffins' dog. When it barked, the neighbor told Mrs. Griffin and her daughter that he would shoot it. Later that evening, the Griffins found tacks strewn across their driveway. Five days later, someone broke another window at the home. On May 14, police officer J. Moore, who lived next door, threw a party. The revelers, including Mrs.

Moore, hurled racial slurs and began throwing rocks at the Griffins' roof. Problems continued through the month.[16]

As Edwards kept up the police guard, he noted that "the expense in manpower and money was egregious, even more so since quite obviously the officers detailed to the duty were deliberately violating their orders for vigilant protection of the premises." After six more weeks of unsuccessful efforts, Edwards decided to try a new tactic. He summoned Thomas R. Nolan to his office. Nolan, who joined the force in 1936, had a reputation for "playing it by the book," and was respected by his fellow officers. Nolan worked in the busy 2nd Precinct, downtown, but he lived in the 16th. Edwards asked Nolan's help and advice about how to safeguard the Griffin house. Miraculously, after his discussion with Nolan, the police took firmer action. Their testimony provided evidence for the Griffins' attorney, William Cain, to obtain an order from a Wayne County Circuit judge barring the neighbors on either side from harassing the African-American family. In early July, a policeman heard Mrs. Moore cursing at Mrs. Griffin. With the policeman's testimony, Cain went back to court and obtained a contempt citation against Mrs. Moore. At a meeting with the district attorney, the Griffins agreed to drop the matter if the neighbors stopped bothering them. Two weeks later, the police guard was removed and there were no more complaints about violence against the family. Edwards mused, "One of the features of the police grapevine is that everybody on it gets the relevant information. Quite obviously, Inspector Nolan was on the grapevine." Edwards rewarded Nolan with a promotion from uniformed lieutenant to uniformed inspector.[17]

While the Griffin case was still unfolding, Edwards ordered action in another incident. May 26, Detroit police arrested three white men who attempted to torch a vacant house at 19128 Rosemont after learning that it had been shown to prospective African-American buyers. The *Michigan Chronicle* said the arrests were a positive step and "marked the first time throughout a series of incidents of vandalism and attempted arson in the Northwest area that arrests have been made."[18]

Despite Edwards's decisive action in the Griffin and Rosemont cases, problems continued. In early October, there was another wave of violence against African-American families moving into the area of northwest Detroit, south of the John Lodge Expressway between Livernois and Wyoming. Trouble began on September 29 when Leroy Church and his wife moved into a house at 14875 Tuller. Crowds ranging in size between six to two hundred gathered in front of the home, yelling racial epithets and throwing rocks. Even though the first incident lasted three hours, Senior Inspector William E. Icenhower's men did not make one arrest. Edwards summoned Icenhower for an explanation. The inspector, who was an organizer of the "Pizza Parlor Putsch," became "flushed and confused." Icenhower initially tried to downplay the incident, claiming that not much had happened. When Edwards pressed him, the inspector changed his story, claiming the mob was so unruly he would have risked his men's lives by ordering arrests. Later, Edwards admitted it was not all Icenhower's fault: "There probably wasn't an officer or sergeant in the 12th Precinct who would arrest a white man in an anti-Negro mob without a direct order."[19]

Edwards called on James M. Lupton, then serving as the department's director of personnel, and asked him to take charge. When problems broke out the next night, police acted swiftly. They barricaded the block to keep out crowds. Vandals moved on to three other homes in the neighborhood owned by African Americans. The police identified the ringleaders and arrested seven people—five boys and two adults, including one woman who tried to stop police from putting the boys in a squad car. As Edwards later noted, "That had been that. No shots. No blood. When the Youth Bureau arrested the 15-year-old son of the [Neighborhood] Association president . . . and Judge Lincoln put him on $5,000 bond, there was no more trouble at Tuller Avenue."[20]

In the fall of 1962, the Common Council also took steps to address racial changes in Detroit's neighborhoods. On September 12, Councilman James H. Brickley introduced a measure to prohibit the use of "racial scare tactics" in real estate transactions. The Common Council passed the so-called Fair Neighborhoods Practices Ordinance on November 21, and it went into effect eight days later. The new law made it illegal to induce panic sales based on the suggestion that an area was about to undergo racial change. The council gave Detroit's Commission on Community

Relations power to investigate and file complaints. Violators faced a maximum ninety-day jail term and $100 fines. Although racial strife between blacks and whites was the most obvious, it was not the only form of bigotry in demographically complex Detroit. During July Reuben Schwartz, secretary of the city's Jewish Cultural Coordinating Committee, wrote to Cavanagh and Edwards about "secret hate groups in our community whose tactics resembled those used by Hitler's early followers." Edwards promptly assigned a detail to investigate.[21]

Edwards recognized that it would be an uphill battle to mitigate unfair housing in Detroit. Although he ordered police officers to respond swiftly and forcefully to attacks on black homeowners, their efforts in the face of determined resistance had only limited effectiveness. In July 1963, Councilmen Mel Ravitz and William Patrick tried to ease housing integration by introducing an open occupancy ordinance. The measure drew heated opposition, and, even with Cavanagh's support, the Common Council rejected it by a 7-to-2 vote on October 8, 1963. The NAACP decried the outcome, saying it "has laid bare for all to see the harsh reality of white opposition to Negro rights."[22]

Edwards's opposition to segregation was based on his belief that separate housing, along with separate schools and public accommodations, fostered broken homes and dashed hopes, and bred a cynicism that led to delinquency and crime. In June 1960, Edwards asked a national convention of juvenile court judges: "Who can deny that a Negro youth denied the right to go to a school maintained by his state for his age group, denied the right to eat at a lunch counter in a store which solicits public trade, denied the right to vote for the public officials who will determine his future, denied a job because of his color, is not denied equality of opportunity in its most meaningful terms?" Edwards argued, "There is a waste of human potential which results from deprivation of opportunity for our young," and he urged his listeners to join in the fight to "remake our cities into places fit for children to live in." In December 1960, Edwards claimed that the nation's growing murder rate demonstrated that Americans were failing their children. "If we would meet the challenge of the '60s, we must bring light and space into the core of our cities by tearing down slums, replanning to include parks and recreation space, and rebuilding. Decent schools and parks and housing must be looked upon as just as essential to the heritage of the central-city child as they are to the heritage of the child who lives in suburbia." He said it was no accident that federal statistics showed that slum dwellers were involved in 60 percent of all murders and 55 percent of all delinquency cases.[23]

Given his background and national reputation as an expert on juvenile justice, it was not surprising that Edwards believed fighting delinquency was an essential part of curbing crime. In a 1960 article for *The New Republic,* he outlined his two assumptions about the problem. "The first is that no child is born predestined to be a criminal. The second is that we can cure a far higher percentage of our juvenile delinquents than we do." Edwards and other juvenile justice policy makers of the era believed that the "cure" for delinquency rested with rehabilitation rather than punishment. Edwards wrote that "aside from lack of a national program, the most destructive influence in the battle for adequate antidelinquency facilities is undoubtedly the influence of the 'Get Tough' school of thought." He said such "revenge theory" resulted in increased jail space at the expense of probation programs.[24]

One leading advocate of the "Get Tough" school was Los Angeles Police Chief William H. Parker. Police across the nation admired Parker as the epitome of professional and aggressive policing, while Edwards reviled him as an example of all that was wrong with law enforcement. Parker and Edwards disagreed about almost everything. Parker blamed working mothers for the nation's ills, saying "I believe that raising a family is a full-time job." Parker was insensitive to racial injustice, claiming that the problem existed only in the minds of minority leaders who were trying to distract attention from the deplorable crime statistics in their own communities. The Los Angeles chief saved his greatest wrath for those who put an "exaggerated or misplaced emphasis on the possibilities of rehabilitating hardened criminals."[25]

In the early 1960s, Edwards and like-minded reformers found a more receptive audience for their views than Parker and his cohorts—at least among members of the Kennedy administration. One sign of the change came on September 22, when President John F. Kennedy signed the Juvenile Delinquency and Youth

Offenses Control Act of 1961. His brother, Attorney General Robert Kennedy, explained the need for the new legislation, which provided federal guidelines and financial assistance to local authorities. "Our failure as a Nation to halt the rising tide of law violation among our young people is a matter of serious national concern. . . . We have talked a lot about preventing delinquency but have not acted with equal vigor. . . . I do not object at all to more police, improved court procedures, or more effective treatment facilities. . . . But we should be pouring as much, or even more, money, manpower and imagination into preventing those early law violations that start criminal careers."[26]

The Kennedys' battle against juvenile delinquency won support in Detroit, even before Edwards took over the police department. On December 7, 1960, Cavanagh's predecessor, Mayor Miriani, appointed a Study Committee on Crime and Crime Prevention in response to "a growing concern in the community about the increase in crime, particularly in juvenile levels." The committee was weighted heavily with such law enforcement officials as Chief Hart, Louis Berg, and Wayne County Prosecutor Samuel Olsen, but its forty-two members also included such civic leaders as Richard Cross, chair of the Community Relations Commission, Roy Reuther of the UAW, and John C. Dancy, retired president of the Detroit Urban League.[27]

The committee's report fell far short of what Edwards and other liberals advocated because most of its suggestions were administrative. The committee suggested that more personnel be assigned to high crime areas, the vice bureau, the women's division, and the traffic bureau. It also urged the department to construct a new building for the police academy, update its communication systems, and buy heavier cars with higher speed motors. In terms of improving juvenile justice, the committee recommended that the department expand its youth bureau on a new site closer to Juvenile Court.[28]

Miriani responded to the recommendations by creating the permanent Action Committee on Crime and Crime Prevention. Like its predecessor, it was headed by Father Ronald L. Heidelberger, the director of Catholic Charities Youth Service. Between the time of its inception and the eve of Cavanagh's election, it met only five times. Its activities included supporting the creation of a boys' vocational school at Whitmore Lake, advocating higher salaries for juvenile probation officers, and setting up three subcommittees to organize inner-city recreational activities, study school drop-out rates, and establish a Family Life Bureau. But just as the subcommittees began their work in earnest, Cavanagh defeated Miriani in the election. Heidelberger's group stopped work until it could determine its role under the new mayor. Because the Action Committee's work was incomplete, Heidelberger forwarded a copy of its predecessor's report.[29]

Cavanagh turned it over to Edwards, who read it carefully. Despite his belief in the social causes of crime, Edwards recognized that there was a sharp distinction between social work and policing. Although many of the proposals were sound, Edwards said, they fell outside the purview of his department. Nevertheless, he agreed to "encourage their implementation to the degree possible." Edwards agreed with all of the committee's recommendations about the police department and promised to work for a new police academy building, more personnel, a better communications system, and a new Youth Bureau building.[30]

On June 22, he staged his own conference on juvenile delinquency as part of his program to encourage citizen cooperation with the police department. He invited clergymen from across the city, and more than 750 attended. The day-long conference began with a meeting in Ford Auditorium, at which Edwards announced: "The simple message of this conference is that we need your help and, more importantly, the help of your parishioners." Inspector Blake Wallace of the Community Relations Bureau added that 4,330 police "simply cannot control the number of law breakers in a city of almost one million and three quarter population." Other speakers included Monsignor Arthur M. Karen of the Archdiocese of Detroit and Rabbi Morris Adler of Congregation Shaarey Zedek. The biggest attraction of the day was an appearance by Raymond Burr, better known to millions of television viewers as the invincible defense attorney Perry Mason. After lunch the clergymen broke up into smaller groups at Veterans Memorial Hall to discuss neighborhood problems with their precinct inspectors.[31]

On November 1, Edwards scheduled another all-day conference, attended by about six hundred public and private school officials, to discuss ways that police and educators could work together to stop youth crime. It followed the same format as the clergy meeting—morning meetings at Ford Auditorium, lunch at Veterans Memorial Hall, and afternoon sessions at precinct stations to discuss local concerns. In addition to Cavanagh and Edwards, other speakers included U.S. District Judge Wade McCree, who addressed the need for equal justice. Edwards's brother-in-law, Semon E. Knudsen, the vice president of General Motors, discussed traffic safety. Margaret Conway, head of the department's women's division, described how teachers could bring problems to her attention. Educators were enthusiastic after the meeting. One called it an "imaginative" way of providing a "a close look at police problems." Dr. Harold J. Harrison, an administrator with the Detroit School District, said it "was one of the best things that could have happened."[32]

In 1962, Edwards also joined hands with Wade McCree, Mildred Jeffrey, Horace Sheffield and many other civic leaders to obtain a $202,000 federal grant to help Detroit launch a broad attack on juvenile delinquency. The program was funded by the President's Committee on Juvenile Delinquency, which provided similar grants to New Haven, Los Angeles, Philadelphia, Cleveland, Minneapolis, Chicago, and New York. In announcing the grant to Detroit in August, Cavanagh said, "Community Action for Detroit Youth, is one step in Detroit's effort to mobilize the total community to work together to solve the problems of youth." The mayor appointed a twelve-member board of directors, which included Edwards, to develop research and development programs. The following year, when President Kennedy introduced the Youth Employment Act, Edwards issued a press release urging Detroit to enact a similar program. He said, "The Detroit Police are very much concerned about the young people, out of school, out of work, who become offenders. A great increase in the number of out-of-work people could be socially calamitous."[33]

Edwards convened meetings with citizens, but unlike his predecessors he never appointed citizen task forces to tackle such problems as delinquency. His vision of community cooperation with the police was much broader and included all law-abiding citizens. Community cooperation was not a novel notion among

law enforcement officials in the early 1960s. Faced with the inex-
orable rise in crime, many excused away their failure to stem the
tide by deeming it a larger social problem. For example, in August 1962, FBI Director J. Edgar Hoover called on community
leaders to "lead the fight to halt the lawless hordes who prey
on society. No amount of rationalization can justly place this
responsibility on the shoulders of law enforcement alone." Edwards and other liberals in the early 1960s put their own stamp
on the traditional message offered by such law-and-order advocates as Hoover. The FBI director, along with most police,
assumed that citizens had an innate duty to respect law enforcement officials. Such a belief rested on the assumption that police
were beyond reproach. Liberals, such as Edwards, viewed the
matter more critically. They argued that the duty of improving
community relations rested with police and not average citizens.
Police had to earn respect by behaving more professionally. It
was their responsibility to foster community cooperation by seeking and cultivating citizen contacts.[34]

Early in his tenure, Edwards implemented concrete changes
to improve policing. He hired more police and shifted existing
officers to peak crime periods and neighborhoods. Nevertheless,
Edwards believed none of those changes would bring about lasting improvement without increased community cooperation. As
he told one reporter, asking for citizen help "hasn't been the attitude here in the past. The basic police attitude . . . is 'Leave it to
us.' But that is wrong. The truth is, we can't handle it alone.
We must have the active cooperation of law-abiding citizens."
Edwards believed that most people wanted to help police. He
cited an incident that occurred when he addressed an African-
American church congregation. "After I spoke, a man got up and
said, 'Commissioner there is a numbers drop right on my block.
My kids see what is going on and I don't like it.' That numbers
drop has been wiped out. From other such informants—white
and Negro—we've had information not only on gambling, but on
prostitution, narcotics, traffic, and other crimes." When Edwards
took command, the department already was sponsoring six hundred block clubs. He urged his men to contact all of them and
enlist their aid.[35]

In order to win support for his programs, Edwards had to

show that his sociological approach to crime did not undermine the effectiveness of law enforcement. This was particularly challenging in the early 1960s, when statistics indicated that Detroit, along with the rest of the nation, was experiencing a dramatic increase in crime. In August 1962, the FBI released its Uniform Crime Reports for the previous year. Based on information by local police departments, the report showed an all-time high in the national crime rate. From 1956 to 1961, FBI Director Hoover noted, "crime has outstripped the growth of the population five to one." The statistics showed an average increase of 2 percent in cities with populations over 25,000. Detroit far exceeded this rate: crime was 8.2 percent higher for the first six months of 1962 than it had been for the same period in 1961. Crime for July 1962 appeared to be up 21.8 percent over July 1961.[36]

Predictably, Hoover and Edwards offered different explanations for the increases. The FBI director said that even though there was no single cause of crime, "We shall see no abatement in widespread lawlessness as long as there is wholesale disrespect for law and order in our Nation. Indulgence and materialistic selfishness are eroding the tried and true American traditions of honesty, integrity and fair play." Perhaps because the crime statistics compiled by local authorities did not reflect badly on the FBI's own efforts, Hoover felt no reason to explain them. Instead, he took them at face value and used them as an excuse to pontificate about the nation's deteriorating morals and his own vigilance in the war against crime.[37]

Edwards, by contrast, recognized the statistics as a potential public relations disaster. He attacked their validity by arguing that they were misleading. Edwards claimed that the increase in reported crimes did not mean more crimes had been committed. Instead, they only showed that more crimes had been detected by the police. In other words, Detroit's higher crime rate reflected better efficiency by his men and more community cooperation. The proof, he said, lay in the fact that the highest increases in crime were reported in the precincts where he assigned more men to work during peak crime hours. These were the same areas that had the highest citizen distrust of police in 1961—the 1st and 10th precincts. In these neighborhoods, African-American complainants accounted for a 71 percent increase in crime reporting for the first six months of the year. By contrast, there were no measurable increases in crime in the 4th, 11th, 14th, 15th, and 16th precincts, white areas where cooperation with the police was always forthcoming. Edwards predicted that more citizen cooperation "may continue to have an effect on increasing crime statistics for sometime to come, but the ultimate effect of uncovering previously unreported crime should be a somewhat safer city." Edwards was not alone in decrying the unreliability and politics of crime statistics. In March 1963, he attended a national meeting of police administrators in Chicago. Michael J. Murphy, New York City police commissioner, received accolades from fellow delegates when he complained that some departments were reluctant to keep statistics because of a "tendency to charge the crime rate against the police rather than against the community." He also criticized "the temptation to draw from such statistics broad generalizations concerning the relative efficiency of various police forces."[38]

To Edwards's critics, however, the statistics reflected a real increase in crime that had nothing to do with changes in reporting habits. Instead, the fact that crime remained the same in white areas but increased dramatically in the city's two African-American precincts seemed to prove what they already assumed. First, blacks committed more crimes. Second, Edwards's overtures to Detroit's African-American community only encouraged more criminal behavior. The *Free Press* reflected these sentiments when it dismissed the commissioner's explanation and lambasted his "political" approach to law enforcement. "Rightly or wrongly, and we wouldn't profess to say which, a good deal of the rank-and-file thinks that these are days to be wary in the pursuit of a suspect lest an officer wind up as a victim of political exploitation. He figures that the merits of the case won't have much bearing if it falls out that he is the goat in a situation that might snare a few votes. This doesn't have to be so, but the consequence is all the same so far as the citizen's safety from criminals goes. It declines." The newspaper said Edwards bore the burden of convincing his men and the public "that this . . . is not the way Mayor Cavanagh intends the department to be run. For the feelings a good many policemen have confided to newspaper men come out as cynicism—and in a police department cynicism is the seed of corruption."[39]

Newspaper stories about the city's alleged increase in crime inspired a spate of critical letters. One voter, Jack Humphrey, sent Cavanagh a copy of the *Free Press* editorial and wrote: "I would suggest you read this . . . and think about exactly what it means to the working public of this city." Cavanagh responded with aplomb, saying: "As you know, Detroit is not unique in this serious situation. All large cities and many smaller ones in the United States are faced with a rising crime rate and are doing their utmost to control the situation." The mayor pointed out that he and Edwards managed to get more money for the police department and better pay for its officers.[40]

The *Free Press* editorial and public outcry reflected a faith in the accuracy of crime statistics. Edwards's explanations, however, may have been closer to the mark. For a variety of reasons, the FBI and law enforcement agencies across the country encouraged public faith in crime statistics. Among other things, if statistics showed a drop in crime, then police and politicians could take credit for their effectiveness. By contrast, when crime statistics show an increase, law enforcement agencies can seek larger budgets. Studies have shown that statistical reports about crime are flawed. They depend on variables, some of which Edwards mentioned, including warmer weather, declining job opportunities, and changes in victim reporting habits. Perhaps the most common reason why statistics are misleading is paperwork errors. The Bergs made Edwards look bad by adding crimes from December 1961 into the January 1962 report. In the department's report for the first six months of 1962, officers in three precincts miscounted domestic quarrels as more serious felonious assaults.[41]

As would be true throughout his tenure, whenever his enemies within the department sensed he was vulnerable, they attempted to publicly undermine his authority. Amid the controversy about the crime statistics, they thought they had found a perfect opportunity to embarrass him at the department's 36th Field Day exercises on August 13, which 35,000 Detroiters showed up to watch. Proceeds from the annual event held at Tiger Stadium went to help widows and orphans of police officers. Each division of the department participated in some activity. The motorcycle unit fielded a "commando" squad. The mounted division showed its horsemanship. The department band provided music. The pistol team gave an exhibition of marksmanship. Other police officers competed against counterparts from Toronto in athletic competitions.[42]

The day got off to a bad start for Edwards when his driver, Jack Jenson, gave him the wrong time for the starting ceremonies. When he found out that the festivities began at 1:30 instead of 2 P.M., Edwards called Inspector Icenhower and asked him to delay the opening review until he could get there. But Icenhower said the program had already begun. When Edwards showed up just in time to miss the beginning, he realized that Icenhower lied to him. Instead of joining the department's command officers on the field, he sat in the stands and pondered what to do next. He decided not to punish Jenson, because he believed that the Bergs and Icenhower ordered him to lie. He also remembered a line from Machiavelli, "Never do an enemy a small injustice."[43]

Outwardly Edwards kept his calm. When he finally did take the podium, he stressed the ways in which Field Day exercises fit in with his community policing philosophy. He told the assembled audience that

> The occasion is a very significant one for its brings together many of our citizens and their police officers. It gives the community an opportunity to see their police department in some less serious . . . moments. It gives Detroiters an opportunity to witness and be a part of the ceremony at which officers who have distinguished themselves in the performance of their duties receive the department's highest awards for that service. It likewise gives the members of the department an opportunity to see enthusiastic examples of public interest in and support for law enforcement. All of this is important because it helps to build that spirit of community understanding and cooperation which is so essential to the operation of the department and to the safety and well-being of the city.[44]

Edwards presented medals to four police officers for outstanding heroism. Then, along with the rest of the audience, he sat back to enjoy the show. Police units performed close ordered drills. He stood side-by-side with Louis Berg cheering on his men as they defeated a tug-of-war team from the Toronto Police Department. Like others, he expressed disappointment when heavy rain forced cancellation of the afternoon and evening aerial and juggling acts. That evening he hosted a cocktail party for the Toronto police. After they arrived home, Peg told him that the Canadian police commanders' wives asked her why Edwards put up with defiance from his own men. Edwards went to sleep asking himself the same question.[45]

He had tried to work with the Bergs, in part, because he knew they enjoyed wide support within the department and the community. The Bergs tolerated Edwards because they assumed his command would be short-lived. But the veneer of civility did little to conceal the fact that the three men disagreed about almost every aspect of police work. The Bergs believed in defending their men at all costs, even when the officers brutalized suspects, discriminated against African Americans, or engaged in corrupt activities. They disdained Edwards's sociological views as naive and thought his "do-gooding" would undermine the effectiveness of law enforcement. As an outsider, Edwards had little comprehension or tolerance for the brotherhood that linked members of the force through a code of defensive silence. He took a much broader view of police work. Rather than seeing it as the ultimate force for law and order, he viewed it as just one piece of a larger mosaic. Despite the Bergs' opposition, Edwards managed to go a long way toward implementing his program of racially unbiased and constitutional policing. But when it came to fighting the entrenched criminal enterprises that could only flourish with police corruption, Edwards needed to have command officers who would work with him. Thus, it was inevitable that the Bergs and Edwards would clash, but the Bergs miscalculated in thinking they could win the battle. For the next several weeks, Edwards pondered what action to take against the Bergs. Then he decided it was time for a showdown. Under Detroit's city charter, he had no power to fire or hire police officers, but he could reassign them. In September, he called Cavanagh and said he planned to demote the Bergs by sending them back to the traffic division. Edwards recalled that the mayor was "obviously disturbed by the news," but he agreed to back his police commissioner. The next morning Edwards took Louis Berg to breakfast at the Cadillac Hotel to break the bad news. The superintendent became upset and protested that the demotions would reflect badly on his entire family. He asked for more time to prove his commitment to

Edwards's program. Edwards agreed but warned Berg: "Louie don't spend three months trying to take me out of here. You might succeed, but you would go first, and if you do, I'll guarantee that you will never work in law enforcement again." During the next six weeks, the Bergs did nothing to help Edwards's program, but they also did nothing to undermine it. Quietly, they began looking for other job opportunities.[46] With the Berg matter temporarily settled, Edwards focussed his attention on the last part of his long-term agenda—fighting organized crime.

8

A Crusade Begins

How can I teach my children to support law enforcement when the Gotham stands there in full operation and in plain view?
—A Detroit African-American citizen in spring 1962

To those who cared about such matters, the existence of organized crime in Detroit and the identity of its leaders had never been much of a secret. Previous police commissioners and department heads like the Bergs tolerated its presence because they were intimidated by the complications involved in fighting powerful crime syndicates, were blasé about the omnipresence of vice, or worried that exposing such deep-seated crime could reveal police corruption. By contrast, Edwards believed that countenancing any criminal activity was a mistake. It reflected badly on the police department and encouraged lawlessness. Edwards also viewed organized crime as more than a matter of vice. His early career in the labor movement shaped his opinion that racketeers posed a much more sinister threat. He was at the hospital bedsides of Walter and Victor Reuther after Santo Perrone's gang attempted to assassinate them in the late 1940s. He watched with disdain as James Hoffa rose to a leadership position with the International Brotherhood of Teamsters. As police commissioner, Edwards wanted to persuade average Detroiters that organized crime was an evil corrupting many aspects of economic and social life.

He was not alone. Many other liberal Democrats across the

country, including Illinois Senator Paul H. Douglas, Tennessee Senator Estes Kefauver, and Attorney General Robert F. Kennedy, argued that organized crime threatened major American institutions. They were especially concerned that racketeering in some unions would tarnish the entire labor movement. Their fears worsened during the 1950s when belief in a nationwide crime empire run by Sicilians gained currency. In 1950 and 1951, the Senate's Special Committee to Investigate Organized Crime in Interstate Commerce, headed by Edwards's friend Sen. Kefauver, garnered national headlines for its revelations in Detroit and other large cities. The committee concluded, "There is a Nationwide crime syndicate known as the Mafia, whose tentacles are found in many large cities. . . . Its leaders are usually found in control of the most lucrative rackets in their cities. There are indications of a centralized direction and control of these rackets, but leadership appears to be in a group rather than in a single individual." Many establishment figures, including FBI Director J. Edgar Hoover, rejected the existence of the Mafia as ludicrous. Then more evidence began to surface.[1]

In January 1957, the Senate created the Select Committee on Improper Activities in the Labor or Management Field to investigate whether organized criminals were infiltrating labor unions to gain access to lucrative pension and welfare funds. The committee became popularly known by the name of its chair, Arkansas Democrat John L. McClellan. Because of their differing views of labor, committee members split along political lines in their definitions of racketeering. Republicans wanted to investigate activist, liberal labor leaders whose agenda included political and social change. Democrats, on the other hand, decried corrupt labor leaders and racketeers who looted union treasuries and used locals as shields for their illegal enterprises. Arizona Republican Barry Goldwater typified the split when he proclaimed: "Mr. Walter Reuther and the UAW have done more damage and violence to freedom than was accomplished by all the peculiar financial transactions of Mr. Dave Beck." He defended Beck, the Teamsters's ex-president, who was removed for misappropriating funds, and his replacement, Jimmy Hoffa, because both supported Republican candidates and avowed their allegiance to the free enterprise system. As chief counsel of the committee, Robert

F. Kennedy developed a loathing for Hoffa, whom he believed was worse than other corrupt labor bosses because of his ties to the underworld. In 1960, with the help of newspaperman John Siegenthaler, Kennedy wrote *The Enemy Within,* a book that described his belief that organized crime posed a threat to American values.[2]

In November 1957, Mafia conspiracy theories gained more credence when the New York State Police happened upon a national conference of underworld bosses at the tiny, upstate hamlet of Apalachin. Alerted by a large influx of black limousines, the police set up roadblocks around a house owned by Joseph Barbara. Fifty-eight crime bosses from across the nation became ensnared in the dragnet. At least twenty-two of them had connections to unions. The Apalachin meeting convinced many skeptics. As historian Arthur Schlesinger, Jr., noted: "What had seemed in 1951 a loose-knit organization was beginning to appear as something far more menacing: a monolithic, formally organized, ethnically homogenous, strictly disciplined secret society, based on esoteric rituals, commanding the absolute obedience of its members and controlling all organized crime—in short, an invisible government of the underworld."[3]

When Kennedy became U.S. Attorney General he made fighting organized crime a major part of his agenda. His well-publicized crusade galvanized many state and local politicians. Edwards was an enthusiastic convert. In March 1961, while still a state Supreme Court justice, he asked a mutual friend, labor writer John Herling, for an introduction to Kennedy. After their brief meeting at the Justice Department, Edwards wrote an enthusiastic thank you letter. He vowed to use his position with the National Council of Crime and Delinquency to pass a resolution supporting Kennedy's efforts, and he urged the attorney general to come to Michigan for an upcoming crime conference. Kennedy sent back a cursory reply, declining the invitation and thanking Edwards for his support.[4]

Edwards's experiences growing up in Texas helped explain his willingness to believe in a secret, underworld syndicate which ruled by fear and engaged in strange rituals. Years later he described the parallels that he saw between the Ku Klux Klan and the Mafia. "Secrecy is, of course, the most valuable weapon which a criminal conspiracy can have. The Ku Klux Klan had for many years after the Civil War, dominated the South, including the State of Texas in the '20s and '30s when I was growing up as a boy." Both relied on intimidation tactics and corruption of law enforcement officials. Edwards never forgot how the KKK members who kidnapped his father got away with their crime because no witness would agree to testify against them in open court.[5]

Although his knowledge of the Klan was based on real experience, Edwards and other organized crime "experts" of the late 1950s and early 1960s based their views of the Mafia on an accepted wisdom that was a hodgepodge of reality infused with hyperbole. Because of its secret nature, law enforcement knowledge of the Mafia was, in fact, hazy. So-called experts layered one piece of information on top of another, making little attempt to verify the underlying facts. As a result, law enforcement officials and journalists had ample room for speculation and exaggeration. They saw signs of a criminal conspiracy, but they had no real way to piece hidden parts of the jigsaw puzzle together. Historians have spent decades trying to separate the myths from reality. Judicious evaluations are still difficult; in the 1960s, when even the FBI was caught flat-footed by the presence of organized crime, they were impossible.

The degree to which Edwards relied on such accepted wisdom became apparent in his first major speech on organized crime, delivered before he became police commissioner. In May 1961, Edwards spoke in place of Robert Kennedy at a Michigan crime conference. His speech would have been worthy of the absent attorney general. Edwards called organized crime an "obscenity to American life," and said "the existence of a known, protected, and profitable national crime conspiracy" was a major factor in promoting disrespect for the law. He ridiculed skeptics who doubted the reality of "the mob," citing the work of Sen. Kefauver, the Apalachin gathering, and Kennedy's book, *The Enemy Within*. Besides, he claimed, average citizens did not have to read books or newspapers; they could just look around their neighborhoods to recognize the influence of organized crime on local government. "If you know where a bookie or a house of vice is in operation and has existed to your knowledge for a month this almost certainly means corruption in the police department in the area." If it had existed for more than six months, then corruption exists in city hall and police headquarters. He insisted that local police investigations were inadequate against the "syndicate" because of "its code of silence, enforced by nationally-organized gangsters, and corruption in local situations." He exhorted his listeners to join Kennedy's efforts to make fighting the Mafia a national effort.[6]

During his first year as Detroit police commissioner, Edwards made overtures to Kennedy. While he was in Washington to attend a White House correspondents' dinner with his friend John Herling, Edwards arranged to meet with the attorney general on April 27, 1962. They discussed how many racketeers got their start as bootleggers in Detroit during Prohibition, then used their profits to fund gambling, labor, prostitution, and narcotics rackets in other states. After he returned home, Edwards thanked Kennedy and expressed optimism that their meeting would "have real meaning in future cooperation between national law enforcement agencies and our department." Several weeks later, when Edwards was speaking to a luncheon of civic leaders, a member of the audience asked him how many racketeers who made their early fortunes in Detroit still ran illegal enterprises in the city. Edwards answered, "That's a corker. Obviously the quick and easy answer is, I don't know. It also needs to be said that I intend to do every last thing I can to find out." He spent the next year trying to learn the answer to that question. He began by contacting federal prosecutors and agents working in Detroit to discuss the possibility of joint operations. He continued to try to develop his relationship with Kennedy. In June, he asked U.S. Supreme Court Justice Douglas to put in a good word about him to the attorney general. Douglas agreed and afterwards wrote Edwards: "I hope you cultivate your acquaintance with Bobby Kennedy. I talked with him about you. . . . He remembered you, and favorably."[7]

Edwards was very concerned about Kennedy's opinion of him, and he worried what Kennedy might think in April 1962 when Hoffa asked him to mediate a Teamsters strike. It is unclear why Hoffa asked the police commissioner to intervene. Edwards never hid his disdain for Hoffa. He publicly worked against the Teamster boss's efforts to infiltrate local politics, and he cheered

201

when his old friend, Senator Douglas, succeeded in keeping Hoffa out of the Chicago taxicab union. Edwards agreed to mediate the newspaper strike as a public service and presided over a successful thirty-three-hour marathon bargaining session with Local 372. At its conclusion on April 26, a photographer for *The Detroit News* snapped a picture of Hoffa and Edwards shaking hands. It was the only time the two ever met, and Edwards worried that their relationship could be misinterpreted. He fired off an explanatory letter to Herling: "Hoffa and I have never been friends, either personally or politically." Edwards said that years earlier he had helped fight Hoffa's attempts to kill a grand jury investigation into his running of the Teamsters. In 1950, Hoffa tried to gain a foothold in Michigan's Democratic party by hand-picking a slate of precinct delegates in Wayne County. Edwards led the effort to disqualify many of the candidates whose "petitions were patently forged and fraudulent." Edwards told Herling: "These two things I think you would want to know in case the topic were ever to be raised down there."[8]

Although Edwards's hatred of organized crime was based largely on his knowledge of labor racketeering, most of his focus as police commissioner was on gambling. Along with Kennedy and other law enforcement officials across the nation, he believed gambling profits were the lifeblood of the Mafia and provided the money to fund its other illegal activities. Soon after taking over the police department, he read a Canadian crime commission report that named Vito "Billy Jack" Giacalone as the gambling czar of Detroit. Edwards had never heard of Giacalone or his older brother, Anthony, although later they would become Detroit's best-known crime bosses. Their father, Giacamo, from Sicily, immigrated to Detroit and raised his seven children in the "Little Italy" section on the East Side between Mack and Kercheval. Vito, who was born in 1923, dropped out of school in the eighth grade and quickly earned a reputation as a "tough guy." He first gained public attention in December 1949, when he was arrested for taking part in a horse betting ring. Throughout the 1950s, he was arrested several more times for gambling, but none of the charges stuck. He served his first jail sentence in 1959—ninety days for running a gambling operation at the Lebanese-American Club at 535 Orleans. In the early 1960s, the

Giacalones ran many gambling enterprises in Detroit, including the Lesod Club, which took its name from its original location on the Lower East Side of Detroit. Several years earlier, the Lesod Club moved downtown to 106 Columbia. Ironically, Edwards first learned about the gambling haven from a friend of his wife, who complained that it was operating openly across the street from the Detroit Women's Club.[9]

Edwards ordered the Bergs to shut down the Lesod. They protested, but forwarded his request to the vice squad. That, according to Edwards, began a "farcical period." He received numerous reports about illegal gambling at the club, along with detailed reports about how police could not penetrate the Lesod's sophisticated defenses. Customers had to check with a lookout posted in a car parked in front of the two-story building. The sentry asked newcomers for their names, addresses and occupations, then sent them home until the club could conduct a background check that usually ferreted out undercover police. The sentry sent regular customers through the front door and up a staircase to another door that was locked from the inside. A guard posted upstairs watched through a peephole to ensure that no unwanted guests slipped past the lookout. On the rare occasions when vice detectives got through the front door, they were still delayed by the locked door. Several times they stood by helplessly as they heard people inside the room hiding gambling paraphernalia. Because the club specialized in barbut, a game of Greek origin that required only a pair of dice and level floor space, there wasn't much to secrete. By the time the door was unlocked, police were confronted by a tame scene. On one 6 A.M. raid, they found twenty-five people playing chess and checkers. Even though most of the playing pieces were out of order, police were unable to make any arrests. Customers, who admitted gambling but refused to testify about their activities, further hampered police action.[10]

Previous commissioners, confronted by their inability to gather the evidence or produce the witnesses necessary for a criminal prosecution, gave up. Edwards took a more lawyerly approach to the problem. He posted police to watch the club and interview its patrons. Owners of three neighboring businesses— two restaurants and a bar—complained that police were also badgering their customers. Sims Realty Company, which owned the building, responded by filing a harassment suit against the city, seeking an injunction against the police department. The city filed a counter suit, saying that if Sims did not take action to stop gambling at the Lesod Club, the building would be declared a public nuisance. At the hearing before Wayne County Circuit Judge George E. Bowles on June 6, Edwards proved to be a feisty witness. Acting more like a state Supreme Court justice than a police commissioner, Edwards sparred with Sims's lawyer, rephrasing his questions and correcting his logic. Attorney Larry S. Davidow became so frustrated that he asked Bowles to instruct Edwards "to forget his past position of prominence" and simply answer the questions.[11]

In order to gather evidence to support his contention that the Lesod Club constituted a nuisance, Edwards ordered his men to stand outside the building for three nights, issuing subpoenas to every customer who walked past them. The first thirteen "made poor witnesses," according to the *Free Press*, because they all invoked their Fifth Amendment right against self-incrimination. Before Judge Bowles could issue a ruling, the Lesod Club closed its operations in Detroit and moved to Highland Park, where it opened two weeks later. Edwards wrote a triumphant letter to Supreme Court Justice Douglas, "The light of publicity and the filing of a suit to abate a nuisance plus the surveillance seemed to convince them that were more desirable locations for business than the city of Detroit."[12]

Edwards also hatched a scheme to make it more difficult for other gambling clubs to operate in Detroit. In June, he proposed an ordinance that would close all of Detroit's four hundred to five hundred nonprofit social clubs from 2 A.M. to 8 A.M. They could stay open after hours only when police investigated each establishment and authorized an exception. Edwards argued that the ordinance would give police the power to close gambling operations without having to go through the arduous efforts involved in gathering the evidence for search warrants. He believed the statute would also help Detroit's legitimate bars by closing down operations that siphoned off their business. When he appeared before the Common Council in the fall to argue for the ordinance, Edwards estimated it would affect only twenty clubs in the city. The measure passed over the objections of Councilmen William Patrick and Mel Ravitz who argued that police could misuse the law to harass legitimate businesses and violate Detroiters' right to assemble.[13]

Edwards was also eyeing a much larger target. In meetings with African-American civic and church groups, he heard recurring complaints from citizens about vice activities in their neighborhoods. One man left a deep impression when he came up after a meeting and asked Edwards, "How can I teach my children to support law enforcement when the Gotham stands there in full operation and in plain view?" The Gotham Hotel at 111 Orchestra Place was the center of the city's numbers rackets. Albert Boyntown and Alice Harz built the Detroit landmark in 1924 during the first year of their marriage. By 1943, the neighborhood had changed, and they sold the hotel to John White, Jr. Under his management, the Gotham thrived by catering to African Americans shut out of the city's upscale white establishments. White also made money by renting space to numbers runners. As the *Free Press* noted, "Despite its frequent raids, the hotel had a reputation as being the finest Negro hostelry in the United States. It had excellent restaurants and rooms and suites."[14]

Edwards came to believe that "stopping gambling at the Gotham was mandatory for the reputation of the city and the police department and, for that matter, of the police commissioner." He thought closing the hotel would show concerned members of the African-American community that police were serious about helping them clean up their neighborhoods. When Edwards asked the Bergs to move against the Gotham, however, they expressed little enthusiasm. They invoked the same excuse they had used for not prosecuting the Lesod Club—the difficulty of obtaining a search warrant.[15]

By late summer, the Bergs still had done nothing about the Gotham. Edwards worried that the hotel's continued presence as a numbers center indicated some kind of law enforcement corruption, but he had no proof. Looking back years later, Vincent Piersante agreed that the Bergs probably realized that the Gotham's gambling could exist only with police corruption. He explained, "The Bergs were not corrupt. They just could not believe that some of the people they had relied on for years were corrupt. I compare it to something happening in your own family. The feeling of family is very intense in a police department. You really don't want to see any part of it harmed or exposed as rotten."[16]

It would take several more months of planning and preparation to close the Gotham. When the raid came, Edwards made sure that the Bergs got none of the glory. Given their inaction against organized vice, Edwards had turned for help to others, including Piersante and his CIB, which had solved the DPW corruption case. Edwards recalled that "it took some time for me to conclude that the Department's most skilled investigative unit should actively participate in making cases against organized crime." Part of his reluctance stemmed from the fact that "all of the illegal businesses of organized crime operated within the jurisdiction of traditional police squads. Gambling and prostitution were the specific territory of the vice squad." Nevertheless, Edwards also took notice of the fact that "the numbers racket operated freely in Detroit even in its public buildings and few cases were brought against numbers operators. No effort had ever been made to gain a search warrant for the Gotham Hotel."[17]

Gambling was not the only open illegal activity in the city. Citizens complained to Edwards about narcotics dealers, prostitutes, and an abortion clinic. He investigated at least two of the reports himself. Theodore Souris, his former colleague on the Michigan Supreme Court, told him about a whore house operating within a block of the Detroit College of Law. Edwards drove by and was astonished to find the most "explicit prostitution advertisement I had ever witnessed in Detroit or any other city. There in three big bay windows in broad daylight seated in rocking chairs were three females obviously advertising sex for sale by smiles, gestures and scantiness of clothing." They saw Edwards standing outside a police car and "vanished." When precinct officers checked later, they found no sign of prostitution. Edwards wondered how they could have missed it before. Edwards also verified a tip about an abortion clinic operating on a corner of West Six Mile Road. He contacted the precinct inspector, who later reported that the operation had moved to Macomb County.

Edwards said, "The result did not strike me as a very significant law enforcement victory. The timing of the move did interest me." He ultimately concluded "that there did not seem to be prosecutions in any of these areas which came close to matching the police manpower assigned to the activity."[18]

In an interview with the *Detroit News* in September, Edwards said that his experience as police commissioner reinforced his belief that there was a "framework of nationally syndicated organized crime which represents a serious menace to public morality and law enforcement." He claimed the "syndicate" was "particularly active in such affairs as importing and distribution of narcotics, organization and banking of horse betting, and in gambling and vice generally." The national and international scope of organized crime created headaches for local law enforcement. As a result, police were "frequently engaged in seeking to kill this particular tree of crime by pulling the leaves off rather than chopping it down." Although he supported Robert Kennedy's request for federal legislation, Edwards maintained that the problem was too serious to wait for Congressional action. "Although we need vigorous national attention to this problem, an alert citizenry and vigilant police department can make [for] a very unprofitable area of operation. I think that to some degree this is already true."[19]

When Edwards began circumventing them, the Bergs realized their days were numbered. They finally decided to open their own security consulting business in the Buhl Building. On November 2, Louis Berg announced that he and his brother were retiring. The *Free Press* reported that the Bergs's departure was "a solar plexus blow for Edwards and touched off shock and dismay in the 4,394-man Detroit Police Department." Edwards found descriptions of him being "shocked and disheartened" amusing. As he said later, "Nothing could have been further from the truth. I much preferred for the Bergs to retire by their own volition than by my having to demote them."[20]

Publicly the Bergs and Edwards refused to comment on their disagreements. Edwards, disengenuously, denied that he forced the brothers out, telling reporters: "I don't think I created an atmosphere that would lead them to think I wanted them to leave." Edwards insisted that the Bergs had given him a friendly reception and continued to support him. The Bergs offered a similar version of events, saying they were leaving only because they could not turn down a compelling business opportunity. Within the department there was little doubt about what had really happened. As Piersante recalled, "The Berg brothers were unquestionably anti-Edwards. He did give them a chance, but I think they believed he was going to try to get rid of them come hell or high water, so they wanted to get rid of him and they believed they could get rid of him." Piersante explained that the Bergs wanted a commissioner who would let them run the department without "civilian" interference. He said the brothers could "not understand that it just doesn't always work that way."[21]

By retiring without publicly criticizing their boss, the Bergs followed the example set by their father, who left the force in 1944 under similar circumstances. The senior Berg resigned after Mayor Jeffries appointed John Ballenger, a social worker, as police commissioner. Berg saw Ballenger as a political appointee whose do-gooding philosophy would undermine the force's effectiveness. As the *Free Press* reported, "Louis Berg, as a good policeman, hates all political interference. From the beginning, he and Ballenger could never see eye to eye. There were other reasons. Mr. Ballenger thinks that a police department should be more of a sociological division of our community. . . . Superintendent Berg, being of the Old School, looks upon the criminal as an enemy of society, and not as a problem child. The end was inevitable."[22]

News of the Bergs' retirement prompted predictable responses. The NAACP issued a statement saying that even though the Bergs may have been good policemen, "we are compelled to welcome the passing from the scene of the architects and executioners of the most infamous attack ever levelled against the Negro community in the history of Detroit in the guise of a so-called crackdown against crime in late 1960 and early 1961." The NAACP welcomed the fact that Edwards would now be free to hire "the best possible high-level personnel of the department who will conscientiously work to accelerate the progressive and enlightened program which he has inaugurated under the greatest of handicaps." In sum, the NAACP said, "All citizens should be grateful for the better police department yet to come with the passing of the Berg brothers."[23]

In the white community, word of the retirements prompted some citizens to see an almost overnight increase in crime. Mrs. Robert Miller wrote Cavanagh describing how her eighty-one-year-old mother had been attacked by two "six-foot Negroes in broad daylight." In grabbing the elderly woman's purse, the attackers pushed her to the ground and left her unconscious with a fractured hip. Mrs. Miller said a black youth snatched her purse in late September, also in broad daylight. She told Cavanagh, "I am not the only one who is perturbed by this situation. I am not blaming the police officers as I think they are doing a fine job but all they can do is obey orders from their superiors." Another Detroiter complained: "There has been a great change in our neighborhood since Edwards has been commissioner. The folks used to be afraid to go out at night—now they're afraid to go out in daytime. . . . The capable police officials are quitting, the patrolman who pounds the beat or rides a scout car looks nauseated at the very mention of the name 'Edwards.' . . . You'd better give Edwards back to the NAACP."[24]

While citizens and newspapers debated the meaning of the Bergs' retirement, Edwards took advantage of their departure to move against the Gotham. He called Inspector Arthur C. Sage, who had just taken charge of the vice squad, and ordered him to close the gambling den. Within the next week, Sage came back with interesting information. The Gotham, which had long been slated for demolition to make way for Detroit's new medical center, had exhausted its appeals to the city. Hotel patrons moved out, and the only remaining residents were numbers runners. From a law enforcement standpoint that was significant. As long as the Gotham remained a residential hotel, police needed search warrants for each of its rooms. Once it became just a gambling spot, police needed only one search warrant. Edwards contacted the U.S. attorney's office, and Sage began planning a joint raid with agents of the Internal Revenue Service (IRS) and the Michigan State Police.[25]

Symbolically, for Edwards at least, the IRS chose the same day for the Gotham raid as the Bergs chose for their retirement party. "I probably could have prevented the coincidence, but I did not," he recalled. Instead, Edwards presided over the retirement party that morning, and by 2 P.M. the Bergs cleared out their desks and left. At about the same time, federal prosecutors went to U.S. District Judge Fred Kaess to get a search warrant. The raid would be a formidable undertaking. The huge building had a lobby, a cafe, and drug store on the first floor, 174 rooms on the next eight floors, and a penthouse on the top floor. Security was tight. Sentries posted around the hotel, a closed-circuit television system, and an alarm system on every floor could alert gamblers when police entered the building.[26]

Law enforcement agents had the element of surprise in their favor. To maintain secrecy federal agents from elsewhere had been brought in the night before. Very few of the police involved in the raid had been told about it beforehand. Detroit Police commanders chose men from the afternoon shift for the special detail without describing what it was. At 5 P.M. the operation began innocuously when two Detroit Street Railway buses pulled into the bus stop in front of the Gotham. One hundred-twelve policemen and IRS agents poured out. As they entered the hotel, an undercover agent working in the lobby beat the desk clerk to the alarm buzzer, while the other law enforcement men swept through the building with axes breaking down locked doors. They arrested forty-one people and seized $60,000 in cash and 120,000 betting slips.[27]

Edwards learned about the success of the raid a few hours later. With all the enthusiasm and purple prose of an excited police reporter, he recounted: "That evening the phone rang at eight thirty—once. I had been waiting since five. The jubilant voice on the other end of the line was that of Inspector Arthur Sage, the new head of the Vice Squad of the Detroit Police Department. 'Boss, we got it. We got the whole schmozzle.' "[28]

The next day Edwards toured the wreckage with Sage and IRS Agent Tony Getto. As he recalled, "The halls were littered with splintered doors. On one floor, a group of intent federal revenue agents were gathered around a safe which an expert locksmith had just cracked. They were counting $38,000 in cash which was spilled out on the floor. In another hallway, other agents were wrestling with sacks of coins." Each floor contained a numbers office, with tables pulled together to create a work space with adding machines to calculate the bet slips. Edwards also noted how "in each of these rooms, the windows were carefully blanketed to exclude any shred of daylight or possible prying eye." Perhaps the most telling evidence was in the linen closets. "In place of blankets, sheets, and pillow cases, these contained boxes and boxes of coin wrappers—more coin wrappers than I have ever seen in any bank."[29]

The raid added further evidence to support Edwards's belief that the Mafia's tentacles stretched far and wide in Detroit. Adding machines and other items found at the Gotham had been reported stolen from legitimate businesses, which indicated that the hotel's owner, John White, Jr., had connections to Detroit fencing operations. In addition, White's telephone directory, seized during the raid, included the names of two of Detroit's most notorious mobsters—Anthony Giacalone and Pete Licavoli. Edwards knew that Giacalone owned the Lesod Club. Licavoli was even better known as an old-time hoodlum with many arrests and convictions. Licavoli's parents immigrated from Sicily and settled in St. Louis. Licavoli came to Detroit in 1927 and played a major role in the gangland wars of the 1930s. In the late 1950s, he was convicted of tax evasion and spent thirty months in prison. He was paroled in the fall of 1960.[30]

Law enforcement hyperbole was the order of the day after the raid. Federal agents claimed the investigation of the Gotham as one of the most successful they ever conducted. From seized evidence they estimated that the gambling operations at the hotel netted $15 million annually. Edwards's press conference took on a colorful note when he revealed that the department had hired a magician to examine the dice and cards taken from the scene. The "expert" found that fifteen of the eighteen pair of dice he examined were loaded, and he verified that many of the card decks were marked. Edwards conceded that numbers operations still existed in Detroit, but he quickly added up the achievements of the Gotham case. "First, there is no gambling location boasting immunity in our city. Second, many of the numbers operators have moved their processing operations out of the city. Third, those who remain stay rather continually on the move with additional chances for surveillance and mistake. And, fourth and finally, we know that the numbers business has diminished as a result of the raid and its disclosures that Detroit's professional gamblers are not only crooks but crooked crooks in the bargain."[31]

Sage put it more succinctly. "This may not put them out of business, but it will hurt them plenty and it'll be a while before they recover." Four days later, Herbert M. Boldt, of the Detroit *News* reported that "the numbers racket here has been operating in a state of utter confusion, according to vice bureau officers. Unaware that police officers were on the other end of the line, several persons have telephoned the hotel to ask, 'What do I do with all this stuff.' "[32]

The case took on other comic overtones when Gotham owner John White, Jr., tried to convince the African-American community that he was a victim of police racism. He complained to the *Michigan Chronicle* that the raiders "broke in here like members of the Notre Dame football team armed with sledgehammers and broke down every door in the hotel." Had they asked for a pass key, White said, he would have given them one. But they did not. Instead, he claimed, they wielded their axes for an hour before even showing him a warrant. Then they drank his whiskey and soda pop, ate all the food they could find, and then stole ten packs of unopened pinochle cards. White took offense at Edwards's assertion that gamblers at the Gotham cheated their customers. He claimed to know nothing about marked decks or loaded dice. But even if they were being used, he added, the club was private and "if we were cheating, we were cheating ourselves." White's claims of victimization, dubious as they were, might have held some sway against another police commissioner. But Edwards made a difficult target given his policy of equal law enforcement.[33]

Plaudits for the Gotham raid rolled in. The U.S. Attorney for Eastern Michigan, Lawrence Gubow, told Edwards: "I want to take this opportunity to congratulate you and your Department for a job well done in connection with last Friday's raid on the Gotham Hotel. The obvious security problems involved because of the large number of officers and agents assigned to the task were well-handled." A. F. Brandsatter, director of Michigan State University's School of Police Administration and Public Safety, wrote, "Congratulations on 'knocking off' the Gotham

Hotel. It is hard to believe that this numbers factory could operate for so many years in one place."[34]

Amid the praise there were also skeptics. When Edwards gave a speech soon after the Gotham raid, members of the audience complained that he gave the impression that police eradicated all numbers rackets in Detroit. Edwards agreed that gambling still existed in the city, but he insisted that his efforts had put pressure on the illegal enterprises. He was also surprised to find little support among other members of the Cavanagh administration. The first rebuff came when he discussed the raid with Common Council President Edward Carey, who warned him that Cavanagh did not share his enthusiasm. Carey quoted the mayor as saying Edwards "would arrest his own grandmother." A few days later, when Edwards asked for a meeting with Cavanagh and department heads to discuss and solicit information about organized crime, the mayor did not come. DPW Commissioner Glenn Richards, perhaps still smarting from the scandal that rocked his department, offered the most vigorous objections. He accused Edwards of engaging in "McCarthyism" and finding "guilt by association." Others complained that police should be pursuing more important cases rather than fighting such "insignificant" crimes as gambling. Edwards left the meeting convinced that it had been "a well orchestrated effort to tell me that City Hall was not with me in attacking the Gotham or Detroit's other organized crime problems."[35]

In subsequent years, Edwards continually referred to the Gotham in speeches about police and organized crime. He used the hotel's long existence to decry citizen and political indifference to illegal activity, and he cited the successful raid as an example of how joint cooperation between police agencies could succeed against organized crime. The hotel itself, however, soon faded from the scene. In July 1963, the Arrow Wrecking Company demolished what was left of the ten-story, thirty-nine-year-old landmark. The following year White died before he could be tried for tax evasion in federal court.[36]

The day after the Gotham raid, Edwards capitalized on its excitement by announcing the Bergs' replacements. As Herbert M. Boldt, the *News* police reporter, noted, the appointments were "a touchy decision for Edwards" because "a choice unacceptable to the department's top echelon could apparently rock the force with more resignations." Boldt speculated about ten possible candidates, but Edwards considered only three. Frederick F. Wright, the department's director of training, was the sole high-ranking officer who expressed any support for Edwards's program. But because of his reputation as a dissenter, Wright had been left out of field command jobs, and Edwards feared that he would not inspire confidence among the rank and file. The second candidate was James M. Lupton, 61, a thirty-eight-year veteran of the department who had been director of personnel since 1950. Edwards had known Lupton since he had served on the Common Council. The Luptons and Edwards fished and dined together, and the Luptons visited Edwards's cottage on Saginaw Bay. The third candidate was Eugene A. Reuter, 58, a robust six-footer, who was a thirty-three-year veteran of the department. Reuter started out as an Illinois coal miner before coming to Detroit to work for the Hudson Motor Car Company. He had been in charge of the department's West Side precincts since 1958. As Edwards recalled, Reuter was "a policeman's policeman. . . . He had come up from the ranks to high command with no blemishes on his record. The men called him the 'Bull of the Woods' and 'Black Bart' " because of his coal mining background.[37]

Edwards weighed Reuter against Lupton. Finally, he decided on the former coal miner as his superintendent. He was impressed with the way Reuter handled several tense strike situations and how he went, unarmed, into a barricaded building and persuaded a gunman to surrender peacefully. More importantly, Edwards was swayed by Reuter's reputation for following the police manual. "I figured that if Reuter could get the Department to do its job by its own regulations, life in Detroit would calm down a long way." Edwards decided that Lupton would be "a natural" for deputy superintendent. "He knew more about the gritty side of the Department than Reuter ever would. His presence might keep the Bull of the Woods from being too rough on policemen who made an honest mistake. And I trusted his courage and tactical judgment for on-the-scene leadership."[38]

At the swearing-in ceremony on November 10, Edwards praised Lupton and Reuter and offered consolation to the other candidates by saying that his biggest problem in making a decision had been choosing among "an overabundance of fine command officers." Edwards also took advantage of the occasion to announce other personnel changes. He acknowledged Wright's support for his program by moving him into Lupton's job as director of personnel. Among other things, he hoped that Wright would make more progress recruiting African-American police officers. He rewarded Sage's handling of the Gotham by promoting him from inspector to senior inspector. He also promoted Glenn C. Chittick to replace Reuter as head of the West Side precincts. Chittick was the precinct inspector who told him about the Willie Daniels beating. As Edwards explained, "Although Chittick's role in telling the truth about the Daniels case had never become public, my guess was that 4,500 police officers would know why he was moved up." Edwards also promoted three officers who had impressed him to inspector rank: Robert H. Kerr, Raymond J. Glinski, and Robert H. Potts. The promotions allowed Reuter to make changes at the precinct level.[39]

Three days later Edwards, with Reuter's advice and consent, announced further changes. He appointed Senior Inspector William J. Bourke to take over Wright's duties as head of research and planning. That allowed Edwards to move Sage into Bourke's old slot to head the department's efforts against liquor, gambling, and vice. He then named Lieutenant John O'Neill, who also participated in the Gotham raid, to head the vice bureau. O'Neill, 41, had joined the force in 1945 and received six citations for meritorious service. Before the unusual swearing-in ceremony in the vice squad room, Edwards presented the officers with a unit citation for outstanding service in the Gotham raid. Reuter then announced new assignments for the inspectors Edwards promoted three days earlier. Glinski went to the McGraw station to replace Marvin Frank, who was transferred to the Davison Precinct. Robert Kerr succeeded Fred Kirby, who went to the parking enforcement bureau. Robert Potts filled a vacancy at the Woodward station. Inspector Eugene R. Geibig, who earned Edwards's contempt for his leadership of the vice bureau, was transferred to head the Jefferson Precinct. Reuter denied that the reshuffling constituted a shake-up. Instead, he explained, some of the transfers, particularly in precinct commands, were made to give senior officers assignments closer to their homes.[40]

Edwards's appointments won wide praise. Mayor Cavanagh expressed satisfaction that Lupton and Reuter "bring an abundance of talent and experience to these positions." Former police commissioner Edward Piggins, who had become a judge on Wayne County's 3rd Circuit Court, wrote Edwards, "Congratulations on your recent promotions. You have chosen an able staff and I know that they will give you their wholehearted support in building a splendid police department. Keep up the good work because every citizen who loves this town is behind you." Brandsatter, of Michigan State, wrote Edwards, "It was quite startling to read about the resignations of Louie and Jim Berg." Then knowing how Edwards felt about the pair, he added, "How lucky can a guy be. I think your choice of Reuter for superintendent is excellent. . . . [T]hrough the years everything I have heard about him has been very good. The combination of Reuter and Lupton should be a good one—one being the rough and ready type and the other being suave and smooth."[41]

Even the rank and file of the police department seemed pleased with Edwards's choice for superintendent. As Herbert Boldt reported, "Reuter, in the opinion of several officers, is a respected policeman. They said he would be able to keep the department running smoothly." Many reserved judgment on Lupton, because as director of personnel, he was not involved in day-to-day policing activities. Edwards hoped that his appointment of Reuter and Lupton would further his goal of creating a closely knit command structure throughout the department. He formally introduced the pair to precinct inspectors at their regularly scheduled November meeting by saying he wanted commanders at all levels to increase their supervisory efforts. Reuter urged the inspectors to instill a sense of pride in the officers under their command. He told them to advise their men that if they did their jobs but made honest mistakes, their superior officers would back them up. "It is when they fail to do their jobs, that they get into trouble," he warned. Edwards and Reuter both commented on the city's increasing crime rate and urged precinct officers to continue visiting schools and churches to encourage citizen cooperation.[42]

Temporarily, at least, the department's focus shifted to more mundane matters in the closing months of 1962. In October, the

National Safety Council gave its highest honor, the Flame of Life Award, to Detroit for being the safest large city in the nation. Its commendation cited Detroit's accident prevention programs, especially among school children. Five pedestrian deaths during the first week of November endangered Detroit's reputation as a pioneer in traffic safety. The five brought the total of traffic-related fatalities for the year to seventy-eight, ten higher than the same period in 1961. In a press release, Edwards said, "I would like to warn all pedestrians about the danger of crossing between intersections and the added danger during the hours of darkness." He suggested that pedestrians wear light-colored clothes after dark and cross only at intersections. He asked drivers to adjust their speed to existing road conditions.[43]

In late November, Edwards announced deployment of special traffic enforcement teams during the Christmas shopping season. The extra police were assigned to Downtown streets to deter jaywalkers and reckless drivers. On December 2, he provided more details of the program at a traffic safety symposium sponsored by the Detroit Council of Churches. Four days later he attempted to humanize the dull subject of traffic safety in a press release about the 106 families of traffic fatality victims for the previous five Decembers. "When you and I are looking forward to the Holiday Season, they know only heartache." To avoid future tragedies, he advised drivers to stay alert, keep hands on the wheel, obey traffic signals, and observe the speed limits. He told pedestrians to stop, look, and wait before venturing out into busy streets. He also announced a crackdown on drunken driving. The program proved successful. The month of December set a record for the lowest number of fatalities and accidents.[44]

Edwards's program received another boost at the end of the year when the police department became the only one in the nation ever honored by the Freedoms Foundation of Valley Forge. The association gave its awards to individuals and groups that promoted constitutional principles. Edwards proudly read the citation, which praised the department for "enlisting the cooperation of community and religious leaders, the newspapers and the general public in aiding the police in fighting crime and race prejudice, bringing to the citizens of Detroit a greater awareness and understanding of each individual's responsibility in helping to

217

maintain law and order." The award fit in well with Edwards's own philosophy of law enforcement. As he noted, citizen responsibility "is ultimately the place where we secure a sound balance between freedom and liberty, because it is in the search for the support of every law-abiding citizen that we have the greatest amount to gain."[45]

In early January, Edwards was able to put the finishing touches on his management reorganization when Walter J. Wyrod, the chief of detectives, resigned after thirty-one years on the force to accept a job as public safety advisor for the Agency for International Development in Saigon, Vietnam. As the department's third ranking officer after the Bergs, Wyrod was once considered by some to be a shoo-in for the superintendent's job, but that became unlikely after he voted against Edwards in the Willie Daniels case and joined the "Pizza Parlor Putsch." Nevertheless, both Edwards and Wyrod publicly denied their disagreements. Edwards told reporters that Wyrod "has served the department with intelligence, skill, and great courage and I am sure every man in the department regrets his departure." Wyrod said he could not resist an opportunity to work overseas.[46]

Wyrod's retirement allowed Edwards to put more supporters in key management positions. On January 10, he named Thomas R. Cochill, 50, to replace Wyrod as head of the detective bureau. Cochill, a Detroit native who followed his father into the department in 1937, received thirty-three citations for meritorious service and served as Wyrod's deputy for the previous two years. Edwards also promoted Piersante, 43, to senior inspector's rank and appointed him to become Cochill's top assistant in the detective bureau. His promotion made him one of the youngest senior inspectors in the history of the department. It also put him in a position to help Edwards launch a dramatic crusade against Detroit's most entrenched and powerful organized crime bosses.[47]

9
BATTLING ORGANIZED CRIME

For reasons I can't tell you, I have decided to write you a letter. It is written and I have turned it over to a close friend with instructions to deliver it to you if anything should happen to me. . . . [I]f you ever get to publish it—which I hope you won't—I guarantee you'll have the damndest newspaper story you have ever seen.

—George Edwards, Jr., to *Detroit News* Editor Martin Hayden, early 1963

E dwards began his second year in office with a dramatic announcement that he hoped would win wider support for his fight against organized crime. On January 7, he called a press conference to announce that members of his department observed Detroit Lions football players socializing with the Giacalones and other unsavory characters. His revelations rocked the National Football League (NFL) and provided a fitting opening salvo in his year-long crusade against the Mafia—a battle that would bring him as much personal satisfaction as his efforts to promote racially unbiased policing. By tackling the potential corruption of professional athletes, Edwards hoped to prove his contention that the tentacles of organized crime reached into every part of society. In April, rumors of Edwards's nomination to the Sixth U.S. Circuit Court of Appeals added extra impetus to his campaign. Frustrated that traditional law enforcement methods would take too long, Edwards began planning a dramatic way to focus the public spotlight on the shadowy corners of Detroit's underworld.

The football scandal became public during the first week of January 1963, but the police investigation actually began months earlier. At 3 A.M. on August 18, 1962, Sergeant William DePugh and other Detroit police officers went to the Grecian Gardens at 562 Monroe in Greektown to investigate a complaint about illegal liquor sales. The *Free Press* described the tavern as the "glitter spot in a drab block of coffee houses and curio shops only a block south of Detroit Police Headquarters." Two years earlier, the Grecian Gardens made headlines when a newspaper story nicknamed its owner, Gus Colacasides, the "Kingpin of Greektown gambling." When DePugh and his men entered the club, they noticed Detroit Lions linebacker Wayne H. Walker seated at a table in the back with the Giacalone brothers. The police officers became curious and set up watch outside. At 4:10 A.M. the revelers left the club through the back door. Most climbed into what later became known as the "party bus" while Walker got into his white station wagon. The two vehicles headed to Cleveland, where the Lions were playing an exhibition game against the Dallas Cowboys. Vince Piersante contacted Cleveland police, who saw three other Detroit Lions players join the group for the ride home. The three were defensive end Darris McCord, guard John Gordy, and all-pro defensive tackle Alex Karras, who had been a Heisman Trophy winner at Notre Dame.[1]

After reading DePugh's report, the Berg brothers notified Detroit Lions management. On August 21, Inspector Eugene Geibig and Lieutenant John O'Neill of the vice bureau met with Lions's Coach George Wilson at the Fox and Hounds Restaurant in Bloomfield Hills, near the football team's practice field at Cranbrook School. Wilson said he gave his players permission to travel home on the party bus because he believed it was owned by legitimate businessmen. Wilson also said he knew about Karras's love of gambling. It had already become an issue with the NFL because of Karras's and Walker's close friendship with Jim Butsicaris, the owner of the Lindell Bar at 1519 Cass. The two Lions players frequented the bar until NFL Commissioner Pete Rozelle declared the place off limits because of its alleged ties to gamblers and prostitutes. When Karras appealed, arguing that he was buying a part interest in the business for $45,000, Rozelle relented. Wilson said he knew that several members of the team frequented the Grecian Gardens, and he promised to declare it off limits to them.[2]

In December, the Lions went to Miami to play a game

against the Pittsburgh Steelers, and Piersante asked local police to watch and photograph the party bus revelers. Miami police snapped photographs of Lions players socializing with the Giacalones and Anthony Zerilli, a part owner of the Hazel Park racetrack; Anthony Thomas, a convicted murderer and burglar; Odus Tincher, a convicted gambler who had been secretary of the Lesod Club; Mike "the Enforcer" Rubino and Anthony J. Corrado, whose father had been one of Detroit's most famous Prohibition-era gangsters. The Miami trip made it clear that Wilson had not talked to his players about police concerns. Edwards contacted Frederick Nash, the Lions general counsel, and asked him to pass the information on to the team's president, William Clay Ford. After it became clear that Lions management still was not taking action, Edwards sent a summary of the police surveillance reports to NFL Commissioner Rozelle.[3]

A Chicago reporter broke the story the following week, and Edwards held a press conference. He told reporters, "We feel the matter of association is primarily a matter for the football league and I called it to their attention for that reason. However, the business of knowing gamblers who bet heavily on football games is police business and we intend to make it our business in the future." Edwards likened the party bus revelries in Miami to "a small Apalachin meeting from the box score of hoodlums on them." Although the players did nothing illegal, Edwards believed they showed poor judgment and may have violated NFL rules. Concerns about gamblers corrupting athletics was a timely concern because of a point shaving scandal in college basketball the previous spring.[4]

Detroit's newspapers picked up the football scandal with colorful coverage. The *News* described the party bus, which was outfitted with a bar and pull-down bunk beds, as "a classy pumpkin coach for the Cinderella Lions who lived in the open-handed, booze-running world of Detroit gamblers." The newspaper reported how the bus "frequently tooled across the streets of Detroit, the Grosse Pointes, and Mt. Clemons loaded with gambling partiers and their girls. . . . Once it pulled up abruptly at a downtown night spot, summarily 'captured' the bar's owner and his entire case of entertainers and wheezed away from the curb into the night."[5]

221

The Lions story became even more of a sensation when Alex Karras appeared on the nationally televised Huntley-Brinkley News program and admitted he bet on NFL teams. Karras defended his right to gamble, as long as he did not bet on his own team. But as Edwards noted later, "Commissioner Rozelle apparently took Karras's announcement as a challenge from a player who felt he was too important to be touched." On April 18, after interviewing more than seventy players and holding a hearing, Rozelle suspended Karras for a year and Green Bay Packers "golden boy" Paul Hornung indefinitely. Karras admitted that he had placed bets on football games at least six times. Hornung admitted that he bet as much as $500 a game on pro and college teams from 1959–61. Rozelle fined Lions management $4,000 for failing to take action on the information supplied by the Detroit Police Department. The biggest surprise came when Rozelle fined five Lions players $2,000 each for betting on the championship game between Green Bay and the New York Giants. As the *Free Press* reported, "there had been no inkling" of the investigation into the other five players who received fines: Gordy, team captain Joe Schmidt, linebacker Wayne Walker, safety Gary Lowe, and defensive end Sam Williams. The fines stemmed from the December trip to Miami for the Steeler's game. Karras invited his teammates to watch the Packers–New York game at the home of his friend, Archie Stone, head of the dog-racing parimutuel clerks in Miami. Karras bet $100 on Green Bay, and his five teammates each bet $50 on the Giants.[6]

Reaction in Detroit varied. William Clay Ford criticized Rozelle: "Speaking for myself and the Detroit Football Company, I consider your fines unduly harsh. You have not helped pro football and locally you have damaged it. It is hard to believe that in the entire NFL only seven players are guilty of gambling, and of these six are on the Lions team. They bet on the championship game, one they weren't even involved in and after their season was over. And it was obviously a social thing. . . . The worst thing they did was to be honest enough to admit it." The *Free Press,* by contrast, sided with Rozelle. Its editorial noted: "If a star player were to get deeply into gambling debt through spirited betting on his own team, or 'innocent' betting on other games, he might one day be sorely tempted to take advantage of his inside

222

position. . . . At the very least, as Rozelle said, betting and associating with gamblers can give the appearance of evil and thereby affect . . . the integrity of the sport."[7]

Edwards seized on publicity surrounding the Lions case to galvanize his own men. At the February precinct commanders' meeting, he announced an all-out drive against organized crime. Saying that most of the previous year's efforts had been directed at traffic violations and unorganized crime, Edwards proclaimed it was time to open a "third front" against organized crime. The department had approximately seventy men in the CIB. In the past, they had little contact with officers working out of the precincts. Edwards wanted to change that. "Do not turn from anything you have been doing but should you run into something that indicates organized crime, contact men who have been working with it." Organized crime activities included narcotics peddling, fencing of stolen property, and gambling. Of these, Edwards said, gambling was the most visible, and in some ways, the most menacing. "[H]ow can people live in a neighborhood where it goes on . . . and how can they raise their children decently and with respect for the law if we do nothing about it?"[8]

The Lions case convinced executives at the *News* that Edwards's crusade against organized crime would continue to be newsworthy, and they wanted the inside track on future stories. Managing Editor Harvey Patton and reporter John M. Carlisle invited Edwards to lunch in late January at the Detroit Athletic Club. Patton suggested that the newspaper's Washington Bureau could act as a go-between if Edwards wanted to provide information to the Senate investigation of organized crime headed by John L. McClellan. Later, Edwards said he was skeptical of the proposal. He was not sure that his department "had the capability to put together a comprehensive picture of the Detroit area Mafia and if we concluded we did, whether or not it would be appropriate for us to do so." He worried that Mafia lawyers would sue him for slander or libel if he publicly accused their clients of being mobsters without adequate evidence. Finally, Edwards anticipated attacks from the American Civil Liberties Union, "an organization whose objectives I supported and with whom, up to that point, I had maintained warm relations." On the other hand, Edwards did not want to give critics the chance to say that his department conducted a crusade against the mob that had ended with the prosecution of only small-time criminals. As he noted, "Our major successes against [the Mafia] had been in driving open and obvious illegal activities off of the street, but we had no success at all, up to that point, in reaching its top operators, let alone controlling dons." Edwards agreed to cooperate with the *News*.[9]

On February 12, Carlisle wrote a long memo summarizing the information that Edwards provided during several off-the-record interviews. Edwards said he wanted to launch a full-fledged multi-front war against Detroit's Sicilian gangsters. He began by reopening the investigation into Ubal E. Calabresse's murder the previous February. Calabresse was a small-time numbers racketeer who had worked for the Giacalones. Police believed his troubles began when he unwisely took a larger cut of the gambling profits. When Mafia enforcers approached him, Calabresse threatened to go to the police. He never had the chance. Police found his rotting corpse, trussed and strangled in the trunk of a car left in the parking lot of a suburban grocery store. A week later patrons at an East Side bar that Calabresse frequented heard a loud bang at the rear door. They found a dead pig had been thrown against it. As Edwards noted, "The message was clear, 'Squealers die.' " The murder angered Edwards. "I took the flaunting of Mafia power in the Calabresse murder as a personal challenge in much the same way I had the open operation of the Lesod Club by Vito Giacalone." Edwards also told Carlisle about police efforts to uncover Mafia links to several legitimate businesses in Detroit, including the Home Juice Company on East Palmer, the Tri-County Sanitation Company on Russell, and the Valley Platers, Inc., in Bellevue.[10]

Carlisle, a veteran reporter, provided his own assessment of Edwards's crusade to identify and expose Detroit's Mafia bosses, and then put them out of business. "Edwards is a little enthusiastic, if not a bit hepped on this subject. . . . Frankly, I am inclined to be a little skeptical over Edwards and the Mafia. Senator McClellan with all the power of the Senate Rackets Committee did no more than name some of them. The Apalachin crime conference put floodlights on sixty of them. But it all hangs up in mid-air like a blood-and-thunder old-time Hearst expose." Despite his misgivings, Carlisle conceded that "Edwards has brought a brilliant, on-the-target mind to police investigations. It is possible that he may be able to achieve what no police executive has ever been able to do—expose and put the Mafia out of business in his area. I would never sell him short. It is incumbent on a reporter covering a man like Edwards to run the plays out with him."[11]

Edwards hoped to bring Detroit mobsters to trial. Failing that, however, he planned to bring the Mafia's membership and unsavory activities to public light through the McClellan Committee. As Carlisle related, "With his Washington connections he could probably get the Senate Rackets Committee in here for some hearings, put some of his boys on the witness stand, and we could shoot our pop guns at the Sicilian-Mafia gangsters and underworld financiers." Edwards and Piersante also met constantly to discuss the information that they would present to the McClellan Committee. They pored over court records to chart the criminal records of Detroit's leading mobsters. Edwards also reread the grand jury records that he obtained for the Kefauver hearings in 1950 and 1951. He assigned Piersante to update the old information with modern surveillance reports and other information.[12]

By early April, Piersante's CIB had mapped a general outline of the Mafia in Detroit. The explosive information was kept in an ordinary, plain blue, three-ring notebook, marked: "MAFIA: Members-Relatives, Associates-Suspects, Detroit Police Department." The first page was a cover letter from Edwards to "police personnel on restricted distribution lists." He wrote: "It is of paramount importance that we, as police officers, acquaint ourselves with 'the people' and their activities, both legitimate and illegitimate. It is noteworthy that as the years have passed, the offspring of the older and best known members of this group have inherited the knowledge and abilities in the criminal lines of their forbears and are 'taking over' and continuing those well-established operations." Edwards added, "Of equal importance to the furtherance of the fight against crime is the continuous accumulation of information. You, therefore, are directed to report immediately or in writing any contacts with people mentioned in this book or any intelligence concerning them which may come to your attention." Finally, because much of the information was "raw and unevaluated" and contained CIB opinions that had not yet been substantiated, Edwards warned that the "material is furnished for closely restricted police use solely, and *under no circumstances* for public distribution."[13]

The next page contained a table of contents that indexed a virtual *Who's Who* of the seventy-six men suspected of leading Detroit's Mafia. Each entry contained detailed biographical information, including place and date of birth, current addresses, unsavory relatives, arrest records, and legitimate and illegitimate business interests. One early entry was for Joseph M. Barbara, Jr., of 23833 Fenton Drive in Mount Clemons, who was born in 1936. His father was the New York gangster who hosted the infamous Apalachin meeting in 1957. Barbara Jr. married Josephine Vitale, whose father, Joseph, was a well-known Detroit mobster. Together the Vitales and Barbara Jr. ran the Tri-County Sanitation Company at 3425 Russell in Detroit. Barbara's arrest record included charges for indecent exposure and perjury. Barbara's was a relatively minor entry. The book contained more information about the Giacalones and others who would figure prominently in Edwards's testimony before the McClellan hearing.

Edwards was so proud of the CIB's effort that he sent a copy of the information contained in the book to Attorney General Kennedy, with a caveat: "Distribution of these materials is solely and exclusively for police purposes. Of necessity, much of the matter contained therein represents raw and unevaluated information not subject to legal proof; and some, of course, represents opinion. . . . We believe it would be appropriate to have a copy of this material available in your Organized Crime Division for such restricted Justice Department reference as you may deem appropriate." Kennedy thanked him several weeks later, "Your interest and consideration in making this material available . . . is indeed greatly appreciated."[14]

Throughout the late spring and summer, Edwards worked with his own men and two staff members of the McClellan Committee to sort through and verify the information in the blue book. Edwards was impressed at how much the Senate staffers already knew about Detroit's leading criminals. In retrospect, their knowledge was not surprising. Many Detroit mobsters were related through marriage to well-known gangsters in New York. Two Detroit Mafiaoso—Joe Zerilli and Mike Tolizzi—attended the Apalachin meeting. Finally, the investigators used earlier information gathered for the Kefauver hearings. Edwards was pleased that the McClellan staffers shared his concern "in seeing to it that we took no chances on the authenticity and detailed accuracy of our testimony."[15]

Their efforts would take months to bear fruit. In the meantime, Edwards began to worry that he would become a Mafia target. Remembering the assassination attempts against the Reuthers and Ken Morris, he decided to take out his own form of life insurance. First, he contacted his friend, *Detroit News* editor Martin Hayden, and invited him to lunch at the Detroit Athletic Club. Years later, Hayden wrote an article describing their meeting. Edwards began by saying, "I don't want you to think I've developed a cops-and-robbers mentality. What I'm going to tell you is serious. It is also brief and I'm not going to be able to give you supporting details." Hayden was intrigued as Edwards continued, "For reasons I can't tell you, I have decided to write you a letter. It is written and I have turned it over to a close friend with instructions to deliver it to you if anything should happen to me. . . . [I]f you ever get to publish it—which I hope you won't—I guarantee you'll have the damndest newspaper story you have ever seen." Edwards said he had told Piersante to "pass the word to the mob that the letter exists."[16]

Edwards's letter to Hayden was contained in a manila envelope that he sent to John Herling in Washington, D.C. On the outside, he wrote: "For Robert Kennedy, to be opened only in the event of my death by violent means or by unnatural causes where certainty of the cause of death cannot be determined." In his cover letter to Herling, he wrote: "Enclosed is an envelope which represents a little bit of extra life insurance. I have taken care that the Mafia here in Detroit knows that this is placed somewhere—but you may be certain that they do not know where." Edwards hoped that if he became a victim of foul play, Kennedy would make sure the information was reprinted in the Congressional Record.[17]

In retrospect, it was not clear whether Edwards's fears were justified. Unbeknownst to Edwards, the FBI bugged Anthony Giacalone's office from 1961 to 1964. Transcripts of his wiretapped conversations became public in 1976. They revealed that the Giacalones were as obsessed with Edwards as he was with them. In a conversation on January 21, 1963, in the wake of the Lions scandal, Vito and his brother complained about their inability to "get to" Edwards. Vito suggested they make it look as if they had corrupted the police commissioner. In its expurgated version of the transcript, the *Detroit News* quoted Vito telling friends, "I'm going to haul my (expletive) bus out. I'm going to get a great big picture of Edwards and put it on there and say we . . . every hoodlum . . . we love him. This will knock his (expletive) wheels off. Hoodlums love Edwards and are voting for him." Two months later in a conversation with an underling, Nick Ditta, Anthony Giacalone referred to Edwards and Piersante and said he was in favor of killing cops. There was never any indication that Giacalone took action to carry out the threat. He probably realized that killing Edwards would draw too much attention. Years later, Piersante said, "I do not believe that there was a real possibility of an Edwards hit by the mob. It was discussed and rejected." Even Edwards conceded, "My previous experiences made me aware that the Mafia didn't specialize in killing police commissioners. However, in 1963, I fully expected to be back in the practice of law within a year, probably never to return to public office. I didn't feel that the Detroit Mafia's aversion to killing police commissioners would necessarily hold true for ex-police commissioners."[18]

Edwards's comments were a bit disingenuous. In reality, he hoped for an appointment to a federal judgeship after he left the police department. The *News* first mentioned his name as a candidate in a January 25 story that detailed the politicking involved in finding a replacement for Thomas F. McAllister of Grand Rapids who was retiring from the Sixth U.S. Circuit Court of Appeals. J. F. Ter Horst reported how former Governor John B. Swainson was trying to wangle a judgeship for himself. After losing the 1962 gubernatorial election to George Romney, Swainson visited John F. Kennedy in the White House. The president, who had campaigned for Swainson in Michigan, promised to help get him "situated." Swainson followed up the meeting by saying if one of the current federal district judges in Detroit were promoted to the Sixth Circuit, then Swainson would accept a nomination to replace him. He sent copies of the letter to Michigan's two Democratic senators, Philip A. Hart and Robert McNamara. Neither senator would comment on the matter, but Ter Horst reported that both were miffed at Swainson's actions; they believed the former governor should have followed protocol by requesting a nomination from them not the president. Ter Horst added that McNamara strongly favored Edwards for the appointment, and he quoted sources "close to Edwards," who claimed that the police commissioner "may be ready to move on to other things in a few months—either law practice or another court post."[19]

Edwards and McNamara discussed the appointment in early March. The two had been close friends for many years. Both had been active in union work. Later, as a city council member, Edwards helped launch McNamara's political career when he recommended him to head the city's rent-control program in the early days of World War II. Edwards suggested McNamara for the post because of all the "qualifications I saw in this blunt, direct Irishman with a quick tongue, delightful sense of humor and a contagious laugh." His faith proved justified, and he declared that "McNamara made an outstanding success of an almost impossible job." Edwards later supported McNamara's elections to city council, the board of education, and the Senate. In two earlier conversations, McNamara urged Edwards to consider taking a job on the Sixth Circuit. The senator believed his friend would be a like-minded replacement for McAllister, who was known as one of the liberals on the Sixth Circuit. Edwards rejected the suggestion both times because he still had much to accomplish as police commissioner. McNamara finally persuaded him by pointing out that the nomination process would take up to eight months. That would give Edwards enough time to complete his two-year term as head of the police department.[20]

Edwards said later it had been a difficult decision. "I knew the appointment would mean the end of active political life—a life which I had greatly enjoyed. But the tradition in the Sixth Circuit was for judges to live in their hometowns and only go to Cincinnati, the base of the court, for hearing sessions. We would not have to leave my beloved Detroit." Edwards also recognized that he would have to leave the department by the end of the year in order to avoid hindering Mayor Cavanagh's reelection. "Although I viewed everything that we had done to bridge the river of hate between the police department and the black community as fitting easily under the title of simple justice, the total program I brought to the Department was highly controversial. I was well aware that as the election neared, I would be less and less of a political asset and more and more of a political liability. I was also well aware that Cavanagh knew this and although he had never said so, would be more than happy to see me move on." Edwards called McNamara and said he would be "deeply honored" by the nomination.[21]

McNamara's plans to nominate Edwards quickly became an open secret in Detroit. On March 9, the *Free Press,* reported that "Edwards Expected to Join U.S. Court; Would Quit as Head of Police." The newspaper described Edwards and McNamara as close friends. It quoted McNamara insisting that no final choice had been made but that Edwards "is very well qualified and . . . would have to be given serious consideration." Edwards refused comment, saying that such an announcement "would have to come from someone else." He insisted he was happy in the police job. Ray Girardin, whom the *Free Press* described as Edwards's likely successor, and Mayor Cavanagh insisted they knew nothing about it. The *Free Press* described how McNamara blocked Swainson's bid for a federal judgeship, and conceded that there were at least three other potential nominees. They included two friends of Edwards, Wade McCree, and Talbot Smith, Edwards's ally from the Supreme Court who was then serving on the federal district court, and a third candidate, Thomas Thornton. The newspaper said Edwards was favored because he was younger than Smith and had the appellate court experience that McCree and Thornton lacked.[22]

On April 4, Michigan Democratic party leaders met in Washington, D.C., and agreed to endorse Edwards for the judgeship. The group, which included McNamara and Mildred Jeffrey, first contacted him to see if he would agree to take the post. Edwards consented, and senators Hart and McNamara forwarded his name to Robert Kennedy. Meanwhile, Edwards told reporters that he "greatly appreciated the expression of confidence." Edwards was less pleased when Cavanagh leaked Girardin's name as his successor. The mayor's action seemed to give credence to rumors that he was unhappy with his police commissioner and was eager to replace him. Edwards worried that speculation about his replacement and his alleged rift with Cavanagh would undermine his effectiveness during his final months in office. He complained to the mayor, and, on April 5, Cavanagh publicly denied that he was unhappy with Edwards. "I still feel that one of the great accomplishments of this administration was to obtain the talents of such a man as Edwards. . . . His contributions to this community to date as police commissioner have been exceptional. He took over a situation which was recognized by almost everyone as a bad one, and he has, in 15 months, redirected and changed the situation." The mayor said he would not consider any appointment for the police commissioner's post until Edwards formally resigned.[23]

Despite Cavanagh's denials, stories about Edwards's possible departure prompted a renewed debate about his effectiveness. One citizen spoke for many when he wrote Mayor Cavanagh, urging him to find a new commissioner immediately. William H. Merrill said he had known Edwards for twenty-five years and had voted for him for Common Council and for mayor. Even so, he explained, "I frankly feel that he is not the man to have been made Police Commissioner because of his 'social worker' attitude toward crime. . . . It is surely well known to you that most, if not all, of the high ranking officers of the department are opposed to Edwards. My own work takes me in contact with many officers . . . and I have yet to find ONE who felt that Edwards's approach to crime was right. All these fine professional police officers can not be wrong, and Edwards' theories right." Another correspondent was even more blunt. After reading the story indicating that Girardin would replace Edwards, he wrote: "Thank God and you, Mayor Cavanagh, for making that magnificent move—all intelligent Detroiters will rejoice. . . . Believe me the morale of our Police Department will rise 100%. . . . Now let's get the Bergs back. . . . With Ray and the Bergs back in control crime will cease shortly or be cut drastically." Not all the comments were negative. A. F. Brandsatter at Michigan State University praised the mayor for defending his police commissioner. "Under the circumstances, Edwards has done an excellent job. . . . The task he assumed as commissioner was not an easy one; it required great courage and intellectual integrity."[24]

Edwards did his best to rise above the fray. During the spring, he took to the hustings, presenting a series of speeches outlining the menace posed by organized crime. These melded information he garnered as police commissioner into the accepted knowledge of a national crime conspiracy known as the Mafia. Perhaps the most noteworthy of his addresses that spring was to fellow members of the Advisory Council of Judges of the National Council on Crime and Delinquency. He announced: "Organized crime is, in my opinion, very much like an iceberg. One tenth of it is available to public view and nine tenths of it are hidden. And yet what we can see shows us that it is a continuing and a successful threat to law enforcement—a threat with which America has not learned to cope." Typically, he drew on information from other parts of the nation—a *Saturday Evening Post* article that described Youngstown, Ohio, as the "Crime Capital of the USA," the recent assassination of Chicago Crime Commission director Virgil Peterson, and Robert Kennedy's estimate that organized crime made $7 billion annually from gambling.[25]

Since becoming Detroit's police commissioner, Edwards said, he had become even more convinced of the existence of the Mafia. He dismissed critics who denied the reality of a national crime syndicate, citing his own department's intelligence.

> If research into the leadership of organized crime leads again and again to a group of families of Sicilian extraction, closely interrelated by marriage and by strong ties in legal and illegal enterprises; if the frustrations of the police center around a code of absolute silence and a positive refusal of all forms of cooperation with legal authority on the part of these families; and if there is strong evidence that in our large cities these illegal enterprises are backed by the threat of planned, carefully executed and highly professional murder, then a name more descriptive than "the Syndicate" seems called for.[26]

Edwards added authenticity to his speech by providing other details of his department's forays against Mafia figures. He described U.S. Supreme Court Justice Douglas's visit the previous summer and their observation of the sophisticated security at the

Lesod Club. He described the Gotham raid. But, despite these successes, Edward said, there was still the likelihood of failure. He cited a recent investigation of Santo Perrone, the gangster allegedly behind the Reuther assassination attempts. A witness had identified Perrone at the scene of a 1961 gas station bombing. Nevertheless, despite round-the-clock protection, the witness stated he could not remember anything. "Just when, or how, he later had been reached is something that I am not prepared to say. However, I have no doubt that the methods of terror employed by organized crime were a major factor in the failure of that prosecution of Perrone." He repeated his prescriptions for fighting the problem: less public tolerance of gambling, closer alliances between federal and local authorities, a determined federal drive against organized crime, increased authority for wiretaps, and harsher penalties for Mafia bosses.[27]

Throughout the spring, Edwards and Piersante worked on a case that they hoped would dramatically demonstrate the corrupting influence of organized crime. The investigation began in February when Sergeant James Thomas led a raid on a Giacalone gambling house on Detroit's West Side. Several days later, Claude Williams, a numbers operator working for Giacalone called Thomas and offered to pay him protection money. In exchange, he asked Thomas to help deter raids against the Giacalones' gambling houses and step up raids on their competitors. Thomas reported the conversation to his commanding officer in the McGraw Precinct on the West Side, Inspector Ray Glinski, who then contacted Reuter and Edwards. They assigned Piersante and the CIB to launch an investigation.

Using wiretaps, the CIB documented six telephone conversations between Thomas and Giacalone between February and June. During the first call on February 23, Giacalone identified himself and agreed to pay Thomas $50 each month. On April 11, they spoke again to arrange a pick-up. This time Thomas warned Giacalone that a new team of vice cops was working out of the precinct. Instead of the department's periodic raids, this team was getting search warrants to close down gambling places. Thomas said Edwards was impressed with the method that had worked so well against the Gotham, and he had ordered it used in other cases. Giacalone said he was not concerned. "Oh, you

233

mean that old . . . bull. . . . Oh that's old farce anyhow. After Edwards leaves that'll be dead." In a conversation in early June, Giacalone asked Thomas's opinion of Edwards. Thomas replied that he had never met Edwards. Giacalone tried again, "Well, you know what I mean. He's for the Niggers. You're not for the Niggers, are you?" Thomas agreed he was not. Giacalone reassured him, "Well, he'll be gone pretty soon and we'll be through with all that search warrant bullshit." Police filed bribery charges against Giacalone, relying on the taped conversations, CIB observations of Thomas talking on the phone, and the $250 in payoff money. Piersante arrested Giacalone hiding in a closet at the Home Juice Company on June 20.[28]

The *Free Press,* usually critical of Edwards, enthusiastically reported: "George Edwards capped his career as Detroit's police commissioner Thursday with the arrest of a man he described as 'a top figure in organized crime in Detroit.' " Giacalone's lawyer subpoenaed Edwards to appear at the preliminary hearing. It was the first time he ever saw the gambling czar in person, but he recognized him from photographs. Edwards recalled the reaction when he walked into the courtroom and took a seat in the front row. "I saw heads move together at the defense table and suddenly Giacalone hitched his chair around and fixed his eyes on me in a hard stare. It seemed an obvious challenge and I stared back. He was in a no-win situation. He had his back to the judge on the bench. My lack of attention to his honor was not nearly so obvious. It seemed to me that this weaponless duel went on for ten minutes. It probably in fact was close to sixty seconds. But Giacalone broke it off."[29]

Edwards worried that Thomas would be in danger, and he looked for a way to raise the sergeant's public profile to deter the Giacalones from taking out a contract on him. Edwards also hoped that by making an example of Thomas, he could "secure some emulation of his loyalty to the Department and the public good" among other officers. A week after Giacalone's arrest, Edwards gave Thomas a "field promotion" to lieutenant. The action received widespread publicity, much to Piersante's chagrin. Piersante considered Thomas one of "the most unqualified sergeants I ever knew. . . . I told George, 'He's not even a good sergeant; I don't see how he'll make a good lieutenant,' but

George wanted to make a big deal of the case." Initially, Piersante believed that Thomas fabricated his story. Even after he verified the story and Thomas played his undercover role to the hilt, Piersante worried that something would go wrong.[30]

Edwards shared none of his friend's concern. He took great pride in the Giacalone prosecution and announced it to friends across the nation who had been following his crusade against organized crime. James C. Otis, an associate justice of Minnesota's Supreme Court, wrote an enthusiastic response, thanking Edwards for keeping him posted about the case and adding his hopes for "what I sincerely hope is the downfall of Anthony Giacalone." He said he was particularly amused with Giacalone's claim that search warrants were a "farce" which would end when Edwards left office. "That is about as high a compliment as you can be paid. Keep up the Good Work!"[31]

Although Edwards saw the case as a success, it ended disastrously after he left office. The first stumbling block was the animosity of Recorder's Court Judge John A. Gillis, who presided over the trial. Edwards described Gillis as "a genial Irishman of a free-wheeling populist persuasion—whom I had known for years and considered a friend." Edwards knew that Gillis did not share his concern about vice. Early in 1962, Gillis asked Edwards to lunch so he could complain about the police department's crackdown on prostitutes working downtown. Gillis argued that police should recognize a "safe" zone where the women could work without interference. As Edwards recalled, Gillis "reminded me that prostitution was the oldest profession in the world. He also told me that he had known many prostitutes who were more honest than the majority of their more fortunate sisters." Edwards countered that prostitution was illegal and as commissioner he had to enforce city and state laws. Besides, he said, prostitution was run by male pimps, who in turn, received help from Mafia figures. Gillis denied the existence of the Mafia in Detroit, and the lunch deteriorated into stony silence. Edwards left with the feeling that Gillis opposed his program.[32]

Gillis's hostility became apparent at trial. Giacalone's lawyers asked that the charges be dismissed, arguing among other things, that Edwards had prejudiced their client by announcing the case with such fanfare. During a hearing on March 21, 1964,

Gillis lambasted Edwards's remarks as "a drastic example of the misuse of police power given to some individuals." Edwards would not respond to the criticism, telling reporters, "My contact with this case was in the pursuance of my duties as police commissioner." Because he was no longer in that job, Edwards said he had no other comments.[33]

Gillis denied defense motions on April 10, and the case went to trial. That proved even more embarrassing for the Detroit Police Department. Giacalone hired a raft of lawyers to represent him, including Robert L. Weinberg, who worked with legendary defense attorney Edward Bennett Williams in Washington, D.C. As a witness, Thomas proved no match for Weinberg. The lieutenant folded under the pressure of the case, according to Piersante, who said he "was like most Americans. When he realized who was involved he got scared to death."[34]

During the investigation, Thomas insisted on typing his reports at the precinct station or at home rather than in the CIB office at police headquarters. He feared if he came downtown, Giacalone might get word that he was working with Piersante. Thomas's decision, which seemed relatively minor at the time, proved disastrous when he decided to lie about it on the stand. In cross-examining Thomas about the accuracy of his reports, Weinberg asked Thomas where he had typed them. The police officer said he had written them at the precinct, but it was clear that the reports had been typed on two different typewriters. When court recessed for the afternoon, Piersante told Thomas to tell the truth the next day. He refused and Weinberg had "a bonanza." In the face of skilled cross-examination, Thomas finally blurted out, "I lied." Thomas meant he had lied about typing the reports, but the confession tainted the rest of his testimony. Piersante recalled that Thomas's remark "was like an explosion in the courtroom." Weinberg was also stunned. Thirty years and thousands of cases later, he still remembered the Giacalone trial. "I never had another experience of a police officer admitting he was lying on the stand."[35]

Piersante was philosophical about the loss. "We had all of these tapes. We had the surveillance of the calls. It was the most solid case I've ever seen." But, he added, Weinberg was a "smart young lawyer" who had "destroyed Thomas on the stand. The verdict came back not guilty. We were beat fair and square." Piersante never became too upset when police lost a case against organized criminals because he recognized that "they keep going and that's what gets them caught eventually." Indeed, many cases would be brought in state and federal courts against the Giacalone brothers on a variety of charges. A handful succeeded, but most failed. Neither Piersante nor Edwards were surprised. Both recognized the difficulties of traditional law enforcement methods in organized crime cases, which was why they continued to gather information for the McClellan hearings during the summer of 1963.

10
HOPE AND DESPAIR IN RACE RELATIONS

We Detroiters know that in many ways we are ahead of the nation in respecting the rights of man. But we are not so presumptuous that we are satisfied. We know that there is much to be done. But we know that we as a community are well on our way.
—Mayor Jerome Cavanagh, June 27, 1963

E ven as Edwards launched his crusade against organized crime, his attention was never far from the city's racial problems. During his first year in office, he defused the explosive situation between Detroit's African-American community and the police, but underlying tensions continually threatened his fragile peace-keeping efforts. The year 1963 would prove to be a particularly volatile time for racial harmony in Detroit and other parts of the country. It marked the centennial of the Emancipation Proclamation, and the NAACP and other civil rights groups celebrated by staging marches, protests, and rallies. Some of the most famous confrontations of the Civil Rights movement occurred that spring in Birmingham, Alabama. The hostility of Alabama police and the brutality they meted out to Martin Luther King, Jr., and his followers stirred the nation's conscience. On August 28, 1963, more than 200,000 people rallied for a "March on Washington for Jobs and Freedom" and heard King deliver his famous "I Have A Dream" speech. Detroit experienced its own version of these highs and lows. In June, whites and blacks, led by Martin Luther King, Jr., staged a Detroit precursor to the national Freedom March. But the glow from that hopeful day, perhaps the most hopeful day in the city's racial history, was soon dashed on the rocks of yet another police brutality case. Edwards's efforts for race relations would never be more severely tested.[1]

Edwards's second year in office started off with signs of success. In early February, the *Michigan Chronicle* named him and Mayor Cavanagh as the only two whites among eight recipients of its citizen-of-the-year awards. At the February 15, 1963, precinct inspectors meeting, Edwards noted the fact that patrol officers were stopping suspicious people on the streets without endangering community relations. His program also drew praise from other cities. For example, in early March, George Schermer, executive director of Philadelphia's Commission on Human Relations, wrote that "Detroit is a substantially better community today, I am sure, because you are its police commissioner."[2]

Even though Detroit's African-American leaders were impressed with Edwards, some feared that he had not gone far enough to implement reforms that would survive after he left the department. One recurring source of controversy was Edwards's refusal to implement a civilian review board for police brutality cases. On one occasion, police mistook a sick man for a drunk and arrested him rather than taking him to the hospital. Congressman Charles C. Diggs, Jr., complained to Edwards about the incident: "Admittedly we have made a lot of progress in police-community relations under your valuable leadership. However, you will not be police commissioner always and some machinery should be set up which would assure that when you move out into another venture we will continue to make progress." Edwards continued to insist that the department could handle its own problems. When it could not, he told Diggs, complainants could air their grievances through the courts, the mayor, Detroit's Common Council, and the city's Community Relations Commission. Down the road, Edwards conceded, it might be necessary to mandate civilian overview of the department. In the meantime, he told Diggs, "I have found one of the strengths of this job to be that it contains both the responsibility for hearing complaints and the power to make needed corrections. I do not believe I would care to serve . . . if this power were divided." As for the incident that prompted Diggs's original letter, Edwards said he discussed the matter with his top command officers who instituted procedures to prevent a similar problem in the future.[3]

Edwards's agenda continued to draw public criticism from whites who believed he had gone too far to mollify African-American complaints. One of his most vocal critics was Councilman William G. Rogell, who in January, told an enthusiastic audience of homeowners in the Greenbriar neighborhood, "George Edwards doesn't deserve to be police commissioner. . . . He can't appease crime with self love. Edwards' main goal in his job is to appease the Negro . . . but does it stop there? . . . We don't have police protection in this town anymore." Rogell asked, "Who is trying to kid who?" He estimated that crime had risen 21.8 percent. Using dubious arithmetic, Rogell arrived at the figure by adding a 12.2 percent increase in crime over the previous year to a 9 percent decline in arrests.[4]

The following month, Edwards and Rogell squared off during a council meeting when Edwards recommended abolishing the department's mounted police division to save money. Rogell, whose brother Edward had been inspector in charge of the horse division before his retirement, disagreed. He accused Edwards of not caring about the police department. According to the *Free Press* reporter covering the meeting, Rogell continued to goad Edwards about many issues, including the city's rising crime statistics. Finally, an angry, exasperated Edwards retorted, "There is no point, Mr. Rogell, in your making the people of Detroit think the problem is worse than it actually is."[5]

Complaints that Edwards's policies were undermining police effectiveness seemed to gain credence on February 24, 1963, when a drunken African American killed one police officer and wounded two others. At 2:45 A.M. Sergeant Stanley Sech and two teams of patrolmen answered a domestic disturbance call at 13475 Dequindre in northeast Detroit. Charles L. Washington, a thirty-four-year-old tool grinder, became irate when he arrived home from his job at DeFoss Manufacturing and found that his wife was out. When she arrived, they had a violent argument and he threatened her with a revolver and threw her out of the house. Sech arrived and found Mrs. Washington standing barefoot in the snow. After talking to her, he walked up to the porch and knocked. Washington told him to leave. Sech knocked again.

After the third knock, Washington fired a shotgun blast through the storm door. The pellets hit Sech, who slumped to the porch. The flying glass temporarily blinded two of the patrolmen. The others shot at Washington, and arrested him trying to crawl away. Sech died en route to Holy Cross Hospital. The other four officers were injured by flying glass as the bullet shattered the front window.[6]

After Edwards learned of the shooting, he visited Mrs. Sech to break the bad news. Later he told reporters it was "the hardest thing I've ever had to do." Follow-up stories revealed that Sech, a father of two, joined the Detroit Police force in 1949 for its job security. Both Edwards and Cavanagh attended his funeral on February 27 at St. Ignatius Church. Six months later, a jury found Washington guilty of second-degree murder, and Recorder's Court Judge Frank G. Schemanske sentenced him to life in prison.[7]

Sech's murder provided new ammunition to Edwards's critics. On March 6, radio commentator Lou Gordon dismissed Edwards's claims that crime fighting had increased on his watch as "mumbo jumbo." Said Gordon, "Police Commissioner Edwards is a fine, bright and well-meaning man. There is no question about his integrity." Still, Edwards's "noble experiment" had failed. "In addition to a considerably higher crime rate, it is common knowledge that more and more streets in our city become less and less safe to walk on after dark. Police officers tell me they have great hesitation in making arrests, because inevitably they become the accused rather than the accuser." Although he decried racial hatred, Gordon said that "the breakdown occurring in law enforcement may be even worse. Morale in the Police Department is declining steadily and communication between the police commissioner and his subordinates becomes poorer and poorer."[8]

Edwards did not let such criticism affect his efforts. Instead, he continued his speaking program and found signs of growing support. After he spoke at Northeast High School in early March, principal W. M. Rea wrote:

> Never before have I heard said, in such simple language, the basic philosophy of the Police Department as you stated it last night. . . . You are reaching the people of Detroit as they have never been reached before.

241

You are creating a new image of the Detroit policeman, a very desirable one. If your strength holds out you will have accomplished more than all the flowery oratory of the last hundred years. It is heartwarming to those of us who have labored at building this kind of human relations to find someone in the "high places" who gives the help, the cooperation and the assurance that you are giving the citizens of Detroit.[9]

Controversy broke out again on March 24, when a drunken African-American motorist shot another white policeman. The incident began when George E. Colby, Jr., a twenty-two-year-old factory worker, argued with his wife. He grabbed their one-year-old son and went for a drive to cool down. Officer Selwyn Adams spotted Colby driving erratically on the Ford Freeway and chased him to the Russell exit. When Colby pulled over, Adams grabbed his keys and told him to get out of the car. Colby pushed the policeman down, grabbed his service revolver, and shot Adams once in the abdomen and twice in the chest, puncturing his heart and lung. Adams, 46, a twenty-year veteran of the force with three children, died on the way to Henry Ford Hospital.[10]

Feelings ran high in the department after Adams's murder, and Edwards worried that the ill will could undermine relations between his men and members of the African-American community. On March 25, he issued a statement over the department's loudspeakers. "It is inevitable that an incident of this kind, tragic as it is in its effect upon the family, and tragic as it is in its effect upon the department, should arouse many bitter feelings and some bitter words. But these are times when a disciplined organization reverts to doing things in accordance with the law and the manual. I ask you not to listen to rumors and not to listen to those who offer panic advice." Edwards cautioned against rogue behavior and urged his men to do their jobs effectively while following the procedures set out in the police manual. "This is the road to success in our efforts to build a city which is safe for all inhabitants and for the department as well."[11]

African-American leaders tried to help Edwards defuse the tension caused by the two shootings. On March 26, Dr. DeWitt T. Burton, a member of the Wayne State Board of Governors; Dr. Alfred Thomas, Jr., an owner of several Detroit hospitals, and Horace L. Sheffield joined with the *Michigan Chronicle* to raise money for the Adams and Sech families. In a public statement, the committee said, "We, as an enlightened community, cannot afford hysteria when a ruthless murder has resulted from a completely irresponsible act." The civic leaders added that in creating the fund, the African-American community hoped to send a message that there were no racial overtones to the police killings despite such implications from "some irresponsible persons." The group raised $2,000 for the two policemen's widows.[12]

Ironically, Adams's March 27 funeral came at the same time George and Peg Edwards became the first couple to receive the Amity Award—one of the city's premier honors for civic achievement. On January 22, Detroit's Episcopal Bishop Richard S. Emrich, who served as a judge for the annual award from the Detroit Women's Division of the American Jewish Congress, told Edwards that he and his wife were being honored for their roles in furthering racial harmony in the city. The other judges included Arthur Poinier, the cartoonist for the *News;* Frank Angelo, managing editor of the *Free Press;* Judge Wade McCree; and Richard Cross, chair of the American Motors Corporation. George's award stemmed from his work with the police department. Peg received recognition for her efforts as head of the Episcopal Society for Cultural and Racial Unity. Among other things, she escorted African-American couples to all-white churches in an attempt to open racial dialogues.[13]

Edwards left the Amity Awards ceremony at the Adas Shalom Synagogue to attend Adams's funeral at Epiphany Lutheran Church. He expected a eulogy to Sergeant Adams and a message to the grieving family. Instead, Rev. Dr. E. T. Bernthal delivered a scathing sermon about rising crime in Detroit. "Two policemen have been murdered within a month in cold blood and crimes of violence are increasing. . . . Our wives and children are afraid to walk the streets, people are afraid to visit their loved ones in hospitals and we are terrified in our homes. We might well ask who is responsible for turning our city into a jungle of crime." Bernthal decried the fact that police were underpaid by a society that had money to build freeways and give welfare to the unworthy and lazy. In a remark partly directed at Edwards, he said: "We agree that all men are innocent until proven guilty, but we cannot understand those who advocate the easy parole and soft approach to crime." He found it a "mystery" how this soft approach could continue when "honest and sincere police officers tell us in confidence this coddling of criminals is all wrong and that because of it all they look forward to is early retirement." As Edwards recalled, "The church was packed with Sergeant Adams's motorcycle division comrades. The message seemed to give moral sanction to them to avenge Sergeant Adams's death on some black who had no possible involvement in the murder. It was certainly not the gentle Jesus who spoke that day."[14]

Had Rev. Bernthal known how the case would end, he might have been even more upset. George Colby went on trial for killing Adams in February 1964. Jurors rejected his lawyer's contention that Colby was innocent by reason of insanity, and he was sentenced to life in prison. Seventeen years later, however, the Michigan Court of Appeals reconsidered the case. This was unusual because so much time had elapsed, but the court ruled that Colby was entitled to a hearing because of his lawyer's negligence. The court ruled that the original trial was marred by the judge's failure to adequately instruct the jury on the issue of malice. It remanded the case, and on May 8, 1982, Recorder's Judge Robert L. Evans reduced Colby's sentence from life to 19–55 years.[15]

Nevertheless, the pastor's remarks had their intended effect of reaching the police commissioner. Edwards was seething when he returned to the Amity banquet just in time to receive his award. Trying to maintain his composure, he asked the 250 members of the audience to stand in silent tribute to Adams. He then said, "Amity is a lovely word. It really stands for something not achieved, but a goal we seek to reach. It reminds us of an ugly problem which has been with us three centuries and is with us today. It is not always easy to put our deep beliefs into practical application. The battle for freedom, order, and equal treatment goes on and on. We deeply value your award because it means we have to some degree been able to participate in the great cause of our day." Edwards returned to Police Headquarters late that afternoon and called in William Polkinghorn, the head of the traffic division, to discuss his concerns about possible revenge for Adams's murder. Polkinghorn was confident that his men would remain calm, and they did.[16]

A week after the awards ceremony, Edwards wrote to Frank

244

Angelo about that day's events. He thanked the *Free Press* managing editor for his kind remarks at the luncheon and said they "came as encouragement on a day of great difficulty." Switching to a more positive note, he added, "I should also record my appreciation for your understanding and support during the fifteen months just concluded. Perhaps many others do not know it, but I feel and I believe you know that we have turned a corner away from a very hazardous road for this City."[17]

In early April, Edwards sent a glowing letter explaining the city's latest crime statistics to Detroit's major newspapers. He recounted his three goals when he took over as police commissioner—delivering effective law enforcement, mobilizing African-American support, and defusing serious racial strife. He said,

> I think that the first quarterly report of 1963 indicates that we have made great gains in relation to all of these objectives. I suspect that not only the future of the program, which I feel you likewise believe in, but also the future of the city to no small degree depends upon how much the people now realize what has occurred. No one can guarantee a great city against individual violence and tragedies which result from such acts. But the gains recorded in police effort and in community support can probably not be matched in any big city in the United States at the present time.[18]

One more barometer of how well Edwards's program was working came after another police shooting. Officer Doyal Johnson, answering a domestic disturbance call on May 16, shot Kirby Brown who had holed up in his home at 3035 Bagby. Superintendent Eugene Reuter moved quickly to suspend Johnson and two other officers, Clair Martin and Eugene Rodegher, after the incident. Ernest Mazey, executive director of the ACLU, responded with a laudatory press release about the police department's "prompt and dispassionate handling of this tragic episode." Mazey noted that Johnson had received "no special treatment because of his position as a police officer." He said that it indicated the "important growth in confidence and respect" that had taken place between the police and the African-American community.[19]

During that spring, Edwards took time out to speak against capital punishment. Michigan had abolished the death penalty, and Edwards believed other states' use of it violated civil rights.

In keeping with his belief that the criminal justice system should focus on rehabilitation rather than punishment, Edwards testified before the California legislature in April. He favored the pending McMillan Bill, a four-year moratorium on the death penalty. Months later, he testified before a New York legislative committee considering a similar ban. At both hearings, Edwards said that capital punishment promoted disrespect for the law by preventing the justice system from correcting its most dramatic mistakes, by furthering "the most brutal proof possible of the ultimate effect of race discrimination in our society," and by making a mockery of law by prompting long delays in punishment. Edwards also rejected the notion that capital punishment deterred crime. Instead, he argued, "Capital punishment tends to brutalize the society which employs it and hence may serve to increase criminal tendencies." He said it was not surprising that the death penalty had been common on the lawless American frontier and was used in modern dictatorships.[20]

In May, Edwards delivered a speech to the Ninth Annual Institute on Police and Community Relations at Michigan State University. His experience as Detroit's police commissioner gave his long-held views about constitutional policing a more practical edge. Edwards described a community relations meeting the previous month in the troubled 10th Precinct at which 450 citizens showed up and stayed for three hours. Remarkably, no one complained about police brutality or racial discrimination. Instead, he said, they offered information about stills, blind pigs, and other illegal activities. "This is the kind of information which makes the law enforcement job so much easier." In addition, Edwards said, the department gave out ten citations during the previous month to citizens who helped police. Three of those honored were African-American men who chased two gunmen after a hold-up and held them until the police arrived. Edwards concluded that such citizen support provided evidence that inner-city residents wanted more vigorous law enforcement, as long as it was tempered by racial fairness.[21]

Too many departments, Edwards said, still followed "the occupation army alternative" which "means that the police officer in walking his beat, or riding his scout car, sees every person as a hostile figure; doesn't see a friendly face, and when he talks to somebody the person he talks to 'doesn't know nuthin.' " The "occupation army" approach guaranteed that every interaction between police and minority citizens would be exaggerated out of context and that hostility to police would translate into hostility toward all whites. He urged police to follow Detroit's example down a better path. "It is the way of the Constitution; it's the way of our essential morality in America. It's the way of practicality also. It calls for vigorous law enforcement which is equal and which has the support of all law-abiding people."[22]

When Edwards coined the phrase "occupation army," he may have been thinking about recent events in Birmingham, Alabama, where Martin Luther King, Jr., led a drive to desegregate stores and public facilities. On April 12, Birmingham police arrested King as he spearheaded a Good Friday procession to City Hall. His placement in solitary confinement sparked national concern and prompted Mrs. King to call the White House seeking federal intervention with local authorities. Two weeks later, Birmingham's Public Safety Commissioner Bull Connor became the subject of national opprobrium when he turned fire hoses and police dogs on African-American youths who had joined the protest movement. As author David J. Garrow writes: "Striking photographs of the snarling dogs and the high-pressure hoses appeared everywhere. One popular picture depicted a Birmingham officer holding a black citizen with one hand and a police dog's leash in the other while the dog attempted to sink its teeth into the man's stomach. News reports stated that five black children had been injured by the police hoses or police clubs, and that one black woman bystander had accused police of knocking her in the stomach intentionally."[23]

Edwards, like many other Americans, was outraged by Connor's behavior, and he was pleased to learn that Detroit's African-American leaders planned to stage a sympathy march. The demonstration was delayed at least once because of animosities between local NAACP leaders and King's closest associate in Detroit, Rev. Clarence L. Franklin, the pastor of New Bethel Baptist Church and the chair of the Detroit Council for Human Rights (DCHR). As author Taylor Branch writes, "Franklin's people levied charges that the NAACP leaders were 'a bunch of Uncle Toms,' and were answered by public claims that the NAACP was 'the real and only voice of the Negro community.' " The newly formed DCHR finally scheduled the march for June 23, and Franklin announced that its purpose would be to protest segregation in the South and the "unequal treatment of Negroes in jobs, education, and housing in Detroit."[24]

The announcement of the parade date drew negative comments and dire prophesies from extremists. One writer, W. Jones, implored Edwards to call off the "nigger march . . . where those attempting to overthrow the government expect to assemble . . . on the Lord's Day! . . . Do you fully realize the tension that is FURTHER AROUSED when you allow 100,000 niggers . . . to get to such an emotional pitch. . . . They are an emotional race anyway. We cannot believe you realize the tension already in this city anyway, without authorizing this holocaust next Sunday." Jones predicted bloodshed from people, like him, who resented providing welfare to blacks, whom he claimed were "idle" and kept having "illegitimate kids . . . by various men."[25]

Edwards was sanguine about the march. He had met King several times and "had no fear that any parade planned with his sanction would be other than peaceful in purpose." He ordered members of the department to follow the same procedures they had used during Malcolm X's visit. As soon as the newspapers carried names of the Detroit sponsoring committee members, Edwards had the police contact them to begin planning. Later, he hosted a meeting at police headquarters to discuss the final details. "We wanted to show as clearly as possible by word and deed that whatever happened to Martin Luther King and his adherents in Alabama" would not happen in Detroit. Edwards's major concerns were not from his own men; rather, he worried about white troublemakers. To provide extra insurance against problems, he offered to have a unit of the mounted division and the police band lead the march. Committee members accepted the idea "unanimously and eagerly." As the date neared, Edwards called Inspector Paul Sheridan of the First Precinct and told him, "I want this event to be peaceful and happy. I want you to talk to everyone of your details personally. Tell them we expect no trouble. Tell them to leave their clubs in the station house, and Paul, tell them all the time they are on Woodward Avenue to smile."[26]

Edwards assigned George Harge, the African-American lieutenant he had promoted the previous year, to act as King's bodyguard. Edwards planned to meet King at the Book Cadillac Hotel, where he was to stay, and then take him in the commissioner's car to the assembly point. King's plane arrived late from Washington, D.C., however, so Edwards instead met him at the airport with the assurance that "you'll see no dogs and fire hoses here." By the time Edwards and King arrived, the march had already started. The mounted division never arrived because the commander refused to take his horses into the large crowd. The police band led the way with King, C. L Franklin, Mayor Cavanagh, Walter Reuther, and a host of other dignitaries following behind the marchers already ahead of them. As Edwards noted later, no one really cared about the confusion. "After all, there were far more thousands behind. The final crowd estimates ranged from 125,000 to 250,000. How anyone could even reasonably be sure, I do not know."[27]

There was a joyous mood on Woodward Avenue that day. According to Taylor Branch, the marchers "raised spontaneous choruses of 'We Shall Overcome' and 'Battle Hymn of the Republic.' One woman wore a gaudy hat in the shape of a birdbath, with a sign saying 'Birds of any color can bathe here.' To bystanders, strutting marchers shouted, 'Come on, get out here. You ain't in Mississippi. Let's walk.' " Edwards recalled, "Never in Detroit had I seen a bigger crowd, nor one in a happier mood. . . . The police on duty seemed to share in the sense of an important civic occasion."[28]

In the press of the crowd, Edwards, who was marching with city dignitaries, and Peg, who was marching as part of the Michigan Chapter of the Episcopal Society for Cultural and Racial Unity, each became separated from their respective contingents. In the middle of the march, Peg looked up, and to her alarmed amusement, found herself walking behind a man carrying a placard that said, "Kill the Pigs." Edwards found his way inside the auditorium where all 12,000 seats were taken and people were standing in the aisles. It was so crowded that King and his entourage had trouble finding their way to the podium. When the civil rights leader finally stood on the platform, he proclaimed that Detroit's march had been "the largest and greatest demonstration

249

for freedom ever held in the United States." King spoke for forty-eight minutes "on his standard themes, so magnified by the occasion that cheers followed nearly every sentence." The audience "reached its crescendo," according to Edwards, when King concluded with a longer version of the "I have a dream" passage that would become so famous during the march on Washington, D.C., two months later. "I have a dream that one day 'every valley shall be exalted, every hill and mountain shall be made low, the rough places will be made plain and the crooked places will be made straight, and the glory of the Lord shall be revealed and all flesh shall see it together.' I have a dream this afternoon that the brotherhood of man will become a reality."[29]

Detroit's Freedom March marked the high point of racial good will in the city. The following week, Mayor Cavanagh confidently told a national convention of newspaper publishers that the parade "commemorated the new spirit that has grown in Detroit—a spirit of fairness and fellowship." He added, "We Detroiters know that in many ways we are ahead of the nation in respecting the rights of man. But we are not so presumptuous that we are satisfied. We know that there is much to be done. But we know that we as a community are well on our way." He pointed out that there had been no violent confrontations on June 23. "Think of that. Could that happen in a city where there is deep-seated racial distrust, where men fear their fellows who are of another color?" Cavanagh concluded that Detroit's Freedom March, "like so many of the fast-moving events of our time, is evidence that the unsavory traditions of prejudice are being shaken to their roots. Those who still cling to these discredited beliefs in inequality have only to open their eyes and their ears to learn that theirs is a shrinking minority—and perhaps the only minority for which there is no room in America."[30]

The march also represented the pinnacle of Edwards's efforts for racially unbiased policing. Despite dire predictions from white racists, the demonstration came off without any problems. Instead, police records showed "crime took a holiday" on June 23. The only trouble in Detroit that day stemmed from one broken window and one disoriented man in the middle of the street whom police quickly removed without incident. On June 24, Edwards spoke over the department's public address system: "I have been receiving congratulations on the work of the Police Department from all walks of life in the City of Detroit." Despite the huge crowds of the previous day, Edwards reported that there had been no violent incidents. He told his officers, "it was a tremendous tribute to the work of the Police Department of this community and every single officer who was on duty yesterday. I suggest to you that the discipline, the skill, the strength with which all details handled the problems of this parade and meeting constituted a high water mark of professionalism."[31]

Plaudits rolled in. Bishop Emrich wrote Edwards, "Just a note to express gratitude and appreciation for your part in the quite wonderful March to Freedom. Your wisdom and cooperation kept the March from being a divisive thing in our community." Rolland O'Hare, chair of Michigan's chapter of the ACLU, wrote, "On behalf of the 300 people, of all races, who marched beneath the banner of the American Civil Liberties Union last Sunday, I wish to express our genuine admiration and real respect for the sensitivity and delicacy with which the Detroit Police Department performed their duty that memorable day."[32]

African Americans also voiced their approval. The Cotillion Club issued a press release saying, "Detroit's FREEDOM MARCH was a MASTERPIECE in police community relations. . . . The entire police force of the city of Detroit rose a shoulder higher in the estimation of those who witnessed their efficient, mannerable concern. . . . For the first time, Negroes in Detroit looked with honor and pride on our police force. This newly discovered impression probably has been building up for a period of time, particularly since George Edwards was appointed Police Commissioner." Perhaps the most moving tribute of all came from Martin Luther King, Jr., who wrote Edwards a thank-you note on June 27. "As one who bears both the physical and psychological effects of brutal and inhuman police forces in the South, I was both uplifted and consoled to be with a police force that proved to be a genuine protector and a friend indeed."[33]

The next few weeks brought more good news for Edwards. The American Legion honored the Detroit Police Department with the 1962 Freedoms Foundation Award. A week later, Edwards received a distinguished service award from an African-American association of neighborhood block clubs. At its fifth annual banquet, the Community Improvement Association praised his efforts at making Detroit a city "where human beings can walk the streets without fear of the Police Department and the public has learned that the police are here to protect and uphold the law."[34]

On July 1, the department's new budget, which included raises for most officers, went into effect. The pay hikes averaged $150 for patrolmen, $200 for detectives, and $370 for supervisors. Edwards repeated his belief that increased pay translated into increased professionalism. He pointed out that during his two-year tenure, the average police officer's pay had gone up 8.7 percent or $534.25. "Historically, you have to go back ten years to find a two-year period when police officers of this city made so great a gain." Although it was not as much as he had requested, Edwards said, it was still more than other city employees had received and it would probably have been higher if the city's fiscal situation had been stronger. Still, he concluded, "As we seek higher professionalism in the service which the Police Department in this community renders to its citizens, we also have a right to expect higher professional pay for these services. A down payment has been made in these two years and a fine basis for future progress has I think been laid with all citizens of this community and with the city government for future budgetary considerations."[35]

Two days later Edwards announced improved crime statistics for the first six months of 1963. The city recorded 2,600 fewer crimes than it had for the same period in 1962, and the number of homicides declined from 67 to 59. At the same time, Edwards said, increased enforcement had led to a higher prosecution rate for felonies and an increase in the number of traffic violations cited. These trends were especially noteworthy, he claimed, because in other parts of the nation crime was rising and prosecution rates were declining. "This enforcement record . . . is testimony to the high quality of professional leadership which our Department is receiving from Superintendent Reuter, Deputy Superintendent Lupton, and Chief of Detectives Cochill. It is also a tribute to every patrolman and detective on the force." Ultimately, however, Edwards concluded that the improved crime statistics provided proof "that fair and equal law enforcement

goes hand in hand with vigorous and effective law enforcement."[36]

That same morning, Edwards broke ground for a new police
station at Livernois and Elmhurst in the 10th Precinct. Both Edwards and Cavanagh spoke about how the up-to-date, $791,000
building symbolized the continuing improvement of police services in Detroit. The Livernois structure replaced the thirty-eight-
year-old ramshackle station on Petoskey near Joy Road. The precinct encompassed a six-mile area with more than 175,000 residents, bounded by the Detroit Terminal Railroad and Grand
River Avenue on the west, West Grand Boulevard on the south,
the Lodge Freeway and Highland Park on the east, and the Detroit Terminal Railroad on the north.[37]

On July 4, Edwards and his wife left for a month in Europe,
confident that the Detroit Police Department was running
smoothly. Edwards and nine other lawyers and judges accompanied U.S. Supreme Court Justice Brennan to London to participate in an Anglo-American Judicial Exchange. After the
conference ended, Edwards and Peg planned a two-week vacation in England and France. They were not scheduled to return
until August 7. But as Edwards visited Scotland Yard and the Old
Bailey, toured prisons, and met with members of Parliament, a
crisis was unfolding that threatened to undo all of his best efforts
and wreck his pending judicial nomination.[38]

The trouble began the day after Edwards left. At 3 A.M. two
police officers—Theodore Spicher, 28, and Robert Marshall,
33,—spotted Cynthia Scott at the corner of John R. and Edmond
Place. Scott was hard to miss. She was six feet tall and weighed
193 pounds. She had eight convictions for prostitution and one
for wrecking a bar during a drunken rampage. When the patrolmen spotted her, Scott had one arm around a man and held a
huge roll of dollar bills in her other hand. Knowing that there
had been several complaints about prostitutes robbing their customers in the area, the policemen got out to investigate. When
they attempted to put Scott into their scout car, she pulled a
knife, slashed Spicher's hand and bolted. Marshall heard his partner cry, saw Scott trying to get away, and gave chase. Spicher
joined the pursuit. When he caught up to her, she turned on him,
again wielding the knife. He told her to stop, she turned to walk

away, and he shot her in the back. The bullet pierced her heart, and she was dead by the time a police ambulance took her to Receiving Hospital.[39]

Edwards first learned of the shooting while he was crossing the Atlantic on an ocean liner. Superintendent Reuter told him that the patrolmen acted correctly, the situation was well in hand, and there was no cause for alarm. Then, shortly before the end of the judicial mission, Edwards received a call from his friend, Mildred Jeffrey, who was director of the UAW's Community Relations Department. She said the Scott case was turning into a public-relations disaster and urged Edwards to come back as soon as possible. He and Peg abandoned plans for the last week of their vacation and returned. Edwards arrived home on July 28 to find his community-relations program in shambles. Reporters met him at the airport, and he tried to defuse the situation by expressing support for Reuter while promising an investigation. "We want no reckless or wanton use of deadly weapons by anyone, least of all by police officers. But we have also assured our police officers that when they follow the police manual they are protected by the law." As he recalled later, "I found the department and the city administration hunkered down endeavoring to weather the storm."[40]

African-American citizens inundated city officials with letters and telegrams. The Detroit Fellowship of Urban Renewal Churches, for example, telegrammed Cavanagh: "The civilized citizens of Detroit are greatly disturbed about the brutal shooting of the Negro woman by Detroit police. . . . We are amazed that the Police Department did not suspend these men. . . . While we as a fellowship neither condone prostitution nor willful resistance to law enforcement we also cannot condone the brutality nor the malicious and indiscriminate slaying of any human being by a police officer." On July 13, three hundred people showed up for Scott's funeral at St. John's A.M.E. Church at Blaine and Woodward. That same day, four hundred people picketed Police Headquarters carrying signs with such messages as "Killer Cops Must Go," and "Give Us Liberty, Not Death." Speakers included Wilfred X., head of the Detroit Temple of the Nation of Islam, and Richard B. Henry, Jr., president of the Negro Group on Advanced Leadership (GOAL). On July 25, GOAL sponsored another rally at the City-County Building. The one hundred picketers were vastly outnumbered by the three hundred police officers on hand. Meanwhile, the Detroit Council for Human Rights asked the U.S. Justice Department to investigate the shooting.[41]

During the ten days after his return, Edwards read reports, interviewed the two police officers, and talked to several eyewitnesses. He also read decisions by Michigan's attorney general and the Wayne County district attorney's office declining to take action against Spicher. Edwards announced that he agreed with their conclusions in a radio and television broadcast over WWJ on August 7. Edwards calmly recounted the progress towards racial justice that the department had made during his eighteen-month tenure. He then concluded that Spicher was justified in shooting Scott. Although in retrospect Spicher's action may not have been wise, there was little doubt that the officer feared for his life when he fired at her. Edwards rejected rumors circulating in Detroit's African-American community that Scott had no knife and that her death resulted from "a motive other than normal law enforcement." Had he found any evidence to support those speculations, Edwards said, he would have ordered disciplinary action against the officers. After consulting with Spicher's superior officers, he agreed with them that the officer should no longer be assigned to scout car duty. He also announced an amendment to the police manual that required formal investigations of police shootings that ended in fatalities. Under the new procedure, three senior officers, none of whom worked in the same unit as the police officer involved in the shooting, would conduct an immediate inquiry.[42]

At the August 14 precinct inspectors meeting, Edwards referred to July as a trying month "all the way around." Crime statistics showed an increase and, along with the Cynthia Scott case, did a considerable amount of damage to the department's community-relations efforts. But, Edwards added, the best way to confront the problem was to continue working with "high professional standards and devotion to duty." As he noted, "These are not the easiest times in the world for anyone and certainly not for police departments in big cities in the United States. There isn't a single police department in the country which isn't under a great deal of pressure and criticism." To would-be critics within the department, Edwards said his backing up of Spicher should have put to rest all complaining that officers received no support from their superiors.[43]

Privately, Edwards continued to worry about the Scott case. He stewed over the fact that neither Ray Girardin nor the mayor had called him when the incident first happened, and he wondered if the outcome would have been different if the department had conducted a prompt, vigorous investigation. Edwards also wondered if he had been in Detroit "would Spicher have fired three shots or two shots or one shot, or any?" He finally concluded "that my decision to leave Detroit in the summer of 1963 . . . was one of the worst mistakes of my life. I had been over-confident about what we had achieved and over-confident about the people I was leaving behind." Even if the outcome had been the same, Edwards believed if he had been present, "a great deal of the public concern and confusion could have been avoided." He knew Scott's shooting created a tense atmosphere in which every negative encounter between African Americans and police would become magnified and he worried about the possibility of a blow-up. In sum, "The controversy had cast a blemish on the equal rights program which I had brought to the department. I knew that I couldn't dissipate it completely during the balance of my tenure as police commissioner." Finally, Edwards was concerned that the incident would endanger his nomination to the Sixth U.S. Circuit Court of Appeals.[44]

Edwards's public statement won plaudits from both Detroit newspapers and many members of the white community. However, some of his traditional allies were disappointed at his failure to take harsher measures against Spicher. The ACLU claimed Edwards's decision was "unsatisfactory" and called for further investigation. Richard Henry, president of GOAL, demanded equal television time to rebut Edwards's explanation, which he called "shabby" and "an attempt to whitewash." One hundred fifty representatives from such African-American and civil rights groups as the ACLU, NAACP, TULC, and the Wolverine Bar Association met on August 9 and agreed to form a citizen watchdog group to investigate future charges of police brutality. Even worse, the Wolverine Bar Association and GOAL argued that

Edwards's handling of the Scott case demonstrated his unfitness for a judicial appointment. They wrote letters to Attorney General Kennedy and Michigan senators Hart and McNamara to protest his nomination. In an attempt to offset criticism, Edwards sent copies of his findings along with favorable editorial comments to Kennedy and the two senators.[45]

He need not have worried. Many African Americans who disagreed with his handling of the Scott case still wanted to see him appointed to the federal bench. The *Michigan Chronicle* editorialized that its disagreement with Edwards "does not alter our long-time respect for George Edwards, the humanitarian. . . . Edwards has been bold and daring in living up to his honestly felt convictions. During most of his tenure as police commissioner, he had been the object of the racial hostility and contempt from the police rank and file and bigoted whites." The newspaper concluded that it was unwise to alienate friends with unfair attacks. Other African Americans agreed. Anne Lowndes of 16595 Princeton, for example, wrote to senators Hart and McNamara. She admitted that the Scott case was unfortunate, that the officer should have shown better judgment, and that Edwards should not have supported the officer. But, she added, "This still is not sufficient for Mr. Edwards to be denied a post which he so rightly deserves and would add honor not only to the citizens of Detroit but to the entire country." In a separate letter to Edwards, she wrote, "Certainly you must know that there are many other Negro citizens in Detroit who feel the same way as Russell and I feel toward you. . . . I am not one to make big speeches but I cannot sit quietly by and see you crucified."[46]

After she heard Edwards's broadcast, Mrs. Edward Davis of 2020 West Chicago Boulevard wrote that she was sure of his "moral integrity and professional responsibility." She added:

> One could not know you and believe otherwise. . . . I think that you should know that hundreds and hundreds of the citizens, particularly Negroes, share this opinion. Many of them may never take the time to write and tell you, perhaps, this is because they are really paying you tribute in reverse; they are taking for granted that you know of and believe in their good will, their faith. Detroit will be losing the finest Police Commissioner we have ever had in my life-time, but, the Federal Judges of these United States will be richer because they have you as a member of the family.

She said her husband was writing to President Kennedy to support Edwards's nomination.[47] Even with their support, Edwards would face one of the toughest Senate confirmation battles in U.S. judicial history.

11
FINAL DAYS IN OFFICE

It can hardly be said that George Edwards departs the Police Department as one of the commissioners best loved by his men. But respect there is—grudging in some quarters, perhaps, and hardly admitted out loud—and more important, some understanding of what he has tried to do and why.

—*Detroit News,* December 22, 1963

Appointments to the lower federal courts do not normally attract much attention, but in keeping with earlier chapters of his life, Edwards's judicial nomination became mired in controversy. The Sixth U.S. Circuit Court of Appeals, based in Cincinnati, encompasses four states—Ohio, Michigan, Kentucky, and Tennessee. Edwards's union activism and stand for racial justice made him an attractive candidate in the two northern states and an unpopular candidate in the two southern states. Conservative leaders of the Tennessee Bar Association worked especially hard to defeat the nomination, and they found willing allies in senators Everett M. Dirksen of Illinois and John Sherman Cooper of Kentucky. Meanwhile, Edwards's supporters rallied around, and the confirmation battle took so long that it was interrupted by President Kennedy's assassination in November. His successor, Lyndon B. Johnson, renewed the appointment and gave Edwards the unusual distinction of being one of the few judicial candidates ever to be nominated by two presidents. With his appointment pending, Edwards worked even harder to leave his mark on the police department. He continued his struggle to insure racially unbiased policing. More importantly, he continued his drive against organized crime by testifying before the McClel-

lan Committee in October. Using information gathered by Vince
Piersante, Edwards turned the spotlight on crime bosses who preferred anonymity. His testimony provided a fitting conclusion to
his two-year tenure as police commissioner, which ended as con-
tentiously as it had begun.

Problems with Edwards's judicial nomination started even
before it reached Congress. After Michigan Democrats, led by
Senator McNamara, forwarded Edwards's name to Attorney
General Kennedy in April, the FBI began conducting a background check. It did not take long for Edwards's experience as a
socialist and labor organizer to surface. FBI agents were especially taken aback by his two arrests—one in Fort Smith, Arkansas, as an organizer for the LID, and the other in Detroit as a
UAW organizer in the Yale and Towne strike. J. Edgar Hoover,
who never forgave Edwards for criticizing him several years earlier, believed he had enough evidence to shoot down the nomination. He contacted Attorney General Kennedy with the damaging
information.[1]

The *Detroit News* missed the Hoover connection, but it
knew the nomination was in trouble and said, "Reports circulated that Edwards had run into a snag in Washington, that he
had changed his mind, that the administration was looking elsewhere for a nominee, that McNamara and Hart had lost influence on this one." Sources at the Justice Department refused
comment. The *News* reported that members of the American Bar
Association's judicial review committee had done a "doubletake"
when they learned about Edwards's arrests, but it predicted that
Senator Hart, who was a member of the Senate Judiciary Committee, could defuse that issue. The *News,* however, said James
O. Eastland, the Democrat from Mississippi who chaired the subcommittee that would hold the confirmation hearings, could
cause trouble because as "an ardent segregationist [he] might be
expected to oppose Edwards, a liberal Democrat and a strong
supporter of civil rights."[2]

Despite Edwards's efforts to cultivate Kennedy, the attorney
general caved in to pressure from Hoover and southern segrega-
tionists. When it looked like the nomination would prove too
controversial, Kennedy tried to persuade McNamara to with-
draw Edwards's name. The senator refused. According to Robert

Perrin, then McNamara's chief aide, Kennedy asked if McNamara would recommend Edwards for the federal district court instead of the appellate court. McNamara again refused. Kennedy tried a new tack by sending an aide to "make regular pilgrimages . . . trying to convince McNamara that the Edwards nomination was not in the best interests of the White House." Finally, Perrin said, "after one visit too many, McNamara came as close to throwing someone out of his office as I saw in my ten years with him. McNamara . . . had had enough. His final words to the White House: If Edwards doesn't get the nomination, no one gets confirmed by the Senate for the vacancy." McNamara's threat succeeded, and the president sent Edwards's nomination to the Senate along with other executive appointments on September 9, 1963.[3]

Edwards knew nothing about Kennedy's maneuvering against his candidacy, and he was optimistic about his chances. He had worked hard to earn the nomination by cultivating his ties to prominent politicians and jurists. His work as a state trial and appellate judge helped compensate for his lack of experience as a lawyer. He was also a nationally recognized expert on juvenile justice. Although that expertise had little relevance to the kinds of cases before the Sixth Circuit, it put him in contact with judges and legal advocacy groups in other parts of the nation. His work on Michigan's appellate court gave him a taste of the many issues of civil and criminal law that he would face as a federal judge. But, his police commissionership, more than anything else, set him apart from other nominees, giving him a certain cachet as a man of practical wisdom and street smarts. Edwards bolstered his credentials as an expert on criminal law by writing chapters on parole and cruel and unusual punishment for a book, *The Law of Criminal Correction,* published in 1963.[4]

While still a member of the Michigan Supreme Court, Edwards cultivated relationships with members of the U.S. Supreme Court, including Chief Justice Warren and associate justices Douglas and Brennan. As police commissioner, Edwards stayed in contact. He explained his decision to take the police job to Brennan, who said he had mixed feelings about the change because Edwards had been such a fine jurist. "At the same time," he wrote, "I so admire the reason you have undertaken what I know must be an extraordinarily difficult assignment. Successful discharge of it, however, must in the long run be as, if not more, important than your judicial contributions. So I am reconciled."[5]

Only a handful of liberals failed to back Edwards for the Sixth Circuit. One surprising critic was his friend, Wade McCree. McCree believed that Talbot Smith, Edwards's ally from the Michigan Supreme Court who was then serving as a federal district judge, would be a more suitable candidate for the Sixth Circuit than Edwards. As he wrote a friend, "I have absolute respect for George Edwards' integrity and ability but I think he would be better employed at the trial court level than on the appellate level since the alternative would be Talbot Smith, whose appellate experience and legal scholarship is demonstrably superior." Even though McCree favored Smith, he conceded that if Edwards got the appellate post, he "could discharge the responsibilities of that office in an entirely creditable manner."[6]

Edwards arrived in Washington, D.C., on September 30 for his confirmation hearings and stayed with Justice Brennan. The U.S. Senate, Subcommittee on the Judiciary, began proceedings the next day. Eastland opened by reading letters of recommendation from Edwards's supporters who included, among others, Nathan B. Goodnow, president of the Michigan Bar Association; New Jersey Governor Richard J. Hughes, a former judge who knew Edwards through their work for the NPPA; Richard E. Cross, a Detroit attorney who served as chairman of the board of the American Motors Corporation; Leland W. Carr, chief justice of the Michigan Supreme Court; Episcopal Bishop Richard S. Emrich; Frank J. Kelley, attorney general of Michigan; and Mayor Cavanagh. The letters praised Edwards's integrity, intelligence, industry, temperament, fairness, and his devotion to family and public service.[7]

In a harbinger of opposition to come, Eastland also introduced a letter from Dick L. Lansden, the president of the Nashville Bar Association. The association's board of directors met and decided to express "deep concern" over the appointment because of a September 26 article in the *Memphis Commercial Appeal* that reported Edwards's arrest years earlier in the Kelsey-Hayes strike. Lansden said, "This background indicates a lack of basic qualification for judicial office." He concluded, "Confirmation of a man with this controversial background will under-mine confidence in the courts."[8]

Actual testimony began when McNamara appeared and said, "I have been before this and other Senate committees on past occasions—in behalf of Michigan citizens who have been nominated for high Federal office. However, I think no appear-ance has given me greater personal pleasure than being present today with George Edwards." Senator Hart agreed. Then Sam Ervin, the Democrat from North Carolina, began the question-ing. After asking about Edwards's judicial and legal experience, Ervin honed in on his radical activities in the 1930s. Ervin asked Edwards to explain a "rather foolish" article favoring isolation-ism that he wrote for the *Student Advocate* in December 1936. Edwards said history proved his youthful views false and added that he had served proudly in the army during World War II.[9]

Next, Ervin brought up Edwards's father's socialist convic-tions. Edwards gave an impassioned defense: "Senator, my father was the most religious man that I have ever known, and one of the best educated; he was a wonderful father and he certainly did influence my life." Even though he eventually rejected some of his father's teachings, Edwards said, "the fact of the matter is that most of the time while he was engaged in advocating various and sundry things in the State of Texas, he was really just advo-cating things which now the United States of America accepts almost without quibble, such as child labor laws and unemploy-ment compensation, social security and old-age pensions." In sum, Edwards said, his father, "advocated equality of all men. This was a hazardous thing to do for a lawyer in the state of Texas in the 1900s."[10]

Ervin recognized that many Americans did not distinguish between socialism and communism, and he pointed out that the House Un-American Activities Committee named the American Student Union as a front organization. Edwards admitted that he had run into communists in the student movement, and added: "It was a very interesting experience to run up against these folks relatively early in life. It is not an experience which you need to have repeated very many times in order to learn." Edwards said that socialists were the most ardent opponents of communists, and he added, "I can say that for all of my life I have sought in every way possible to use my discretion or any discretion which lay with me so as to reduce and defeat Communist intrigue and power." Ervin seemed satisfied.[11]

Edwards went on to explain his activities as a student and union organizer and his arrests in Detroit and Arkansas. One of the lighter moments of the proceedings occurred when Edwards explained that police in Fort Smith arrested him for singing the national anthem. Ervin joked, "I would like to go on record as saying that I have every confidence that if I took to singing in public, I would be justly charged with disturbing the public peace." The frivolity lasted only a minute. Senator Dirksen interrupted to provide more details of the Kelsey-Hayes strike. He cited newspaper accounts which said the strikers hurled weights and tear gas bombs at the police. Edwards denied that he participated in the attacks. Dirksen then read a portion of the judge's decision decrying the union's lawlessness. Edwards, as he had done many times, said he now agreed with the judge's decision. Finally, Dirksen raised a more serious question about whether Edwards should have disqualified himself when writing a 1959 opinion for the Michigan Supreme Court in *Clark v. the Michigan Employment Security Commission* because the UAW was a party to the suit and Edwards had once been a UAW organizer. Edwards pointed out that he had not worked for the union since 1939. He added "that various and sundry times I have been rather heatedly criticized by labor people for the view of the law which I took. I do not believe that there is any reason why I cannot sit and enforce the Constitution of the United States and the law of this land impartially in relation to any litigant which comes before the court."[12]

Four Edwards supporters spoke next. Each attempted to anticipate and allay objections to his candidacy. His friend Theodore Souris, who had since joined the Michigan Supreme Court, said Edwards never showed any judicial favoritism to labor organizations. He cited Edwards's 1960 opinion in *Scholle v. The Secretary of State* that went against the AFL–CIO's position. Michigan Bar Association President Goodnow addressed the question of Edwards's participation in the Kelsey-Hayes strike. "I have observed through the years that as newspapermen and citizens and even lawyers have talked about Justice Edwards's

264

participation in that sit-down strike, there have been so many errors, so much baseless scuttlebutt, that I just feel it is my duty to reveal to you that there was never a scintilla of evidence of any throwing of anything by Justice Edwards toward any policeman." Goodnow, who was a Republican, said, "I personally regard Judge Edwards to be the possessor of the classical attributes for a fine jurist." Damon Keith, speaking as an African American and a commissioner for the state bar association, praised Edwards's tenure as police commissioner and said that despite "this long hot summer when extremists" were advocating trouble, Detroit remained peaceful because of "faith in our police department [and] faith in our commissioner."[13]

Even before Edwards appeared before Congress, members of the Tennessee Bar Association began organizing to defeat his nomination. Years later, syndicated columnist Jack Anderson reported that J. Edgar Hoover, upset that Attorney General Kennedy had not withdrawn Edwards's name, decided to take surreptitious action on his own. Hoover leaked information about Edwards's two arrests and his father's work as a socialist in Texas to four Tennessee lawyers, including S. Sheppard Tate of Memphis, president of the state bar association. Tate led the charge against Edwards by calling an October 11 board meeting in Nashville to organize a formal protest. After a lengthy debate, board members decided to write a letter to Senator Eastland asking for an opportunity to have their objections heard. Their demand delayed the confirmation process.[14]

The *Detroit News* offered its opinion of the controversy in Washington. "Sure, Edwards's nomination is less than popular with the local right-wing crowd who make careers of writing letters and circulating tracts which cast doubt on the integrity—if not the loyalty—of anyone slightly to the left." Nevertheless, the editorial concluded, "All the objections boil down to ancient political grudges, of no significance now, save as they indicate that George Edwards was, as in a different context he is now, a man of conviction and spirit." In a question that would become much more common during the 1980s when contentious federal court nominations became the rule rather than the exception, the newspaper asked if Edwards's critics would "prefer some party hack, noncontroversial simply because he never had the brains or the nerve to commit himself to anything?"[15]

Edwards also grew nervous. He complained to friends in Washington, including Sen. Hart, who wrote back: "If we could find a formula to move the nomination along faster I know you know it would be applied." Hart said he had spoken to Sam Ervin, who promised to fix a date soon to air the Tennessee Bar objections to Edwards. Other than that, Hart said he had no advice to offer, unless somehow Edwards could persuade the Tennessee Bar Association to drop its objections.[16]

Edwards had already begun trying to muster support in Tennessee. He contacted Michigan Supreme Court Justice Otis M. Smith, who asked Robert Lillard, an African-American lawyer in Memphis, to start a letter writing campaign for Edwards. One lawyer who responded to the appeal was John D. Black of Knoxville, who wrote to Ervin and Tennessee Sen. Albert Gore. He pointed out that many of the events that Tennessee Bar Association President Tate complained about had occurred decades earlier. "When considered in the context of the economical and political tenor of the times, even these activities are understandable, if not excusable. Certainly, the laudatory record subsequent to that period, together with his impeccable character, far outweigh this possible criticism."[17]

Efforts by Edwards and his supporters did little to hasten the process, and Edwards turned his attention to the McClellan Committee. His timing could not have been better. On September 27, Joseph Valachi, a sixty-three-year-old criminal turned government informant, appeared before the committee to discuss his life as a member of what he called La Cosa Nostra, literally translated as "our thing." His testimony about the inner workings of the Mafia fascinated television viewers nationwide. As Ronald Goldfarb, then an attorney in the U.S. Department of Justice, writes: "For days, Valachi tore away at the Mafia's veil of secrecy and publicly exposed its hierarchical chain of command. For the first time the American public heard about omerta, and blood oaths, and bosses, and soldiers, and buttons, and capos, and consiglieri, and all the exotic appellations of a vast and organized criminal syndicate." Valachi's testimony was, according to Attorney General Kennedy, "the biggest intelligence breakthrough yet in combatting organized crime and racketeering in the U.S."[18]

Valachi's testimony helped clear a path of credibility for Edwards's appearance before the McClellan Committee on October 11. His five hours of testimony marked the culmination of Edwards's twenty-two month crusade against organized crime in Detroit. He gave his message timely appeal by referring to Valachi's comments two weeks earlier. Edwards said he regretted the fact that no member of his police department had had an opportunity to interview the famous informant. Nonetheless, he said, the information Piersante's men had gathered about Detroit's underworld supported Valachi's portrait of a tightly knit Mafia. The evidence led "again and again to a small group of families of Sicilian extraction, closely interrelated by marriage and by strong ties in legal and illegal enterprises." Attempts to learn more had been frustrated by the Mafia's "code of absolute silence and a positive refusal of all forms of cooperation with legal authority." Edwards said the Mafia's power in Detroit was based on its members' "threat of planned, carefully executed and highly professional murder."[19]

Edwards also declared that Detroit was "the cleanest and least racket ridden big city in the country." Nevertheless, he quickly added, "This does not for a moment blind me to the fields of organized crime, both within and without its boundaries." Edwards predicted that many Detroiters would be shocked by his comments because "most respectable and law-abiding citizens . . . see little evidence of gambling, narcotics or prostitution. And in their daily lives they have never been threatened by, or pushed around by the element which dominates these activities." He warned citizens not to be misled by the "Jekyll and Hyde characters" who publicly cultivate reputations as successful businessmen and donors to charity while privately engaging in activities that "constitute a continuing menace to law enforcement."[20]

The most controversial and dramatic moment of Edwards's testimony came when he unveiled a chart showing the relationships between the city's top sixty-three organized crime bosses and their various legal and illegal enterprises. Edwards claimed the Mafia netted more than $200 million in Detroit annually. At the top was the ruling council, that consisted of Joseph Zerilli,

Angelo Meli, Peter "Horseface" Licavoli, William "Black Bill" Tocco, and John "Papa John" Priziola.[21]

All five men were familiar to anyone who followed organized crime in Detroit. Joseph Zerilli, 66, a native of Sicily, was known as the head of illegal gambling in the city. He allegedly reinvested his gambling profits in car dealerships, an Italian bakery, and other enterprises. Meli, 56, of 1326 Devonshire, Grosse Pointe, invested his Prohibition profits into legitimate businesses, including a cleaners and an auto-supply company. Between 1919 and 1963, police arrested Meli sixteen times on charges ranging from murder to disorderly conduct. During the 1920s and early 1930s, the Detroit Police Department labelled him "Public Enemy Number 1." Licavoli, 61, of 1154 Balfour, Grosse Pointe, also got his start during Detroit's booming Prohibition era when he and Joe Moceri controlled liquor coming across the Canadian border to the city's East Side. Later, Edwards said, Licavoli branched out into gambling and invested heavily in real estate in Detroit and Arizona. He had been convicted of bribery and income tax evasion. Tocco, 66, also a native of Sicily, also made his initial fortune selling beer during Prohibition. He then invested some of the money in a bakery, a bus line, a food distributor, real estate, and the Hazel Park Racetrack. According to Edwards, he was grooming his son, Jack, to take over his numbers racketeering enterprises. Tocco had no convictions, but he had been arrested a number of times since 1920 on charges ranging from armed robbery and gambling to suspicion of murder. Priziola, 80, a native of Sicily, had been arrested seventeen times during his years in Detroit. Police believed he made money from drug smuggling and invested his profits in an oil company and real estate.[22]

The next level in the Mafia pyramid included eleven administrators, whom Edwards characterized as the "Big Men" or the "Heirs Apparent." These men, often sons of the leaders, operated the more lucrative operations and acted as front men for money handling. The third tier included "Chiefs of Operating Units" who ran such rackets as gambling, loansharking, narcotics, and prostitution. They, in turn, hired lieutenants. The fourth tier included "section leaders" whom Edwards characterized as "Sicilians working their way up the ladder or those of non-Sicilian extraction who can't go higher." These were the men most likely to be caught in gambling or vice raids. At the bottom level were the "field men"—the runners, errand boys, and hooligans for hire—who were not technically part of the Mafia.[23]

The Mafia was not merely a problem for Detroit; its tentacles stretched to the surrounding area. Edwards pointed out that most of the Mafia bosses lived in the wealthy suburbs of Grosse Pointe, Grosse Pointe Park, Grosse Pointe Woods, and Grosse Pointe Shores. Two others lived in Florida. Increasingly, the Mafia was also moving its operations out of the city to surrounding areas. He cited his department's success in forcing the Lesod Club out of the city and the joint investigation that led to the closing of the Gotham. Still, his department's success had created another host of law enforcement headaches by pushing Mafia enterprises into outlying jurisdictions where small, local police departments lacked the resources to combat the problem.[24]

Ultimately, the solution to fighting organized crime, Edwards argued, rested in joint law enforcement efforts, and he called for Congressional action to improve coordination between federal and local agencies. He also favored federal jurisdiction of gangland killings, a federal wiretap statute, statutory provisions for granting immunity to witnesses, and changes in sentencing guidelines that would give special latitude to judges confronting organized crime bosses. Edwards's suggestions were not original. Indeed, prosecutors since the 1930s had been pushing for similar measures. Federal jurisdiction of gangland killings made sense because the hitmen were often brought in from other states. Law enforcement officials argued that wiretapping was essential to permeate the upper, hidden levels of organized crime where the bosses gave orders but rarely participated directly in the kinds of activities that could lead to arrest. Edwards, along with other organized crime fighters, said police often were forced to indict organized crime bosses for such trivial kinds of crimes as perjury or gaming license violations. These tended to carry light sentences which did not reflect the far-reaching and sinister nature of their activities. After he completed his testimony, Vince Piersante and Inspector Earl Miller provided more details to the committee.[25]

Edwards's recommendations put him at odds with many

civil libertarians. The Michigan chapter of the ACLU, for example, issued a press release summarizing its long-standing objections to wiretapping. The ACLU pointed out that unlike ordinary searches conducted under the Fourth Amendment, "Wire-tapping is by its very nature indiscriminate. All conversations of all persons using the tapped phone, including in-coming and out-going calls by persons in no way connected with the activity under suspicion are recorded. Add this fact to the ease with which tapes and other recordings can be doctored, and the frightening totalitarian possibilities of official eavesdropping become clear."[26]

Michigan's ACLU took issue with all of Edwards's testimony before the McClellan Committee. Its executive director, Ernest Mazey, said criticizing a long-time ally like Edwards was "not a pleasant responsibility but one we felt obligated to fulfill." The organization's press release said it was unclear whether Edwards's testimony would help efforts against the "Mafia conspiracy." Nevertheless, it was clear, the ACLU opined, that Edwards had "done tremendous damage to the basic principles of our constitutional faith and heritage" by naming people without having the evidence to bring criminal charges against them. The ACLU concluded that such a "hit-and-run tactic" taken under "the cloak of Congressional immunity . . . is reminiscent of the days of Joe McCarthy" and especially egregious given Edwards's "background, knowledge and public character." In the end, Edwards had "an obligation to put-up or shut-up," according to the ACLU. "Either he must proceed promptly to seek warrants for the arrest of persons he has accused of criminal activity or stand convicted of seriously damaging the basic concepts of due process of law and ordered liberty he has sworn to uphold."[27]

The *Free Press* offered a similar assessment. Its editorial said, "The mantle of Congressional immunity is a wonderful garment. It allowed Joe McCarthy to accuse scores of innocent people of being Communists. It allowed songbird Joe Valachi, covered by it as a witness, to defame a Connecticut citizen who was ten years old when his purported criminal activities occurred. Thursday it allowed Detroit Police Commissioner George Edwards to harmonize with Valachi in listing sixty-three people as leaders of the Detroit Mafia conspiracy, and to accuse others of guilty by association." Edwards said organized crime posed a threat to democracy. Ironically, the newspaper argued, that "in seeking to defend the security of our democracy, Edwards used methods which are the antithesis of the democratic system. He accused these men of crimes which he cannot prove they committed. And they have no recourse by law to defend themselves." The newspaper also criticized Edwards's argument in favor of stronger wiretap laws as "dubious at best." The editorial concluded, "What surprises us is that Edwards' testimony is contrary to his long record as a defender of civil liberties. He would be the first to scream if one of his police officers accused or arrested a citizen without enough evidence to take him to court."[28]

Some of the people named in Edwards's testimony also complained. Michael Polizzi, whom Edwards had characterized as a member of the Mafia's second tier of administrators, complained to Mayor Cavanagh about being called an "underworld chief." Polizzi said he was proud to be the president and sole stockholder of Valley Die Cast Corporation, which made auto parts, and the only owner of the Living Room Lounge at 58 Lothrup. He told the mayor, "I cannot conceive a reason why anyone would be prompted to inject my name into this chart, without cause or justification, and thus inflict great harm upon my family and me. The basic principles of freedom, justice, and liberty which we all cherish so deeply have been fractured by this baseless and unfounded attack upon me." William E. Bufalino of Wilkes-Barre, Pennsylvania, levelled a similar complaint in a telegram. Edwards had not named Bufalino, but Miller testified that the Pennsylvanian had unsavory connections in the trucking business. He wrote: "I challenge the Detroit Police Department or any other law enforcement agency to show that I assisted anyone directly or indirectly in any such enterprise. . . . I request that you investigate this matter and come forward with any proofs you have."[29]

Perhaps the strangest reaction came from Edwards's recurring nemesis—the suburban newspapers that had always opposed his racial views. The Warrendale and Parkland issues of the *Courier* managed to tie Edwards's testimony before the McClellan hearings, his racial views, and his judicial nominations into one illogical, conspiratorial bundle. If Edwards had been forced to produce evidence to substantiate his Senate testimony, he would have fallen "flat on his back in the center of the aisle." But his political enemies did not publicly criticize his testimony because they did not want to undermine the judicial appointment that would take him out of Detroit politics. This was especially true of Mayor Cavanagh, who according to the newspaper, "is almost prayerful in his desire to be rid of Edwards." The editorial darkly hinted that Edwards and top-ranking officers of the department had gathered dirt on Cavanagh and that even if he were appointed to the bench, Edwards could continue wielding influence in the department through his hand-picked henchman, Piersante. Finally, the *Courier* accused Edwards and Detroit's African-American community of hypocrisy in their discussions of organized crime. Although it was a well-known fact that many areas of vice were controlled by blacks, the newspaper said, Edwards and African-American leaders had tried to shift the blame to Sicilians.[30]

Edwards also garnered many defenders. One, Harold K. Daniels, vice president of personnel for Parke, Davis & Co., said he was disappointed with Edwards's critics whose comments "betray a lack of awareness of the gravity of the problem which we face and which you have attempted to expose to public view." Paul E. Dietrich of Grosse Pointe wrote Senator McClellan, "We never knew much about Detroit Police Commissioner George Edwards in the past, but his stature has definitely risen tremendously in our opinion. His courageous testimony and particularly his definite suggestion for doing something about this terrible gangster blight in our country is very much to be admired."[31]

Months later, the *Saturday Evening Post* ran an article praising Edwards's program as a model for the rest of the nation. Writer James Atwater reported, "By exposing the Mafia leaders who had been posing for years as reformed bootleggers, George Edwards gave the campaign against Detroit's underworld an important psychological boost." In addition, Edwards provided more than just talk. Atwater described how the police commissioner ordered the CIB to gather more intelligence, how he fought entrenched gambling enterprises, and how he increased cooperation between Detroit police and state and federal agents.[32]

Amid the criticism and praise, Edwards never harbored any

doubts about his decision to testify before the McClellan Committee. The morning after he returned from Washington, D.C., an attorney for the Hazel Park Racetrack called him and demanded that Edwards retract his testimony that Santo Perrone and Joseph Zerilli had invested in the track through front men. Edwards refused. As he said later, no one else came forward to challenge his testimony. "No libel suits were ever filed. The reasons why Mafia chieftains . . . don't sue for libel are first, because truth is a complete defense to libel and second, a libel plaintiff must be prepared to be called to the witness stand and testify under oath and face penalties for perjury."[33]

Edwards returned home to find that Superintendent Reuter had assigned a police guard to his house. Edwards did not think the protection was needed. As he wrote later, "The judgment was not due to any doubt that the Mafia would like to see me dead or that they had the capability of accomplishing that end. I didn't think, however, they would do it because it would serve to underline the truth of everything I had said and would probably produce a stronger effort against them." After three nights, Edwards called off the police guard because he slept with the bedroom window open and had been kept awake by the police officers running their patrol car's engine to keep warm in the chilly October weather. "On the fourth night," he said, "we slept without qualms or motor noise." Their next door neighbors were not so sanguine. Fearing that Mafia hitmen might mistake their house for the Edwards home, they continued to use the heavy curtains they had bought and installed after his testimony.[34]

It would take another thirteen years for the full impact of Edwards's efforts against organized crime to become public. Unbeknownst to the Detroit police, the FBI was wiretapping the Giacalones. The revelations would provide a fitting chapter in Edwards's later career on the bench. For the time being, however, he turned his attention to more immediate problems. In early October, he cancelled a trip to Washington because the NAACP planned a sit-in for October 4 at the First Federal Savings and Loan Association at Griswold and West Lafayette. First Federal was Detroit's largest home loan institution, and the NAACP charged that it discriminated by not hiring blacks or loaning money to them. Pickets and sit-in demonstrations continued until

October 18, when police arrested eighteen protestors. Finally, the bank's board of directors agreed to meet and discuss policy changes. When the board made no changes, protests and arrests continued into the following month. Finally, the bank agreed to hire two black tellers, although it took another year to implement a "full equity program."[35]

Edwards also used his last months in office to make symbolic personnel changes. He promoted his closest ally within the department, Picrsante, to deputy chief of detectives. He replaced Carl W. Falk, who resigned to become chief of the Port Huron Police Department. The following month, Edwards promoted Lieutenant George W. Harge to the rank of inspector. In his new position, Harge, whom Edwards had promoted to lieutenant the previous year, took command of the Parking Enforcement Bureau. Francis Kornegay, executive director of the Urban League, praised the promotion on behalf of Detroit's African-American community. Damon J. Keith wrote Edwards that his action "once again demonstrated that the philosophy you preach is also practiced in that you consider the ability of the individual as the measuring rod for advancement in the police department. This action has given added inspiration to other officers of the department because they now feel that there is a chance to be promoted based solely on their ability."[36]

On November 21, the Senate Judiciary subcommittee resumed its hearings. The first witness, as expected, was Sheppard Tate of the Tennessee Bar Association. He pointed out that Edwards's union activities, arrests, and connection with a student group that had communist members had received widespread publicity. Tate said that the Sixth Circuit Court of Appeals was one of the great courts of the nation, and, he added, "I would not like to see anyone appointed to it who might in any way create a lack of confidence in it." He was followed by Dick L. Lansden, president of the Nashville Bar Association, and Thomas Crutchfield, president of the Chattanooga Bar Association. Crutchfield offered perhaps the most unique argument of the day when he told the senators, "Rudyard Kipling wrote a story many years ago in which he concluded that a leopard does not change its spots. And one might say that the Chattanooga Bar Association's opinion in opposing George Edwards is based upon this conclusion." After Senator Hart countered the objection by introducing Edwards's many court opinions into the record, Crutchfield tried another tack by bringing up Edwards's father. "Ordinarily, I would say this is dirty pool to bring up something like that, but since it has already come up in the record, we might just as well comment upon it. . . . I cannot for the life of me believe that a person can be brought up to have the faith and the trust and the respect for his father that he states in the record, who was the leader of the Socialist Party, and not have a part brush off on him." Cooper Turner, Jr., the immediate past president of the Memphis Bar Association, concluded the anti-Edwards contingent. He endorsed the criticisms of his fellow Tennesseeans and added that he felt Edwards lacked the kind of experience as a lawyer and judge that would be needed for the federal appeals court.[37]

For the next three weeks, Edwards's nomination was in limbo, as the nation grappled with President Kennedy's assassination on November 22. At the same time, Edwards's supporters and opponents continued to fight each other behind the scenes. Edwards called old friends to gather their support. One, Alfred P. Murrah, chief judge of the Tenth U.S. Circuit Court of Appeals, offered help and encouragement. "I will surely see what I can do in Tennessee. Meanwhile be steadfast and confident." On December 11, the Judiciary Committee approved Edwards's nomination and sent his name to the full Senate despite the objection of committee's Chair James Eastland, who vowed to vote against Edwards.[38]

A rancorous debate broke out the following week when Edwards's nomination came up on the full floor. McNamara recommended Edwards as "a very fine citizen of Michigan and a very fine family man." Hart agreed. As a member of the Judiciary Committee, Hart said he had heard all the questions raised by Edwards's opponents, and they had strengthened his conviction that Edwards was an unusually worthy candidate. "I know that history's verdict of George C. Edwards as an appellate judge of the Sixth Circuit will reflect the same character and sheen that attaches to his already luminous record in other positions."[39]

Senator Dirksen weighed in with a lengthy indictment. He cited Edwards's alleged participation in union violence. Although supporters pointed to Edwards's youth at the time, Dirksen countered that Edwards "certainly was at the age of discretion and understanding." He criticized Edwards's union activism and his membership in the LID. Dirksen pointed out that the House Committee on Un-American Activities had charged the LID "with calling for the disarmament of the capitalist state and the army of the proletariat state." Finally, the Illinois senator said, "It may be true that he has learned; that he has changed since his youth; and that, as he says, he regrets some things which he has done." But the larger question was whether litigants could have faith in a judge with Edwards's "ultra liberal" background. "So we have the case against George C. Edwards's nomination. It does not go to the activities of his turbulent youth, his defiance of the police and the courts or his espousal of Communist-approved causes, or to the ability and experience he may have gained in later years. It goes directly to whether the people he will be judging have confidence they will receive a fair trial from him. They have said emphatically that they do not." Senator John Sherman Cooper challenged Edwards's commitment to the law. "I know that the appointee holds today a very important position—that of police commissioner of Detroit. But it does seem strange to me that one who is devoted to the law . . . should quit the bench to become the police commissioner of a city."[40]

Edwards's staunchest defender was Hubert H. Humphrey, the Senate whip and Democrat from Minnesota. The two men had been friends since the mid-1940s when Humphrey served as mayor of Minneapolis and Edwards was on the Detroit Common Council. Initially drawn to each other by their interest in city government, their friendship deepened because of their liberal politics. "I feel in this nominee we have a man of judicious temperament, qualified in the law, brilliant, and one who has earned the respect and the admiration of all walks of life. If there is any one quality that George Edwards has above all others it is his deep sense of social justice and his sense of fairness. I can think of nothing more needed today than that the law be tempered with a sense of humanity and compassion, and yet administered fairly, honestly, and courageously." Humphrey argued that Edwards's leadership of the Detroit police set a standard for the nation. He conceded that Edwards had his critics, but he concluded, "That is all the more reason why his nomination should be confirmed. A man who does not have critics is a man who apparently has no convictions, sense of purpose, or sense of idealism."[41]

Hart suggested that given the complexity of the hearings, it was necessary to include a transcript of the hearings in the *Congressional Record*. Dirksen disagreed, saying there was no need to include all seventy-eight pages. They bickered back and forth, finally reaching a compromise to put some excerpts of the hearings in the record. Those filled more than three pages. Despite Dirksen's best efforts, the Senate voted to confirm Edwards that afternoon. Humphrey asked that President Johnson be notified immediately.[42]

After the protracted floor battle, Humphrey telegrammed, "Congratulations, Your Honor. Delighted." Edwards wrote him later, "Thanks so much for your wire. Thanks even more for your help throughout the confirmation process and on the floor the day of the vote. But thanks even more for what you continue to mean for this country." A relieved Edwards wrote McNamara, "While I never doubted the outcome, it was still good to see the finale. . . . Without forgetting for a second Phil's skill and patience and perseverance, I know that your influence was the crucial factor."[43]

The following day Edwards handed in his resignation as police commissioner to be effective December 19, 1963. Cavanagh told reporters he regretted Edwards's departure and released a letter saying: "Our police department and our community is considerably better today as a result of your services. Your contribution has been a tremendous one and will be acknowledged in an even greater degree as years go on." Richard V. Marks, secretary-director of the Detroit Commission on Community Relations, wrote: "We are convinced that during your tenure as police commissioner both law enforcement and intergroup understanding were improved." The *Detroit News* probably summed up the situation most aptly in its editorial on Edwards's departure. "It can hardly be said that George Edwards departs the Police Department as one of the commissioners best loved by his men. But respect there is—grudging in some quarters, perhaps, and hardly admitted out loud—and more important, some understanding of what he has tried to do and why."[44]

The following day, Edwards was sworn in as a judge of the Sixth Circuit Court of Appeals in Cincinnati. In Detroit, Cavanagh formally appointed Ray Girardin as the new police commissioner. It seemed a fitting appointment. Edwards and Girardin were old friends. Edwards recommended Girardin as chief probation officer of Wayne County in December 1960. Later, as an advisor to Cavanagh during his mayoral campaign, Girardin returned the favor by suggesting Edwards for the police commissioner's job. On June 1, 1962, Cavanagh had appointed Girardin as his top aide to replace Joseph B. Sullivan. In that job, he and Edwards had worked together again.[45]

Despite their similar views about law enforcement, it became immediately apparent that Girardin did not share Edwards's staunch idealism. His comments on taking over as police commissioner provided a stark contrast to Edwards's early days in the post. Girardin eschewed lofty pronouncements and simply told reporters, "There are too many people running around with nickel solutions to million-dollar problems. I have some ideas but I don't claim any cure alls." To many members of the department, Girardin offered a welcome relief from Edwards. He fell in love with the romance of police work as a young reporter; he never lost his sense of awe for the men in blue. After his appointment, one critic aptly predicted, "There may be too much cop in him. He may become one of the boys and forget that the commissioner is a citizens' representative to a quasi-military force."[46]

CONCLUSION

The states have been the silent spectators of urban plight. Most state legislators are typical of most whites, who live in suburbs or small towns. They don't know about slums, hospital emergency rooms with blood and guts flowing across the floor. They don't see that. Their city visions are striped expressways, sparkling buildings. Our metropolises remind me of an ocean liner, majestic like the Queen Mary, slowly sinking.

—Jerome Cavanagh, 1969

Although he ascended to the Sixth U.S. Circuit Court based in Cincinnati, Edwards did not immediately move to Ohio. Instead, he remained in Detroit and commuted to his new job. During the tumultuous 1960s, he watched with despair as the city and nation he loved were torn apart by the racial hatreds and social inequities that he had spent decades fighting. Yet Edwards never lost hope. Although others used endemic race riots, violence, and social chaos as excuses to change their philosophies, Edwards remained an outspoken liberal and continued to lobby for social justice. Until his death in 1995, Edwards sounded the same themes that he had as police commissioner—the need for racial justice, the need to address the root causes of crime, the need for fairness in law enforcement, and the need to battle organized crime.

Edwards took the police commissionership with four goals in mind—to prevent a riot like the one Detroit had experienced in 1943, to leave the department more professional in terms of performance and pay scales, to fight organized crime—especially as it affected police corruption—and, finally, to defuse racial tensions between police and African-American citizens by recruiting more minority officers, promoting racially unbiased policing, and

279

encouraging citizen cooperation. Edwards achieved his first aim and made progress toward the others. Nevertheless, because his program never had much resonance among members of the force or his successor, he did not leave a long-term legacy. Girardin lived up to his critics' worst fears. At a time when Detroit needed a forceful visionary to lead the department, Girardin was a throwback to a string of lackluster predecessors. His tenure was rocked by problems.

Girardin attempted to build on some of Edwards's reforms. In 1965, he strengthened the department's Community Relations Bureau, changing its name to the Citizens Complaint Bureau and giving it more autonomy and power. The inspector of the bureau reported directly to the commissioner and could initiate his own investigations. Under the system that had been in place when Edwards was in charge, there were several intervening layers of administration, and the bureau could only investigate complaints assigned to it by the deputy superintendent. Girardin also improved in-service training and established a Youth Services Corps to afford minority teenagers opportunities to witness police work first hand. Despite his best efforts, Detroit's African-American leaders never believed that Girardin was as effective as Edwards. In 1965, leaders of the Cotillion Club complained that police brutality had increased since Edwards's resignation. They contrasted Girardin's "good intentions" with Edwards's "more vigorous program."[1]

Even though Edwards had not been well liked by his rank and file, he had worked hard to get them pay raises. Girardin, perhaps because of his background working for Cavanagh, was more willing to bow to the city's budget pressures. As a result, the Police Officers Association, which was relatively compliant under Edwards's leadership, became a militant union during the Girardin years. In the spring of 1967, police officers began a ticket-writing slowdown, and Cavanagh ordered Girardin to take disciplinary action to end the protest. The two sides reached a dramatic impasse in June 1967, when police walked off the job for five days to demand a pay increase. It was the first police strike in the nation since Boston's force struck in 1919.[2]

Girardin also failed to follow through on Edwards's crusade against organized crime. This upset Edwards who continued to worry about mobsters in Detroit. His first cause for alarm came in early 1964, when his old nemesis, Santo Perrone, was the victim of a gangland hit. On January 20, when Perrone tried to start his car, which was parked adjacent to the Aladdin Cleaners at 12809 Gratiot, a bomb exploded, blowing off most of Perrone's right leg and mangling his left leg and testicles. Perrone was taken to Saratoga General Hospital while police pored over the remains of his car. In the trunk, they found a .22-caliber rifle with a telescopic sight and a copy of the October 11, 1963, edition of the *Detroit News* detailing Edwards's testimony about Perrone before the McClellan Committee.[3]

Piersante contacted Edwards about the incident, and Edwards concluded that Perrone was planning to kill him. Edwards theorized that Perrone was acting alone and his threats worried other Mafia leaders who realized that an attack on a federal judge would inevitably bring unwanted scrutiny to their activities. So, Edwards reasoned, they decided to kill Perrone before he could kill him.[4]

When Perrone survived the attack, Edwards worried that the threat to his life remained. On January 21, 1964, he contacted the Detroit office of the FBI which, much to his chagrin, did not share his fears. An agent interviewed Edwards, then seven weeks passed without action. On March 10, Edwards wrote a scathing letter to the agent in charge of Detroit's FBI office.

> While I fully recognize that the above facts and inferences are far from sufficient to warrant charging anybody with any federal crime, I do suggest that there is sufficient information to occasion investigation by the FBI. . . . I assure you that I am not a particularly nervous person, nor do I believe that there is ever any certainty of protection against a determined and clever assassin. But, in dealing with people as dangerous as these . . . I want the advantage of as much information and protection as can reasonably be made available.[5]

After the FBI still took no visible action, Edwards complained to Robert Kennedy. In a three-page letter detailing his frustrations, he wrote: "One part of my reluctance to write . . . has been my profound hope that no hint of this should reach public view. My wife has already suffered sufficiently from the public repercussions of my activities in the Police Department." He suggested that FBI agents interview Perrone and his two sons-

281

in-law as a way of intimidating them. Kennedy wrote back promptly, apologized for any misunderstandings, and informed Edwards that the FBI had already talked to the three men.[6]

Edwards remained skeptical of the FBI, and his suspicions increased the following year when Perrone became the leading suspect in the murder of Pete Lombardo. In April, police found the sixty-four-year-old hoodlum's body, riddled with bullets, lying face down in his St. Clair Shores home. He had been dead for at least two weeks. Lombardo, a long-time associate of Perrone, had a checkered past. He served five years in a federal penitentiary for counterfeiting engine numbers and papers for stolen cars. He lost part of his jaw in a gun battle with Detroit police in 1950. Four years later, along with Perrone, he was charged with taking part in the assassination attempt against Walter Reuther. Two weeks after Lombardo's body was found, a Macomb County grand jury completed its unsuccessful investigation by calling Perrone as its last witness.[7]

Although Perrone was never tried in the case, Edwards was convinced of his guilt. In the bomb attempt on his life, Perrone lost one leg, and his testicles were mangled. Edwards reasoned that once Perrone identified Lombardo as one of his attackers, he sought a fitting revenge. Thus, it was no coincidence that Lombardo's murderer stabbed him in the rectum and knifed his testicles before shooting him with a .22-caliber revolver. Edwards was troubled by the fact that the FBI never contacted him when Perrone became active again. By then, the FBI had a new agent in charge of its Detroit office, Paul Stoddard, and Edwards ordered him to his chambers in July. Edwards recounted the meeting in a memo, "I mentioned to Mr. Stoddard my belief that if any attempt were made in relation to me, the probability would be strong that care would be taken to disguise it as an accident." He predicted that any such attempt probably would be made away from Detroit.[8]

Given what he perceived to be the FBI's indifference, Edwards decided to add to his "life insurance policy." In September, he gathered all the information about the Perrone assassination attempt, the Lombardo case, and his own memos and letters to the FBI and sent them to his friend, labor writer John Herling, in

Washington, D.C. As police commissioner, Edwards had already sent information to Herling about his McClellan testimony.[9]

Two years later, Edwards's concerns with Perrone took another bizarre twist when a drunken man with a heavy Italian accent called the FBI's Detroit office on January 29, 1967. He refused to give his name, but he did mention a man he called "Pirrini" whose legs had been blown off in a bomb. The caller said that Edwards was going to be "gotten." William B. Soyars, the agent in charge of the Cincinnati FBI office, notified Edwards who, in turn, contacted Warren Olney III, director of the administrative offices of the federal court system. Edwards wrote: "Anyone who wishes can be contemptuous in relation to Mr. Perrone's capacities for assassination, but I am not one of them." He insisted that his need for help from the FBI was more dire now than before because Ray Girardin had gutted the Detroit Police Department's organized crime efforts. "Absent some attention to the matter from federal sources, I do not believe that there is any protection of any consequence available to me from any source."[10]

Despite Edwards's fears, there was little actual evidence that Perrone ever seriously considered killing him. Perrone died in January 1974, and Edwards was never harmed. FBI surveillance tapes that surfaced two years later, however, showed that Edwards's fears were not entirely imaginary. The tapes revealed that while Edwards was police commissioner, Anthony Giacalone discussed killing him because of his drives against the Lesod Club, the Gotham raid, and the Detroit Lions scandal. Giacalone's complaints provided evidence that Edwards's crusade against organized crime were more effective than even he realized.[11]

Perhaps nothing pointed up Girardin's failure to continue Edwards's crusade against organized crime more than the Grecian Gardens raid. In August 1965, Wayne County Judge Edward Piggins launched a one-man grand jury investigation into a traffic ticket scandal. The police department assigned Piersante, who by then had become chief of detectives, to help. After hearing reports that Grecian Gardens owner Costa "Gus" Colacasides and his night manager, Peter Vitale, were bribing police, Piersante dispatched an officer posing as a crooked cop to visit the Greektown restaurant at 544 Monroe. On six occasions, while the policeman wore a wiretap, Colacasides and Vitale paid him bribes to overlook a barbut game they were hosting. The officer's testimony provided enough information for a search warrant, but Piersante worried about whether to tell Commissioner Girardin. Under grand jury rules of secrecy, Piersante was technically barred from discussing the case. Yet, he also felt that he had an obligation to tell his boss. Piersante called Edwards and they discussed the dilemma for more than an hour. Edwards advised Piersante to follow Piggins's instructions not to discuss the case with any of his superiors.[12]

Piersante and his men raided the Grecian Gardens in the early morning hours of January 22, 1966. They discovered two small black books that contained the names of more than forty policemen and what appeared to be a schedule of payoffs. The books took on a symbolism far beyond the information they contained. Girardin convened a board of inquiry in June consisting of three civilians and two career police officers. In December, after interviewing 119 police, the board recommended suspensions and disciplinary actions against four ranking officers, major personnel changes in the vice bureau and 1st Precinct, and other changes in vice investigation procedures. Meanwhile, during a nineteen-month investigation the grand jury indicted twenty-one police officers, seventeen of those for perjury. Girardin suspended eighteen policemen—five based on the board's recommendations and thirteen others based on the grand jury indictments. He also transferred all of the police named in the books from the vice squad and the 1st Precinct.[13]

At the same time, Girardin was furious with Piersante and accused him of disloyalty. Other career officers in the department agreed. Before the Grecian Gardens scandal, Piersante was the police department's rising star. Afterwards, he was persona non grata. Fellow officers isolated him by not providing him with routine paperwork. According to the *Detroit News,* "The entire matter was passed off as an unnecessary embarrassment for the department." Rumors began that the department would retaliate by investigating Piersante for his possible misuse of stolen equipment. The investigation of that allegation came to nothing, but Piersante realized his effectiveness as a Detroit policeman had ended. In February 1967, he took a job as chief of the Michigan

Attorney General's Organized Crime Division. Girardin did not come to the retirement party. Instead, he attended a meeting and sent his regrets.[14]

Edwards watched the entire Grecian Gardens case with disgust. He believed that Girardin should have promoted Piersante and taken further action to root out corruption within the department. But that would have been impossible for a man who, as Detective Inspector Charles H. Gentry said several years later, was known by his men "as a friend as well as police commissioner." For the next decade, police department observers debated the meaning of the little black books. Edwards was convinced that they were records of police payoffs. He viewed Girardin's failure to discipline all of the officers named in the books as a sign of corruption, and he would remain convinced for the rest of his life that the Mafia had "reached" both Girardin and Cavanagh. Defenders of the department continued to insist that "the books were nothing more than 'Christmas' lists for hardworking lawmen." In 1976, when the FBI surveillance tapes of Giacalone became public, Piersante and Edwards were partially vindicated. It became clear that the books did list police payoffs and incriminated two of Edwards's top officers— Inspector Paul Sheridan of the 1st Precinct and John O'Neill, who supervised the vice squad. But, there was no evidence that either Girardin or Cavanagh ever received any bribes.[15]

Edwards continued to worry about organized crime, but most of his attention—like that of the nation as a whole—turned to race riots. His views of racial justice and his experience as Detroit's Police Commissioner seemed particularly relevant as cities across the nation burned with the flames of inner-city discontent. He was especially passionate about the role that police played in fomenting all of the major civil disturbances of the decade. In the aftermath of the Watts riot in Los Angeles, Edwards told the U.S. Conference of Mayors, "The police function is in trouble in every section of our nation." He attributed the problems to four historic factors—increased urbanization, growing African-American migration to cities, the Civil Rights Movement, and the U.S. Supreme Court's stricter mandates requiring police compliance with the Bill of Rights. "I do not decry any of these trends," Edwards told his listeners, "but it is quite evident that each of them imposes certain problems upon the metropolitan police function." The changes had increased white prejudice, and the best antidote was strong law enforcement. Edwards joined the law-and-order advocates in saying that black offenders should be quickly removed from the streets, but he added it was necessary to simultaneously guarantee unbiased law enforcement.[16]

He believed the reforms that he had tried to implement in Detroit could work nationwide. He advocated harsh, swift action against police who abused their positions by misstating evidence and brutalizing defendants. In cases where troublemakers could not be fired, they should be transferred to "noncritical" jobs. He also believed police departments should require officers to be polite, discourage them from using racially inflammatory words, ban "investigative" arrests, increase law enforcement in high-crime precincts, drive out organized crime, integrate police teams, and seek better pay and training for officers. When he implemented some of these changes, Edwards said, there were "many predictions of dire consequences from prophets of doom both inside and outside of the Police Department." None took place. Instead, crime statistics for Detroit remained below the national average. In his conclusion, Edwards identified a trend that would continue to plague policing in inner city America when he said, "Citizen support for law enforcement is basic in a democratic society. Without it, the police effort can degenerate into an occupation army attitude."[17]

Edwards was a man before his time in his sensitivity to and analysis of the problems of urban policing. Nevertheless, as historian Sidney Fine argues, "Although police-community relations took a turn for the better while Edwards was police commissioner, it is doubtful that the Police Department changed very much during his two years at the helm. His efforts at reform had been resisted from the start by the department's bureaucracy, and as a police official who headed a special squad at the time asserted, Edwards was commissioner for too short a time to have had any real impact at the 'rank-and-file' level."[18]

Criminologists looking at failed attempts to reform police departments during the 1960s offered other theories, some of which applied to Edwards's experiences in Detroit. In a 1968 pamphlet written for the Michigan Civil Rights Commission, Burton Levy provided an insightful commentary on reformers like Edwards, who advocated increasing professionalism, establishing police community-relations programs, and recruiting more African-American officers. Levy argued that such approaches tended to be unsuccessful because they attempted to change "a few bad apples" rather than ingrained police culture. There was no evidence, he wrote, that increased education, pay, or training ameliorated prejudice. In addition, community-relations programs tended to focus on meetings between police officers in special bureaus or high-ranking officers and well-meaning citizens; they had little effect on street interactions between prejudiced beat cops and hostile citizens. In sum, Levy and other criminologists argued, most police departments recruited working-class officers who were more likely to be prejudiced than other men their age, then socialized them in a system with strong racist tendencies, then compounded the problem by assigning police with the worst records to ghettos.[19]

Arthur Niederhoffer in his landmark book, *Behind the Shield: The Police in Urban Society,* pointed up other reasons why police culture worked against change. He claimed that many officers chose their jobs, in part, to avoid further schooling. Thus, it was not surprising that they viewed "in-service training" and community understanding courses as a waste of time. Niederhoffer also described how many police became alienated from minorities in ghettos. Faced with overwhelming violence and crime, many officers gave up, rationalizing their negligence by assuming that citizens in high-crime areas would not cooperate with them. Lastly, Niederhoffer argued that improving police-community relations by attempting to reform police behavior was doomed to fail because it addressed only one side of the equation. No amount of police reform could work in the face of citizen hatred and mistrust.[20]

Sadly, the realization of failure and the search for answers came only in the aftermath of the violence that rocked many American cities during the 1960s. In Detroit, it took the 1967 riot to prompt city fathers to wholeheartedly adopt many of the reforms that Edwards had advocated five years earlier. Trouble began at 5:30 A.M. on July 23, a muggy Sunday, when police raided a suspected blind pig on 12th and Clairmount on the West Side. As they herded the African-American patrons and bartender into a paddy wagon and scout cars, an angry crowd gathered. Within two hours the city was in flames; it took eight days to bring the worst riot in the nation's history under control.

To many liberals, including Edwards, the civil unrest in what many considered the Model City was incomprehensible. Edwards was not alone in saying, "Yes, we can understand Watts; yes, we can understand Newark, but in Detroit we tried." Pundits came up with three explanations: there had not been enough progress toward equality for African Americans, the police had not reacted quickly enough to the brewing trouble, and Black Power groups had turned a local riot into a city-wide conflagration. Edwards believed all three explanations contained kernels of truth, and he argued more money and effort were needed to solve the problems.[21]

Edwards was not alone in his soul searching. Mayor Cavanagh later wrote, "The overwhelming trauma—the ignominious assault—was almost beyond our capacity to comprehend. I must confess that I was shaken by those terrible events. Ever since taking office as Mayor in 1962, I had directed a considerable amount of the attention of my administration toward building a climate of decency, hope and opportunity for all of our citizens. In retrospect, however, it was evident that a great deal of this effort was superficial and illusory."[22]

In the wake of the riots, Governor Romney appointed department store chairman Joseph L. Hudson, Jr., to chair the New Detroit Committee. In an attempt to find solutions for Detroit's inner-city problems, the committee consulted some of the nation's leading experts, including Harvard Professor Daniel Patrick Moynihan. It did not take long for the committee to focus attention on the police. As had been true in Detroit, police actions began most of the 150 riots that had beset 120 American cities in 1967. A month after the Detroit conflagration, Frank Angelo, managing editor of the *Free Press*, lamented the suspicion that African Americans held for police. He said improvements had been made under Edwards and Girardin. But, he added, "It is also true that no more than a handful of Negroes in

Detroit, down deep, feel that police have any concern for Negroes as human beings."[23]

Edwards believed that one way of eliminating inner-city residents' hostility was by recruiting and promoting more African-American police. Girardin agreed, but his efforts were largely unsuccessful. On the eve of the riots, the department had only 191 black officers compared to 4,049 white policemen. Harge, whom Edwards had promoted to inspector, was still the highest ranking African American in the department. At lower management levels the statistics were equally dismal. There was only a single black among 156 lieutenants, 9 blacks among 349 sergeants, and 8 blacks among 364 detectives.[24]

Recognizing the depth of the problem, in September 1967 the Detroit Chamber of Commerce established a committee to help the department with minority recruitment. It raised $400,000 in donations and launched an advertising campaign in November with television, radio, newspaper, and magazine advertisements featuring future police chief Isaiah McKinnon, who was then a patrolman. The department also formed a special recruiting task force made up of twelve African-American officers who visited schools, churches, and sports events. On July 1, 1968, the mayor and council approved higher police salaries, raising a four-year veteran's annual pay to $10,300. In addition, during the first three months of 1968, six hundred officers attended an in-service program in community relations at Wayne State University.[25]

There were other, even more visible changes in the department's command structure. In the aftermath of the riots, Girardin announced his retirement in October 1967. On February 8, 1968, Eugene A. Reuter, whom Edwards had made superintendent, and Arthur C. Sage, whom Edwards had promoted to senior inspector after the Gotham raid, both retired. When Girardin died two years later, the *Free Press* summed up his weaknesses as commissioner, and, so doing described the failings of a whole generation of 1960s police executives nationwide: "Mr. Girardin's service as Detroit police commissioner was more of a footnote to a long and honorable career than anything else. He served as a police commissioner at a time when the old techniques didn't work anymore."[26]

The city launched a nationwide search to find Girardin's replacement. The mayor chose Johannes F. Spreen, a veteran of the New York City Police Department who retired to teach political science as a university professor. Spreen took over in July 1968 and began building on existing efforts to recruit more African-American police and improve community relations. Among other things, he created a motor-scooter patrol unit manned by volunteers who received special training in human relations, sociology, and psychology. Their job was to help reduce crime and community tensions by bringing police closer to neighborhoods.

In early July 1968, the Common Council passed and Mayor Cavanagh signed a so-called Crime Control Ordinance. Its goal was to provide stepped-up policing without giving police a license to violate civil liberties. In other words, it was a new version of Edwards's dictum mandating more vigorous but fair law enforcement. Department guidelines explained that "mere unexplained hunches or sixth senses do not alone furnish the reasonable cause required by the ordinance." In addition, the police could only stop citizens in public places, treat them civilly, and pat them down without searching pockets or inner garments. Even then, the guidelines said, "the officer has no right routinely to search every person whom he stops for questioning. A search is authorized only when the officer is justified in believing that the person is armed and presently dangerous."[27]

By May 1969, it was clear that the department's efforts were making slow but visible progress. The number of African Americans on the force had almost quadrupled to 445. Harge remained the highest ranking black man in the department and had been promoted from inspector to one of eight district inspectors. In addition, the department increased the number of African Americans in other ranks. There were two black inspectors, three black lieutenants, sixteen black sergeants and five black detectives. Nonetheless, in 1969 the Police Community Relations Project Committee recommended still more action. It complained that the department continued to hire suburbanites despite a city residency requirement and used culturally biased written tests.[28]

Given the symbiotic relationship between police and Detroit politics, it was not surprising that it took a political revolution in city government to remake the department. In 1969, Cavanagh declined to run again. He expressed frustration at the problems of Detroit and other U.S. cities: "The states have been the silent spectators of urban plight. Most state legislators are typical of most whites, who live in suburbs or small towns. They don't know about slums, hospital emergency rooms with blood and guts flowing across the floor. They don't see that. Their city visions are striped expressways, sparkling buildings. Our metropolises remind me of an ocean liner, majestic like the Queen Mary, slowly sinking." In a June 1969 appearance on the national news program "Meet the Press," Cavanagh predicted that the era of "progressive white mayors" was ending. He said it was growing increasingly difficult for politicians in his mold to survive in an urban political landscape where they were caught in the middle between African-American activists and "white law and order types."[29]

Wayne County Sheriff Roman Gribbs replaced Cavanagh in the mayor's seat. After two years in office, Gribbs instituted a controversial undercover, anticrime campaign called Stop the Robberies, Enjoy Safe Streets (STRESS). Critics complained that the STRESS program's unorthodox tactics, including the use of decoys, unfairly targeted African Americans. Other problems exacerbated objections to STRESS. As author Wilbur Rich wrote, "During a thirty-month period in the early 1970s, there were an estimated four hundred warrantless police raids and twenty-two related deaths (mostly of blacks). Detroit had the highest number of civilian killings per capita of any American police force." Just as they had in 1961, police excesses galvanized the city's African-American voters behind Coleman Young, who won the 1973 mayoral race.[30]

Significant change in the department also came with passage of the City Charter of 1973, which gave more impetus to Edwards's belief in civilian control of the police department. Under the new system, the commissioner was replaced by a board of five commissioners appointed by the mayor and approved by city council. A chief replaced the superintendent. To appease worried white Detroiters, Young appointed Douglas Fraser of the UAW to chair the police board. He also retained former FBI Agent Phillip Tannian as police chief. To meet supporters' demands, Young appointed Frank Blount, an African American, as deputy chief. Three months into office he disbanded the STRESS program.[31]

Like Edwards, Young recognized the importance of recruiting and promoting more black officers. In September 1975, he appointed Detroit's first African-American police chief, William Hart. In 1991, when Hart was convicted for embezzlement and sentenced to prison, Young replaced him with another African American, Stanley Knox. Young also moved quickly to hire black officers. The department opened recruitment offices in inner-city neighborhoods and scrapped tests that smacked of racial bias. Young also called for enforcement of the city's residency requirement and instituted an affirmative action program that required promotion of one black officer for every white officer promoted. His efforts eventually bore fruit. By 1990, Detroit was far ahead of the nation's other large cities; its force was 58.7 percent African American. The next closest was Philadelphia, where 25.7 percent of police were black.[32]

Ironically, as Detroit took a more responsive turn to meet its problems, the nation as a whole retrenched. The tone and tolerance level began to change after the 1968 presidential election when Richard M. Nixon promised to restore order to American streets. Edwards spoke out against the trend toward a hardline approach to inner-city problems. On December 11, 1968, in a speech to the Human Rights Day Recognition Dinner at the Veteran's Memorial Building in Detroit, he said, "In this year, we have had some voices raised that would, I think, have desired to move America back in the direction of a police state. . . . The issue of whether there will be civilian control of the police . . . is one of the most critical issues of our time." In a veiled criticism of Girardin, Edwards said, "The person who functions as the executive head of the police department should have his eye on the civilian need for his department, not whether he is popular with his rank and file."[33]

The following year, Edwards pointed out that fears of street crime were largely exaggerated. Out of every 100,000 Americans, 25 died in car accidents, 12 died in home and industrial accidents, 12 died in falls, and 5 died in homicides. He agreed that the homicide rate was too high, but he said the solutions advocated by hardliners would pose an even more sinister threat to the nation's well-being. Edwards deemed as dangerous approaches typified by such slogans as "Take the handcuffs off the police," and "Impeach Earl Warren."[34]

He added that encouraging police misbehavior would only exacerbate an impossible law enforcement situation in which ghetto residents viewed police officers "as an occupation army" and tried to undermine their efforts. Blaming the courts was equally misleading. In reality, Edwards pointed out, the courts freed very few dangerous criminals. Even if such landmark civil rights cases as Mapp, Gideon, Mallory, and Miranda were abandoned, the nation would still have street crime. Edwards concluded that the "advocates of 'tough' law enforcement and the critics of the Supreme Court are really concerned about the revolution in Negro rights which is taking place."[35]

The following year, Edwards recognized that his views, once seen as wise, were now dismissed as irrelevant. In a speech to the Michigan Welfare League, he said, "I speak to you not as a judge, but as a citizen deeply concerned about our state and our nation. I also speak as one of that hardy (and I trust not vanishing) breed known as American liberals—a title which I have worn all of my adult life and wear now with pride and without apology to anyone, including Spiro Agnew and the equally shrill voices of the far left." Edwards invoked the best of American liberalism, "The interest in hearing both sides . . . , the tolerance for a point of view of another, however mistaken one may feel it to be."[36]

As a member of the Sixth Circuit Court of Appeals, Edwards continued to offer a liberal voice. Perhaps his most publicized decision came in the case of Dr. Sam Sheppard, a suburban Cleveland osteopath who was charged with murdering his wife, Marilyn, on July 4, 1954. Sheppard claimed that a long-haired intruder had beaten her to death, but police charged him with the killing. The case quickly turned into a media circus. The coroner's inquest was broadcast by radio from the local gymnasium. The trial was even worse, eventually spawning a television series and movie titled *The Fugitive*. When Sheppard filed suit to get his conviction overturned, arguing that the media pandemonium had prevented him from receiving a fair trial, Edwards agreed in a lonely dissent. In 1966, the U.S. Supreme Court adopted Edwards's logic and granted Sheppard a new trial.[37]

His most significant decision came in 1971, when Edwards wrote a majority ruling that the executive branch did not have the power to authorize wiretapping in internal security cases without judicial review. The ruling arose from the trial of Lawrence Robert Plamondon, a white Panther Party member awaiting trial on a charge that he and two others bombed a CIA office in Ann Arbor in 1969. Plamondon's lawyer, William Kunstler, argued that wiretapping without court approval violates the Fourth Amendment. The U.S. Justice Department appealed to the Sixth Circuit, arguing that Attorney General John Mitchell had the power to authorize wiretaps to gather information about threats to national security.[38]

Edwards disagreed. He wrote, "The government has not pointed to, and we do not find, one written phrase in the Constitution, in the statutory law, or in the cases of the United States, which exempts the president, the attorney general, or the federal law enforcement agencies from the restrictions in the case at hand." The U.S. Supreme Court upheld Edwards's decision, and the case provided the legal underpinnings for the Watergate proceedings that led President Nixon to resign.[39]

Edwards's career on the Sixth Circuit further cemented his faith in the U.S. Constitution. In a newspaper article he wrote in 1975, he cited his eighteen years as an appellate judge on the Michigan Supreme Court and Sixth Circuit deciding cases based on the Bill of Rights. "Gradually I have come to think of these amendments as the finest representation of the American genius. I have come to believe that they undergird and protect the magnificent diversity which is the greatest characteristic of our land."[40]

In 1973, Edwards moved to Cincinnati, but two years later he took one last opportunity to describe how he believed the Constitution applied to the city he had loved so dearly in *Bradley et al. v. Milliken et al.*, more commonly known as the Detroit busing case. In 1974, the U.S. Supreme Court overruled the federal district court and the Sixth Circuit Court of Appeals, both of which said integration of the city's schools could only be accomplished by including white suburbs in a busing plan. Although the main issue had been decided, there were still a few legal details to complete so the case came back before the appellate court in

1975. Edwards took the opportunity to lambast the Supreme Court's earlier ruling. "Presumably this means that if and when the Detroit School District becomes 95% or more black, immediately surrounded by suburban school districts 95% or more white, no problem of federal constitutional significance arises." He warned that unless the Supreme Court or Congress changed the thrust of the decision "it can come to represent a formula for American apartheid. . . . I know of no decision made by the Supreme Court of the U.S. since the Dred Scott decision . . . which is so fraught with disaster for the country." In 1990, Edwards resigned from the bench, beset by Alzheimer's and Parkinson's disease. But his prophesy came true. At the time of his death on April 8, 1995, Detroit and its suburbs constituted the most segregated metropolitan area among the nation's ten largest cities. The nation's metropolitan areas, as a whole, were only 17 percent black compared to its cities, which were more than 50 percent black.[41]

NOTES

Chapter 1

1. Ernest Dunbar, "Detroit's Jerry Cavanagh: The Mayor Who Woke Up a City," *Look*, 21 September 1965, box 7, file 5, Papers of Jerome P. Cavanagh, Walter Reuther Archives, Wayne State University (hereafter cited as Cavanagh Papers).
2. "Girl Knifed by Robber in Office," *Detroit News*, 7 December 1960; "Then They Took Her Upstairs and She Died," *Detroit News*, 8 December 1960.
3. "News Offers $10,000 for Capture of Killers," *Detroit News*, 3 January 1961; Herbert M. Boldt, "Police Sift 400 Murder Tips, Arrest 1,000," *Detroit News*, 1 January 1961.
4. Hart obituary, *Detroit News*, 6 April 1995.
5. Tom Nicholson, "Detroit's Surprising Mayor," *Harper's Magazine*, December 1963; Orpheus C. Kerr, "Facts in the News," *Michigan Chronicle*, 14 January 1961; George Edwards, Jr., untitled autobiographical manuscript, 18 (hereafter cited as Edwards Manuscript), Papers of Mary M. Stolberg, Walter Reuther Archives, Wayne State University (hereafter cited as Stolberg Papers).
6. "Six-Day Work Week Suspended," *Michigan Chronicle*, 14 January 1961; "News Offers $10,000 for Capture of Killers," *Detroit News*, 3 January 1961; "Council Offers Hart Full Backing," *Detroit Free Press*, 6 January 1961.
7. "January Drop in Crime'Unbelievable' Hart Says," *Detroit News*, 4 February 1961; "Hart Hails Force for Crackdown," *Detroit Free Press*, 4 February 1961.
8. Elaine Latman Moon, *Untold Tales, Unsung Heroes: An Oral History of Detroit's African American Community, 1918–1967* (Detroit: Wayne State University Press, 1994), 259, 297; Nicholson, "Detroit's Surprising Mayor."
9. Charles Wartman, "The Spectator," *Michigan Chronicle*, 14 January 1961; "Council Offers Hart Backing: More Funds, Men Available to Aid His Battle on Crime," *Detroit Free Press*, 6 January 1961.

297

10. "Do Police Infringe on Liberties?" *Detroit Free Press,* 15 January 1961.

11. Orpheus Kerr, "Facts in the News," *Michigan Chronicle,* 14 January 1961; "State Sets Parley on City Crime," *Detroit Free Press,* 14 January 1961; "Detroit Chapter, ADA, January 13, 1961," box 54, Papers of George Edwards, Jr., Walter Reuther Archives, Wayne State University (hereafter cited as Edwards Jr. Papers).

12. "Police Abuse Sparks Meeting," box 46, file "Invitations, March 1961," Edwards Jr. Papers; "Hart Asserts NAACP Won't Back up Its Charges on Police," *Detroit News,* 17 January 1961.

13. "Police Chief Hails Crash Program, Blasts NAACP," *Michigan Chronicle,* 14 January 1961; "Hart Asserts NAACP Won't Back up Its Charges," *Detroit News,* 17 January 1961; "Supt. Berg Denies Police Aim Crackdown at Negroes Alone," *Detroit Free Press,* 11 January 1961; "Northeast Council Lauds City's Crackdown on Crime," *Northeast Detroiter,* 12 January 1961.

14. "Do Police Infringe on Liberties?" *Detroit Free Press,* 15 January 1961; Robert C. Fassett, "The President's Column," *Tuebor,* February 1961.

15. Edwards Manuscript, 18; "Study Group Urged on Police Tactics, Crime," *Detroit News,* 12 January 1961; "Wayne State Sociologists Call for City Crime Conference," *Detroit Free Press,* 2 February 1961; Sidney Fine, *Violence in the Model City: The Cavanagh Administration, Race Relations, and the Detroit Riot of 1967* (Ann Arbor: University of Michigan Press, 1989), 15–16.

16. Moon, *Untold Tales,* 259; "Study Group Urged on Police Tactics," *Detroit News,* 12 January 1961; Jack Manning, "The Big Five Don't Know Our City," *Detroit Free Press,* 5 February 1961; Jack Manning, "Who Wants Job, Except to Serve," *Detroit Free Press,* 6 February 1961.

17. Editorial, *Detroit Free Press,* 6 March 1961.

18. "Crime-Rate Cut Cited by Police," *Detroit Free Press,* 18 January 1961; Bill Lane, "People, Places 'n' situawayshuns," *Michigan Chronicle,* 28 January 1961; "Crash Program Ends: No Solution," *Michigan Chronicle,* 11 February 1961.

19. Wilbur C. Rich, *Coleman Young and Detroit Politics: From Social Activist to Power Broker* (Detroit: Wayne State University Press, 1989), 76–77; Fine, *Model City,* 6.

20. Moon, *Untold Tales,* 180; Rich, *Coleman Young,* 77.

21. Edwards Manuscript, 5–6; Fine, *Model City,* 16.

22. "Statement in Connection with Filing for Office of Mayor," 29 July 1961, box 1, file 3, Cavanagh Papers.

23. Edwards Manuscript, 6.

24. Undated press release, box 1, file 5, Cavanagh Papers; Speech to Metropolitan Civic League for Legal Action, Olivet Baptist Church, 3 October 1961, box 1, file 10, ibid.

25. Rich, *Coleman Young,* 75; Undated radio speech, box 1, file 4, Cavanagh Papers; Testimonial dinner speech, 23 October 1961, box 1, file 12, ibid.

26. Television speech, 2 August 1961, box 1, file 5. ibid.; Press release, 2 November 1961, box 1, file 4, ibid.; Talk for WXYZ, 3 November 1961, box 1, file 4, ibid.; B. J. Widick, *Detroit: City of Race and Class Violence* (1972; reprint, Detroit: Wayne State University Press, 1989), 155.

27. Herb Levitt and Earl B. Dowdy, "Upset by Cavanagh Biggest in 32 Years," *Detroit News,* 8 November 1961; Herb Levitt, "Newcomer Unseats Miriani by 41,605 in Mayor Race," ibid.; "Unknown, 33, Beats Veteran," *Detroit Free Press,* 8 November 1961; "For Our New Mayor, A Need for Greatness," ibid.

28. Fine, *Model City,* 16; Widick, *Detroit,* 155; Nicholson, "Detroit's Surprising Mayor"; Rich, *Coleman Young,* 77.

29. The other mayors included Richard Lee of New Haven, Joseph Barr of Pittsburgh,

Ivan Allen of Atlanta, Arthur Naftalin of Minneapolis, Floyd Hyde of Fresno, Joseph Alioto of San Francisco, John Lindsay of New York, Carl Stokes of Cleveland, and Richard Hatcher of Gary. Fred Powledge, "The Flight From City Hall: Four Mayors Who Aren't Running Again," *Harpers,* November 1969, 69–86.

30. Undated speech (after election), box 1, file 3, Cavanagh Papers; Inaugural speech, 2 January 1962, box 52, file 1, ibid.
31. Ernest Shell, Pioneers Club, to Cavanagh, 30 November 1961, box 2, file 14, ibid.
32. Raymond C. Jenkins to Cavanagh, 11 November 1961, box 2, file 15, ibid.
33. Jack Mann, "Ray Girardin: Pro Among Cons," *Detroit News,* 30 June 1963; "Girardin: Tough But Fair," *Detroit Free Press,* 30 November 1971; Edwards to Frank G. Schemanske, presiding judge Wayne County Recorder's Court, 30 December 1961, box 44, Edwards Jr. Papers; Edwards to Milton G. Rector, Director, National Council on Crime and Delinquency, 19 December 1960, ibid.
34. Ronald M. Ryan, President, State Bar of Michigan, to Edwards, 31 October 1961, appointing him to 1961–62 Committee On Crime Prevention Center, box 61, ibid.
35. Edwards Manuscript, 4.
36. Ibid., 3–5.
37. Ibid., 4–5.
38. Ibid., 5–6.
39. Ibid., 7–8.
40. "Cavanagh Picks Chief Appointees," *Detroit News,* 7 December 1961; Frank Angelo, "He Weighs Leaving High Court for Post," *Detroit Free Press,* 7 December 1961.
41. Edwards Manuscript, 8.
42. "Mr. Cavanagh Bids for a Man of High Promise," *Detroit Free Press,* 8 December 1961.
43. "Cavanagh's First Job Choices—'Bold' is the Word," *Detroit News,* 7 December 1961.
44. Robert J. Baker to Edwards, 6 December 1961, box 64, Edwards Jr. Papers; Charles C. Diggs, Sr., to Edwards, telegram, 8 December 1961, ibid.
45. "George Edwards—Personal Data," prepared for American Bar Association, 1963, Stolberg Papers.
46. Edwards Manuscript, 9–11.
47. Romans 13:9–12; Edwards Manuscript, 9–10; Edwards to the Rev. Gordon Jones, Rector, All Saints Episcopal Church, 19 December 1961, box 39, Edwards Jr. Papers.
48. Edwards Manuscript, 11; Edwards to Kitty and George Edwards, III, 14 December 1961, box 64, Edwards Jr. Papers; "Mr. Justice Edwards," press release, 12 December 1961, box 2, file 14, Cavanagh Papers; Jack Casey, "Edwards In; 'No Big Changes Now,' " *Detroit Free Press,* 13 December 1961; "Bible Text is Guide for Edwards," *Detroit News,* 12 December 1961; Girardin to Edwards, 14 December 1961, box 64, Edwards Jr. Papers.
49. Edwards to Selig Harrison, 15 December 1961, ibid.; Harrison to Edwards, 20 December 1961, ibid.; Edwards to John Herling, 15 December 1961; Edwards to Philip Hart, 19 December 1961, ibid.; Hart to Robert F. Kennedy, and Hart to Arthur Goldberg, 15 January 1962, ibid.; Edwards to Goldberg, 31 December 1961, ibid.

Chapter 2

1. James N. Gregory, "The Southern Diaspora and the Urban Dispossessed: Demonstrating the Census Public Use Microdata Samples," *The Journal of American History* 82, no. 1 (June 1995): 111.

2. George Edwards, Jr., *Pioneer-at-Law: A Legacy in the Pursuit of Justice* (New York: W.W. Norton & Co., Inc. 1974), 29–33, 43.
3. Ibid., 76.
4. Ibid., 107–9, 115; "Memoirs of George C. Edwards of Dallas, Texas," 110–12, in George Edwards Sr. Papers, Walter Reuther Library, Wayne State University (hereafter cited as Edwards Sr. Papers).
5. Edwards, *Pioneer-at-Law*, 114–15, 117–20.
6. *The Cardinals*, unidentified photocopied pages, 104–5, Stolberg Papers.
7. George Clifton Edwards, Sr., to A. E. Hindmarsh, secretary of the scholarship committee at Harvard, 1 September 1930, box 8, file 3, Edwards Sr. Papers; Edwards Sr. to Henry Pennypecker, Harvard Committee on Admissions, 17 October 1932, box 8, file 14, ibid.; *The Cardinals*, 316.
8. Manuscript notes, series 9/27/91, box 7, Edwards Jr. Papers.
9. Edwards, *Pioneer-at-Law*, 138.
10. Manuscript notes, series 9/27/91, box 7, Edwards Jr. Papers.
11. Ibid.
12. Ibid.
13. Edwards, *Pioneer-at-Law*, 148, 150; "Student Mob Near Riot When Pacifist Meet Becomes Melee," *The Harvard Journal*, 14 April 1934, box 103, file "College Newspapers," Edwards Jr. Papers.
14. Edwards, *Pioneer-at-Law*, 155–56.
15. "Memorial Gathering for Mary Fox Herling," 2 December 1978, unpublished pamphlet, Stolberg Papers.
16. Testimony in the trial of State of Arkansas v. Rev. C. C. Williams, 22 February 1935, box 9, file 9, Edwards Sr. Papers; article about barratry, *Arkansas Gazette*, 19 February 1935, ibid.
17. Mary Fox Herling Memorial; "Memoirs of George C. Edwards," 58; Edwards to his parents, 1935, box 9, file 20, Edwards Sr. Papers; Earl Dunn, Fort Smith attorney, to Edwards Sr., 26 June 1935, box 9, file 14, ibid.
18. Mary Fox Herling Memorial.
19. Edwards Sr. to Edwards Jr., 2 March 1935 and 3 April 1935, box 9, file 12, Edwards Sr. Papers.
20. Edwards to his parents, 17 November 1935, box 9, file 19, ibid.
21. Edwards to his parents, 2 December 1935, box 9, file 20, ibid.; clippings from *New York Herald-Tribune*, December 1935, box 10, file 1, ibid.
22. Edwards to his parents, 2 December 1935, box 9, file 20, ibid.; Edwards to his parents, 9 March 1936, box 10, file 2, ibid.; Edwards to his parents, October 1936, box 10, file 14, ibid.
23. Edwards Jr. to Edwards Sr., 3 November 1936, box 10, file 14, ibid.; John Herling, interview with Edwards, 15 May 1978, John Herling Papers, Walter Reuther Library, Wayne State University. The CIO changed its name to the Congress for Industrial Organizations in 1938. Edwards often told the story of his desire to write a novel in Detroit. See, for example, Edwards, *Pioneer-at-Law*, 159, and *The Cardinals*, 316; Edwards Jr. to Edwards Sr., 3 November 1936, box 10, file 15; Edwards Sr. Papers; story and correspondence, box 9, file 6, ibid.
24. Edwards Jr. to Edwards Sr., 3 and 15 November 1936, file 10, box 14, ibid. While attending College of the City of Detroit, Walter and Victor formed a club affiliated with the LID, Victor Reuther, *The Brothers Reuther and the Story of the UAW: A Memoir by Victor G. Reuther* (Boston: Houghton Mifflin Company, 1976), 59; Nelson Lichtenstein, *The Most Dangerous Man in Detroit: Walter Reuther and the Fate of American Labor* (New York: Basic Books, 1995), 50–51.

25. Benjamin Stolberg, *The Story of the CIO* (New York: Viking Press, 1938), 156–59; Anthony Carew, *Walter Reuther* (Manchester: The University of Manchester Press, 1993), 18.

26. Lichtenstein, *Most Dangerous Man*, 55–57; Sidney Fine, *Sit-down: The General Motors Strike of 1936–1937* (Ann Arbor: University of Michigan Press, 1969), 122.

27. Ibid., 132; Edwards to his parents, 30 November 1936, box 10, file 14, Edwards Sr. Papers; Edwards Jr. to Edwards Sr., 1 December 1936, box 10, file 17, ibid.; Herling Interview.

28. Reuther, *The Brothers Reuther*, 128, 133–35; Lichtenstein, *Most Dangerous Man*, 63.

29. Edwards to his parents, 1, 3, and 4 December 1936, box 10, file 17, Edwards Sr. Papers; Edwards, Jr. to his parents, 2 and 4 January 1937, box 10, file 1, ibid.; Edwards, *Pioneer-at-Law*, 159; Herling Interview.

30. Fine, *Sit-down*, 132; Edwards letters, box 10, file 17, Edwards Sr. Papers; Reuther, *The Brothers Reuther*, 140.

31. Handbill, and Edwards to his parents, 9 December 1936, box 10, file 17, Edwards Sr. Papers; Herling Interview.

32. For a list of other sit-downs in Detroit, see Fine, *Sit-down*, 132. Membership figures for this period are elusive. Victor Reuther says UAW membership at the West Side local increased from 78 to 3,000 (*The Brothers Reuther*, 141), but Fine says the UAW started with 200 in Kelsey-Hayes alone (*Sit-down*, 132).

33. ASU meeting, 29 December 1936, box 10, file 17, Edwards Sr. Papers; Edwards to his parents, 2 January 1937, box 10, file 1, ibid.

34. Edwards was laid off 8 January 1937. Edwards to his parents, 8 January 1937, box 11, file 1, ibid.; Herling Interview.

35. Edwards, Jr. to his parents, 19 February, box 10, file 17, Edwards Sr. Papers.

36. Fine, *Sit-down*, 331.

37. Edwards mentions eight strikes in a letter to his parents, 14 March 1937, box 11, file 3, Edwards Sr. Papers; see also Edwards, *Pioneer-at-Law*, 177–78; Christopher H. Johnson, *Maurice Sugar: Law, Labor and the Left in Detroit, 1912–1950*, (Detroit: Wayne State University Press, 1988), 200.

38. Ibid., 200; Senate Committee on the Judiciary, Hearings on the Nomination of George Clifton Edwards, Jr., of Michigan, to be United States Circuit Judge, Sixth Court, 88th Cong., 1st sess., October 1, 1963, 18.

39. Edwards, *Pioneer-at-Law*, 178–84; Edwards to his parents, 28 April 1937, box 11, file 3, Edwards Sr. papers.

40. Incomplete clipping, *Detroit News*, 3 May 1937, box 11, file 5, ibid.

41. Edwards Sr. to his wife, 1 and 2 May 1937, box 11, file 11, 5, ibid.; George Addes to Frank Murphy, 3 May 1937, box 11, file 10, ibid.

42. *The Cardinals*, 317; Edwards, *Pioneer-at-Law*, 176.

43. Edwards to his family, 27 May 1937, box 11, file 5, Edwards Sr. Papers.

44. Edwards to his family, 21 and 27 May, and 1 June 1937, box 11, file 5, ibid.; Carew, *Walter Reuther*, 20.

45. Fine, *Sit-down*, 329; Carew, *Walter Reuther*, 26; Lichtenstein, *Most Dangerous Man*, 113–31; Herling Interview; Edwards to his family, 8 and 30 September 1937, box 11, file 7, Edwards Sr. Papers.

46. Ibid.; Edwards to his family, 7 November 1937, box 11, file 8, ibid.

47. Reuther, *The Brothers Reuther*, 206–8; Herling Interview; Lichtenstein, *Most Dangerous Man*, 102–3.

48. By the end of 1937, car production dropped from two-thirds of its 1936 rate, and

the automakers began laying off workers. By January 1938, the UAW estimated that 320,000 of 517,000 auto workers were jobless and the rest were employed only part-time. Statistics in a report by the Michigan Emergency Welfare Relief Commission. See James J. Lorence, "Controlling the Reserve Army: The United Automobile Workers and Michigan's Unemployed, 1935–1941," *Labor's Heritage,* Spring 1994, 25–28, 30–31.

49. Edwards Jr. to Edwards Sr., 12 June 1938, box 11, file 15, Edwards Sr. Papers. Getting the job was tough, but keeping it proved even more difficult. The following month, Edwards wrote to his family that Martin and other UAW opponents constantly threatened to fire him, 9 July 1938, box 11, file 16, ibid.

50. Carew, *Walter Reuther,* 28; Lorence, "Controlling the Reserve Army," 34.

51. Lichtenstein, *Most Dangerous Man,* 95–96; Edwards to his family, 6 February 1940, box 13, file 1, Edwards Sr. Papers.

Chapter 3

1. Edwards Senate Nomination Hearings, 15.

2. Edwards, *Pioneer-at-Law,* 184–85; Edwards to his family, 23 March, 23 April, and 25 May 1939, box 12, file 15, Edwards Sr. Papers.

3. Dominic J. Capeci, Jr., *Race Relations in Wartime Detroit: The Sojourner Truth Housing Controversy of 1942* (Philadelphia: Temple University Press, 1984), 15–16.

4. Edwards to his family, 6 February 1940, box 13, file 1, Edwards Sr. Papers.

5. "Dallas Intellectual to Guide Detroit's Housing Program," *Detroit News,* 8 March 1940; "Jeffries Receives an AFL Protest," *Detroit News,* 10 March 1940; "Ed Thal Protested Edwards Appointment," *Detroit News,* 15 March 1940.

6. Edwards to his family, 6 May 1940, box 14, file 1, Edwards Sr. Papers. See also, Edwards Jr. Papers, box 8.

7. Box 8, file "Housing, Zoning, Housing Scandal, 1941–1956," ibid.; Edwards to his parents, 25 January, and 20 March 1941; box 13, file 1; Edwards Sr. Papers.

8. Edwards to his family, 23 April and 25 January 1941, box 13, file 2, ibid.; Capeci, *Race Relations,* 33.

9. Edwards Jr. Papers, box 8; Capeci, *Race Relations,* 7.

10. Ibid., 76–77.

11. Ibid., 76–100, 122–45; August Meier and Elliott Rudwick, *Black Detroit and the Rise of the UAW* (New York: Oxford University Press, 1979), 178–83.

12. Ibid., 199–201; Capeci, *Race Relations,* 13; Margaret Edwards to Edwards Sr., 8 March 1940, box 14, file 1, Edwards Sr. Papers.

13. Edwards to his family, 3 April 1941, box 13, file 2, ibid.; Edwards to his family, 13 August 1941, box 13, file 3, ibid.

14. Edwards to his family, 25 January 1941, box 13, file 1, ibid.

15. *Detroit News,* 6 November 1941; *Detroit Times,* 11 November 1941.

16. "Ku Klux Klan, Free Press Fight Sen. Diggs' Election," *Michigan Chronicle,* 25 October 1941; "Next Tuesday," *Michigan Chronicle,* 1 November 1941.

17. Edwards to his family, 19 October 1941, box 13, file 4, Edwards Sr. Papers.

18. Margaret Edwards to Edwards's parents, 4 November 1941, box 13, file 4, ibid.; Edwards to his parents, 5 November 1941, ibid.; Edwards Jr. to Edwards Sr., 9 December 1941, ibid.

19. Edwards to his parents, 19 December 1941, box 13, file 4, ibid.; Capeci, *Race Relations,* 82; Meier, *Black Detroit,* 179.

20. Edwards Jr. to Edwards Sr., 2 and 9 February 1942, box 13, file 7, Edwards Sr. Papers.

21. Capeci, *Race Relations,* 88; Geraldine Bledsoe, interview by Norman McRae, 1970, Walter Reuther Archives, Wayne State University.

22. Meier, *Black Detroit,* 187–93; Capeci, *Race Relations,* 75–100, 122–44.

23. Janet L. Langlois, "The Belle Isle Bridge Incident: Legend Dialectic and Semiotic System in the 1943 Detroit Race Riot," *Journal of American Folklore* 96, no. 380 (1983): 183–99; Widick, *Detroit: City of Race,* 99–112; Senate, Confirmation Hearings, 70.

24. James A. Wechsler column, *PM,* 30 July 1943, box 8, file "Minority Groups, 1943–1948," Edwards Jr. Papers; Widick, *Detroit: City of Race,* 104; L. Alex Swan, "The Harlem and Detroit Riots of 1943: A Comparative Analysis," *Berkeley Journal of Sociology* 16 (1971–72): 85.

25. Capeci, *Race Relations,* 168; Harvard Sitkoff, "The Detroit Race Riot of 1943," *Michigan History* 53, no. 3 (1969): 183–206; Swan, "The Harlem and Detroit Riots," 75–93.

26. Edwards Jr. to Edwards Sr., 13 September 1943, box 13, file 4, Edwards Sr. Papers; Edwards Jr. to Edwards Sr., 27 October 1943, box 13, file 5, ibid.

27. "Floyd McGriff, 77," *Royal Oak Tribune,* 12 April 1968; "Expose Edwards' Radical Career," *Home Gazette,* 26 October 1943.

28. Radio talk, 4 October 1943, and Edwards to his parents, 27 October 1943, box 13, file 5, Edwards Sr. Papers; Meier, *Black Detroit,* 202–4.

29. Returns in "Unofficial Canvas of Votes of Primary October 5, 1943," and Edwards to his parents, 27 October 1943, both box 13, file 5, Edwards Sr. Papers; Meier, *Black Detroit,* 204.

30. Edwards to his parents, 24 November 1943, box 13, file 15, Edwards Sr. Papers.

31. Edwards to his parents, 13 May 1940, box 14, file 1, ibid.

32. "Once Backed by CIO, Edwards Gets War Job," *Detroit Free Press,* 9 April 1943; Edwards, *Pioneer-at-Law,* 199.

33. "News by Karl Sieffert," *Detroit News,* 9 January 1944; "George Edwards," *Detroit News,* 13 January 1944.

34. Edwards, Jr., letter to the editor, *Detroit News,* 2 March 1944.

35. Dominic Capeci generously provided a chronology of Edwards's army career, which he compiled for his book *Detroit and the "Good War": The War-Time Letters of Mayor Edward Jeffries and Friends* (Lexington: University of Kentucky Press, 1996); Sgt. 1st Class Ronald Beasley of the U.S. Army Infantry, assigned to the Reserve Officer Training Corps at Appalachian State University, gave general information about infantry training during World War II in an interview, 21 August 1995.

36. "Bring Edwards Back," *Detroit Free Press,* 3 October 1945; "Council Asks Army to Free Edwards," *Detroit News,* December (date unclear) 1945.

37. " '46 Council Takes Over with Newcomer Oakman," *Detroit Free Press,* 31 December 1945; "Edwards Makes Council Head," *Detroit News,* 7 November 1945; UAW flyer, 28 October 1947, box 21, file "Edwards 1947 Candidacy," Edwards Jr. Papers; "Edwards Would Open All Bowling Alleys to Negroes," *Home Gazette,* 23 October 1947.

38. Clipping, *Detroit News,* 22 December 1947, box 15, file 4, Edwards Sr. Papers.

39. Edwards to his parents, 19 December 1947, box 15, file 4, and 8 January 1948, box 15, file 16, Edwards Sr. Papers.

40. Draft and final version, box 15, file 5, Edwards Jr. Papers.

41. Ibid.

42. Blair Moody, "Mrs. FDR Organizes New Political Group: Reuther, Edwards Help Launching: 3rd Party Idea Rejected," *Detroit News,* 5 January 1947; Helen Ber-

thelot, *Win Some Lose Some: G. Mennen Williams and the New Democrats* (Detroit: Wayne State University Press, 1995), 41–49; D. Duane Angel, *Romney: A Political Biography* (New York: Exposition Press, 1967), 7.

43. "Edwards Ready to Seek Mayoralty," *Detroit Free Press*, 19 September 1948.

44. "Hats In: Edwards in Race for Mayor," *Detroit News*, 6 April 1949; "Mayoral Nominees Write," *Home Gazette*, 23 October 1947; "ADA, PAC in Detroit Will Face New Poll Test," *New York Times*, 11 September 1949; "Edwards Files $100 Fee to Establish Candidacy," *Detroit News*, 22 June 1949.

45. "Edwards Calls for New Deal for American City Dwellers," *United Automobile Worker*, August 1949, box 3, file "Edwards, 1949 Candidacy," Edwards Jr. Papers.

46. "Patrolman Justified, Court Says," *Detroit News*, 20 December 1948.

47. "Judge Frees Slayer of Mosely," *Detroit Free Press*, 20 December 1948; "Patrolman Justified, Court Says," *Detroit News*, 20 December 1948; "Toy Answers Critics of Melasi Shooting," *Detroit News*, 24 December 1948.

48. "NAACP Raps Mayor, Toy," *Detroit News*, 10 January 1949; "Toy Offer to Quit Post Rejected," ibid.

49. "Press Argues Loyalty Oath," *Detroit News*, 23 January 1949; "Toy Reverses on Card Oath: Anti-Red Pledge Left at Last to Editors," *Detroit News*, 25 February 1949; "As We See It," *Detroit Free Press*, 15 July 1949; "Sticker Test Lost by Toy: Judge Dismisses Case After Inspecting Car," *Detroit News*, 26 September 1949.

50. "Toy Defends Arrests Without Warrants," *Detroit Free Press*, 28 August 1949.

51. Edwards quoted from his August 25 speech in a letter to the editor, "Why Mr. Edwards Dislikes Mr. Toy," *Detroit News*, 27 August 1949.

52. Letter to Editor, *Detroit News*, 9 September 1949.

53. "Expect Organized Labor to Renew Battle for Control of the City Hall," *Detroit Times*, 30 July 1949; "Edwards Plagued by Schisms as Mayor Rivals Reap Benefits," *Detroit News*, 7 August 1949.

54. "Cobo Explains Slum Clearance," *Detroit Times*, 23 August 1949; "Cobo Outlines Stand on Campaign Issues," *Detroit News*, 8 September 1949; "Speech at YMCA: Albert Cobo Takes Stand Against Bi-Racial Housing," *Michigan Chronicle*, 29 October 1949.

55. Berthelot, *Win Some*, 86; "Civic Group Endorses Candidates," *Grand River Record*, 27 October 1949; "Democrats Rush to Deny They're All for Edwards," *Detroit News*, 27 September 1949; "Cobo Blasts that Man," *Detroit News*, 25 October 1949; "Cobo Wins Backing of Civic League," *Detroit Free Press*, 30 October 1949; "Boss Rule," *Detroit Free Press*, 3 October 1949.

56. Margaret Edwards to Eleanor Roosevelt, 22 August 1949, box 15, file "Correspondence," Edwards Jr. Papers.

57. "ADA PAC in Detroit Will Face New Poll Test," *New York Times*, 11 September 1949; Editorial, *Pittsburgh Courier*, 10 September 1949; Manuscript, box 1, file 7, Papers of Robert J. Greene, Walter Reuther Archives, Wayne State University (hereafter cited as Greene Manuscript).

58. *Time*, 26 September 1949, and election returns, box 15, file "Miscellaneous," Edwards Jr. Papers; "Cobo's Edge Found Hard to Explain," *Detroit Free Press*, 15 September 1949.

59. "Edwards Runs as 'Dem' Scraps Non-Partisan Rule," *Detroit Times*, 24 September 1949; "Edwards Brands Cobo B of C Man," *Detroit Times*, 14 September 1949; "They—the Board of Commerce," speech, 3 November 1949, WWJ-TV, box 13, file 2, Edwards Jr. Papers.

60. "Boss Rule," *Detroit Free Press*, 3 October 1949; "Cobo Wins Backing of Civic League," *Detroit Free Press*, 30 October 1949.

61. "Cobo by 105,000; Record Set as 529,360 Cast Votes," *Detroit News,* 9 November 1949.
62. Greene Manuscript; "Cobo's victory over Edwards," *Michigan Chronicle,* 8 November 1949.
63. William Morosco to Edwards, 9 November 1949, box 3, file "Edwards, 1949 Candidacy," Edwards Jr. Papers.
64. Edwards Jr. to Edwards Sr., 25 December 1949, box 15, file 7, Edwards Sr. Papers.

Chapter 4

1. Edwards Sr. to Edwards Jr., 4 May 1938, box 11, file 18, Edwards Sr. Papers.
2. Edwards to his parents, 2 December 1938, box 11, file 16, ibid.
3. Salaries in a Congressional survey Edwards filled out for his nomination to the Sixth U.S. Circuit Court of Appeals, Stolberg Papers.
4. Reuther, *The Brothers Reuther,* 270–74; John Barnard, *Walter Reuther and the Rise of the Auto Workers* (Boston: Little, Brown and Company, 1983), 130.
5. Edwards Manuscript, 215–16; Reuther, *The Brothers Reuther,* 270.
6. Barnard, *Walter Reuther,* 128–29; Reuther, *The Brothers Reuther,* 270–86; Edwards Manuscript, 218.
7. Ibid., 219–20.
8. Ibid., 222–23.
9. Reuther, *The Brothers Reuther,* other information 297–300; Barnard, *Walter Reuther,* 130; Edwards Manuscript, 222. See also ibid., 219–23.
10. Berthelot, *Win Some,* 59–60, 70–71.
11. Margaret Edwards to Edwards's parents, undated letter August 1950, and undated letter October 1950, box 15, file 9, Edwards Sr. Papers.
12. Margaret Edwards to Edwards's parents, undated, and Edwards to his mother, 7 October 1951, box 15, file 13, ibid.
13. Edwards to his parents, 6 January 1952, box 16, file 1, ibid.
14. "George Edwards—Personal Data," prepared for American Bar Association, 1963, Stolberg Papers; Edwards to his parents, 21 October 1953, and Edwards's speech to Detroit Rotary Club Statler Hilton, 2 December 1953, box 16, file 11, Edwards Sr. Papers.
15. "Speed Juveniles Court Hearings, *Detroit Times,* date unclear, and clipping, 24 January 1952, box 16, file 1, ibid.
16. Margaret Edwards to Edwards's parents, 3 May 1952, and 5 May 1953, box 16, file 3, ibid.; *Conveyor,* May 1952, box 16, file 7, ibid.; Edwards to his parents, telegram, 6 August 1952, box 16, file 5, ibid.
17. Newspaper clippings, *Detroit News,* undated (1952), and 30 April 1952, box 16, file 7, ibid.
18. Margaret Edwards to Edwards's parents, 30 May 1952, box 16, file 3, ibid.
19. Estes Kefauver to Edwards, 19 May 1954, box 22, file "May 1954," Edwards Jr. Papers.
20. Edwards to his parents, 25 March 1952, box 16, file 2, Edwards Sr. Papers.
21. J. Edgar Hoover, "The 'Mollycoddling' Charge," *Law Enforcement Bulletin,* February 1957, reprinted in *NPPA News* 36, no. 3 (May 1957); Alexander Charns, *Cloak and Gavel: FBI Wiretaps, Bugs, Informers, and the Supreme Court* (Champaign, The University of Illinois Press, 1992), 136. See also Jay G. Hayden, "Feuds On," *Detroit News,* 1 December 1964; John Gill, *Detroit News,* 5 January 1976.
22. Edwards to Robert E. Henshaw, 1 December 1956, box 35, Edwards Jr. Papers. Edwards testified in Washington before the Senate Committee for the National Child

Welfare League on a bill that would have established a federal delinquency bureau and a national council on delinquency, and would have provided $5 million in local aid. Margaret Edwards to Edwards's parents, 7 July 1955, box 17, file 3, Edwards Sr. Papers.

23. "Justice Edwards Says: For Real Criminal Take One Healthy Baby—Mix Well," *Detroit Free Press*, 31 August 1958; "Attack Crime at Roots, Edwards Tells Lawyers," *The State Journal* (Lansing), 26 August 1958.

24. Correspondence regarding NPPA, box 27, and speeches and schedule of groups he addressed, box 21, Edwards Jr. Papers.

25. Edwards to Phillip W. Sarles, 22 September 1954, box 22, ibid.

26. "George Edwards—Personal Data."

27. Pat Taylor to Edwards's supporters, 8 May 1954, and Margaret Edwards to Edwards's parents, 9 June 1954, box 17, file 2, Edwards Sr. Papers; Edwards to his parents, 5 April 1955, box 17, file 6, ibid.; "Edwards Appointed Black, Jesse Eggleston, As His Clerk Effective December 1," *Michigan Chronicle,* 17 December 1955.

28. *Theodora Dahlstrom, Administratrix of Estate of Charles E. Dahlstrom v. Mohawk Lumber & Supply Co. and Playford Jackson,* 26, Edwards Jr. Papers.

29. *The Cardinals,* 325; *May E. Fisher v. City of Detroit,* box 26, Edwards Jr. Papers.

30. Edwards to his parents, 1 May 1955, box 17, file 7, Edwards Sr. Papers.

31. Edwards to his parents, 4 October 1955, box 18, file 1, ibid.

32. Edwards to his parents, 4 October 1955, box 18, file 1, ibid.; Talbot Smith to Edwards, 28 December 1955, and other letters, box 25, file "Circuit Court relations with Supreme Court, 1955," Edwards Jr. Papers.

33. George Edwards, Jr., "The Dissenting Opinions of Mr. Justice Smith," *University of Detroit Law Journal* 34, no. 1 (October 1956): 81–91.

34. The other four Circuit Court judges who attended were John V. Brennan, George B. Murphy, Theodore R. Bohn, and Wade H. McCree, Jr. See box 31, file "Misc., 1956," Edwards Jr. Papers; *The Cardinals,* 318.

35. "George Edwards—Personal Data."

36. *Bishop v. New York Central Railroad,* 349 Mich. 345 (May 1957), 351, 362; James Robinson, "State Supreme Court Ends Five Revolutionary Years," *Detroit Free Press,* 8 January 1962.

37. *Comstock v. General Motors,* 358 Mich. 163 (November 1959).

38. Robinson, "State Supreme Court Ends Five Revolutionary Years."

39. "5 of Michigan Justices Defend U.S. High Court," *Detroit News,* 28 August 1958; Tom Cameron, "Supreme Court's Stand Defended," *Los Angeles Times,* 28 August 1958.

40. Edwards to Mennen Williams, 22 September 1958, and Earl Warren to Edwards, 15 September 1958, box 61, file "U.S. Supreme Court, 1958–1960," Edwards Jr. Papers; Will Mueller, "Political Court System 'Cancer,' Black Charges," *Detroit News,* August 1960, box 41, file "Clippings, 1957–1961, Miscellaneous," ibid.

41. Speech files, box 53, ibid.; Edward S. Piggins to Edwards, 10 March 1955, box 33, ibid.; "BVS Lacks Facilities, Says Judge," undated, unidentified newspaper clipping, box 40, ibid.; G. Mennen Williams to Edwards, 22 September 1956, box 34, ibid.; Senate talks, box 55, ibid.; "President's commission on Juvenile Delinquency and Youth Crime," box 79, ibid.; Mrs. David Littauer, general conference chair, to Edwards, 26 October 1956, box 34, ibid.

42. "Court 'Partisanship' Denied by Edwards," *Detroit News,* 6 September 1957; "Edwards Wears Big Liberal Tag," *Detroit Free Press,* 7 December 1961.

43. Edwards to William McClow, administrator, Amalgamated Clothing Workers of America Insurance Fund Board, 3 August 1961, box 42, Edwards Jr. Papers.

44. Box 39, ibid.; Joe Rauh to Edwards, 29 January 1957, box 34, ibid.; Israel Goldstein of American Jewish Congress to Edwards, 27 December 1956, and Edwards to Goldstein, 21 January 1957, box 35, ibid.; Edwards to Rev. Tracy M. Pullman, chair Selection Committee of the ACLU, box 41, ibid; "Justice Calls Cure Goal of Penal System," *Detroit Free Press,* 9 September 1958. On Edwards, Jr.'s work for the Child Welfare League, see box 43, Edwards Jr. Papers.

45. Arthur Johnson to Edwards, 19 September 1958, box 51, file "NAACP, 1957–1961"; George M. Zimmerman to Edwards, Jr., 9 September 1956, box 34, ibid.

46. *The Cardinals,* 323–25.

47. Frank D. Eamon to Edwards, 31 October 1956, box 34, Edwards Jr. Papers.

48. *In Re Maddox,* 351 Mich. 359 (March 1958).

49. *People v. Gonzales,* 349 Mich. 572, (September 1957); *People v. Gonzales,* 356 Mich. 251 (June 1959).

50. Edwards to William O. Douglas, 17 June 1959, box 44, Edwards Jr. Papers; Edwards to William J. Brennan, 27 April 1960, box 39, ibid.; *Frank v. Maryland,* 359 U.S. 360 (1959); *Abel v. United States,* 362 U.S. 217 (1960).

51. Edwards, Jr., draft of opinion, box 32, file "DeBarr v. Oakland Circuit Judge, Long v. Cass Circuit Judge, Fineder v. Oakland Circuit Judge," Edwards Jr. Papers; Edwards to William J. Brennan, 3 November 1960, box 39, ibid.

52. Boxes 27–28, 31, ibid.; George Edwards, Jr., "The Constitution, The Citizen, and The Police," *Michigan State Bar Journal* 40, no. 4 (April 1961).

53. Boxes 28–29, 31, Edwards Jr. Papers; Edwards, Jr., "The Constitution, The Citizen"; Curt Gentry, *J. Edgar Hoover: The Man and His Secrets* (New York: W.W. Norton & Co., 1991), 449.

54. Boxes 31–32, Edwards Jr. Papers; Edwards, Jr., "The Constitution, The Citizen."

55. Ibid., 32.

56. David M. O'Brien, *Constitutional Law and Politics,* vol. 2 (New York: W.W. Norton & Co., 1991), ch 4.

Chapter 5

1. Edwards Manuscript, 9.

2. "Attorney F. Eaman Dead at 84," *Detroit Free Press,* 25 October 1962.

3. "He Left Footprints," *Detroit News,* 24 October 1962; "What are the Major Problems of Law Enforcement in Metropolitan Detroit," Edwards's speech to the Economic Club of Detroit, 14 May 1962, Stolberg Papers.

4. Edwards Manuscript, 14.

5. "Edwards Wears Big Liberal Tag," *Detroit Free Press,* 7 December 1961; Edwards Manuscript, 15.

6. Edwards Manuscript, 19; "The Police Look at Edwards," *Detroit Free Press,* 12 December 1961.

7. Edwards Manuscript, 19–20.

8. Ibid., 11–12; Herbert M. Boldt, "Rapid Rise of Brothers No Surprise," *Detroit News,* date unclear, Stolberg Papers; "Lieutenant Berg Moving Up," *Detroit News,* 14 October 1945; "Louis J. Berg, 69, Ex-Police Superintendent," *Detroit News,* 8 June 1980.

9. Edwards Manuscript, 16; "Fast Changes Are Ruled Out," *Detroit Free Press,* 4 January 1962.

10. Statement on taking office, 3 January 1962, box 79, file "Press Releases, 1962–1963," Edwards Jr. Papers; Edwards Manuscript, 16.

11. Fine, *Model City,* 19; Robert Battle to Cavanagh, telegram, 7 December 1961, box

2, file 4, Cavanagh Papers; George W. Crockett, Jr., president Cotillion Club, to Cavanagh, telegram, 12 December 1961, ibid.; L. M. Quinn to Cavanagh, 8 December 1961, ibid.; Broadus N. Butler to Cavanagh, 8 December 1961, ibid.; "Broadus Butler, 75, Ex-Tuskegee Airman and Education Aide," *New York Times,* 13 January 1996.

12. Robert F. Allen to Cavanagh, 7 December 1961, box 45, file 22, Cavanagh Papers; John S. Humphrey to Cavanagh, telegram, 14 December 1961, box 2, file 14, ibid.; "Disillusioned Already, Says Cavanagh Voter," *Detroit News,* 17 December 1961.

13. "Edwards Bars New Quiz into Shooting by Officers," undated newspaper clipping attached to letter from Cavanagh to NLG Chapter President Bernard J. Fieger, 2 March 1962, box 29, file 17, Cavanagh Papers.

14. Herbert M. Boldt, "Edwards Starts in at the Beat Level," *Detroit News,* 11 February 1962.

15. Edwards Manuscript, 144; *Proceedings of the Sixth Annual National Institute on Police-Community Relations,* May 15–20, 1960, Michigan State University, box 53, Edwards Jr. Papers.

16. Edwards Manuscript, 21.

17. George W. Crockett, Jr., to Edwards, 16 March 1962, box 29, file 20, Cavanagh Papers; Edwards Manuscript, 22–23.

18. Ibid., 26.

19. Ibid., 37–38.

20. "Night Police Stepped up by Edwards," *Detroit News,* 17 February 1962; Edwards, "What are the Major Problems."

21. Edwards Manuscript, 38–39.

22. Ibid., 39–40; "Message Delivered Over Police Inter-Com to All Officers of the Detroit Police Department by Commissioner Edwards on Saturday, February 17, 1962," box 29, file 8, Cavanagh Papers; Statement, 17 February 1962, box 80, file "Speeches 1962–1963," Edwards Jr. Papers.

23. Edwards Manuscript, 27–29.

24. Ibid., 24.

25. "Edwards, in Sermon, Tells Why He Took Police Job," *Detroit Free Press,* 19 February 1962; "Police to Treat All Equal, Edwards Tells Negroes," *Detroit News,* 19 February 1962.

26. B. Kliff to Cavanagh, 19 February 1962, box 29, file 17, Cavanagh Papers.

27. "Audit Report for Police Department Ended December 31, 1961," box 13, file 16, ibid.; Edwards, "What are the Major Problems"; Edwards address, 26 January 1962, box 80, file "Speeches 1962–1963," Edwards Jr. Papers; Herbert M. Boldt, "Extra Pay for Nights Key Issue with Police," *Detroit News,* 27 January 1962.

28. "No Letup in Detroit's War on Crime—Edwards," *Detroit News,* 9 March 1962; "Edwards Gets Boost by Negroes," *Detroit Free Press,* 9 March 1962; Al Barbour to Cavanagh, 26 March 1962, box 29, file 20, Cavanagh Papers; NAACP to Cavanagh, 7 March 1962, box 29, file 17, ibid.

29. Dunbar, "Detroit's Jerry Cavanagh," 21 September 1965, *Look,* box 20, file 6, ibid.; George W. Kuhn to Cavanagh, 28 February 1962, ibid.

30. Edwards, "What are the Major Problems."

31. Ibid.

32. Normal civil service promotions were based 60 percent on written tests, 10 percent on seniority, 10 percent on service ratings, and 20 percent on oral interviews. The figures for the police department were 40 percent on written tests, 10 percent on seniority, 20 percent on service ratings, and 30 percent on a vague standard called

promotion ratings. "Community Coordination Council Recommendations Concerning the Police Department," undated memo, box 29, file 6, Cavanagh Papers.

33. "A Study of Detroit Police Department Personnel Selection Practices Prepared by the Research Division of the Detroit Commission of Community Relations at Request of Detroit Common Council, Confidential," 15 January 1962, box 29, file 7, ibid.

34. Detroit Police Department, inter-office memorandum to Edwards, 24 January 1962, box 14, file 11, ibid.

35. "A Study of Detroit Police Department Personnel."

36. Detroit Police Department, inter-office memorandum, to Commissioner Edwards from Personnel Examiner Robert A. Lothian, 24 January 1962, box 14, file 11, Cavanagh Papers.

37. Joseph B. Sullivan to Cavanagh, undated memo, and Sullivan to Edwards, undated memo, both box 29, file 15, ibid.

38. "Highlights of the Commission Meeting: Detroit Commission on Community Relations, February 1962," box 39, file 1, ibid.; Edwards to Detroit Commission on Community Relations, box 39, file 2, ibid.

39. "Edwards Gives Views on Study of Hiring," *Detroit News*, 27 February 1962.

40. Executive Order Number 1, 22 February 1962, box 4, file 7, Cavanagh Papers.

41. Speech at program meeting of the Coordinating Council on Human Relations, 22 February 1962, box 52, file 2, ibid.

42. "Negroes Get Police Job Pledge," *Detroit Free Press*, 29 March 1962; "Police Personnel Policy in Proper Perspective," *Michigan Chronicle*, 24 March 1962.

43. Ibid.

44. Detroit Police Department, inter-office memo to Commissioner Edwards from Personnel Examiner Robert A. Lothian, 4 April 1962, box 39, file 2, Cavanagh Papers.

45. "Negro is Raised to Lieutenant in List of Police Promotions," *Detroit News*, 16 May 1962.

46. Ibid.; "Detroit's Top Black Officer Retires," *Detroit News*, 28 January 1972; "Ex-Inspector Named School Security Boss," *Detroit News*, 11 February 1976; "Top Police Job is Filled by Negro," *Detroit Free Press*, 10 July 1969; "Top Black Officer Leaves a Happy Police Career," *Detroit Free Press*, 28 January 1972; Irah M. Charles, "Mediocrity Not His Dish," *Michigan Chronicle*, 23 August 1969.

47. Memo 22, February Inspectors meeting, box 80, file "Staff Meetings and Precinct Inspector Meetings, 1962–1963," Edwards Jr. Papers; Edwards Manuscript, 25.

48. "Edwards Makes Public 3-Point Police Program," *Detroit News*, 14 March 1962; "Edwards Calls for Close Tie Between Police and Citizens," *Detroit News*, 28 March 1962.

Chapter 6

1. "Inner City is Chief Target in Crime Reduction Drive," *Detroit Free Press*, 9 July 1962.

2. "Lawyer's Guild Irked by Governor's Riot Report," *Michigan Chronicle*, 18 September 1943.

3. "The Fifth Anniversary of an Idea," 1948 Annual Report, City of Detroit's Interracial Committee, box 8, file "Minority Groups, 1943–1948," Edwards Jr. Papers; "Inner City is Chief Target in Crime-Reduction Drive," *Detroit Free Press*, date unclear, Stolberg Papers.

4. "Police Brutality Against Negroes in Detroit: A Statement by Arthur L. Johnson, Executive Secretary, Detroit Branch of the NAACP," prepared for the U.S. Commission on Civil Rights in Detroit, Michigan, December 15, 1960, Cavanagh Papers.

5. Ibid.
6. Ibid.
7. "Report of the Detroit Bar Association Committee on Civil Liberties on Detroit Police Department Policy of 'Arrests for Investigation,' " box 41, file "Civil Liberties, 1956–1960," Edwards Jr. Papers; "Police Brutality Against Negroes in Detroit."
8. Ibid.
9. Ibid.
10. "Well-Meaning But Without Cause," *Detroit Free Press,* 23 January 1961.
11. "Two Investigations Pledged of NAACP Complaints," *Detroit News,* 17 May 1961; Editorial, *TUEBOR,* August 1961.
12. "Police Bid for Better Relations," *Detroit News,* 17 May 1961; "NAACP Takes Dim View of New Police Board," undated, newspaper clipping, box 9, file 2, Cavanagh Papers.
13. Civil Rights Commission Report quoted in *Keesing's Research Report: Race Relations in the U.S.A.,* 129; *New York Times,* 21 March 1962.
14. "The Police: An Interview by Donald McDonald with William H. Parker, Chief of Police in Los Angeles," box 65, file "May 16–31, 1962," Edwards Jr. Papers.
15. "Police Officials Overrule Edwards in Brutality Trial," *Detroit News,* 16 March 1962; Edwards Manuscript, 41–42.
16. Ibid., 42–43.
17. William P. Doran, assistant corporation counsel, to Lee H. Kozol, assistant attorney general of Massachusetts, 12 March 1963, box 88, file 3, Cavanagh Papers.
18. "Standard Operating Procedure," *Michigan Chronicle,* 24 March 1962; Edwards Manuscript, 43.
19. Ibid., 43–44.
20. Ibid., 44–46.
21. Ibid., 46–47; "Police Officials Overrule Edwards in Brutality Trial," *Detroit News,* 16 March 1962.
22. Edwards Manuscript, 47.
23. Ibid., 48.
24. Ibid., 48–49.
25. Ibid., 50.
26. Ibid., 51.
27. Ibid., 52.
28. Ibid., 53–54.
29. "Standard Operating Procedure"; "Police Officials Overrule Edwards in Brutality Trial"; Edwards Manuscript, 54.
30. Ibid., 55.
31. Ibid., 54; "Both Stories Can't Be True," *Detroit Free Press,* 17 March 1962.
32. Edwards Manuscript, 56–57.
33. Ibid., 57–58.
34. Ibid., 58–59.
35. Ibid., 60–61.
36. Annual Report, 1962, Detroit Police Department, box 87, file 2, Cavanagh Papers; Edwards Manuscript, 61–62.
37. Dr. D. T. Burton to Cavanagh, 19 March 1962, and Cavanagh to Burton, 26 March 1962, box 29, file 20, Cavanagh Papers.
38. "Standard Operating Procedure."
39. John E. Beckley, "A Negro v. Police," *Detroit News,* 5 April 1962.
40. Edwards Manuscript, 62; Edmund J. Papineau, Sr., to Edwards, 24 March 1962, and other letters, box 29, file 21, Cavanagh Papers.

41. Edwards Manuscript, 63–68. Edwards's account was apparently based on an undated interview with Piersante, found in Stolberg Papers.

42. Richard Strichartz, special assistant to the mayor, to Edwards, 25 April 1962, box 29, file 21, Cavanagh Papers.

43. Edwards Manuscript, 69–70, 82.

44. Ibid., 73.

45. Ibid., 74–77.

46. Ibid., 82; Martin Hayden to Edwards, 22 May 1962, box 65, Edwards Jr. Papers.

47. "2 Police Officials Outvote Edwards in Brutality Case," *Detroit News,* 16 March 1962; "The Way to Bring More Negroes into Police Uniforms," *Detroit Free Press,* 28 March 1962.

48. Victor J. Baum to Edwards, 10 April 1962, and Edwards to Baum, 11 June 1962, box 65, Edwards Jr. Papers. Philadelphia Mayor Richardson Dilworth appointed a citizen review board on 30 September 1958, after a policeman who assaulted two citizens attacked a superior office. Police claimed the board undermined their authority and was beholden to minorities, but an independent review did not support those contentions. See "Philadelphia: Policing the Police," *The Reporter,* 19 June 1962.

49. Edwards Manuscript, 82–83.

50. Monthly report, July 1962, box 29, file 1, Cavanagh Papers.

51. "How One City is Making a Dent in Its Crime Rate," *U.S. News & World Report,* 21 May 1962, 66–67; Edwards Manuscript, 71.

52. Ed Breslin, "Justice Watches as Police Work," *Detroit Free Press,* 7 June 1962; William O. Douglas to Edwards, 27 May 1962, and 7 June 1962, and Edwards to Douglas, 15 June 1962, box 65, Edwards Jr. Papers.

53. Edwards Manuscript, 84.

54. Malcolm X Little with Alex Haley, *The Autobiography of Malcolm X,* (New York: Grove Press, Inc., 1966), 206–9.

55. Ibid., 238, 247.

56. *New York Times,* 16 May 1962.

57. Edwards Manuscript, 85–86.

58. Ibid., 86–87.

59. Ibid., 87–88.

60. Ibid., 88, 90–91; "Muslims Hear Chief at Olympia," *Detroit Free Press,* 11 June 1962; "Muslim Rally Uneventful," *Michigan Chronicle,* 16 June 1962.

61. John Millhone, "Where Police Face the Biggest Test," *Detroit Free Press,* 11 July 1962.

62. John Millhone, "City's Police Are Using a 'Soft Sell,' " *Detroit Free Press,* 8 July 1962.

63. John Millhone, "Inner City is Chief Target in Crime-Reduction Drive," *Detroit Free Press,* 9 July 1962.

64. "Where Police Face the Biggest Test."

65. John Millhone, "How Crime Picture Looks to Edwards," *Detroit Free Press,* 10 July 1962.

66. John Millhone, "2 Way Task Confronts Edwards," *Detroit Free Press,* 12 July 1962.

67. "Crime Not Race Issue—Edwards," *Detroit News,* 26 July 1962; Edwards Manuscript, 128–29.

68. Community Relations Report of August 6, 1962, and Detroit Police Department, Annual Report, 1962, both box 87, file 2, Cavanagh Papers; Memo, October 11, meeting of Precinct Inspectors, box 80, file "Staff Meetings and Precinct Inspectors Meetings, 1962–1963," Edwards Jr. Papers.

Chapter 7

1. Memo, 13 April 1962, meeting of Precinct Inspectors, box 80, file "Staff Meetings and Precinct Inspector Meetings, 1962–1963," Edwards Jr. Papers.
2. Announcement to Department, 7 May 1962, ibid.
3. Edwards Manuscript, 97; Vincent Piersante to Edwards, memo, 9 July 1962, box 30, file 31, ibid.
4. Edwards Manuscript, 98–100.
5. Herbert Boldt, "Accuse 30 in DPW Graft," *Detroit News,* 10 July 1962.
6. Herbert M. Boldt and Herb Levitt, "Bribe Plot Laid to Contractors," *Detroit News,* 10 July 1962; "List Firms, Persons in DPW Case," *Detroit News,* 10 July 1962.
7. Edwards Manuscript, 99; "Cavanagh to Put Out Anti-Graft Directive," *Detroit Free Press,* 12 July 1962.
8. "Edwards Wears a Big Liberal Tag," *Detroit Free Press,* 7 December 1961; "George Edwards—Personality in the News," news clipping, 11 April 1963, Stolberg Papers.
9. Edwards Manuscript, 96; Widick, *Detroit: City of Violence,* 7–11.
10. Ibid., 5–6, 11–21; John Hope Franklin, *From Slavery to Freedom: A History of Negro Americans* (1967; reprint, Alfred A. Knopf, Inc., 1969), 484.
11. Ibid., 610–11; Widick, *Detroit: City of Race,* 140–45; Chester Bulgier, "Study of Housing Traces Climb of Segregation Here," *Detroit News,* 23 September 1962.
12. Edwards Manuscript, 96–98.
13. "Dreams Realized, Dreams Faded," *Detroit Free Press,* 21 February 1988; "Law and Order is Now the Sole Issue," *Michigan Chronicle,* 2 September 1961.
14. Edwards Manuscript, 92; "Highlights of the Commission Meeting: Detroit Commission on Community Relations," bulletins for February 1962 and April 1962, Papers of the City of Detroit Commission on Community Relations (hereafter cited as CCR), part I, series IV, box 3, Walter Reuther Archives, Wayne State University. Other details in the commission's meeting minutes for December, 1961, and February, May, and July, 1962, ibid.
15. Edwards Manuscript, 93–94.
16. Ibid., 95–96; Minutes of Community Relations Council meetings, 16 April 1962, 21 May 1962, and 18 June 1962, box 39, file 2, Cavanagh Papers.
17. Edwards Manuscript, 95–96; Department Monthly Report, June 1962, box 29, file 2, Cavanagh Papers; Minutes of the Community Relations Council meeting, 18 June 1962, box 39, file 2, ibid.; Edwards Manuscript, 96; "Edwards Promotes 4 Policemen," undated news clipping, June 1962, series 9/10/91, box 1, Scrapbook "DPD 1962," Edwards Jr. Papers.
18. Isaac Jones, "Arrest Trio for Arson," *Michigan Chronicle,* 26 May 1962.
19. Edwards Manuscript, 124, 146–47; "Highlights of the Commission Meeting: Detroit Commission on Community Relations," October 1962, box 39, file 1, Cavanagh Papers.
20. Edwards Manuscript, 147; "Negro Homes Terrorized in Northwest Community," *Michigan Chronicle,* 13 October 1962.
21. "Highlights of the Commission Meeting: Detroit Commission on Community Relations," October 1962, and November 1962, box 39, file 1, Cavanagh Papers; Reuben Schwartz to Cavanagh, 5 July 1962, and Girardin to Schwartz, 20 July 1962, box 30, file 17, ibid.; Tom McPhail, "Council Approves Measure to Curb Panic Homes Sales," *Detroit Free Press,* 21 November 1962.
22. Index file, "Housing: Negro: Detroit," *Detroit News* library; Hal Cohen, "Law to Ban Housing Bias Rejected by Council, 7–2," *Detroit Free Press,* 9 October 1963.
23. "Justice Speaks: Racial Bias Cited as Crime Cause," *Detroit Free Press,* 21 June

1960; Edwards to Detroit Urban League, speech, 1 December 1960, box 54, file "Detroit Urban League," Edwards Jr. Papers.

24. George Edwards, Jr., "Judge I Told That Boy," *The New Republic* 142, no. 13 (28 March 1960): 16.

25. "The Police: An Interview by Donald McDonald with William H. Parker, Chief of the Police of Los Angeles," box 65, file "May 16–31, 1962," Edwards Jr. Papers.

26. "Testimony on the Juvenile Delinquency and Youth Offenses Control Act of 1961 Given in July 1961 before Special Subcommittee on Education, House of Representatives," box 55, file "White House Regional Conference 'Problems of Youth, Detroit,' " ibid.

27. "Mayor's Study Committee on Crime and Crime Prevention: Report Submitted to the Hon. Louis C. Miriani, Mayor City of Detroit," 7 December 1960, box 29, file 13, Cavanagh Papers.

28. Ibid.

29. Ronald L. Heidelberger to Cavanagh, 29 December 1961, box 29, file 10, ibid.

30. Edwards to Cavanagh, 26 June 1962, box 30, file 1, ibid.

31. "Police Enlist Clergy in Crime War," *Detroit Free Press,* 23 June 1962.

32. "Principals, Policemen at All Day Meeting," *West Side Courier,* 8 November 1962; Harry Golden, Jr.,"Police Applaud Educators for Boosting Co-Operation," *Detroit Free Press,* 2 November 1962; Harry Salsinger and Herbert M. Boldt, "School Police Co-operation Strengthened by Conference," *Detroit News,* 2 November 1962.

33. Press release, "President's Committee on Juvenile Delinquency and Youth Crime," 20 August 1962; box 6, file 26, Edwards Jr. Papers; Press release, 26 August 1963, box 79, file "Press Releases, 1962–1963," ibid.

34. "Message from the Director," *FBI Law Enforcement Bulletin* 31, no. 8 (August 1962), box 29, file 10, Cavanagh Papers.

35. "How One City is Making A Dent in Its Crime Rate," Mayor's Study Committee report.

36. "Message from the Director," Cavanagh Papers; George Edwards, undated report, box 29, file 15, ibid.; Editorial, *Detroit Free Press,* 7 July 1961.

37. "Message from the Director," Cavanagh Papers.

38. George Edwards, undated report, Cavanagh Papers; Minutes, meeting of Large City Police Administrators, Chicago, 7 March 1963, box 67, Edwards Jr. Papers.

39. Editorial, *Detroit Free Press,* 7 July 1962.

40. Jack Humphrey to Cavanagh, 10 July 1962, and Cavanagh to Humphrey, 16 July 1962, box 30, file 2, Cavanagh Papers.

41. The literature on the unreliability of crime statistics is vast. One particularly useful study is Stanley A. Scheingold, *The Politics of Law and Order: Street Crime and Public Policy* (New York: Longman, Inc., 1984).

42. "36th Police Field Day Will Be a Real Circus," *Detroit Free Press,* 6 August 1962.

43. Edwards Manuscript, 110–13.

44. Press release, undated, box 79, file "Press Releases, 1962–1963," Edwards Jr. Papers.

45. "35,000 See Police Field Day in Rain," *Detroit News,* 13 August 1962; Edwards Manuscript, 115–17.

46. Ibid., 120–21.

Chapter 8

1. Gus Tyler, *Organized Crime In America* (Ann Arbor: University of Michigan Press, 1962), 343.

2. Arthur M. Schlesinger, Jr., *Robert Kennedy and His Times* (Boston: Houghton

Mifflin Company, 1978), 177. See also Robert F. Kennedy, *The Enemy Within* (New York: Harper & Brothers, 1960).

3. Schlesinger, *Robert Kennedy,* 175.

4. Edwards to Robert F. Kennedy, 31 March 1961, and Kennedy to Edwards, 4 April 1961, box 54, file "Attorney General's Crime Prevention Conference, Lansing, May 19, 1961," Edwards Jr. Papers.

5. Edwards Manuscript, 214.

6. Draft of speech, box 54, file "Attorney General's Crime Prevention Conference, Lansing, May 19, 1961," Edwards Jr. Papers; Herb Levitt, "Edwards Calls Syndicate Major U.S. Crime Factor," *Detroit News,* 19 May 1961.

7. Edwards Manuscript, 79, 122; Edwards to Robert F. Kennedy, 4 April 1962, and Edwards to Kennedy, 7 May 1962, box 65, Edwards Jr. Papers; William O. Douglas to Edwards, 29 September 1962, box 66, ibid.

8. Photo in *Detroit News* library; Edwards to Paul H. Douglas, 25 July 1959, box 44, Edwards Jr. Papers; Edwards to John Herling, 31 May 1962, box 65, ibid.

9. Allan Lengel, "Giacalone: A Saga of Cops, Courts and Prison," *Detroit News and Free Press,* 22 May 1994; Edwards Manuscript, 105–6.

10. Ibid., 106; Edwards, "Organized Crime in the United States, May 29, 1963, to Advisory Council of Judges of the National Council on Crime and Delinquency at New York City," speech, box 80, file "Speeches 1962–1963," Edwards Jr. Papers.

11. Robert D. Kirk, "Edwards as a Witness Clashes with Attorney," *Detroit News,* 14 June 1962. See also Don Schram, "In Gambling Case, Landlord Sues to Banish Police," *Detroit Free Press,* 10 June 1962.

12. "Club-case Witnesses Take Fifth," *Detroit Free Press,* 15 June 1962; Edwards to Douglas, 18 September 1962, box 66, Edwards Jr. Papers.

13. "Police Seek Rule to Limit Clubs," *Detroit Free Press,* 10 June 1962; "Edwards Asks Curb on All Private Clubs," *Detroit News,* 12 September 1962.

14. Fragment of early manuscript by George Edwards Jr., Stolberg Papers; John White, Jr., obituary, *Detroit Free Press,* July 9, 1964.

15. Edwards Manuscript, 29, 159.

16. Ibid., 119; Vincent Piersante, interview by author, 22 March 1996.

17. Edwards Manuscript, 100.

18. Ibid., 101–3.

19. Ibid., 136–37.

20. "Berg Brothers Quit; Police Department Rocked," *Detroit Free Press,* 3 November 1962; Edwards Manuscript, 121.

21. Herbert M. Boldt, "Fear Rash of Police Retiring," *Detroit News,* 3 November 1962; Piersante Interview.

22. "Berg is Fired," *Detroit Free Press,* 2 September 1944.

23. Boldt, "Fear Rash of Police Retiring."

24. Mrs. Robert Miller to Cavanagh, 14 November 1962, box 30, file 8, Cavanagh Papers; Disgusted Native Detroiter to Cavanagh, 22 January 1963 (and similar letters), box 87, file 14, Edwards Jr. Papers.

25. Edwards Manuscript, 122; Edwards, Jr. "Detroit: A Lesson in Law Enforcement," *The Annals of the American Academy of Political and Social Science* 347 (May 1963): 68.

26. Edwards Manuscript, 126; Edwards, "Detroit: A Lesson," 68.

27. Ibid., 69–70.

28. Ibid., 67.

29. Ibid., 68.

30. Ibid., 73; Edwards Manuscript, 262–63.

31. Ibid., 166; Edwards, "Detroit: A Lesson," 72–73.

32. Neal Shine, "Blow Cripples Detroit Racket," *Detroit Free Press,* 10 November 1962; Herbert M. Boldt, "Numbers Men Battle Heavy Odds," *Detroit News,* 14 November 1962.

33. "John White Tells Story of Raid," *Michigan Chronicle,* 17 November 1962; " 'Those Aren't My Cards,' Owner John White Claims," *Michigan Chronicle,* 15 December 1962.

34. Lawrence Gobow, to Edwards, 14 November 1962, and A. F. Brandsatter to Edwards, 26 November 1962, box 66, Edwards Jr. Papers.

35. Edwards Manuscript, 169–70.

36. Harry Golden, Jr., "Echoes of Music and Dice Mix as the Gotham Passes," *Detroit Free Press,* 18 July 1963; John White, Jr., obituary *Detroit Free Press,* 9 July 1964.

37. Herbert M. Boldt, "Reuter, Lupton Get Top Police Jobs; 6 Others Promoted," *Detroit News,* 10 November 1962; Edwards Manuscript, 122–23. Boldt also listed William Polkinghorn, Walter Wyrod, Thomas Cochill, Peter Soncrant, William Icenhower, William J. Burke, and James Dunleavy in "Fear Rash of Police Retiring."

38. Edwards Manuscript, 124–25.

39. Ibid., 125; Boldt, "Reuter, Lupton Get Top Police Jobs"; "New Police Boss Shifts Top-Level Commands," *Detroit News,* 13 November 1962.

40. "Name O'Neill as Head of Vice Bureau," *Detroit Free Press,* 14 November 1962; "New Police Boss Shifts Top-Level Commands," *Detroit News,* 13 November 1962; "O'Neill is Promoted, Heads Vice Bureau," *Detroit News.*

41. Boldt, "Reuter, Lupton Get Top Police Jobs"; Piggins to Edwards, 10 November 1962, and A. F. Brandsatter to Edwards, 26 November 1962, box 66, Edwards Jr. Papers.

42. Boldt, "Reuter, Lupton Get Top Police Jobs"; Memo, 14 November 1962, meeting, box 80, file "Staff Meetings and Precinct Inspector Meetings, 1962–1963," Edwards Jr. Papers.

43. "Detroit's Traffic Safety Program," 2 January 1963, box 80, file "Speeches 1962–1963," ibid.; Press release, 8 November 1962, box 79, file "Press Releases, 1962–1963," ibid.

44. "Traffic Enforcement Policy from November 21 to December 31, 1962," ibid.; Harold F. Koch, director of General Activities, Detroit Council of Churches, to Edwards, 5 December 1962, box 67, ibid.; Traffic Safety Association of Detroit, *Bulletin,* 20, no. 12 (December 1962), box 80, file "speeches 1962–1963," ibid.

45. Edwards Draft Manuscript, 1–19, Stolberg Papers.

46. "Detective Chief Gets U.S. Post," *Detroit Free Press,* 7 January 1962.

47. Herbert M. Boldt, "Cochill, Falk are Appointed to Direct Detective Bureau," *Detroit News,* 10 January 1963.

Chapter 9

1. "Greek Cafe is Back in Spotlight," *Detroit Free Press,* 9 January 1963; Surveillance report, Detroit Police Department inter-office memorandum, 24 August 1963, Stolberg Papers.

2. Eugene R. Geibig to Edwards, memo, 3 January 1963, ibid.; William J. DePugh to Commanding Officer, memo, Vice Bureau, 3 January 1963, ibid.; John J. O'Neill to Edwards, memo, 3 January 1963, ibid.

3. "How Police Spied on Gambler at Lions Game," *Detroit News,* 9 January 1963; Edwards Manuscript, 227.

4. John M. Carlisle, "NFL Probes Lions' Link to Hoodlums," *Detroit News,* 8 January 1963; "Party Bus Old Joke to Police," *Detroit News,* 9 January 1963.

5. Ibid.

6. Edwards Manuscript, 227–28; George Puscas, "Bar Karras and Hornung, Fine 5 Lions," *Detroit Free Press,* 18 April 1963.

7. Doug Greene, "Press Box," *Detroit News,* 16 April 1963; Edwards Manuscript, 228.

8. Memo, 13 February 1963, meeting of Precinct Inspectors, box 80, file "Staff Meetings and Precinct Inspectors Meetings, 1962–1963," Edwards Jr. Papers.

9. Edwards Manuscript, 212–14.

10. Ibid., 244–46. The Calabresse case was never solved. See Carlisle memo, February 5–11, 1963, notebook, series 9/27/91, box 7, Edwards Jr. Papers.

11. Ibid.

12. Ibid.; Edwards Draft Manuscript, 13.

13. Blue notebook, series 9/27/91, box 7, Edwards Jr. Papers.

14. Edwards to Robert Kennedy, 3 April 1963, and Kennedy to Edwards, 24 April 1963, box 68, ibid.

15. Edwards Manuscript, 225–26.

16. Martin Hayden, "Edwards 'Letter to Editor,' " *Detroit News,* 2 August 1976.

17. Manilla Envelope, series 9/27/91, box 4, Edwards Jr. Papers.

18. Seth Kantor, Robert Pavich and Michael Wendland, "Tony Giacalone Once Talked of Killing 2 Top Detroit Cops," *Detroit News,* 2 August 1976; Piersante in interview with author, 7 May 1996, Stolberg Papers; Edwards Draft Manuscript, 12.

19. J. F. Ter Horst, "Swainson's Plea to Kennedy Perils Bid for Judgeship," *Detroit News,* 25 January 1963.

20. Edwards Manuscript, 183–86.

21. Ibid., 188–89.

22. "Edwards Expected to Join U.S. Court; Would Quit as Head of Police," *Detroit Free Press,* 9 March 1963.

23. "Edwards Gets Party's OK for U.S. Judgeship," *Detroit News,* 4 April 1963; "Angry Mayor Defends Edwards, Blasts Critics," *Detroit News,* 5 April 1963; Robert Kennedy to Hart and McNamara, 12 April 1963, series 9/10/91, box 5, file "Old Matters re: Appointment," Edwards Jr. Papers.

24. William H. Merrill to Cavanagh, 8 April 1963, box 87, file 17, ibid.; Luke Leonard to Cavanagh, 11 April 1963, ibid.; A. F. Brandsatter to Cavanagh, 10 April 1963, ibid.

25. "Organized Crime in the United States, May 29, 1963," speech to the Advisory Council of Judges of the National Council on Crime and Delinquency, New York City, box 80, file "Speeches 1962–1963," ibid.

26. Ibid.

27. Ibid.

28. Edwards Manuscript, 229–40.

29. Bob Pearson, "Case Called Edwards' High Point," *Detroit Free Press,* 21 June 1963; Edwards Manuscript, 241–42.

30. Ibid., 244; Piersante Interview.

31. Letters from Edwards to friends, box 68, file "August 1–15, 1963," Edwards Jr. Papers; James Otis to Edwards, 2 July 1963, box 68, file "July 1–15, 1963," ibid.

32. Edwards Draft Manuscript, 26–27.

33. John M. Carlisle," 'Edwards Prejudices Giacalone Bribery Case,' Gillis Charges," *Detroit News,* 21 March 1964.

34. Piersante Interview.

35. Ibid.; Robert L. Weinberg, interview by author, 5 September 1994.

Chapter 10

1. Franklin, *From Slavery to Freedom: A History of Negro Americans,* 629–34.

2. "The Chronicle Salutes Eight Citizens of the Year," *Michigan Chronicle,* 10 February 1963; Memo, 15 February 1963, meeting of Precinct Inspectors, box 80, file "Staff Meetings and Precinct Inspector Meetings, 1962–1963," Edwards Jr. Papers; George Schermer to Edwards, 4 March 1963, box 68, (misfiled) file "June 8–15, 1963," ibid.

3. Charles C. Diggs, Jr., to Edwards, 9 October 1962, and Edwards to Diggs, 11 October 1962, box 66, ibid.

4. "Rogell 'Tees Off' on City Hall Problems," *Northeast Record,* 28 January 1963.

5. "Rogell and Edwards Square Off in Council Meeting," *Detroit Free Press,* 8 February 1963.

6. "Policeman Slain by Shotgun Blast; Killer Wounded," *Detroit Free Press,* 25 February 1963.

7. James Kerwin, "Dead Officer Loved Police Work, Home," *Detroit Free Press,* 25 February 1963; "Policeman's Killer Gets Life Term," *Detroit News,* 13 September 1963.

8. Transcript of Lou Gordon show, WXYZ Radio, 6 March 1963, series 9/27/91, box 4, file "Incidents 1962–1963," Edwards Jr. Papers.

9. W. M. Rea to Edwards, 6 March 1963, box 67, (misfiled) file "March 16–21, 1963," ibid.

10. "Motorist Tells How Anger Led to Killing of Officer," *Detroit Free Press.* 25 March 1963.

11. "Edwards Advises Caution for Officers," *Detroit News,* 26 March 1963.

12. "Negroes Start Fund to Aid Families of Slain Officers," *Detroit News,* 27 March 1963; Alfred E. Thomas, Jr., to Edwards, 22 April 1963, box 68, Edwards Jr. Papers.

13. Richard S. Emrich to George and Margaret Edwards, 22 January 1963, box 67, (misfiled) file "January 8–15, 1963," ibid.

14. "Half-Mile Long Procession Escorts Policeman to Grave," *Detroit News,* 28 March 1963; Edwards Manuscript, 178–79.

15. "Police Slayer Guilty of Second Degree Murder," *Detroit News,* 19 February 1964; "Policeman's Killer Gets Life Term," *Detroit News,* 3 March 1964; "New Trial in 1964 Murder," *Detroit News,* 11 November 1981; "Judge Resentences Cop Slayer," *Detroit News,* 8 May 1982.

16. "Edwards, Wife Get Amity Award," *Detroit Free Press,* 28 March 1963; Edwards Manuscript, 180.

17. Edwards to Frank Angelo, 3 April 1963, box 68, Edwards Jr. Papers.

18. Edwards to Royce Howes and Frank Angelo (*Detroit Free Press*), Chester Higgins (*Detroit Courier*), L. M. Quinn (*Michigan Chronicle*), and Martin Hayden (*Detroit News*), 11 April 1963, box 68, ibid.

19. "ACLU Lauds Handling of Police Shooting," *Detroit News,* 22 May 1963.

20. Gerald D. Marcus, Northern California Chairman, Californians Against Capital Punishment, to Edwards, 4 April 1963, box 67, Edwards Jr. Papers; Edwards to Ronald R. Entwistle, 1 July 1963, box 68, ibid.; "Outline of Testimony of George Edwards before the California Assembly," box 80, file "Speeches, 1962–1963," ibid.

21. "The Constitution and the Citizen: The Quest for Balance," speech to the Ninth Annual Institute on Police and Community Relations, Michigan State University, May 19–24, 1963, series 9/27/91, box 2, ibid.

22. Ibid.

23. David J. Garrow, *Bearing the Cross: Martin Luther King, Jr., and the Southern Chris-*

tian Leadership Conference (New York: Vintage Books, 1988), 250. See also ibid., 239–49.

24. Edwards Manuscript, 189. Taylor Branch, *Parting the Waters: America in the King Years 1954–63* (New York: Simon and Schuster, 1988), 842; "Deny Local Split in Negro Ranks," *Detroit News,* 22 July 1962; "Throng to March Down Woodward to Protest Bias," *Detroit Free Press,* 23 June 1963.

25. Edwards Manuscript, 189; W. Jones to Edwards, 16 June 1963, series 9/27/61, box 4, file "Incidents 1962–1963," Edwards Jr. Papers.

26. Edwards Manuscript, 190–92.

27. Ibid., 193–95; Branch, *Parting the Waters,* 842.

28. Ibid., 842–43; Edwards Manuscript, 195.

29. Ibid., 195–96; Margaret Edwards, interview with author, 12 July 1996; Branch, *Parting the Waters,* 843.

30. Cavanagh, speech to the National Newspaper Publishers Association, June 27, 1963, the Sheraton-Cadillac Hotel, box 108, file 11, Cavanagh Papers.

31. Edwards Manuscript, 195; Address to Police, 24 June 1963, box 79, file "Press Releases, 1962–1963," Edwards Jr. Papers.

32. Richard S. Emrich to Edwards, 25 June 1963, box 68, (misfiled) file "July 1–15, 1963," ibid.; Rolland O'Hare, quoted in undated Edwards's speech, July 1963, box 80, file "Speeches, 1962–1963," ibid.

33. "Detroit's FREEDOM MARCH," letter released by Cotillion Club to press, 24 June 1963, box 68, (misfiled) file "July 1–15, 1963", ibid.; Martin Luther King, Jr., to Edwards, 27 June 1963, cited in undated Edwards speech, box 80, file "Speeches, 1962–1963," ibid.

34. Edwards to Norman Robbins, Commander Detroit District Association, the American Legion, 4 June 1963, box 68, ibid.; Certificate of Award, the Community Improvement Association of Block Clubs, Inc., 14 June 1963, box 65, ibid.

35. Edwards, message over department speakers, 1 July 1963, box 79, file "Press Releases, 1962–1963," ibid.

36. Press release, 3 July 1963, box 79, file "Press Releases, 1962–1963," ibid.

37. Press release, dedication ceremonies for new 10th Precinct station, 3 July 1963, box 79, file "Press Releases, 1962–1963," ibid.

38. Itinerary and schedule of events, "Third Draft Anglo-American Judicial Exchanges, July 10–24, 1963," series 9/10/91, box 5, file "England, July 1963," ibid.

39. Unmarked, undated speech, box 80, file "Speeches 1962–1963," ibid.

40. Edwards Manuscript, 204.

41. Detroit Fellowship of Urban Renewal Churches to Cavanagh, telegram, 12 July 1963, and other letters, box 88, file 7, Cavanagh Papers; "Pickets at Police Headquarters Seek New Shooting Quiz," *Detroit News,* 14 July 1963; "100 March in Scott Protest," *Detroit Free Press,* 26 July 1963; "Rights Group Asks U.S. Aid," *Detroit Free Press,* 31 July 1963.

42. Undated copy of speech, box 80, file "Speeches 1962–1963," Edwards Jr. Papers.

43. Memo of Precinct Inspectors meeting, 12 August 1963, box 80, file "Staff Meetings and Precinct Inspectors Meetings, 1962–1963," ibid.

44. Edwards Manuscript, 105–7.

45. Ibid., 207; "Edwards TV Talk Assailed by ACLU," *Detroit Free Press,* 9 August 1963; "Officer Clear in Scott Case—Edwards," *Detroit Free Press,* 8 August 1963; "Block Edwards Judgeship, 2 Negro Groups Ask," *Detroit Free Press,* 10 August 1963; Edwards to Robert Kennedy, Robert McNamara, and Philip Hart, 9 August 1963, box 68, Edwards Jr. Papers.

46. "Criticism of Edwards Should Be Fair," *Michigan Chronicle,* 17 August 1963; Anne Lowndes to Robert McNamara, 23 August 1963, and Anne Lowndes to Edwards, 23 August 1963, box 68, Edwards Jr. Papers.

47. Mrs. Edward Davis to Edwards, August 1963, box 68, file "August 22–31, 1963," ibid.

Chapter 11

1. Richard Gibeau, "Judge Edwards says Allegations by Anderson Might be True," *Cincinnati Post,* 6 January 1976.

2. "Edwards Judgeship Gets to Kennedy's Desk at Last," *Detroit News,* 6 September 1963.

3. Robert Perrin, "Remembering Judge George Edwards, Jr.," unpublished essay, Stolberg Papers; *Congressional Record,* 88th Cong., 1st sess., 15697.

4. George Edwards, Sol Rubin, Henry Weihofin, and Simon Rosenzweig, *The Law of Criminal Corrections* (St. Paul, Minn.: West Publishing, 1963).

5. Brennan to Edwards, 3 March 1962, box 65, Edwards Jr. Papers.

6. Wade H. McCree, Jr., to Carl J. Marsh, 8 July 1963, series 9/10/91, box 5, file "Old Matters re: Apt," ibid.

7. Edwards to Brennan, 25 September 1963, series 9/10/91, box 5, file "Lots of Support Re: Confirmation to Federal Appeals Court," ibid.; Confirmation Hearings, 1–6.

8. Ibid., 6–7.

9. Ibid., 6–7, 11–12.

10. Ibid., 13.

11. Ibid., 14.

12. Ibid., 16–19.

13. Ibid., 23, 25, 27.

14. Gibeau, "Judge Edwards says Allegations by Anderson Might Be True."

15. Confirmation Hearings, 44; "Unquestionably Qualified," *Detroit News,* 10 October 1963.

16. Philip A. Hart to Edwards, 25 October 1963, series 9/10/91, box 5, file "Lots of Support Re: Confirmation to Federal Appeals Court," Edwards Jr. Papers.

17. John D. Black to Samuel J. Ervin, 15 October 1963, ibid.

18. Goldfarb, *Perfect Villains,* 149–54.

19. Statement of Police Commissioner George Edwards before Permanent Subcommittee on Investigations of the Committee on Government Operations, box 80, file "Speeches 1962–1963," Edwards Jr. Papers.

20. Ibid.

21. Ibid.

22. Edwards testimony and notebook, "Mafia Members-Relatives, Associates-Suspects, Detroit Police Department," series 9/27/91, box 7, ibid.

23. Ibid.

24. Ibid.

25. Edwards McClellan testimony; Mary M. Stolberg, *Fighting Organized Crime: Politics, Justice, and the Legacy of Thomas E. Dewey* (Boston: Northeastern University Press, 1995).

26. Press release, American Civil Liberties Union, Metropolitan Detroit Branch, 23 October 1963, box 69, Edwards Jr. Papers.

27. Ernest Mazey to Edwards, 24 October 1963, and ACLU press release, 23 October, 1963, ibid.

28. "The Principle at Issue in Edwards Testimony," *Detroit Free Press,* 12 October 1963.

29. Michael Polizzi to Jerome Cavanagh, 12 October 1963, and William E. Bufalino to Edwards, telegram, 17 October 1963, box 87, file 9, Cavanagh Papers.

30. Undated editorial from the *Courier* newspapers of Warrendale and Parkland, box 69, file "October 22–31, 1963," Edwards Jr. Papers.

31. Harold K. Daniels, 14 October 1963, box 69, file "October 22–31, 1963," ibid.; Paul E. Dietrich to McClellan, 29 October 1963, box 69, (misfiled) file "November 1–7, 1963," ibid.

32. James Atwater, "A City Fights Back," *Saturday Evening Post*, 20 May 1964, quoted in Edwards Manuscript, 279.

33. Ibid., 280–81.

34. Ibid., 279–80.

35. Edwards to Robert Kennedy, telegram, 3 October 1963, box 69, Edwards Jr. Papers; "Press Release, 30 September 1963," The Detroit Branch of the NAACP Collection, Walter Reuther Archives, Wayne State University, part I, box 24, file "Press Releases 1963"; "Pickets Return to 1st Federal," *Detroit Free Press*, 19 October 1963; "6 Arrested in Picketing at First Federal," *Detroit Free Press*, 16 November 1963; "First Federal Hires Two Tellers, Clerk," *Michigan Chronicle*, 30 November 1963.

36. "High Detective Post Goes to Piersante," *Detroit News*, 22 October 1963; Francis Kornegay to Edwards, 11 September 1963, box 69, (misfiled) file "September 16–21, 1963," Edward Jr. Papers; Damon Keith to Edwards, 8 November 1963, box 69, (misfiled) file "November 16–21, 1963," ibid.

37. Senate Confirmation Hearings, 45, 51, 54, 60, 63–64.

38. Alfred P. Murrah to Edwards, 27 November 1963, series 9/10/91, box 5, file "Letters of Congratulations," Edwards Jr. Papers; "Edwards Sure of Court Post," *Cincinnati Post*, 12 December 1963.

39. *Congressional Record*, 88th Cong. 1st sess., 16 December 1963, 109, no. 207, 23500.

40. Ibid., 23500–1.

41. Ibid., 23501–2.

42. Ibid., 23503–6.

43. Humphrey to Edwards, telegram, 18 December 1963, Edwards to Humphrey, 17 January 1964, and Edwards to McNamara, 31 December 1963, series 9/10/91, box 5, file "Letters of Congratulations," Edwards Jr. Papers.

44. Resignation letter, box 69, file "December 8–31, 1963," ibid.; Cavanagh to Edwards, 18 December 1963, file "Old Matters re: Appt," and Richard V. Marks to Edwards, 27 December 1963, file "Letters of Congratulations," series 9/10/91, box 5, ibid.; "It can hardly be said," *Detroit News*, 22 December 1963.

45. "Mayor Taps Girardin: Executive Secretary," *Detroit Free Press*, 2 June 1962.

46. E. A. Batchelor, Jr., "Ex-Police Boss Girardin is Dead," *Detroit News*, 29 November 1971; Jack Mann, "Ray Girardin: Pro Among Cons," *Detroit Free Press*, 30 June 1963.

Conclusion

1. "A Report to the People of Detroit on Police-Community Relations by the Subcommittee on Police-Community Relations Citizens Committee for Equal Opportunity," February 1965, box 15, file 14, and "The Police, Law Enforcement and the Detroit Community," Summer 1965, box 15, file 16, both in the Richard McGhee Collection, Walter Reuther Archives, Wayne State University; The Cotillion Club, Inc., to Members of the Citizens Committee on Police-Community Relations," 22 January 1965, NAACP Collection.

2. Batchelor, "Ex-Police Boss Girardin is Dead"; Fine, *Model City*, 122–23.
3. Carter Van Lopik and Harry Golden, Jr., "Auto Bomb Injures Gangster Perrone," *Detroit Free Press*, 20 January 1964.
4. Edwards to FBI Special Agent Bernard C. Brown, 10 March 1964, series 9/27/91, box 4, file "Incidents 1962–1963," Edwards Jr. Papers.
5. Ibid.
6. Edwards to Robert F. Kennedy, 23 April 1964, and Kennedy to Edwards, 28 April 1964, series 9/27/91, box 4, file "Incidents 1962–1963," ibid.
7. "Mafia Leader Found Slain in Shores," *Detroit News*, 18 April 1965; "Perrone Faces Jury After a 2-Day Wait," *Detroit News*, 30 April 1965.
8. Edwards to Warren Olney III, director of the Administrative Office of the U.S. Courts, 3 February 1967, and memo of conversation with Mr. Paul Stoddard, Agent in Charge, Detroit FBI Office, 1 July 1965, series 9/27/91, box 4, file "Incidents 1962–1963," Edwards Jr. Papers.
9. Manilla envelope, series 9/27/91, box 4, ibid.
10. Edwards to Warren Olney III, director of the Administrative Office of the U.S. Courts, 3 February 1967, series 9/27/91, box 4, file "Incidents 1962–1963," ibid.
11. "Santo Perrone, Reputed Member of Mafia, Dies," *Detroit Free Press*, 3 January 1974; Seth Kantor, Robert Pavich, and Michael Wendland, "Tony Giacalone Once Talked of Killing 2 Top Detroit Cops," *Detroit News*, 2 August 1976. The FBI tapes rekindled Edwards's fears, and he sent more material to Herling for the "life insurance file." See Edwards to John Herling, 8 August 1976, series 9/27/91, box 4, manilla envelope, Edwards Jr. Papers.
12. "The Parking Lot Conference at St. Joseph's Church," Edwards Draft Manuscript, Stolberg Papers.
13. Detroit Police Department Board of Inquiry, Summary of Findings, 10 December 1966, box 660, file 9, Cavanagh Papers.
14. "A Good-Bye Party," *Detroit Free Press*, 15 February 1967; Jo Thomas, "Vincent Piersante, That Tough Cop From Detroit, Quietly Works A Net Around Organized Crime," *Detroit Free Press*, 25 May 1975.
15. Edwards Manuscript, 308–10; Batchelor, "Ex-Police Boss Girardin is Dead"; "O'Neill, Cavanagh Deny Receiving Mafia Payoffs," *Detroit News*, 2 August 1976.
16. George Edwards, Jr, "Order and Civil Liberties: A Complex Role for the Police," *Michigan Law Review* 64, no. 1 (November 1965): 48–49.
17. Ibid., 56–59, 61.
18. Fine, *Model City*, 107.
19. Burton Levy, "Cops in the Ghetto: A Problem of the Police System," State of Michigan Civil Rights Commission Pamphlet, March–April 1968, CCR Papers.
20. Arthur Niederhoffer, *Behind the Shield: The Police in Urban Society* (Garden City, N.Y.: Doubleday, 1967).
21. "Lessons from a Summer of Protest," speech to the Michigan Welfare League, 16 November 1967, series 9/27/91, box 1, Edwards Jr. Papers.
22. Jerome Cavanagh, "Justice and Urban Ills: Law for the Poor," *1967–1968: A Compilation of the Virginia Law Weekly*, 19 (1968): 66.
23. Frank Angelo, "It's Time to Listen, At Last, to the Soft, Unheard Voices," *Detroit Magazine of the Free Press*, 3 September 1967, 16.
24. Fine, *Model City*, 108–9; Report on Chronology of Steps Taken by the City and Detroit Police Department in An Attempt to Avert Another Riot, undated, box 582, file 9 Cavanagh Papers.
25. Ibid.

26. Batchelor, "Ex-Police Boss Girardin is Dead"; "Mr. Girardin's Service," *Detroit Free Press*, 30 November 1971; "Girardin: Tough But Fair," ibid.

27. Press release, 9 July 1968, and Guidelines for Police Personnel Functioning in Public Places and Investigating for Criminal Activity, undated, box 585, file 2, Cavanagh Papers.

28. Chronology of steps in Police Community Relations Project Committee, Revised Recommendations, 5 December 1969, box 583, file 2, ibid.

29. Jerome Cavanagh with Al Rothenberg, *Look*, 24 February 1970, and pamphlet transcript of Meet the Press, 15 June 1969, box 7, file 2, ibid.

30. Rich, *Coleman Young*, 94, 208.

31. W. Marvin Dulaney, *Black Police in America* (Bloomington: Indiana University Press, 1996), 99.

32. Rich, *Coleman Young*, 209–214.; Dulaney, *Black Police*, 99–101; Peter T. Kilborn, "New York Police Force Lagging in Recruitment of Black Officers," *New York Times*, 17 July 1994.

33. Gary Blonston, "Edwards Urges Rein on Police," *Detroit Free Press*, 11 December 1968.

34. "Liberty, Equality, and Domestic Tranquility," speech at William Mitchell College of Law, St. Paul, Minnesota, 9 June 1969, series 9/27/91, box 1, Edwards Jr. Papers.

35. Ibid.

36. "Toward a Better Tomorrow," speech to the Michigan Welfare League, Detroit, 17 November 1970, series 9/21/91, box 2, ibid.

37. *Sheppard v. Maxwell*, 385 U.S. 333 (1966).

38. "George C. Edwards, Jr., Dies; Wrote Ruling on Wiretapping," *Washington Post*, 9 April 1995.

39. *United States v. United States District Court*, 44 F.2nd. (6th Ct., 1971).

40. George Edwards, "Opinion: America's Greatest Gift," *Cincinnati Post*, 15 December 1975.

41. *Bradley et al. v. Milliken et al.*, U.S. Circuit Court of Appeals for 6th Circuit, 75–1668, filed June 19, 1975; *1990 Census of Population and Housing: Summary of Population and Housing Characteristics* (Washington, D.C.: GPO, 1992).

BIBLIOGRAPHY

Primary Sources

Archival material at Walter Reuther Library, Wayne State University, Detroit, Michigan

Interviews and Memoirs

> Geraldine Bledsoe by Norman McRae, 1970
> Joseph Coles by Norman McRae, 1970
> The Rev. Charles Hill by Norman McRae, 1970
> Memoirs of George C. Edwards of Dallas, Texas

Collections

> Jerome P. Cavanagh
> The City of Detroit Commission on Community Relations
> The Detroit Branch of the NAACP
> George Clifton Edwards, Sr.
> George Clifton Edwards, Jr.
> Robert J. Greene
> John Herling—Interview with George Edwards, Jr.
> Richard McGhee
> Mary M. Stolberg

Author's Interviews

> Robert Beasley (1995)
> Margaret McConnell Edwards (1996)
> Vincent Piersante (1996)
> Robert L. Weinberg (1994)

Public Records

Hearings Before A Subcommittee of the Committee on the Judiciary, United States Senate, 88th Cong., 1st sess. On the Nomination of George Clifton Edwards, Jr., of Michigan, to be United States Circuit Judge, Sixth Circuit, October 1 and November 21, 1963. Washington, D.C.: GPO, 1963.

1990 Census of Population and Housing: Summary of Population and Housing Characteristics. Washington, D.C.: U.S. GPO, 1992.

Studies in Crime and Law Enforcement in Major Metropolitan Areas II, Field Surveys III, Prepared under a Grant by the Office of Law Enforcement Assistance, United States Department of Justice to the University of Michigan. Washington, D.C.: GPO, 1968.

Court Opinions by George Clifton Edwards, Jr.

Bishop v. New York Central Railroad, 349 Mich. 345 (May 1957).

Bradley v. Milliken et al, U.S. 6th Circuit Court of Appeals, 75–1668.

Comstock v. General Motors, 358 Mich. 163 (November 1959).

In Re: Maddox, 351 Mich. 359 (March 1958).

People v. Cole, 349 Mich. 175 (1957).

People v. Gonzales, 349 Mich. 572 (September 1957).

People v. Gonzales, 356 Mich. 251 (June 1959).

People v. Hildabridle, 353 Mich. 562 (September 1958).

People v. Johnson, 356 Mich. 619 (July 1959).

People v. Reese, 363 Mich. 329 (June 1961).

United States v. United States District Court, 44 F.2nd. (6th Ct., 1971).

Other Court Rulings

Jones v. Alfred H. Mayer Co., 392 U.S. 409 (1968).

Sheppard v. Maxwell, 385 U.S. 333 (1966).

Newspapers

Cincinnati Post 1963–96.

Detroit Free Press 1936–95.

Detroit News 1936–95.

Detroit Times 1941–62.

Michigan Chronicle 1943–63.

New York Times 1949–96.

Pittsburgh Courier 1949–95.

Secondary Sources

Books

Albini, Joseph L. *The American Mafia: Genesis of a Legend.* New York: Meredith Corp., 1971.

Angel, D. Duane. *Romney: A Political Biography.* New York: Exposition Press, Inc., 1967.

Barnard, John. *Walter Reuther and the Rise of the Auto Workers.* Boston: Little, Brown and Co., 1983.

Bayley, David H., ed. *Police and Society.* Beverly Hills, Calif.: Sage Publications, Inc., 1977.

Bibliography

Berthelot, Helen Washburn. *Win Some Lose Some: G. Mennen Williams and the New Democrats*. Detroit: Wayne State University Press, 1995.

Blum, John Morton. *Years of Discord: American Politics and Society, 1961–1974*. New York: W.W. Norton & Company, 1991.

Branch, Taylor. *Parting the Waters: America in the King Years 1954–63*. New York: Simon and Schuster, 1988.

Capeci, Dominic J., Jr. *Race Relations in Wartime Detroit: The Sojourner Truth Housing Controversy of 1942*. Philadelphia: Temple University Press, 1984.

———. *Detroit and the "Good War": The World War II Letters of Mayor Edward Jeffries and Friends*. Lexington: University of Kentucky Press, 1996.

Carew, Anthony. *Walter Reuther*. Manchester: The University of Manchester Press, 1993.

Charns, Alexander. *Cloak and Gavel: FBI Wiretaps, Bugs, Informers and the Supreme Court*. Champaign: The University of Illinois Press, 1992.

Cardozo, Benjamin N. *The Paradoxes of Legal Science*. 1928. Reprint, Westport, Conn.: Greenwood Press, 1975.

Darden, Joe T., Richard Child Hill, June Thomas, Richard Thomas. *Detroit: Race and Uneven Development*. Philadelphia: Temple University Press, 1987.

Dulaney, W. Marvin. *Black Police in America* (Bloomington: Indiana University Press, 1996.

Edwards, George. *Pioneer-at-Law: A Legacy in the Pursuit of Justice*. New York: W.W. Norton & Co., Inc., 1974.

Edwards, George et al. *The Law of Criminal Corrections*. St. Paul, Minn.: West Publishing Company, 1963.

Fine, Sidney. *Sit-down: The General Motors Strike of 1936–1937*. Ann Arbor: University of Michigan Press, 1969.

———. *Violence in the Model City: The Cavanagh Administration, Race Relations, and the Detroit Riot of 1967*. Ann Arbor: University of Michigan Press, 1989.

Franklin, John Hope. *From Slavery to Freedom: A History of Negro Americans*. 1967. Reprint, New York: Alfred A. Knopf, Inc., 1969.

Garrow, David J. *Bearing the Cross: Martin Luther King, Jr., and the Southern Christian Leadership Conference*. New York: Vintage Books, 1986.

Gentry, Curt. *J. Edgar Hoover: The Man and the Secrets*. New York: W.W. Norton & Company, 1991.

Glazer, Sidney. *Detroit: A Study in Urban Development*. New York: Bookman Associates, Inc., 1965.

Goldfarb, Ronald. *Perfect Villains, Imperfect Heroes: Robert F. Kennedy's War Against Organized Crime*. New York: Random House, 1995.

Harrington, Michael. *The Other America: Poverty in the United States*. New York: The Macmillan Company, 1963.

Jackson, T. Kenneth. *Crabgrass Frontier: The Suburbanization of the United States*. New York: Oxford University Press, 1985.

Johnson, Christopher H. *Maurice Sugar: Law, Labor, and the Left in Detroit, 1912–1950*. Detroit: Wayne State University Press, 1988.

Keesing's Research Report: Race Relations in the U.S.A., 1954–68. New York: Charles Scribner's Sons, 1970.

Kennedy, Robert F. *The Enemy Within*. New York: Harper & Brothers, 1960.

Lichtenstein, Nelson. *The Most Dangerous Man in Detroit: Walter Reuther and the Fate of American Labor*. New York: Basic Books, 1995.

Little, Malcolm X with Alex Haley. *The Autobiography of Malcolm X*. New York: Grove Press, Inc., 1966.

Matusow, Allen J. *The Unraveling of America: A History of Liberalism in the 1960s.* New York: Harper & Row, Publishers, 1984.

McClellan, John L. *Crime Without Punishment.* New York: Duell, Sloan and Pearce, 1962.

Meier August and Elliott Rudwick. *Black Detroit and the Rise of the UAW.* New York: Oxford University Press, 1979.

Moon, Elaine Latzman. *Untold Tales, Unsung Heroes: An Oral History of Detroit's African–American Community, 1918–1967.* Detroit: Wayne State University Press, 1994.

Niederhoffer, Arthur. *Behind the Shield: The Police in Urban Society.* Garden City, N.Y.: Doubleday & Company, Inc., 1967.

Niederhoffer, Arthur and Abraham S. Blumberg, eds. *The Ambivalent Force: Perspectives on the Police.* Hinsdale, Ill.: The Dryden Press, 1976.

O'Brien, David M. *Constitutional Law and Politics,* vol. 2. New York: W.W. Norton & Co., 1991.

Reuther, Victor. *The Brothers Reuther and the Story of the UAW: A Memoir by Victor G. Reuther.* Boston: Houghton Mifflin Company, 1976

Rich, C. Wilbur. *Coleman Young and Detroit Politics: From Social Activist to Power Broker.* Detroit: Wayne State University Press, 1989.

Scheingold, Stanley A. *The Politics of Law and Order: Street Crime and Public Policy.* New York: Longman, Inc., 1984.

Skolnick, Jerome H. *Justice Without Trial: Law Enforcement in a Democratic Society.* New York: Wiley, 1966.

Schlesinger, Arthur M., Jr. *Robert Kennedy and His Times.* Boston: Houghton Mifflin Company, 1978.

Stolberg, Benjamin. *The Story of the CIO.* New York: Viking Press, 1938.

Stolberg, Mary M. *Fighting Organized Crime: Politics, Justice and the Legacy of Thomas E. Dewey.* Boston: Northeastern University Press, 1995.

Tyler, Gus. *Organized Crime in America.* Ann Arbor: The University of Michigan Press, 1962.

Viorst, Milton. *Fire in the Streets: America in the 1960s.* New York: Simon and Schuster, 1979.

Widick, B. J. *Detroit: City of Race and Class Violence.* 1972. Reprint, Detroit: Wayne State University Press, 1989.

Wilson, James Q. *Varieties of Police Behavior.* Cambridge: Harvard University Press, 1968.

Articles

Cavanagh, Jerome P. "Justice and Urban Ills, Law for the Poor," *1967–1968: A Compilation of the Virginia Law Weekly* 19 (1968): 66–70.

Dunbar, Ernest. "Detroit's Jerry Cavanagh: The Mayor Who Woke Up a City." *Look,* 21 September 1965.

Edwards, George Clifton, Jr. "The Constitution, The Citizen, and The Police." *Michigan State Bar Journal* 40, no. 4 (April 1961): 26–32.

———. "Detroit: A Lesson in Law Enforcement." *The Annals of the American Academy of Political and Social Science* 347 (May 1963): 67–73.

———. "The Dissenting Opinions of Mr. Justice Smith." *University of Detroit Law Journal* 34, no. 1 (October 1956): 81–91.

Bibliography

———. "Judge, I Told That Boy." *The New Republic* 142, no. 13 (28 March 1960): 11–16.

———. "Order and Civil Liberties: A Complex Role for the Police." *Michigan Law Review* 64, no. 1 (November 1965): 48–61.

Farley, Reynolds. "The Urbanization of Negroes in the United States." *Journal of Social History* 1, no. 3 (1968): 241–58.

Gregory, James N. "The Southern Diaspora and the Urban Dispossessed: Demonstrating the Census Public Use Microdata Samples," *The Journal of American History* 82, no. 1 (June 1995): 111–34.

"How One City is Making A Dent in Its Crime Rate." *U.S. News & World Report* (21 May 1962): 66–67.

Langlois, Janet L. "The Belle Isle Bridge Incident: Legend Dialectic and Semiotic System in the 1943 Detroit Race Riot." *Journal of American Folklore* 96, no. 380 (1983): 183–99.

Lorence, James J. "Controlling the Reserve Army: The United Automobile Workers and Michigan's Unemployed, 1935–1941." *Labor's Heritage* (Spring 1994): 19–37.

Peterson, Joyce Shaw. "Black Automobile Workers in Detroit. 1910–1930." *Journal of Negro History* 64, no. 3 (1979): 177–90.

Sitkoff, Harvard. "The Detroit Race Riot of 1943," *Michigan History* 53, no. 3 (1969): 183–206.

Swan, L. Alex. "The Harlem and Detroit Riots of 1943: A Comparative Analysis." *Berkeley Journal of Sociology* 16 (1971–72): 75–93.

Sugrue, Thomas J. "Crabgrass-Roots Politics: Race, Rights, and the Reaction against Liberalism in the Urban North, 1940–1964." *The Journal of American History* 82, no. 2 (September 1995): 551–86.

Thomas, Richard W. "The Black Urban Experience in Detroit: 1916–1967." In *Blacks and Chicanos in Urban Michigan*, edited by Homer C. Hawkins and Richard W. Thomas, 56–80. East Lansing: Michigan Department of State: 1979.

Acknowledgments

This book is loosely based on a manuscript that George Edwards wrote before his death. Wherever appropriate I have quoted sections of the original manuscript in order to provide a fuller sense of Edwards's ideas and eloquence. Edwards's widow, Margaret McConnell Edwards, and his son, James, entrusted this project to my care, read it with an eye for errors, yet freed me to draw my own conclusions. Unfortunately, because of a backlog at the FBI, Edwards's voluminous file, which would have added more details to some aspects of his life, will not be available for several years.

Arthur Evans of Wayne State University Press and Phil Mason, editor of the Great Lakes Book Series, offered advice and encouragement. Arthur Johnson, who served as executive director of the Detroit Chapter of the NAACP during the years covered by this book and later became a vice chancellor at Wayne State, collected money to offset some of my expenses.

Vincent Piersante granted me an interview and answered many subsequent inquiries. Pat Zacharias, librarian of the *Detroit News,* was equally generous with her time and patience. Dominic J. Capeci, Jr., of Southwest Missouri State University, John Barnard of Oakland University, and Nelson Lichtenstein of the University of Virginia provided insights into the life and times of George Edwards. Although I have not always agreed with their interpretations, their expertise made this a better book. Staff members of the Walter Reuther Library were uniformly professional, friendly, and knowledgeable. Margaret Raucher deserves special credit for going out of her way to find uncatalogued material and to answer long-distance questions.

Finally, I was lucky to have wonderful hosts in James Edwards and Patrick Murray. They put up with my many visits, introduced me to Detroit, and entertained me grandly.

INDEX

331

Dietrich, Paul E., 272
Diggs, Charles C., Jr., 25, 239
Diggs, Charles C., Sr., 35, 70, 72
Dillon, Francis J., 49
Dingell, John, 108
Dingeman, Harry I., 66
Dirksen, Everett M., 259, 264, 275–76
Donohue, Marilyn Lou, 17
Douglas, Paul H., 197
Douglas, William O., 117, 118, 167–68, 201, 261
Dowdy, Earl B., 28
Dunbar, Ernest, 17

Eaman, Frank D., 115, 125–26
Eastland, James O., 260, 262, 275
Economic Club of Detroit, 164
Edgecomb, Charles F., 71–72
Edwards, George Clifton, Jr.: arrival in Detroit, 9–10, 48–49; optimistic liberalism, 12–13, 14; family background, 38–39; memories of southern injustice, 39–41; at Harvard, 41, 42–44; reading of law, 41; undergraduate education, 41; meeting with Franklin D. Roosevelt, 46–47; as chair of American Student Union, 47–48; marriage to Margaret McConnell, 64; switch from Socialist to Democratic affiliation, 69; response to World War II, 77; military service, 77–79; illness with polio, 89; death, 295
  Labor organizer: itinerant socialist organizing activities, 9, 44–48; arrest, 45; hiring by Kelsey-Hayes, 51–52; recruiting for UAW, 52; sit-down strike at Kelsey-Hayes, 52; sit-down strike at Yale and Towne, 54–57; later perspective on strike activities, 57; reaction to Battle of the Overpass, 58; opposition to Martin's reorganization agenda, 59; and attack on Reuther by gangsters, 59–60; as head of relief efforts for UAW, 61–62
  Detroit City councilman: 63; 1941 campaign, 69–71; continued support for African-American housing,

72–73; stand for racial justice after 1943 riots, 74; 1943 campaign, 75, 76; election as president in 1945, 80; battle with Floyd McGriff, 80–81; 1947 reelection, 81–82
  Detroit Housing Commission director: appointment as, 65–66; bribery scandal during tenure, 66–67; Sojourner Truth controversy, 67–68; accomplishments as, 71
  Political aspirations: 1949 mayoral race, 10, 63, 83–90, 92–93; aspirations to U.S. Congress, 82, 108; role in founding Americans for Democratic Action, 82; work for election of Williams as governor, 82, 99; work for Michigan Democratic party, 82; election as precinct delegate and congressional district chairman, 99; as legal advisor to Wayne County Democratic party, 99
  Detroit Police commissioner: concept of community policing, 12–14, 127, 133, 189–90, 246–47; concept of "ordered liberty," 13, 120; on Detroit law enforcement problems, 20–21; decision to accept police commissioner position, 32–37; concern about avoiding race riots, 33, 35, 74; opposition from top command officers, 125, 127–30, 135–38; lessons learned from Frank Eaman, 126–27; emphasis on crime prevention, 127; swearing-in ceremony, 129–30; accolades from African-American community, 130–31; reception by civic and business leaders, 131; efforts to win cooperation of officers, 131–33; efforts to achieve racially unbiased policing, 133–34, 137–38, 148, 164–65, 174, 175; public relations crisis as result of internal sabotage, 135–38; efforts to improve funding, 138–40, 252; efforts for racial justice in personnel policies, 143, 144–46; 3-Point Police Program, 146–47; efforts to eliminate police brutality, 153–67; and Daniels police brutality case, 154–62, 174; nomination for

Index

under AFL, 49–50; affiliation with CIO, 50; West Side Local 174, 50, 53; sit-down strikes of mid-1930s, 50–54; attempts to organize Ford, 57–58; membership growth after sit-down strikes, 58; factionalism, 58–59, 60, 61; Progressive Caucus, 59; Unity Caucus, 59, 61; creation of welfare department, 60–61; support for Edwards's city council candidacy, 70; on Charles Oakman, 80; support for Edwards's mayoral candidacy, 90; struggles with gangster Santo Perrone, 96–97

University of Islam, 169

U.S. Civil Rights Commission report on police brutality, 152–53

U.S. Department of Housing and Urban Development (HUD), 11

U.S. News & World Report, 167

U.S. Senate: Select Committee on Improper Activities in the Labor or Management Field, 198; Special Committee to Investigate Organized Crime in Interstate Commerce, 198; confirmation hearings on Edwards's judgeship, 260, 262–66, 274–75; debate on Edwards's nomination to federal judgeship, 275–76

U.S. Supreme Court: decisions affecting police abuse in 1960s, 13; and application of Bill of Rights, 116–17, 121; decision in Sam Sheppard case, 293

Valachi, Joseph, 266–67
Van Antwerp, Eugene I., 83, 84–86, 167
Van Antwerp, Philip J., 21, 166–67
Vitale, Joseph, 226
Vitale, Peter, 283, 284
Voelker, John D., 111, 112

Wadsworth, James E., 30
Wald, Robert G., 66
Walker, Wayne H., 220, 222
Wallace, Blake S., 167, 188

Warren, Earl, 13, 94, 112, 116, 261
Wartman, Charles J., 20
Washington, Charles L., 240
Watergate, 294
Waters, Ethel, 181
Watts, John D., 86
Watts riot, 285
Wayne County Probate Court, 101
Webster, Arthur, 54, 55, 56, 99
Wechsler, James A., 74
Weinberg, Robert L., 236–37
Weis, William L., 155, 156
Welch, Edward, 155, 157
West Side Local Auxiliary, 61
Whitby, Ira, 30
White, Byron, 121
White, Horace A., 68, 71, 72
White, John, Jr., 205, 211, 212, 213
Whitehead, Alfred, 42
Whittaker, Charles Evans, 121
Widick, B. J., 29, 180
Wilfred X, 254
Williams, Claude, 45, 233
Williams, Edward Bennett, 236
Williams, G. Mennen, 82–83, 109
Williams, Sam, 222
Wilson, Bruce, 55
Wilson, George, 220
Winn, Frank, 49, 59
Witherspoon, John H., 75
Wolverine Bar Association, 256–57
Work Relief Act of 1939, 61–62
Works Progress Administration (WPA), 10, 61, 62
Wright, Frederick F., 214, 215
Wyrod, Walter, 128; and Daniels police brutality case, 155, 157, 158, 159, 163; resignation, 218

Yale and Towne, 54; sit-down strike of 1937, 54–55; agreement to organize all factories, 58
Young, Coleman, 291–92
Young Progressives of Michigan, 85

Zerilli, Anthony, 221
Zerilli, Joseph, 227, 267, 268, 273
Zimmerman, George M., 115

TITLES IN THE GREAT LAKES BOOKS SERIES

Freshwater Fury: Yarns and Reminiscences of the Greatest Storm in Inland Navigation, by Frank Barcus, 1986 (reprint)

Call It North Country: The Story of Upper Michigan, by John Bartlow Martin, 1986 (reprint)

The Land of the Crooked Tree, by U. P. Hedrick, 1986 (reprint)

Michigan Place Names, by Walter Romig, 1986 (reprint)

Luke Karamazov, by Conrad Hilberry, 1987

The Late, Great Lakes: An Environmental History, by William Ashworth, 1987 (reprint)

Great Pages of Michigan History from the Detroit Free Press, 1987

Waiting for the Morning Train: An American Boyhood, by Bruce Catton, 1987 (reprint)

Michigan Voices: Our State's History in the Words of the People Who Lived It, compiled and edited by Joe Grimm, 1987

Danny and the Boys, Being Some Legends of Hungry Hollow, by Robert Traver, 1987 (reprint)

Hanging On, or How to Get through a Depression and Enjoy Life, by Edmund G. Love, 1987 (reprint)

The Situation in Flushing, by Edmund G. Love, 1987 (reprint)

A Small Bequest, by Edmund G. Love, 1987 (reprint)

The Saginaw Paul Bunyan, by James Stevens, 1987 (reprint)

The Ambassador Bridge: A Monument to Progress, by Philip P. Mason, 1988

Let the Drum Beat: A History of the Detroit Light Guard, by Stanley D. Solvick, 1988

An Afternoon in Waterloo Park, by Gerald Dumas, 1988 (reprint)

Contemporary Michigan Poetry: Poems from the Third Coast, edited by Michael Delp, Conrad Hilberry and Herbert Scott, 1988

Over the Graves of Horses, by Michael Delp, 1988

Wolf in Sheep's Clothing: The Search for a Child Killer, by Tommy McIntyre, 1988

Copper-Toed Boots, by Marguerite de Angeli, 1989 (reprint)

Detroit Images: Photographs of the Renaissance City, edited by John J. Bukowczyk and Douglas Aikenhead, with Peter Slavcheff, 1989

Hangdog Reef: Poems Sailing the Great Lakes, by Stephen Tudor, 1989

Detroit: City of Race and Class Violence, revised edition, by B. J. Widick, 1989

Deep Woods Frontier: A History of Logging in Northern Michigan, by Theodore J. Karamanski, 1989

Orvie, The Dictator of Dearborn, by David L. Good, 1989

Seasons of Grace: A History of the Catholic Archdiocese of Detroit, by Leslie Woodcock Tentler, 1990

The Pottery of John Foster: Form and Meaning, by Gordon and Elizabeth Orear, 1990

The Diary of Bishop Frederic Baraga: First Bishop of Marquette, Michigan, edited by Regis M. Walling and Rev. N. Daniel Rupp, 1990

Walnut Pickles and Watermelon Cake: A Century of Michigan Cooking, by Larry B. Massie and Priscilla Massie, 1990

The Making of Michigan, 1820–1860: A Pioneer Anthology, edited by Justin L. Kestenbaum, 1990

America's Favorite Homes: A Guide to Popular Early Twentieth-Century Homes, by Robert Schweitzer and Michael W. R. Davis, 1990

Beyond the Model T: The Other Ventures of Henry Ford, by Ford R. Bryan, 1990

Life after the Line, by Josie Kearns, 1990

Michigan Lumbertowns: Lumbermen and Laborers in Saginaw, Bay City, and Muskegon, 1870–1905, by Jeremy W. Kilar, 1990

Detroit Kids Catalog: The Hometown Tourist by Ellyce Field, 1990

Waiting for the News, by Leo Litwak, 1990 (reprint)

Detroit Perspectives, edited by Wilma Wood Henrickson, 1991

Life on the Great Lakes: A Wheelsman's Story, by Fred W. Dutton, edited by William Donohue Ellis, 1991

Copper Country Journal: The Diary of Schoolmaster Henry Hobart, 1863–1864, by Henry Hobart, edited by Philip P. Mason, 1991

John Jacob Astor: Business and Finance in the Early Republic, by John Denis Haeger, 1991

Survival and Regeneration: Detroit's American Indian Community, by Edmund J. Danziger, Jr., 1991

Steamboats and Sailors of the Great Lakes, by Mark L. Thompson, 1991

Cobb Would Have Caught It: The Golden Years of Baseball in Detroit, by Richard Bak, 1991

Michigan in Literature, by Clarence Andrews, 1992

Under the Influence of Water: Poems, Essays, and Stories, by Michael Delp, 1992

The Country Kitchen, by Della T. Lutes, 1992 (reprint)

The Making of a Mining District: Keweenaw Native Copper 1500–1870, by David J. Krause, 1992

Kids Catalog of Michigan Adventures, by Ellyce Field, 1993

Henry's Lieutenants, by Ford R. Bryan, 1993

Historic Highway Bridges of Michigan, by Charles K. Hyde, 1993

Lake Erie and Lake St. Clair Handbook, by Stanley J. Bolsenga and Charles E. Herndendorf, 1993

Queen of the Lakes, by Mark Thompson, 1994

Iron Fleet: The Great Lakes in World War II, by George J. Joachim, 1994

Turkey Stearnes and the Detroit Stars: The Negro Leagues in Detroit, 1919–1933, by Richard Bak, 1994

Titles in the Great Lakes Books Series

Pontiac and the Indian Uprising, by Howard H. Peckham, 1994 (reprint)

Charting the Inland Seas: A History of the U.S. Lake Survey, by Arthur M. Woodford, 1994 (reprint)

Ojibwa Narratives of Charles and Charlotte Kawbawgam and Jacques LePique, 1893–1895. Recorded with Notes by Homer H. Kidder, edited by Arthur P. Bourgeois, 1994, co-published with the Marquette County Historical Society

Strangers and Sojourners: A History of Michigan's Keweenaw Peninsula, by Arthur W. Thurner, 1994

Win Some, Lose Some: G. Mennen Williams and the New Democrats, by Helen Washburn Berthelot, 1995

Sarkis, by Gordon and Elizabeth Orear, 1995

The Northern Lights: Lighthouses of the Upper Great Lakes, by Charles K. Hyde, 1995 (reprint)

Kids Catalog of Michigan Adventures, second edition, by Ellyce Field, 1995

Rumrunning and the Roaring Twenties: Prohibition on the Michigan-Ontario Waterway, by Philip P. Mason, 1995

In the Wilderness with the Red Indians, by E. R. Baierlein, translated by Anita Z. Boldt, edited by Harold W. Moll, 1996

Elmwood Endures: History of a Detroit Cemetery, by Michael Franck, 1996

Master of Precision: Henry M. Leland, by Mrs. Wilfred C. Leland with Minnie Dubbs Millbrook, 1996 (reprint)

Haul-Out: New and Selected Poems, by Stephen Tudor, 1996

Kids Catalog of Michigan Adventures, third edition, by Ellyce Field, 1997

Beyond the Model T: The Other Ventures of Henry Ford, revised edition, by Ford R. Bryan, 1997

Young Henry Ford: A Picture History of the First Forty Years, by Sidney Olson, 1997 (reprint)

These Men Have Seen Hard Service: The First Michigan Sharpshooters in the Civil War, by Raymond J. Herek, 1997

The Coast of Nowhere: Meditations on Rivers, Lakes and Streams, by Michael Delp, 1997

From Saginaw Valley to Tin Pan Alley: Saginaw's Contribution to American Popular Music, 1890–1955, by R. Grant Smith, 1997

Toast of the Town: The Life and Times of Sunnie Wilson, by Sunnie Wilson with John Cohassey, 1997

The Long Winter Ends, by Newton G. Thomas, 1997 (reprint)

Bridging the River of Hatred: The Pioneering Efforts of Detroit Police Commissioner George Edwards, by Mary M. Stolberg, 1998